26 - interdependent ch—
    ex amp—

40 - 41 coord—— / wy—
    58 - conventions

64 - not persons
    73 - incongruing m— — n—t n—t—
        wholly free—
    79 doxical / dentif—
    57 - f ru—— — m—nt t catch—f w——l
        7 n—l only
    102 - l—y—g— — anth n n——my
        instrum—ll m—
    113 pr——ly 7 nd int—l— — m——l
        attn pr—d—t 7 nd int—l—.
        can't be ass——g

FII - Brandom
    128 ff language / adopt—tion
    159 — crit—c——ms st Brand—
    160 — m—phll— tm—k—f st d—n——
    161 — g—n—t c—nstr—t d— (b—t—m—)
    m—t—l — d——l —bl—
    170 - altruism / f—ee will— p—ll—
    172 — recepro cal altru——— ··
        not enough
    185 — social norm — n—t
        regul—y
    140 — —st culture / biology
    193 — norm— c—f—l d—y—t —t—ad—

Following the Rules

Following the Rules

Practical Reasoning and Deontic Constraint

JOSEPH HEATH

OXFORD
UNIVERSITY PRESS

2008

OXFORD
UNIVERSITY PRESS

Oxford University Press, Inc., publishes works that further
Oxford University's objective of excellence
in research, scholarship, and education.

Oxford   New York
Auckland   Cape Town   Dar es Salaam   Hong Kong   Karachi
Kuala Lumpur   Madrid   Melbourne   Mexico City   Nairobi
New Delhi   Shanghai   Taipei   Toronto

With offices in
Argentina   Austria   Brazil   Chile   Czech Republic   France   Greece
Guatemala   Hungary   Italy   Japan   Poland   Portugal   Singapore
South Korea   Switzerland   Thailand   Turkey   Ukraine   Vietnam

Library of Congress Cataloging-in-Publication Data
Heath, Joseph, 1967–
Following the rules : practical reasoning and deontic constraint / Joseph Heath.
     p. cm.
ISBN 978-0-19-537029-4
1. Deontic logic.   2. Practical reason.   3. Ethics.   4. Duty.   I. Title.
BC145.H43 2008
128'.4—dc22   2007052440

9 8 7 6 5 4 3 2 1

Printed in the United States of America
on acid-free paper

Acknowledgments

My thanks to those who have helped me with this book over the years, along with those who have read and commented on it. Special thanks to Joel Anderson, Benoît Dubreuil, Benoit Hardy-Vallée, Vida Panitch, Patrick Turmel, Scott Woodcock, and Sergio Tenenbaum. Thanks also to my colleague Ronald De Sousa, along with Peter Ohlin and Peter Momtchiloff, both of Oxford University Press, for giving the entire project a boost when it most needed it.

This book incorporates, in revised form, ideas that have been presented in journal articles over the years. My thanks to the editors and referees at these journals, along with all those who helped me with these papers. The formulation of my arguments in this work should be taken to supersede those presented in "Foundationalism and Practical Reason," *Mind* 106, 3 (1997): 452–73; "The Structure of Normative Control," *Law and Philosophy* 17, 4 (1998): 419–42; "Brandom et les sources de la normativité," *Philosophiques* 28 (2001): 27–46; "Rational Choice with Deontic Constraint," *Canadian Journal of Philosophy* 31, 3 (2001): 361–88; "Practical Irrationality and the Structure of Decision Theory," in Sarah Stroud and Christine Tappolet, eds., *Weakness of Will and Practical Irrationality* (Oxford: Clarendon, 2003); and "The Transcendental Necessity of Morality," *Philosophy and Phenomenological Research* 67 (2003): 378–95.

This book covers a lot of ground. I would like to thank those who, at crucial junctures, have introduced me to ideas and bodies of work to which I might otherwise have been oblivious, but which subsequently proved central in the development of my views. These include Thomas McCarthy, James Johnson, Stephen Toulmin, David Davies, Michael Williams, Paul Thompson, and Ronald De Sousa.

I would also like to acknowledge the generous support I have received, over the years, from the Social Sciences and Humanities Research Council of Canada, the Canada Research Chairs Program, along with the Departments of Philosophy at the University of Toronto and the Université de Montréal.

Contents

Following the Rules

Introduction

There are many aspects of morality that are puzzling. Perhaps the most puzzling is that it often requires us to act in ways that are contrary to our self-interest. We may find ourselves *wanting* something, but feeling that morality prohibits us from doing what is necessary to obtain it. Morality therefore presents itself to us in the form of a duty to refrain from the pursuit of individual advantage, or to use the more technical term, in the form of a *deontic constraint*. It is not difficult to see how this aspect of morality could come to seem paradoxical. What is our "self-interest," if not the set of goals that we have good reason to pursue? And if our self-interest is the set of goals that we have good reason to pursue, then any constraint on the pursuit of self-interest would seem to be, by definition, irrational.

These sorts of considerations have led many philosophers to deny the phenomenon, and to suggest that any conflict between morality and self-interest must be merely apparent. After all, it is not just morality that presents itself to us with the appearance of a constraint. We also find ourselves subject to prudential constraints in our practical deliberations. There is often something that we would like to do, but feel that we should restrain ourselves from doing because of the long-term consequences of the act. In this case, it seems clear that while "prudence" seems to express itself as a constraint on the pursuit of self-interest, this is merely an appearance. The illusion is dissolved as soon as one sees that the conflict is not really between a prudential constraint and self-interest, but merely between one's short-term interests and one's long-term interests. Prudence therefore turns out to be not really a constraint, but rather an expression of one's self-interest, correctly understood.

Many philosophers have felt that moral constraints, insofar as they are justifiable, must have an analogous structure. Morality often expresses itself as a duty to perform an action that advances the interests of another, to the detriment of one's own. However, moral actions usually do not occur in isolation, but rather as part of a generalized system of reciprocity (one that stands at the core of the social order in every human society). This system of reciprocity generates benefits for everyone involved (benefits that include many intangibles, such as freedom from worry about certain depredations). If compliance with one's own duties represents the price of admission into this generalized system of reciprocity, then it seems clear that respecting moral constraints also generates benefits. The primary difference between morality and prudence is simply that, in the latter case, the long-term benefits are secured through one's own agency, whereas in the former case, they are mediated through the agency of another, namely, the person whose reciprocity is secured thanks to one's compliance with the moral law.

Thus moral philosophers have labored long and hard to show that morality is also a component of self-interest, correctly understood. Such an argument, were it to be carried through successfully, would not only solve one of the central puzzles in our understanding of morality but would also constitute a decisive refutation of moral skepticism, since it would provide a reason for acting morally that, in principle, any rational person should be obliged to acknowledge. Unfortunately, no one has ever been able to develop this argument in a thoroughly convincing way. When the idea is sketched out at a high level of abstraction, it seems enormously plausible. Certainly it cannot be a coincidence that, on the one hand, people feel obliged to respect moral obligations, and on the other hand, very significant cooperative benefits are realized when everyone respects such obligations. But whenever anyone has tried to work out the details in a rigorous manner—to show how you get from one hand to the other—the argument always seems to require some philosophical prestidigitation at a key point.

Furthermore, no matter how ingenious the argumentation strategy, the phenomenology of moral life remains stubbornly resistant to this sort of reduction. Many people find Immanuel Kant's analysis of common-sense morality, in the first part of the *Foundations of the Metaphysic of Morals*, intuitively correct.[1] Morality imposes duties, in the form of actions that must be performed for their own sake, and not for the sake of some anticipated reward. If morality were just some indirect way of advancing one's personal interests, then it wouldn't really be morality any more. Thus the phenomenology of moral life—the way that moral obligations are experienced by the individual, at the point of action— remains resolutely deontic. And yet if one takes this phenomenology seriously, then the puzzle about deontic constraint imposes itself with renewed force: How is it possible that, even though it may not be in one's interest to act morally, it is still rational to do so?

Much as this may seem like a timeless and eternal question, there have been a number of recent theoretical developments that promise to make it more tractable. The term "self-interest" has always tended to be vague. It is possible to offer a much sharper characterization of the phenomenon of deontic constraint by distinguishing a concern over the character of an action from a concern over its *consequences*. When Kant distinguished a categorical imperative ("do x") from a hypothetical imperative ("if you want y, do x"), what he set up in effect was an opposition between actions valued for their own sake, or for their intrinsic properties, and actions valued for their consequences. The value of an action that is valued for the sake of its consequences is contingent upon those very consequences. The value of an action that is valued for its own sake is independent of its consequences. The fact that morality is a system of deontic constraint is reflected, according to Kant, in the fact that moral value is of the latter type.

Thus one way to approach the puzzle of deontic constraint is to ask whether rational action necessarily has a consequentialist structure, or whether it can incorporate nonsequential considerations. This is another way of asking whether an *instrumental* conception of practical rationality—one that maintains that actions are valued only as *means* to the attainment of certain valued *ends*—is correct. When formulated this way, the puzzle about deontic constraint comes to be seen as just a special instance of a more general puzzle about the rational basis of rule-following behavior. Economists, for example, have long observed (and have sometimes even been troubled by the fact) that people are not nearly as responsive to incentives as a strictly instrumental theory of rational action would lead one to anticipate. In experimental games, people tend to engage in spontaneously cooperative behavior even when the incentives have been carefully aligned to promote failures of cooperation.[2] Some of this can be written off as irrationality. But with irrational conduct, people often correct themselves as soon as the error is pointed out to them. Much of the behavior that has troubled economists (and more lately, game theorists) remains stubbornly resistant to any attempt at correction. People seem to have a good idea what they are doing, and why they are doing it; yet so far the structure of their reasoning has eluded all attempts at formal reconstruction.

The advantage of resituating the puzzle of deontic constraint within this broader sociotheoretic context is that, while many philosophers still use the imprecise vocabulary of "means" and "ends" to discuss consequentialism and instrumental rationality—a vocabulary that has scarcely changed since Kant—the debate among social theorists and economists is structured around a significantly more sophisticated articulation of the instrumental conception of rationality, namely, Bayesian decision and game theory (often referred to jointly as "rational choice theory"). This particular model of rational action was developed in order to update the instrumental conception of rationality in order to incorporate insights arising from the development of probability theory in the nineteenth century. The incorporation of probabilistic elements is flagged by the transition from talk about promoting one's *ends* to talk about maximizing one's *expected utility*.

Seen from this perspective, the type of deontic constraint that Kant took to be a feature of moral action has some interesting characteristics. Most important, because the value of an action is taken to be independent of its consequences, the associated reason for action is one that can be applied without engaging in any sort of probabilistic reasoning. Furthermore, in a social context, this means that such a reason for action is one that can be applied without engaging in any *strategic reasoning*. Given the insoluble regress of anticipations that develops in many social interactions involving interdependent choice, this may turn out to be a very interesting and important characteristic of deontic constraints. Unfortunately, this has been overlooked in much of the philosophical discussion, largely due to the ongoing prevalence of the antiquated vocabulary of "means" and "ends." Indeed, the inadequacy of this vocabulary has been one of the major forces pushing philosophers to reformulate the issue of deontic constraint in terms of the distinction between "agent-relative" and "agent-neutral" reasons for action.[3] I intend to avoid such a reformulation here. When discussing the structure of practical rationality, it makes more sense to start with rational choice theory, precisely because it is the only model that builds in probabilistic reasoning on the ground floor. Within such a framework, there are a variety of quite respectable ways of preserving the folk-psychological distinction between actions and their consequences.

Unfortunately, many theorists (philosophers and social scientists) have been misled into believing that the technical apparatus of rational choice theory, introduced in order to handle the complications of probabilistic reasoning, is also one that *prohibits* the introduction of nonconsequential considerations into the agent's practical deliberations. In other words, it is sometimes thought that decision theorists are necessarily committed to consequentialism, or that consequentialism is simply the *expression* of Bayesian reasoning, when applied to practical affairs. Deontic constraint, or rule-following behavior, according to this view, is either not mathematically tractable, or else violates some elementary canon of logical consistency. Thus a commitment to rational choice theory, or to the view that agents seek to maximize their expected utility, is widely regarded as entailing a commitment to an instrumental conception of rationality.[4]

My first major task, in the argument that follows, is to show that there is no such entailment. There is absolutely no reason that a rational choice theorist cannot incorporate deontic constraints—or any other type of rule-following behavior—into a formal model of rational action as utility-maximization (although, in so doing, it would perhaps be prudent to shift away from the vocabulary of *utility-maximization* toward that of *value-maximization*, given the close connection in many people's minds between utility theory and consequentialism). The commitment to consequentialism on the part of many rational choice theorists is the result of a straightforward oversight that arose in the transition from decision theory (which deals with rational choice in nonsocial contexts) to game theory (which deals with social interaction). Early decision theorists adopted a consequentialist vocabulary, but did so in a way that made consequentialism trivially true, and thus theoretically innocuous. Leonard Savage, for instance, in his canonical development of decision theory, defined an action as simply "a function attaching a consequence to each state of the world."[5] It follows quite immediately that the value of an action will depend entirely on the value of its consequences. When game theorists came along, however, and began to extend decision-theoretic models in order to handle social interaction problems, they began to treat actions as *events*, often ones that could be observed by other players (in sequential move games). In so doing, they inadvertently picked up the largely innocuous use of consequentialist vocabulary among decision theorists and transformed it into a substantive commitment to consequentialism as a thesis about human rationality. This move was always unmotivated. It persisted for so long only because it went largely undetected.[6]

As a result, many rational choice theorists have wasted an inordinate amount of time defending the instrumental conception of rationality, under the mistaken belief that doing so was necessary in order to defend a rationality-based approach to the analysis of social action. My goal in the first three chapters will be to describe the problems that this approach has created for proponents of the instrumental conception of rationality, and show how the "rational choice" model can be modified in order to incorporate deontic constraints and rule-following behavior without compromising mathematical tractability, or the standard analysis of probabilistic reasoning.

At first glance, a model of rational action that incorporates rule-following (as a sui generis element, not an indirect strategy) would appear to go some distance toward showing that it can be rational to respect deontic constraints. But in fact, all it does is eliminate some of the bad reasons that theorists have had for thinking that a model of rational action necessarily precludes deontic constraints. It does not do much to establish the positive thesis, because of the extraordinarily permissive attitude that decision theorists have traditionally taken toward the content of an agent's intentional states. In the traditional analysis, there are two types of intentional states relevant to the agent's decision: beliefs and preferences. Rational choice theorists generally prefer to remain agnostic about the source of the *content* of these states, choosing instead to "treat preferences as given" and to regard beliefs as subjective probabilities. The result, of course, is that a complete madman could turn out to exhibit perfect *practical* rationality, so long as he was able to hook up his delusional beliefs up with his demented preferences in a way that promoted the maximum probability-weighted satisfaction of the latter.

Although the distinction between practical rationality and other forms is quite important, the resulting conception of practical rationality fails to correspond very closely to our everyday use of the term "rational." So even though it is an uphill battle, in the end it is not much of a triumph to show that rule-following can be "rational" in this narrow, practical sense of the term. It does not exclude the possibility that respecting deontic constraints may be "rational" in the same narrow sense in which it may be rational for someone with an obsessive compulsive disorder to wash her hands for several hours a day. Since I am inclined to put rules on the "preference" rather than the "belief" side of the preference-belief distinction, what really needs to be shown is that the preference through which an agent's commitment to a rule is expressed may also be rational. In order to do so, it is necessary to challenge the prevailing noncognitivism about preferences, or the view that desires are somewhat less susceptible to rational reevaluation than beliefs. This involves a lot more work, and raises a number of more profound philosophical questions. In the case of *practical* rationality, even though there is no consensus, there is at least a single, reasonably precise model that has served as a focal point for discussion and debate. When it comes to beliefs and preferences, on the other hand, the philosophical discussion is marked by profound disagreement, and there is nothing like a focal model.

action → why
∧ why → act

In such a field, the chances of making a decisive argument are negligible. As a result, my goal in the remainder of the book is not so much to demonstrate the rationality of deontic constraints as it is to point the fly in the general direction of the exit from the bottle. More specifically, my goal is to take what I consider to be some of the best thinking done in the past couple of decades in epistemology and philosophy of language, and show how it "fits" with some of the most important work being done in evolutionary theory, in order to reveal the deep internal connection between rationality and rule-following. One of the major forces aiding and abetting the noncognitive conception of preference, for well over three centuries, has been a commitment to representationalism in the philosophy of mind (i.e., the view that "representation" constitutes a central explanatory concept when it comes to understanding the contentfulness of our mental states). What theorists of this persuasion have been trying to do, in a sense, is take a concept that was tailor-made for the explanation of belief and extend it to provide an explanation of human action. It is this strategy, I will argue, that has generated the puzzles about the rationality of rule-following.

The alternative strategy, which has recently been developed with considerable sophistication by pragmatist theorists like Robert Brandom, is to start with a set of concepts that are tailor-made for the explanation of human action, and then extend these to explain belief and representation.[7] This is based on the plausible intuition that human action in the world is more fundamental than human thought about the world. Proponents of the instrumental conception of rationality have typically *presupposed* contentful intentional states, then gone on to work up an account of rational action. The results are unsatisfactory, because the explanatory strategy is based on a precise inversion of the correct order of dependence (both logical and developmental). In the second half of the book, I will try to show that a pragmatist strategy along the lines of Brandom's provides a far more persuasive understanding of the nature of intentional states than the type of "psychologism" that has traditionally been assumed by rational choice theorists. Furthermore, I will try to show how this pragmatist strategy has the potential to dissolve a wide range of traditional puzzles about practical rationality—not only the mystery of deontic constraint but also the traditional problem of *akrasia*, or weakness of the will.

At the same time, I hope to pay some acknowledgment to the fundamental consequentialist intuition, which is that there is something odd about following rules for their own sake. It is genuinely strange that we human beings insist on performing certain actions, and refuse to perform certain others, regardless of what actually *happens* as a result of our choices. It is even stranger that morality often demands this of us. Consequentialists do not err in drawing attention to this oddness; the problem arises only when they dismiss it as *irrationality*. I would like to stop short of that, while nevertheless granting that there is an element of cosmic arbitrariness in this aspect of our intentional planning. It is, I will argue, an artifact of the evolutionary process that generated cultural dependence in the human species. However, unlike many products of our evolutionary heritage, such as the fact that we have ten fingers, we cannot freely imagine things being otherwise. This is because the process that generated human culture-dependence is also the process that led to the development of language, and to the advanced forms of cognition that this "language upgrade" supplied to our primate brains. Rationality itself is a form of rule-following, one that we internalize at least partially from our cultural environment (and thus one that is not merely the expression of some innate psychological endowment). So while there may be something odd about rule-following, this does not make it irrational. On the contrary, it merely serves to highlight one of the odd things about rationality.

This analysis serves as the basis for my defense of what I call "the transcendental necessity of morality." What I attempt to show is that the fact that we all find deontic constraints *binding*, to a greater or lesser degree, in our practical deliberations, is a fact about our psychology that is, as they say in German, *nichthintergehbar*. I recognize that transcendental arguments are regarded as somewhat exotic in contemporary philosophical circles. The proof will be in the pudding, as they say, but for now I would merely like to note that a "transcendental" claim, in Kant's sense of the term, denotes the opposite of a "metaphysical" claim. The need for a transcendental argumentation strategy, in my view, is essentially imposed by the willingness to understand practical rationality in its empirical context, taking into account the important facts known to us from the study of human psychology, child development, sociological theory, and evolutionary biology.

Reading the philosophical literature, it has come to my attention that "Kantian evolutionary naturalism" is not a particularly well-represented position in the debates over the foundations of human morality. This is a deficiency I hope to remedy. The basic Kantian claim, with respect to moral motivation, is that there is an internal connection between following the rules of morality and being a rational agent. Even a cursory glance at the current state of play in evolutionary theory is enough to lend considerable prima facie plausibility to this hypothesis. There are a variety of traits that set humans apart from our closest primate relatives. The "big four" are language, rationality, culture, and morality (or in more precise terms, "syntacticized language," "domain-general intelligence," "cumulative cultural inheritance," and "ultrasociality"). Yet the fossil record suggests that these differentia developed within a period of, at most, two to three hundred thousand years (which is, to put it in evolutionary terms, *not very long*).[8] The thought that each of these might have evolved independently (as a separate cognitive "module," for instance) is completely implausible. Not only are all four likely to be the product of a single development, but the development in question is likely to have been more like a "tweak" to existing capacities than a brand-new mechanism. Thus morality is almost certainly part of an evolutionary "package deal," one that includes all of our more prized cognitive abilities, such as planning for the future, developing scientific theories, doing mathematics, and so on. One can posit possible worlds in which these competencies are disaggregated, but such a world is not cognitively accessible to our own. Thus speculation about the "rational amoralist" is metaphysical, in the Kantian (i.e., pejorative) sense of the term.

Three cautionary notes: The way that I contrast "deontic constraint" with "consequentialism" differs from the distinction more familiar to moral philosophers between "deontological" and "consequentialist" moral theories. I am interested in the way that morality imposes constraints on the pursuit of self-interest at an action-theoretic level. However, many moral philosophers also believe that morality imposes constraints on the pursuit of the good. According to the terms of this dispute, "consequentialists" are those who believe that, once the outcome has been identified that is best from the moral point of view, then the morally correct action is the one that best conduces to the attainment of that outcome (according to whatever specification of practical rationality one might care to endorse). The "deontologist," on the other hand, believes that even after the outcome that is best from the moral point of view has been identified, morality may still impose further constraints on the means that one may employ in order to achieve that outcome.[9] Thus, while it would be better, from the moral point of view, for a runaway trolley to crush one innocent bystander, rather than five, that does not make it permissible to push someone under its wheels, so that it will grind to a halt before it hits the other five.

This debate is, in principle, quite distinct from the one that serves as the focal point of the discussion in this book. A rule-utilitarian, for example, believes that practical rationality incorporates genuine deontic constraints—agents must really follow "the rules" at the point of decision, without regard for the consequences. Consequential considerations come in only at a higher level, when it comes to justifying the rules. Here the rule-utilitarian believes that the only justifiable rules are ones that will promote the greatest happiness, when generally adhered to in a deontic fashion. Thus the rule-utilitarian rejects "deontology" as a theory of moral justification, but accepts deontic constraints as an essential element of moral action. (The challenge is then to explain why the consequentialism that prevails at the justificatory level doesn't bleed over into the deliberations that occur at the point of decision.)

Many people think such a theory is incoherent; I mention it only because it provides a helpful illustration of the difference between the two levels at which deontic constraints may be imposed: at the action-theoretic level, as part of the theory of practical rationality, where "the rules" are simply taken as given, and at the justificatory level, as part of the theory of norm-rationality, where "the rules" are subjected to further scrutiny. Kant endorsed "deontology" at both levels—he thought that allowing a categorical imperative to determine one's maxim of action was a perfectly rational way of deciding what to do, and he also thought that the justification for these categorical imperatives (in the plural), which we use in practical deliberation, would be through reference to the categorical imperative (in the singular). I would like to defend the rationality of deontic constraints at the level of action, but am not committed to defending "deontology" as a theory of justification. Naturally, it may be easier to introduce "deontological" considerations at the justificatory level once one has provided a vindication of deontic constraints at the action-theoretic level, but that is not my goal in what follows.

Note also that I use the term "moral" in a very loose sense in this book, to refer to a very wide range of obligations. There are principled reasons for this, but they will not emerge until the final chapter. I do adhere to the increasingly standard terminological distinction between "moral" and "ethical" questions, whereby "morality" refers to questions of what is right and wrong, permissible and impermissible (i.e., normative judgments with a deontic form), whereas "ethics" refers to questions of value, conceptions of the good (or so-called axiological questions). Many moral philosophers, however, also use the term "moral" to refer only to some heavily idealized set of normative judgments, which are presumably timeless and eternal. They then draw an invidious contrast between what is moral and what people *take* to be moral, or what society *tells us* is moral. This way of talking seems to me to beg a variety of important philosophical questions. Furthermore, most of the stock examples of things that are taken to be timeless and eternal moral truths (racism is unjust, cruelty to cats is wrong, etc.) are both culture specific and of comparatively recent invention. Thus my inclination is to use the term "moral" in a quasi-anaphoric sense, to refer to whatever it is that people themselves take (and have taken) to be moral. As a result, while I sometimes talk about "moral constraint" as a subspecies of "deontic constraint," this is not intended to designate any important difference in kind.

There is also an inclination among moral philosophers to draw a sharp distinction between "moral" and what are called "conventional" obligations, such as rules of etiquette, or "social norms" more generally.[10] I reject this distinction, not because I think morality is conventional, but rather because I follow Emile Durkheim in thinking that all social norms (or "conventions" in this way of speaking) have an implicitly moral dimension. As Jürgen Habermas put it, when trying to understand social interaction "one has to take into account the fact that the normatively integrated fabric of social relations is moral *in and of itself.* . . . The basic moral phenomenon is the binding force of norms, which can be violated by acting subjects."[11]

Another way of putting it is to say that the most mysterious features of morality are also features of social norms. We simply tend to ignore the mysterious aspects of social norms, because we are more likely to take norms for granted, and less is at stake in their observance. Nevertheless, it is important to recognize that the theoretical problems that have beleaguered social theorists throughout the twentieth century—concerning the action-theoretic basis of norm-conformity—are structurally identical to the questions that have troubled philosophers since Socrates, concerning the motivational basis of "justice," or moral obligation. In my view, anyone capable of providing a satisfactory answer to the question "Why do people obey social norms?" would do most, if not all, of the work that is involved in answering the question "Why do people respect their moral obligations?"

So even though this book takes as its point of departure the problem of morality, and of moral motivation, what it tries to develop is a general theory of practical rationality, one that is able to represent following the rules (or norm-conformity) as a species of straightforwardly rational action. I happen to believe that solving these action-theoretic puzzles also solves several traditional puzzles of moral philosophy, but I will not be insisting on that here. It is only the arguments of the final chapter that are internally connected to this perspective.

1

Instrumental Rationality

One of Thomas Hobbes's great contributions to the Western philosophical tradition was his extremely disciplined articulation of what we would now refer to as an *instrumental conception of practical rationality*. His ambition, in *Leviathan*, was to establish a series of political recommendations as a deductive consequence of a set of relatively parsimonious assumptions about human psychology and behavior. Thus he begins with a basic philosophy of mind, generalizes this to produce a theory of how each individual is inclined to act, and then derives a series of conclusions about how a group of individuals, so characterized, would interact with one another when given the opportunity. Because his overall approach is deductivist, he attempts to start with a set of initial "axioms" that will be relatively uncontroversial, but still will have bite when it comes to deriving conclusions. In this respect, his argument is strikingly successful. He begins with a series of psychological postulates that look quite innocuous, and yet ends up with his famous characterization of life in the state of nature as "solitary, poor, nasty, brutish and short." And even though most people dispute his conclusions, few doubt that they follow from his premises.

Incredibly, the sort of action theory that is currently considered to be "state of the art" among economists and many other social scientists—variously referred to as "rational choice theory," "decision-theory" or "utility-maximization theory"—is not substantially different from Hobbes's. The only major changes were introduced in the early twentieth century in order to accommodate the development of probability theory. Unfortunately, these changes have also had the effect of obscuring, to some degree, the underlying psychological assumptions of the theory. This is unfortunate, because the theory derives much of its plausibility from the intuitively appealing character of this underlying psychology. And this psychology can be discerned with great clarity in Hobbes's presentation.

Hobbes starts out *Leviathan* by outlining what we can easily recognize as a *representationalist* theory of cognition. Thoughts, he claims, are "every one a representation or appearance of some quality, or other accident of a body without us, which is commonly called an object."[1] He then adds to this an empiricist claim about how these representations are formed, namely, through causal interaction with the object in question. A "train of thought" is then constructed by linking together a series of such representations. Repeated exposure to particular sequences of events leads us to associate certain thoughts more strongly with others; out of this emerges the idea of a causal ordering of events. This in turn allows us either to *explain* a particular event (by following the associated chain regressively) or to *predict* its consequences (by following the chain progressively).

This constitutes Hobbes's basic account of what Kant would later call "theoretical rationality." The way that Hobbes extends it to include practical deliberation is then quite straightforward. Unlike his predecessors, who conceived of practical philosophy as involving a sometimes bewildering array of virtues, vices, and other such substantive dispositions, Hobbes offers a much simpler framework. When considering a possible state of affairs, he suggests, we are beset by one of three passions: attraction (we are drawn toward it), aversion (we are driven "fromward"), or contempt (we are indifferent).[2] Practical deliberation therefore involves considering some action and thinking through the chain of future consequences. The attraction or aversion that one feels toward these imagined consequences is then communicated back through the chain of associations, so that one begins to feel either attracted or averse to the action. Choosing an action will then involve simply selecting the one that is most attractive, or the least aversive.

In order to show that there is nothing more to it, Hobbes goes on to argue that all of the traditional virtues and emotions—the distinct qualities that were normally thought to be associated with actions—can be reduced to some combination of one of these basic attitudes with a belief.[3] Thus, in Hobbes's view, all of the work done by reason in practical contexts involves figuring out the causal chains that will connect up actions with outcomes (in effect, "channeling" our desires toward particular actions). Reason has no specifically practical function, other than establishing such connections. In particular, reason is not at all involved in the determination of the magnitude or polarity of our feelings of attraction or aversion. Practical wisdom is simply born of experience. The more we have seen of the world, the stronger the associations between our ideas will be, and so the more lively and accurate the transmission of attraction or aversion from imagined consequences will be.

One can see quite clearly the sort of underlying mechanism that Hobbes is imagining at work in the mind. Attraction and aversion are like magnetic charges. A thought, or representation, is like a piece of iron, which can receive this charge. When it does, the charge is communicated through the entire set of representations associated with it—the stronger the association, the more completely the charge is communicated. (Think of creating a chain of paper-clips, just by touching one to a magnet, then sticking the second to the first.) Practical deliberation, in Hobbes's view, is simply the experience of being pulled one way or the other by these various forces. We take a set of actions available to us and then "charge them up" by imagining all of the consequences they might bring, allowing our attraction and aversion to these outcomes to flow back to the actions. We are then moved toward the action that has the strongest attractive force, or the least aversive.

It is possible to recognize in this theory a precursor of what we would now call belief-desire psychology. According to this view, the mind is inhabited by two sorts of intentional states—beliefs, which aim to represent states of affairs, and desires, which also take states of affairs as their object, but rather than trying to represent them, instead valorize them. The difference is often expressed in terms of "directions of fit."[4] In the case of beliefs, the goal is to have the intentional state "fit"—correspond to—the way things are in the world. With desires, on the other hand, we hope to remake the world in such a way that it comes to "fit" the intentional state. Practical deliberation involves, roughly, taking a desire for an outcome, then using one's beliefs to determine which actions will be effective in bringing about that outcome. Thus our beliefs are used to "transfer" the desire for an outcome onto some particular action. It is in this respect that reason is said to be instrumental. It is something that we *use* in order to determine how best to satisfy our desires.

Once this basic framework is in place, Hobbes goes on to draw out its implications. One of the most famous consequences is his moral noncognitivism. Moral judgments are not going to count as real thoughts, in Hobbes's view. After all, what sorts of states could moral properties be representations of? And even if there were moral states of affairs, how could we know them? Moral properties are not generally regarded as having causal efficacy, and so are incapable of interacting with our senses. Thus moral judgments must reflect our passions, not our thoughts. And so Hobbes concludes that "whatsoever is the object of any man's appetite or desire, that is it which he for his part calleth good; and the object of his hate and aversion, evil; and of his contempt, vile and inconsiderable."[5] Of course, this would not be a problem for traditional morality, if it were possible to rationally debate the merits of a particular attraction or aversion. What gives Hobbes's position teeth is his further claim that these passions are fundamentally idiosyncratic: "For these words of good, evil, and contemptible are ever used with relation to the person that useth them: there being nothing simply and absolutely so; nor any common rule of good and evil to be taken from the nature of the objects themselves; but from the person of the man."[6]

Using belief-desire vocabulary, it is much easier to explain why Hobbes thinks that reason has no role in the determination of our passions. It is because desires cannot be held accountable to anything outside one's person. Beliefs, because they seek to represent the world, are corrigible. They can be corrected by experience, thus it makes sense to say that they are either true or false. Desires, on the other hand, have the opposite "direction of fit," and so cannot be corrected. They are about states of affairs that do not yet exist. Thus there is nothing that they can be held accountable to. They arise out of our animal spirits. Not only do they differ across individuals, but there is not even any reason to believe that they will remain dynamically stable within an individual. Thus moral judgments, insofar as they reflect our desire to bring about particular states, cannot be either true or false.

This noncognitivism about moral judgment is one of Hobbes's claims that has been widely accepted. It is important, however, not to confuse this issue with the question of whether practical rationality is instrumental. The two theses are closely connected in Hobbes's view, yet they remain analytically distinct. His instrumentalism stems from the claim that practical reasoning involves using our beliefs to discover the best means to the realization of our ends, and that actions are valued only for the sake of these ends. This can be referred to as the *consequentialism* hypothesis. The second claim is that there can be no reasoning about desires or ends. This is his *noncognitivism* about desire. Strictly speaking, it is only the former thesis that defines his view as instrumental, since it is only this thesis that makes a claim about practical rationality.[7] The noncognitivism thesis concerns the origins of our intentional states, not the way they are applied in practical contexts. The question "What is the relationship between reason and desire?" is strictly analogous to the question "What is the relationship between reason and belief?" Both are questions about how intentional states are formed or revised. But once these questions are answered, we must go on to ask the further question "Given these beliefs and desires, what should I do?" This is the sort of question that a theory of practical rationality seeks to answer. Thus I will reserve the term "instrumental conception of practical rationality" for the view that practical rationality serves to determine the best means to the realization of our ends, while setting aside for the moment the question of the cognitive status of desires.

1.1.   Decision Theory

Since Hobbes's time, the instrumental conception of rational action has exercised an extremely profound grip on the philosophical imagination. Many contemporary philosophers find this sort of model so powerfully intuitive that they have difficulty even imagining that it could be incorrect. This phenomenon is, in a certain sense, quite understandable, since there is no denying that the instrumental model has a certain intuitive appeal. When making a decision, every agent is faced with a set of possible outcomes. The agent will naturally prefer some outcomes over others, while remaining indifferent among others. Whatever sort of fancy mental states one might like to invoke in order to capture the nature of the agent's attitudes towards these outcomes, the fact remains that, at the end of the day, the agent is going to have to come up with some sort of ranking of them—preferably a complete ranking from best to worst, with maybe a few ties. In order to decide what to do, the agent must then determine what the chances are of each available action achieving any particular outcome, and then weigh these chances against the possible benefits. This process should yield a contextually specific ordering of possible actions from best to worst, from which the agent can then choose the highest ranked option.

Not only is this an overwhelmingly plausible reconstruction of our actual deliberative processes, but the underlying belief-desire psychology is also attractive in its simplicity. Following through on the logic of this psychological theory, one can regard the elements that are relevant to the success of a decision as being partitioned into three categories: actions, states, and outcomes.[8] The goal of practical deliberation is to select an action. Agents draw on their beliefs and desires in order to do this. First, they consider the outcomes that could possibly arise as a result of the actions that are available to them. They then rank the set of outcomes according to which are more or less desirable, and consider which actions will bring about which outcomes. In order to decide this, they must determine which of the possible states is most likely to obtain. They will then make the decision by hooking up a *desire for an outcome* with a *belief about the state* in order to recommend a particular action. Again, what makes this account "instrumental" (i.e., consequentialist) is that actions are not chosen for their own sake, but rather for the outcomes they are thought likely to produce.

Modern decision theory has not really strayed all that far from Hobbes's original formulation of the instrumental view. In its updated version, the deliberative process is often represented using a decision tree. When there are no probabilities involved, we can think of beliefs and desires as a type of *deliberative constraint*. Agents use these constraints as a filter to throw out possible options. Following Georg Henrik von Wright, we can represent the agent as starting out with a decision tree that contains the full set of action-state-outcome permutations, then pruning this tree by eliminating undesirable outcomes and impossible combinations of events, using these constraints.[9] Within this framework, beliefs and desires can be thought of as doxastic and desiderative constraints, respectively.

This kind of decision tree is represented in figure 1.1. The diagram shows a decision problem with three actions available to the agent $\{a_1, a_2, a_3\}$, three possible states $\{s_1, s_2, s_3\}$, and three possible outcomes $\{o_1, o_2, o_3\}$. Things start off with nature "choosing" which state will obtain. This puts the agent at one of her three decision nodes.[10] However, without knowing which node she is at, the agent will be unable to determine which action will produce which outcome. For instance, if the state is s_1 (i.e., nature has "chosen" branch s_1), then action a_1 will produce outcome o_1. However, if the state is s_2, choosing a_1 will produce o_2, and if the state is s_3, a_1 will produce o_3.

The agent's decision procedure can then be regarded as a process of pruning the decision tree. The agent's beliefs and desires can be introduced into the diagram simply by cutting off some branches. Suppose that the agent is able to ascertain which state obtains, and so believes, for example, that nature has "chosen" s_2. This allows him to cut the s_1 and s_3 branches off at nature's node, a process we may call "doxastic pruning." Once the problem is simplified in this way, the agent knows which node he is at, and so knows which actions will produce which outcome. As a result, he can simply choose the action that will lead to the outcome he most desires. This can be thought of as a desiderative pruning, in which each branch leading to an outcome other than the one most desired is

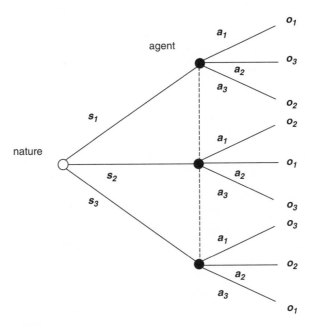

Figure 1.1 Decision tree.

cut off. What is left after this final pruning is a single action, which the agent can then proceed to perform. These two rounds of pruning are shown in figure 1.2.

The situation is more complicated when the agent is less than certain about which state will obtain. In this case, she can only assign probabilities to the occurrence of various states, and so will not know with certainty which action will bring about the desired outcome. As a result, she cannot simply "prune" branches off the tree. Instead, she must select the action that gives her the best chance of getting her favored outcome. But even then, things are not simple. She may face a situation in which she must choose between an action that gives her not only a reasonable chance of getting her favored outcome but also some chance of getting an outcome that is disastrous for her and an action that gives her a guarantee of at least a mediocre outcome. In order to choose between these two options, she will have to consider how *much* she really wants the best outcome, and whether pursuing it instead of the mediocre outcome is worth the risk of disaster. Some desires have much higher priority in her overall set of objectives. So just as beliefs will have to be given confidence levels in order to accommodate probabilities, her desires will have to be assigned (cardinal) priority levels.

The decision tree in figure 1.3 shows the probability with which the agent believes each state will obtain between angle brackets and the priority with which the agent desires each outcome between parentheses.[11] Since one of the three states must obtain, the probabilities assigned to nature's move must add up to 1. On the other hand, whether the numbers used to represent the priority level

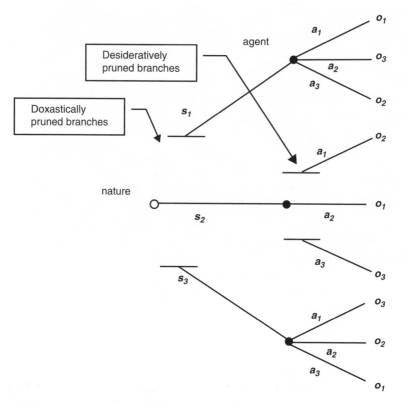

Figure 1.2 Doxastically and desideratively pruned tree.

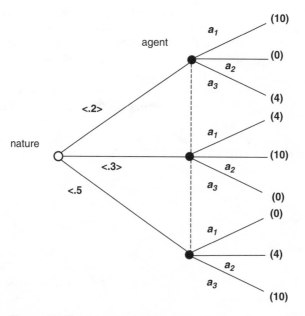

Figure 1.3 Decision tree with uncertainty.

of the agent's desires add up to 1 is not important, since the only thing that matters is the strength that these desires have relative to one another. For simplicity, the most preferred outcome (o_1) is assigned 10, and the least preferred outcome (o_3) a priority of 0.

In order to decide what to do, the agent must calculate the value of each action, in terms of the chances that it gives of achieving the various outcomes. If we assume that a 20 percent chance of getting some desirable outcome is worth half as much as a 40 percent chance of getting the same outcome, then we can calculate the value of each action by multiplying the desirability of each outcome by the probability that it will occur as a result of that action, then adding all of these up:

$$u(a) = \sum_o p(o \,|\, a) u(o) \tag{1}$$

The attractive feature of this rather simplified expression is that it shows quite clearly how the utility associated with an action is simply a function of the utility associated with its possible outcomes (the right-hand side, in English, reads: "For every outcome, o, multiply the utility of o by the probability of o given a, then add these all up"). Applying this to the example given in figure 1.3 generates the following:

$$u(a_1) = (0.2 \cdot 10) + (0.3 \cdot 4) + (0.5 \cdot 0)$$
$$= 3.2$$
$$u(a_2) = (0.2 \cdot 0) + (0.3 \cdot 10) + (0.5 \cdot 4)$$
$$= 5$$
$$u(a_3) = (0.2 \cdot 4) + (0.3 \cdot 0) + (0.5 \cdot 10)$$
$$= 5.8$$

The number that results is known as the *expected utility* of the action. Now, instead of simply selecting the action that produces the outcome the agent most desires, the instrumentally rational agent will select the action with the highest expected utility. The agent is therefore said to *maximize* expected utility. In this example, a_3 is the best choice. This is not obvious without the calculation. Although a_3 gives the agent the best chance of getting her most preferred outcome (50 percent chance of getting o_1), it also gives her a fairly high chance of getting her least preferred outcome, o_3. Action a_2, on the other hand, minimizes the chances of getting the worst outcome, and maximizes the chances of getting the second best. Action a_3 winds up being better because the agent likes the best outcome a lot more than the second-best outcome. If the value of o_2 were increased from 4 to 8, then a_2 would be better than a_3.

This example shows how the conception of practical rationality as utility-maximization follows very naturally from the application of belief-desire motivational psychology to decision problems under uncertainty. However, some theorists have doubted whether it is reasonable to represent beliefs and desires as having specific numerical probabilities or priorities. Obviously, in day-to-day contexts, we have only a vague idea of how convinced we are of something, or of how much we want this or that. There is, however, a very easy procedure we can use to fix these levels. To get the general idea, consider a person who is offered three different kinds of fruit to eat—an apple, an orange, and a banana. He knows that he likes apples best, and prefers oranges to bananas, but is not sure how *much* he likes one over the other. It is easy to find out, using the following procedure. Assign "apple" a value of 10. Now cut a piece off the apple (say 10 percent of it), and offer him a choice between what is left of the apple and the entire orange. If he chooses what is left of the apple, cut off another piece, and repeat the offer. Eventually, so little of the apple will be left that he will begin to prefer the orange. The value of the orange is therefore equal to the portion of the apple that is left at precisely the point at which his preference switches (and in principle there must be such a point). So if cutting off 30 percent of the apple makes him indifferent between the apple and the orange, then an orange is worth 0.7 apples to him. Multiplying this number by the value of the apple yields the priority level of his desire for an orange. The same procedure can be repeated for the banana. In the end, the value of each piece of fruit is expressed as a fraction of the most desired piece.

Clearly, this procedure works because one of the outcomes is near-perfectly divisible. We can cut as many pieces off the apple as we like, and we can make them extremely small. In order to apply the same general idea to any set of outcomes, a more abstract procedure must be devised. To do this, all we have to do is offer the person a set of lotteries that give her a greater or lesser chance of "winning" the best outcome. Again, assign "apple" a value of 10, and "nothing" a value of 0. Oranges and bananas will be somewhere in between. Now offer her a gamble that gives her a 90 percent chance of getting the apple, and a 10 percent chance of getting nothing. (This is called a "lottery over the extremes," as it gives her some chance of getting either her best or worst outcome.) If she prefers this lottery to the orange, offer her a new lottery that gives her a lower chance of getting the apple. Eventually the chances of getting the apple will be so slim that she will begin to prefer the orange. The value of the orange can therefore be set equal to the chance of getting the apple in the lottery at which her preference switches. (So if she is indifferent between the orange and a lottery that gives her a 70 percent chance of getting the apple, then an orange is worth 0.7 apples to her. Multiplying this number by the value of the apple yields the priority level of her desire for an orange.)

The lottery procedure is designed to be formally analogous to the sort of procedure that can be used to fix beliefs. A standard strategy for determining people's level of conviction is to see how much they are willing to bet on the occurrence of some future event.[12] For instance, if someone is quite convinced that p, and he is offered a choice between $10 for sure and $20 if p is true, then he should prefer the conditional offer. But if the value of the sure-thing offer is slowly increased, eventually there will come a point at which he becomes indifferent between that offer and the gamble. This will reveal the probability that he assigns to p. (For example, if he is "90 percent sure" that p, then he will prefer the sure-thing offer once it gets higher than $18—assuming risk neutrality.)

The advantage of these lottery procedures is that they can be applied universally, since a hypothetical lottery can be constructed for any outcome. (It also means that we don't have to worry about discontinuities, or just lumpiness, in people's preferences over, for example, fruit slices.) Furthermore, it has the effect of building whatever attitudes toward risk that the agent may have into her utility function, so that it will necessarily be the case that she will be indifferent between an outcome with a utility of 5 and a 50 percent chance of getting an outcome worth 10. However, this is not really the point. The purpose of the procedure is to provide some reason to think that desires can always be represented as having a certain priority level (and beliefs as having a confidence level). It is much more of a conceptual point than a practical proposal.

There are four things to keep in mind about this definition of utility:

- It is referred to as expected utility because it represents only the expected value of a particular choice, that is, the value ex ante, or before it is known how things turn out. Once the action is performed, the agent will discover which state actually obtains, and so will discover which outcome she receives. Thus the expected utility of an action is distinguished from its *payoff*, which is the value that it has for the agent ex post. In the example above, action a_3 may have an expected utility of 5.8, but it will have a payoff of 10, 4, or 0, depending on which state obtains.

- It is important not to think of utility as some kind of distinct psychological state that agents seek to maximize. As has been emphasized many times, contemporary decision theory marks an unequivocal break with the sort of hedonistic assumptions that still informed Hobbes's view. The "utility" an agent derives from an action is just numerical shorthand for expressing the way the outcome satisfies one or more of her desires. There is no reason to think that these desires have anything in common, or that they can all be reduced, à la Hobbes, to some common underlying currency. The agent's utility-maximizing course of action may be to donate money to famine relief, but this does not mean that she donates to famine relief in order to maximize her utility. She donates to famine relief because she wants to alleviate the suffering of others, and donating to famine relief is the best way of doing this. The fact that it is the "best" way of doing this is indicated by the fact that it is utility-maximizing. Nevertheless, our way of speaking can easily lead to thinking that there is some particular goal—such as the production of utility, pleasure, or happiness—that all actions are intended to achieve.

- The scale of the numbers used to represent the agent's utility are arbitrary. For any given utility function for an agent, one can construct a notational variation on it by multiplying it by any positive number and/or adding any number to it. More specifically, any positive linear transformation ($u' = xu + y: x > 0$) of an agent's utility function yields an equivalent representation of that agent's ranking of actions. This follows from the fact that the numbers assigned to the extremes (the best and worst outcomes) are arbitrary. In the above example, instead of assigning 10 to apple and 0 to nothing, we could have assigned 50 to apple and 10 to nothing, and it would have made no difference in the calculation of which action the agent should perform. The utility function is constructed by translating the agent's desire for an orange or for a banana into a desire for a chance at getting an apple. Once all desires are expressed in terms of apple-chances, then it is possible to balance them against one another. However, instead of performing calculations like (0.3apple + 0.12apple), it is easier to just assign "apple" some numerical value, and forget about the specific content of the desire that is being used as *numeraire*. The danger in this strategy is that it can mislead one into thinking that once this number has been assigned, it is because the intensity of the agent's desire for an apple has also been determined.[13] This is not the case. Two agents could have exactly the same utility function for fruit, yet could hold these desires with vastly different intensities. I may like apples more than oranges and bananas, but not like fruit in general, while my friend is wild about it. We may therefore each get utility of 7 from oranges, but this says nothing about how much happiness either of us get from oranges in the grand scheme of things. As a result, this type of utility measure does not yield meaningful interpersonal comparisons. One person can have a longer life expectancy, or a longer life, than someone else, but no one can have more expected utility, or a larger payoff, than anyone else. It is especially important to resist the idea that someone with a greater numerical utility payoff is in any way "happier" than anyone else. It may be possible to make these sorts of comparisons somehow, but the notion of utility, as defined in decision theory, cannot be used to perform them.

- It is important to remember that the use of lotteries to determine cardinality is not an essential feature of the utility concept. This method is adopted by philosophers primarily because of the pleasing logical properties of models that are developed in this way. Economists and people with more practical concerns do not always follow suit. For example, in health care economics, there are two very common ways of determining the subjective utility associated with various health states (in order to calculate the "quality-adjusted life years" generated by a particular medical intervention). Investigators start out by assigning perfect health a value of 1 and death a value of 0. They then proceed to ask individuals to assess the value to them of life in various states of morbidity. One way of doing so is to ask them to consider whether they would choose to undergo an operation that had an x percent chance of curing them completely and a $1 - x$ percent chance of killing them outright. Varying x then allows one to find an indifference point, which can be used to discount (or "quality-adjust") the value of time spent living with the condition. Another method is to ask them whether they would be willing to undergo an operation that cured them completely, yet shortened their lifespan by x number of days.[14] Thus one might find that a person was indifferent between, say, living for one more year with the condition and living for eight months without it. Again, one can use this to determine the appropriate "quality adjustment." The first procedure uses a lottery, while the latter resembles the procedure of "taking away slices of the apple." The primary difference between the two methods is that the former will generate a set of valuations that incorporates the individual's attitude toward risk, while the latter does not. There are, in certain cases, pragmatic reasons for wanting to ascertain subjective utility independent of attitudes toward risk (or the well-known "framing effects" and biases that judgments under uncertainty are subject to). Philosophers, however, have been inclined to adopt the lottery procedure, simply because it allows them to define the utility concept at the highest level of generality.

1.2. The von Neumann–Morgenstern Procedure

The presentation of basic decision theory given above is somewhat unorthodox. I presented it this way in order to keep the psychological motivation for the theory somewhat closer to the surface, and to show how the standard conception of rationality as utility-maximization represents a natural extension of the instrumental conception of rationality pioneered by thinkers such as Hobbes. However, the more standard way of establishing the utility-maximizing conception of rationality is through what has come to be known as the von Neumann–Morgenstern procedure (after John von Neumann and Oskar Morgenstern.)[15] This approach differs from my own in that it does not directly assign priority levels to desires. Instead, it places only an ordinal preference relation on outcomes, then uses a set of axiomatic constraints on choice behavior to impose a cardinal utility ranking on actions. (One can see here the influence of neoclassical economic thinking, where ordinalism represents an important constraint.)

The von Neumann–Morgenstern procedure, rather than presupposing that the agent has a set of desires with given priority levels, assumes merely that the agent has a set of *preferences* that provide a rank ordering of the set of outcomes. There are certain advantages associated with introducing the term "preference" as a term of art in this context. The most significant is that the term "desire," unlike "belief," is not generally used to refer to an "all things considered" judgment. There is nothing wrong with having conflicting desires, such as a desire to go to the movies and a desire to stay home. The idea of a "preference" cuts out all these complications, by defining the "outcome" to include every aspect of the possible future state of the world that is of interest to the agent, then defining preferences as simply an ordering of this set of complete consequences. If the agent has a desire both to go to the movies and to stay home, then the agent's preference will be whatever ultimately emerges from the weighing of these two contradictory desires against one another. The mechanism through which a reconciliation of these sorts of conflicts between desires is achieved is of no interest to the decision theorist—the theory of practical rationality kicks in only at the point at which the agent has a well-ordered set of beliefs and preferences.

Even though the agent's ordinal preference ordering is taken as a given, it must still satisfy certain formal restrictions. First, preferences should form a complete transitive ordering over the set of outcomes. This is represented axiomatically in the form of two conditions:[16]

Completeness: For every pair of outcomes *a* and *b*, either *a* is weakly preferred to *b*, or *b* is weakly preferred to *a*.[17]

Transitivity: For any three outcomes *a*, *b*, and *c*, if *a* is weakly preferred to *b* and *b* is weakly preferred to *c*, then *a* is weakly preferred to *c*.

These two conditions alone suffice to define *ordinal* utility, which is just any function defined over the set of outcomes assigning a real number to $u(a)$ such that, for all *a* and *b*, $u(a) > u(b)$ just in case *a* is preferred to *b*. This provides a number for each outcome, but it does not say how "far apart" the preferences are from one another, that is, how strongly the agent prefers one outcome to another. The derivation of a *cardinal* utility function (i.e., a function that includes this information) requires four further assumptions. These assumptions presuppose the use of lotteries, understood again as probability distributions over the set of outcomes. Thus the agent can be given a lottery consisting of, for example, a *p* chance of receiving outcome *a*, and a $(1 - p)$ chance of receiving *b*.

Trivially, it is assumed that agents' preferences over outcomes can be extended to yield a complete, transitive ordering on the set of lotteries constructed from these outcomes. The more substantive assumptions are as follows:

Reduction of compound lotteries: A person is indifferent between a simple lottery over the set of outcomes and compound (multistage) lottery that yields exactly the same probability distribution over these outcomes (computed using the standard probability calculus).

Monotonicity: If the agent strictly prefers outcome *a* to *b*, and $0 \le p_2 < p_1 \le 1$, then the lottery that awards $p_1 a + (1 - p_1)b$ is strictly preferred to the lottery $p_2 a + (1 - p_2)b$.

Continuity: If *a* is weakly preferred to *b* and *b* weakly preferred to *c*, then there exists some number *p* such that $0 \le p \le 1$ and the agent is indifferent between *b* and the lottery $pa + (1 - p)c$.

The monotonicity assumption states that, all things being equal, the agent always prefers a higher probability of getting a better outcome. The continuity assumption states that, given any two lotteries, a lottery that gives probability *p* of receiving a better outcome and $(1 - p)$ of receiving a worse one will become better in a continuous manner as *p* increases. This implies that an outcome ranked anywhere between a better and worse outcome will be just as good as some lottery over the two. Let us arbitrarily assign the worst outcome o_w a utility of 0, and the best outcome o_b a value of 1. Clearly, for each point *p* on the number line between 0 and 1, there is a corresponding lottery that gives a *p* chance of getting o_b and a $(1 - p)$ chance of getting o_w. But this line "fills the space" between the best and worst outcomes, so all of the other outcomes, which are ranked somewhere in between, must be equivalent in value to some randomization over the extremes. This motivates the last assumption:

Substitutability: Given any outcome *a*, there is an equivalent lottery that awards some probability distribution over the extremes that is substitutable for *a*.

This means that for any particular outcome, there will be a lottery over the agent's most and least preferred options such that she is not only indifferent between that outcome and the lottery, but willing to accept the substitution of one for the other. The agent's cardinal utility for the outcome can then be represented by assigning it the same value as the probability placed on the most preferred outcome in this equivalent lottery. For example, indifference to a lottery that gives a 70 percent chance to the most preferred outcome would give the equivalent action a utility of 0.7. This provides the correct "spacing" between the numbers (in this example they are all between 0 and 1) and remains unique through any positive linear transformation.

Once a cardinal utility function has been derived to represent the agent's preferences over outcomes, it is very easy to determine how the agent selects an action. By definition, each of the agent's actions will yield one particular outcome, depending on which state of nature obtains. When the agent knows which state will obtain with certainty, she has only to choose the action that yields the best outcome. When there is some uncertainty as to which state will obtain, she chooses the action that yields the highest expected utility, given her beliefs about the relative probabilities of various states. This is easy to calculate: suppose the agent believes that action *a* will yield either outcome o_1 when state s_1 obtains or outcome o_2 when state s_2 obtains. If the agent believes that state s_1 will obtain with probability *p*, then the action *a* is essentially equivalent to the lottery $pu(o_1) + (1 - p) u(o_2)$, and so has the same utility. The agent therefore decides what to do simply by selecting the lottery available to her that has the highest expected utility.

1.3.   Social Interaction

Regardless of how one chooses to derive this conception of practical rationality as utility-maximization, it is important to recognize just how innocuous the principal assumptions have become. Early heroes of instrumentalism, such as Thrasymachus or Machiavelli, endorsed very substantive theories about the sort of desires that motivate people to act. For Thrasymachus, the ultimate interest of the superior man is to acquire power.[18] Machiavelli thought that "one can say this generally of men: that they are ungrateful, fickle, pretenders and dissemblers, evaders of danger, eager for gain."[19] But Hobbes was already moving away from this sort of view. Since the three "passions" he identifies are quite formal, he need not commit himself to such a specific view of human motivation. Courage, for example, he regards as just aversion "with hope of avoiding that hurt by resistance," anger as nothing but "sudden courage," and indignation as anger at an injury done to another. Thus the claim that individuals are motivated by appetites and aversions is intended to be extremely weak. What sort of counterexamples could there be? It is difficult to think of a motive that, at some level, does not amount to the positive or negative cathexis of some state of affairs.

Modern instrumentalism takes this strategy one step further. The concept of preference, or desire, is completely vacuous with respect to content. Thus the claim that rational agents maximize expected utility winds up being, in effect, just a precise development of the idea that agents decide what to do by ranking available outcomes and then choosing the action that they expect to provide the best result with respect to this ranking. Nowhere is it suggested, for example, that agents act from self-interested motives—the content of their desires has been left unspecified. The instrumentalist theory is not committed to any particular account of how agents' beliefs and desires are formed, instead choosing to treat them as exogenously determined. This means that there is nothing to stop one from supplementing this model of action with a characterization of desire-rationality that places substantive constraints on the way agents rank outcomes. (The moral realist could claim, for instance, that just as true beliefs accurately reflect some objective probability distribution over states, good desires accurately reflect some objective order of values. The fully rational agent could then be characterized as one who seeks to believe what is true and desire what is good.[20] In this case, all that the model outlined above would suggest is that knowing the truth, the rational agent then seeks to maximize the good.)

Given the thinness of the theory, one could easily be misled into thinking most of the objections to the instrumental conception of rationality, or at least its decision-theoretic expression, rest on misunderstanding of the theory. After all, it is difficult to think of a conception of rational action that could not, in some sense, be characterized as instrumental. Neo-Aristotelian theories of action, for example, such as the ones promulgated by Alisdair MacIntyre and Charles Taylor, are all perfectly compatible with the sort of instrumentalism expressed in preference-based decision theory.[21] There is, however, one important little wrinkle. The problem arises with the introduction of a second rational agent into the framework. (For simplicity, I shall confine my remarks to two-person cases, with an understanding that everything said can be generalized to n person cases.)

The situation that is of interest arises in the context of what rational choice theorists call "interdependent choice." This is a situation in which the outcome is determined *jointly* by the actions of two separate agents. It was mentioned earlier that actions and states are the two classes of events that combine to cause an outcome. Social interaction refers to a situation in which the action of the first agent combines with the action of a second agent in order to produce an outcome. Thus the action of one agent will be a state for the other, and vice versa. The question that arises is how agents are supposed to develop rational beliefs in such a context. In the decision-theoretic case, beliefs could be treated as exogenous to the choice problem. But when the first agent's state is actually the second agent's action, it is no longer possible to fix beliefs in a way that is exogenous to the choice problem.

In a simple decision problem, the agent could start by assigning probabilities to states and then move on to the problem of deciding what to do. But when agents are interacting with one another, each agent must solve both of these problems simultaneously. In order to decide what to do, the first agent must determine the probability of various states obtaining. But since these states are simply the second agent's actions, the first agent must determine what the second agent intends to do. In order to figure this out, he must figure out what the second agent's beliefs are. But since the second agent's beliefs about what state will obtain are equivalent to her beliefs about what the first agent will do, and since this is precisely what the first agent is still trying to decide, a regress of anticipations arises.

Since the state that will obtain for each agent is no longer given in advance of the decision problem, both agents must solve for two variables simultaneously. Not only must each decide which action to choose, she must also determine which state will obtain. The problem is that which state will obtain depends on which actions will be chosen, and which actions will be chosen depends on which state will obtain. This presents a serious problem for the instrumental conception of practical rationality. Since states provide the link between outcomes and actions, the only way to reason back from a desired outcome to a favored action is via some knowledge of the state. Without some mechanism for pinning down these beliefs, *it will simply be impossible for agents to reason instrumentally in social contexts.*

Von Neumann and Morgenstern were actually the first to recognize the seriousness of this problem. In their introduction to *The Theory of Games and Economic Behaviour*, they wrote:

> Every participant can determine the variables which describe his own actions, but not those of the others. Nevertheless, those "alien" variables cannot, from his point of view, be described by statistical assumptions. This is because the others are guided, just as he himself, by rational principles.... [Thus the traditional "Robinson Crusoe" model of instrumental rationality] is of much more limited value to economic theory than has been assumed heretofore even by the most radical critics.[22]

Two possible programmatic strategies present themselves at this point. One would be to suppose that social interaction presents a fundamentally new type of problem, one that agents will require some additional cognitive resources in order to resolve. Earlier, I presented desires and beliefs as selection criteria that allowed the agent to eliminate choice options. It is always possible that the introduction of some new criterion—corresponding to a new category of intentional states—might be called on to resolve social interaction problems. Given that human beings are, first and foremost, social animals, it would not be surprising to find that we had some dedicated psychological equipment to assist us in resolving social interaction problems.

The alternative to introducing some specifically social form of decision criterion would be to suppose that the regress of anticipations is not vicious, and that agents, given only the basic resources supplied under the decision-theoretic model, would be able to find some way of pinning down states. The idea here would be to explore the regress to see if it stops somewhere.

This second option is what has developed into the program known as *game theory*. The objective of game-theoretic analysis is to find a way of working through the regress of anticipations in such a way as to allow a stable set of beliefs to emerge for all players, without introducing any new sort of selection criterion. A game-theoretic "solution" is therefore an *equilibrium* of beliefs, and game theory is a general mechanism for determining beliefs about the relative probabilities of various states. For each player, *strategic reasoning* operates by working through the cycles of anticipation in such a way as to turn other players' actions (which have not yet been planned or performed), into events that will occur with specific probabilities. When such a reduction is possible, each player's choice can then be handled as a simple decision problem.

In the initial stages of the development of game theory, the idea that interaction problems could be separated out into decision problems showed some promise. The same sort of tree diagrams used to represent choice problems can be used to represent social interaction, with the two agents "playing" against each other, rather than against nature. The only difference is that the payoffs are now given as a vector, showing the payoff to player 1 first, to player 2 second, and so on. Consider the game illustrated in figure 1.4. Here, player 1's actions $A_1 = \{U, D\}$ are states for player 2, and player 2's actions $A_2 = \{L, R\}$ are states for player 1. Obviously, before the players decide what to do, it is impossible to assign any probability to the occurrence of any state. The fact that player 2 does not know what player 1 is going to do is represented by the dashed line between her two nodes.

In this case, it takes only a small effort for both players to determine what the other will do. Agents might begin reasoning like a typical chess player, with an hypothesis of the form "suppose I decide to do *x*." They can then go on to

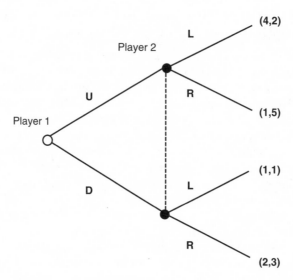

Figure 1.4 Social interaction.

consider how the other player would respond, how they would respond to that response, and so on, in order to see if this process levels off somewhere. With luck, they will be able to find a pair of responses that is consistent with every initial hypothesis. In the game shown in figure 1.4, player 1 might think: "Suppose player 2 expects me to play U. In that case, she will plan to play R. But if player 2 is going to play R, I would be better off playing D. So then what if player 2 expects me to play D? If player 2 expects me to play D, she will continue to play R. So no matter what she expects me to do, she will play R. Therefore, I should play whatever is my best response to R, namely D." In this example, L is a *strongly dominated strategy*, that is, it is always worse for player 2 than R. Since no rational agent would ever play such a strategy, player 1 can predict R with certainty. This effectively changes the game into a decision for player 1 between the (U,R) and (D,R) outcomes.

The solutions generated by the elimination of strongly dominated strategies are not always so obvious, especially when the decision problem is more complex. For more difficult problems, it is often convenient to represent the decision as just a matrix of payoffs (this is known as the normal form, as opposed to the sequential or extended form, representation of games). Consider figure 1.5, which shows a game in which two players each have three actions available to them.

In this example, all of the players' strategies seem to have something to recommend them, and so the interaction seems quite indeterminate. However, on closer inspection, one can see that player 2's strategy R is strongly dominated. No matter what player 1 does, player 2 will always be better off playing M than R. As a result, player 1 can infer that player 2 will not play R. However, if player 2 is not going to be playing R, then player 1 has no reason to ever play D, since either of his other two strategies is better under L and M. In other words, strategy D *becomes* strongly dominated as soon as R is eliminated from consideration. So player 1 should never play D, because it could never be rational for him to assume that player 2 will play R. However, once D is eliminated, then player 2 no longer has any incentive to play M. So player 1 can infer that player 2 will play L, and so he will be best off playing U. Thus there is a single solution to this game,

Player 2

		L	**M**	**R**
	U	(2,5)	(3,4)	(1,3)
Player 1	**C**	(1,3)	(4,2)	(2,1)
	D	(0,2)	(2,7)	(8,4)

Figure 1.5 Iterated elimination of dominated strategies.

(U,L), which can be discovered through the iterated elimination of dominated strategies.

This example is particularly tidy, because the (U,L) outcome has the advantage of being both stable and convergent—stable because neither player would have an incentive to switch strategies if (U,L) is the anticipated outcome, and convergent because every set of initial hypotheses about what either player will choose leads to the selection of this outcome. Thus it is possible for players to "power" their way through to a solution, just by considering all of the implications of all of the options available to them. The regress of anticipations is therefore harmless, because every process of reasoning leads to (U,L). Such a solution might lead one to be optimistic about the prospect that instrumental reasoning in social contexts might turn out to be just a slightly more sophisticated version of the way people reason in nonsocial contexts. Unfortunately, things are not so simple. Figure 1.6 shows a game that has no dominated strategies. Here it is clear that some other sort of solution concept will be required.

The kind of solution proposed for figure 1.5 is called an equilibrium because it contains a set of beliefs and strategies that has no tendency to change. More specifically, it is a set in which the strategies that it contains do not imply any false beliefs. To see this, consider what happens if a player adopts as a proposed solution a strategy that is not in equilibrium. Suppose player 2 decides to play M. In order for this strategy to be rational, she must believe that player 1 is going to play D. But since it would only be rational for him to play D if he believes that she will play R, then she must believe that he believes that she plans to play R. If we assume that player 1 is rational (and that player 2 believes that player 1 is rational, etc.)[23] this ascription of belief must be false. Thus player 2's strategy, because it is out of equilibrium, undermines the set of beliefs that sustains it. There is nothing inconsistent, however, about planning to play L while assuming the player 1 plans to play U. In this case, the interlocking set of beliefs and strategies, on the part of both players, is not self-undermining.

Thus it must be a general property of any proposed solution to a game that it be in equilibrium—that is, that the set of beliefs and strategies not be self-undermining. This is the idea that gave rise to the first general game-theoretic solution concept, proposed by John Nash.[24] According to Nash, a solution will be in equilibrium so long as each player's strategy is a best response to the strategies of

Player 2

		L	R
Player 1	U	(3,1)	(0,0)
	D	(0,0)	(1,3)

Figure 1.6 Battle of the sexes.

the others (and each player believes that everyone else is going to play the strategy specified in the solution).[25] This definition captures the idea that any solution must be self-enforcing. If each player's strategy maximizes expected utility, given the strategies of the others, then no one has an incentive to change strategies, and so no one has any reason to believe that anyone will change strategies. Thus the overall set of intentions and beliefs will have no tendency to undermine itself.

The Nash solution concept allows one to resolve a variety of different games that cannot be solved through elimination of dominated strategies, such as the one shown in figure 1.6. Unfortunately, not all these games have only one equilibrium, so defined. In figure 1.6, the so-called Battle of the Sexes game, both (U,L) and (D,R) are in equilibrium. Under the hypothesis that player 1 will choose U, player 2 will choose L, but under the hypothesis that he will play D, she will play R. Unfortunately, no process of reasoning will lead players to converge on one or the other of these outcomes. Thus, unlike figure 1.5, here it is impossible for players to "power" their way through to a solution.

This is known as the "equilibrium-selection" problem in game theory. To make things worse, there are some games in which no outcome appears to be either stable or convergent. To see this, consider figure 1.7. Again, player 1 can start out: "Suppose player 2 expects me to play U. In that case, she will respond with R. But if player 2 is going to play R, I would be better off playing D. So player 2 should expect me to play D. But if player 2 expects me to player D, she will switch to L. But if player 2 is going to play L, I would be better off playing U … (etc.)." No matter what you take as the initial hypothesis, this vicious cycle of expectations develops. Thus there is no set of pure strategy choices that is not self-defeating—and thus there appears to be no decision that would not depend on an internally inconsistent set of strategies and beliefs.

Nash did have a solution to this "existence" problem, although it has not been universally accepted. The basic idea is to allow players to randomize over their possible strategies, for example, to throw dice to determine what to do. So instead of just playing "pure" strategies like U and D, player 1 could also adopt a "mixed" strategy, like [$\frac{3}{10}$U, $\frac{7}{10}$D]. This is equivalent to expanding the set of outcomes to include not just the "pure" outcomes, but the entire set of randomizations over these outcomes. Subject to a few minor qualifications, this guarantees that every game has at least one stable outcome.[26] In the game illustrated in figure 1.7, the

Player 2

		L	R
	U	(3,0)	(1,3)
Player 1			
	D	(0,3)	(3,1)

Figure 1.7 Absence of pure strategy equilibrium.

strategy profile ([⁴⁄₇U,³⁄₇D],[⁴⁄₇L,³⁄₇R]) a Nash equilibrium. (Since these strategies give both players an expected utility of for either of ¹²⁄₇ their actions, both are willing to play these randomizations over the two.)

While this modification solves the existence problem, it unfortunately only serves to worsen the equilibrium selection problem. The first, more mundane complication arises from the fact that the introduction of mixed strategies increases the number of equilibria in most games. While it serves to provide equilibria where previously none existed, it also adds some new ones in cases where there was already an excess. In figure 1.6, the introduction of mixed strategies adds a new equilibrium to the game: ([³⁄₄U,¹⁄₄D],[³⁄₄L,¹⁄₄R]). Since there are now three equilibria in this game, each the stable outcome of a process of reasoning beginning with one of three different initial suppositions, it becomes even more important to determine where these suppositions come from.

The more exotic complication stems from the type of belief supports that mixed strategy equilibria require. What holds the equilibrium together against deviation is the fact that each player's strategy makes the other completely indifferent between his actions. For instance, in figure 1.7 the expectation that player 1 will play [⁴⁄₇U,³⁄₇D] gives player 2 an expected payoff of, ¹²⁄₇ regardless of whether she chooses L, R, or some randomization over the two. This means that she has no specific reason *not* to play [⁴⁄₇L,³⁄₇R] but of course no specific reason to do so either. But then what grounds does player 1 have for expecting player 2 to play [⁴⁄₇L,³⁄₇R] in the first place? The answer is: none in particular. All the equilibrium does is provide a point on which the regress of expectations can be terminated; it does not provide the agents with any actual guide to action. This effectively drives a wedge between the expectations and the strategic plans of agents. In the equilibrium in figure 1.4, player 2's belief that player 1 is going to choose D happily coincides with the fact that player 1, insofar as he is rational, actually plans to choose D. In a mixed strategy equilibrium, everyone's expectations can be rational, yet systematically false. Furthermore, when it comes to actually deciding what to do, both players are free to ignore the strategies that they assign to themselves under the equilibrium.

This means that in order to arrive at a mixed strategy equilibrium, players must basically set aside the question of what anyone might actually do, and specifically go looking for a set of beliefs that will terminate their regress of anticipations. Players will then adopt these expectations, not because they expect them to come true, or plan to make them come true, but simply because they provide a stop to the regress. This makes these beliefs seem more like useful fictions than serious expectations. This might be set aside as merely a peculiarity of these equilibria, except that it renders even more acute the problem of where the players' initial hypotheses about possible actions are supposed to come from.

There have been a variety of proposals aimed at resolving this difficulty consistent with the overall reductionist ambitions of the game theory project. First, it is worth mentioning that the introduction of *refinements* on the Nash equilibrium concept has resulted in a slight reduction in the size of the solution sets. Some of these refinements, like *subgame-perfection* and *trembling-hand perfection*, simply correct for the fact that the Nash solution concept places no constraints on players' responses to zero-probability events.[27] While these refinements are clearly simple extensions of the formal conception of strategic rationality, a number of other refinements go much further, introducing substantive constraints on the range of admissible outcomes. These include, for instance, restrictions that serve to eliminate Pareto-dominated equilibria.[28] While these are in some sense quite plausible, they introduce principles or considerations that simply are not implied by the instrumental conception of rationality, and so represent an obvious departure from the reductionist program.

Either way, it should be fairly obvious that there is only so much that can be accomplished by way of refinements. In a game like Battle of the Sexes, which has two perfectly symmetric pure strategy equilibria, there is, from a purely rational standpoint, simply no relevant difference between them that could serve as a basis for the elimination of one or the other. Refinements serve to eliminate equilibria that are, in some often subtle sense, defective. It therefore seems quite unlikely that the general equilibrium-selection problem can be adequately addressed in this manner.

The second major hope was that equilibrium selection problems might be due to the fact that simple "one-shot" games, like the ones shown above, represent too short a time frame for agents to effectively coordinate expectations. It was hoped that over repeated plays of the same game, a dominant equilibrium might emerge. This hope was soon dashed by the discovery that over repeated plays of the same game, where players are able to choose actions for each stage game that are conditional on the actions taken by other players in the previous game, the set of equilibria is dramatically enlarged. Most important, proof of the so-called "folk-theorem" established that for infinitely repeated games, or finitely repeated games where there is some uncertainty as to when the sequence will end, the set of sustainable equilibria is infinitely large.[29] Although this wild proliferation of equilibria does not occur in all finitely repeated games, under no circumstances is the number of equilibria reduced. The basic reason is that iteration of the game allows players to adopt strategies that prescribe a complicated pattern of different actions for different stage games. This not only increases the size of their strategy sets, but makes it so that their past actions continue to be an unreliable indicator of their intentions in future play.

The final, and perhaps most widely shared hope, was that the introduction of some kind of communication system would help players select an equilibrium. Naturally, there was never any question of introducing primitive semantic resources into the game (such as a separate class of actions that would carry some coded information content), since this would amount to an abandonment of the reductionist program. The idea instead was that a communicative interaction might be modeled as a special type of multistage game, in which one player's choice of action allowed others to make accurate inferences about his beliefs or intentions. A communication system of this type could then be pegged onto a variety of standard games as a "preplay" segment, allowing one or more players to effectively announce their intentions before beginning the game.

This idea was abandoned when it was discovered that models of this type also have the unfortunate consequence of increasing, rather than decreasing, the number of equilibria.[30] Because the "meaning" of each player's signal is not fixed exogenously but is determined by the effective equilibrium, a new equilibrium can always be created by permuting the mapping of meanings to actions. To illustrate, since the relationship between sounds and meanings is essentially arbitrary, for every equilibrium in which "left" means left and "right" means right, there will be another in which "left" means right and "right" means left. As long as this relationship is common knowledge, no agent has any reason to prefer one over the other.

In addition to this, there is the "problem of neologisms."[31] Since the meaning of messages is determined by the effective equilibrium, the occurrence of any message that is not anticipated under the equilibrium is a zero-probability event. This means that Bayesian reasoning places no constraints on the meaning that players can ascribe to such a message. This gives rise to a new batch of equilibria in which players assign to any message that is not expected the same meaning as one of the messages that is expected, rendering the sender indifferent between the two. Because messages in these games are not directly associated with payoffs, none of the standard equilibrium refinements are able to screen out such deviant interpretations. Thus, assuming that players have available a compositional language, the equilibrium set of every such game will be infinitely large.

The intractability of the equilibrium selection problem creates a serious problem for the game theory project in its strict reductionist form. It appears that instrumental rationality is simply indeterminate—it fails to yield a single practical recommendation in contexts of social interaction. This is a relatively serious flaw, since the Nash equilibrium solution concept does not do anything to specify the mechanism through which agents are supposed to arrive at the beliefs that sustain the equilibrium. All it does it pick out sets of beliefs and intentions that are not self-contradictory. As Cristina Bicchieri puts it:

> [Nash's] admittedly limited definition of mutually rational beliefs would be completely satisfactory were game theory just bound to define what an equilibrium is and the conditions which make it possible.... Yet normative game theory's aim is to prescribe actions that will bring about an equilibrium, which means providing a unique rational recommendation on how to play. Indeed, if the task of the theorist were limited to pointing to a set of rational actions, the players might never succeed in coordinating their actions, since different agents might follow different recommendations. Thus a unique rational action for every player must be recommended, together with a unique belief about the behavior of other players justifying it.[32]

Roger Myerson, one of the strongest proponents of rationality-based game theory, suggests that this indeterminacy problem reveals "an essential limit on the ability of mathematical game theory to predict people's behavior in real conflict situations and an important agenda for research in social psychology and cultural anthropology."[33] If this is correct, then it has significant consequences for the instrumental conception of rationality, since it demonstrates that, in a wide variety of social interactions, agents are simply not able to make the inference from a desired outcome back to a favored action. The "overwhelmingly plausible" idea that agents make decisions by ranking outcomes, then choosing the action that gives them the prospects, relative to this ranking of outcomes, is still overwhelmingly plausible; it is just that agents involved in social interactions *are no longer capable of doing so.*

1.4. The Problem of Order

The indeterminacy problem is the first major difficulty that the instrumental conception of rationality encounters when the attempt is made to extend it from nonsocial to social contexts. It is something of a glaring defect. For example, it raises questions about how rational individuals could manage simple tasks like passing on a sidewalk without colliding.[34] There are two equilibria: the first person goes left, the second goes right; and the first person goes right, the second goes left. Furthermore, regardless of how either one feels about left or right passing, they are both interested in avoiding collisions. This means that each one wants to go left only if the other is going right, and wants to go right only if the other is going left. So how does either of them choose? It would appear that—absent further supplementation—game theory, and hence a strictly instrumental conception of rationality, cannot tell us.

This is not the end of the problems, however. The second major difficulty with the instrumental conception of rationality has a more overtly normative dimension, although it, too, generates an explanatory deficit. The basic problem is that game theory appears to recommend courses of action to us that are collectively disastrous. In fact, many of the "utility-maximizing" courses of action recommended constitute patterns of behavior that, in everyday life, we would usually identify as being "dumb" (or at least "self-defeating"). Specifically, situations may arise in which every agent involved in an interaction could be made better off by being *prevented* from pursuing a utility-maximizing course of action.

The most celebrated instance of this is the prisoner's dilemma. Consider figure 1.8. Both L and U are strongly dominated strategies in this game, so the only equilibrium is (D,R). However, (D,R) gives a payoff of only (1,1), whereas (U,L) gives a payoff of (2,2). Thus (U,L) is better for both players. Unfortunately, (U,L) is unobtainable—if player 2 thought player 1 was going to play U, she would switch to R, and if player 1 thought that player 2 was going to play L, he would switch to D. Actually, it doesn't even matter what either of them thinks about the other—D and R are always the best strategies. And yet they produce an outcome that is worse for both players than (U,L).

In the vocabulary that has become standard in the literature, actions like L and U are referred to as "cooperative" (since if players were to sit down and discuss the situation beforehand, they should be able to agree to perform those actions.) However, when it comes time to act, both players have an incentive to defect from this agreement (thus the noncooperative strategy in this game has become known as "defect"). The person who defects is also called a "free rider," because he is trying to secure the advantages of cooperation, without doing his part to sustain the cooperative solution.

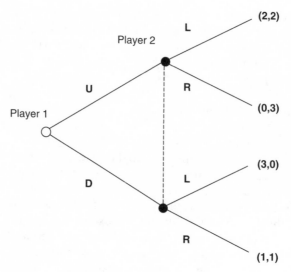

Figure 1.8 Prisoner's dilemma.

The prisoner's dilemma is, in fact, just a special instance of a more general problem, which is that the equilibria of games need not be Pareto-optimal. (A situation is Pareto-optimal just in case it is impossible to increase one person's payoff without lowering someone else's. Thus the fact that equilibria need not be Pareto-optimal means that there may be other outcomes in which at least one person could be made better off, and no one worse off.) Many more complex games exhibit this same characteristic. Consider figure 1.9, which presents a rough sketch of what we commonly call a "race to the bottom." On the first iteration, strategies R and D get eliminated (they are dominated), so it looks like players can get, at best (3,3) rather than (5,5). But on the second iteration, strategies C and M have now become dominated, and so they, too, get eliminated. This leaves (U,L) as the sole equilibrium. As a result, the players wind up each getting a payoff of 1. Thus a race to the bottom consists of a set of "embedded" prisoner's dilemmas, in which the outcome becomes progressively worse with each new cycle of reasoning (or with each new play of the game, if the choices are occurring sequentially).

Finally, it is possible for more than two people to get into a prisoner's dilemma. Whenever individuals are able to improve their own condition in a way that imposes a cost on others, it will normally be the utility-maximizing course of action to do so. However, when everyone does this, the accumulated costs may easily outweigh the advantages achieved through defection—leaving everyone worse off than they were to start with. When this happens in groups it is known as a collective action problem or, more colorfully, as a "tragedy of the commons."[35]

Many theorists have thought that there is something paradoxical about these sorts of situations, and so have tried to come up with a "solution" to the

Player 2

		L	M	R
	U	(1,1)	(4,0)	(4,0)
Player 1	**C**	(0,4)	(3,3)	(6,2)
	D	(0,4)	(2,6)	(5,5)

Figure 1.9 Race to the bottom.

prisoner's dilemma. This has usually taken the form of some abstruse form of reasoning designed to show that it is really "rational" to cooperate in interactions that have this structure.[36] There is good reason to believe, however, that the situation must be more complex than this. After all, real people going about their daily affairs all routinely fall into prisoner's dilemmas—it's usually impossible to drive down a city street for five minutes without getting into one. Furthermore, individuals often continue to defect, even when they know it is contributing to their own problems, simply because they have no incentive to stop. Thus the fact that instrumental reasoning often leads us into prisoner's dilemmas may not be a defect in the theory, but rather just a feature of the human condition—there may be nothing paradoxical about it. As Thomas Schelling put it: "Things don't work out optimally for a simple reason: there is no reason why they should. There is no mechanism that attunes individual responses to some collective accomplishment."[37]

Take some typical examples: Gridlock is a collective action problem that arises when streets are heavily congested. Cars enter an intersection on a green light, but because of congestion ahead, are unable to clear the intersection. As a result, when the light changes, cars traveling on the other road are unable to get through, causing congestion that may lock up the intersection behind *them*. If this happens two more times, the intersections on all four corners of a block can get locked up. The amazing thing about gridlock is that if the streets are one-way it can last forever, since the four obstructions may become mutually reinforcing. Then it can only be corrected if someone somewhere *backs out* of an intersection. So this is clearly a suboptimal outcome. The reason it is so common is that the interaction has the structure of a prisoner's dilemma. Each driver has a choice of either entering the intersection as soon as possible, or else waiting to ensure that the intersection can be cleared before entering. The danger is that if you don't enter the intersection right away, the cars going the other way may lock you out. Furthermore, if you do enter the intersection, the worst that can happen is that you block the cars going the other way—you still get through faster. So while choosing to enter increases the average travel time on the road, those who enter rather than wait nevertheless always reduce their own personal travel time. Thus if everyone reasons instrumentally, then everyone will choose to enter, and average travel time will increase (as shown in figure 1.10).

Because of the nature of traffic flow, this is a "one-shot" prisoner's dilemma. People often get into these situations inadvertently—by the time they realize what they've done, it's too late. However, it is also quite common for people to get into races to the bottom. Here they have ample time to reflect on the consequences of their actions. The fact that they so often persist strongly supports the view that instrumental rationality does in fact recommend defection in these situations. For example, anyone who has lived in an apartment building knows what it is like to listen to a neighbor's music through the wall. Many people respond to the problem by putting on some music of their own, in order to drown out the offensive noise coming from next door. This can generate a typical prisoner's dilemma. Suppose one person puts on some music at fairly high volume. This irritates her neighbor, who responds by putting on some music of his own. Note that he would rather not listen to any music at all, but if he does have to listen to some, he would rather listen to his own than his neighbor's. However, once he puts on his stereo, his neighbor can now hear some of his music filtering through her wall, which diminishes her listening enjoyment. But she can hardly turn off her stereo now, since that would make the music from next door even more irritating. So she turns her stereo up. Now the race to the bottom has begun. If her neighbor responds by turning up his stereo, she may have no choice but to turn her own up again. Eventually they may find themselves listening to their own music at such high volume that they would both prefer silence. But neither is in a position to unilaterally call off the competition.

The first person to suspect that these sorts of collective action problems might be all-pervasive was Hobbes. If our natural inclination is to reason instrumentally, then

> there is no place for Industry; because the fruit thereof is uncertain: and consequently no Culture of the Earth; no Navigation, nor use of the commodities that may be imported by Sea; no commodious Building; no

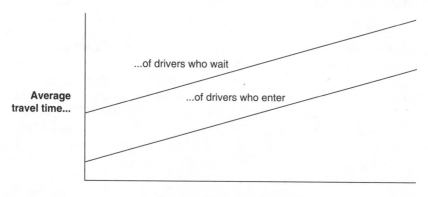

Figure 1.10 Gridlock as prisoner's dilemma.

Instruments of moving, and removing such things as require much force; no Knowledge of the face of the Earth; no account of Time; no Arts; no Letters; no Society; and which is worst of all, continuall feare, and danger of violent death.[38]

All of these activities will be impossible because they require *cooperation*. The state of nature will be unappealing, in Hobbes's view, not because people are evil, or because they have the wrong sort of motives, but simply because they pursue their interests in an instrumental fashion. (Thus Hobbes's characterization of the state of nature does, as I suggested earlier, follow quite directly from his assumptions about the nature of practical rationality.)

All it takes is a little bit of laziness in order to generate a prisoner's dilemma. Take, for instance, Hobbes's claims that people in the state of nature will be incapable of "removing such things as require much force." This seems like a very odd claim, and it has received very little mention in the literature. What could be the reasoning here? Why should people be unable to get together to lift heavy objects? The problem is that work effort, in this case, is unobservable. Suppose a group of six people get together to lift a rock. If every one of them put a moderate amount of effort into it, they could easily pick it up. However, each one might reason as follows: "Why should I throw my back out lifting this rock? If I choose not to push quite as hard, the others will certainly take up the slack." Of course, if they all reason this way, the rock will go nowhere. This is a classic collective action problem. Call it the pallbearer's dilemma.

Some people have taken this prima facie consequence of rational choice theory—that one should always defect in a prisoner's dilemma—to undermine the normativity of instrumental rationality. It leads us to question whether we should always follow the recommendations of the instrumentalist, or whether we might not be better off adopting some other sort of standard of choice. The most explicitly formulated version of this claim is the one developed by David Gauthier, who argues that self-interest should lead us to choose a choice disposition that recommends noninstrumental (or non-utility-maximizing) choice in particular circumstances.[39] However, I would like to set these arguments aside for the moment, in order to focus on a more basic difficulty. Both the problem of indeterminacy and the problem of suboptimality present a challenge to the empirical adequacy of the instrumental conception of rationality. While we often fall into suboptimal interaction patterns, we also have a somewhat mysterious ability to avoid them in many circumstances. Much of the time, people are able to organize their interactions in a way that is both coordinated and cooperative. While we do sometimes experience failures of cooperation—and while we do sometimes run into difficulties passing each other on the sidewalk—the fact is that most of the time we are able to avoid these sorts of problems. We sometimes even act cooperatively—forgoing opportunities for profitable defection—just for fun.

To take just one example of this, patrons at drive-through Tim Hortons donut shops in Canada sometimes like to amuse themselves by playing the following game: One person starts things off by paying not only for his own order, but for the order of the person in the car behind him (which, by the time he is at the window, will already have been placed). Thus the person behind will be surprised to discover, when she finally reaches the drive-through window, that her order has already been paid for by the person ahead, who has at this point driven off. She responds, in turn, by paying for the order of the next person behind. This continues until someone finally defects and simply drives off with his or her free coffee and donut. Employees at Tim Hortons report, however, that during morning rush hour, the "pay it forward" system will often be sustained for half an hour or longer. The fact that cooperation is so *obviously* vulnerable to defection in this system is, presumably, one of the reasons that people take pleasure in creating and sustaining it.

Everyone is presumably familiar with "pay it forward" anecdotes of this sort. More rigorous data is also available. Experimental game theory has demonstrated unequivocally that randomly selected subjects, thrown together into one-shot anonymous interactions, are able to achieve levels of cooperation and coordination that far exceed those predicted by standard rational choice theory.[40] The question is what sort of resources these subjects are using in order to manage their interactions, and to achieve these outcomes. If the resources being deployed can all be modeled within the framework of the instrumental conception of rationality, then there is really no problem, and so no normative issue to be addressed. But if they cannot, it suggests that the reductionist game theory program is a failure, and that the model of action should be expanded in order to incorporate noninstrumental deliberative considerations.

1.5. Conclusion

The two problems outlined above—the problem of coordination and the problem of cooperation—are often bundled together and referred to as "the problem of order." In the following chapter, I will consider the various solutions to this problem that have been proposed over the years. For the moment, I would just like to comment briefly on what is at stake in this discussion. The instrumental conception of rationality derives much of its plausibility from the intuitively appealing character of the psychological assumptions with which it begins. However, this initial elaboration of the instrumental model—including the expected-utility-maximization theorem—is done with respect to completely nonsocial choice problems. It is only after the model has been fully specified that an attempt is made to generalize it to handle social interaction. At this point, the model encounters very substantial difficulties. The regress of anticipations that arises in social interactions threatens to undermine our ability to select an instrumentally rational course of action in these contexts. Furthermore, there is no a priori reason to believe that such a problem should be resolvable. Equations containing two variables are a completely different kettle of fish from equations with only one. Game theorists have made a valiant effort, but the problem of order shows that much of the theoretical debt incurred remains outstanding (in fact, the problem of order just *is* the segment of the debt that remains outstanding).

Not only is there no a priori reason to suspect that the problem of order should be resolvable within the framework of an instrumental conception of rationality, there is good reason to think that it should *not* be. In the background of the instrumentalist strategy is an assumption that, on reflection, can easily be seen to be dubious. The idea that decision theory should provide the "foundations" for game theory amounts to the assumption that all of the "equipment" a rational agent brings to bear on the world is already in place and deployed in nonsocial contexts. It is, as von Neumann and Morgenstern astutely observed, a "Robinson Crusoe" conception of rationality. When other people come along, they get treated as simply more complex objects. The goal of strategic reasoning is, quite literally, to parameterize human behavior, so that the actions of others can be predicted like any other natural event.

The plausibility of this approach has a lot more to do with the popularity of certain sorts of philosophical theories of mind than with any sort of empirical psychological evidence. It's not as though actual human infants learn how to deal with "easy stuff" like tables and balls first, then go on to deal with more complex subjects, like their mothers. They learn to deal with people first. It is in fact a commonplace observation in developmental psychology that human infants begin by treating all objects in their environment as essentially social, and only much later learn to separate out the animate from the inanimate, and the nonhuman from the human. Thus it is quite possible that we do not "build up" from reasoning in nonsocial to social contexts, but rather, we "scale back" our reasoning when we drop down from social to nonsocial contexts. From this perspective, it is quite plausible to think that the resources we deploy in nonsocial contexts might be a subset of the full set of cognitive resources we deploy in everyday social interactions—and thus that a reduction of social to nonsocial choice problems should not be possible.

If this is the view, then the best way to elaborate a theory of practical rationality would be to begin with an analysis of the structure of social interaction, in order to see what sort of resources people appear to be using to organize these exchanges. Once this is done, an attempt can be made to develop a more formal model of the relevant deliberative processes, one that will parallel the sort of elaboration that provided us with the decision-theoretic model of practical deliberation. Unfortunately, the dominant inclination among economists has not been to expand the model of rational action, but rather to drop the rationality postulate entirely, in favor of evolutionary or behavioral models of action. Thus "cooperation" often gets mentioned in the same breath as cognitive biases, framing effects, bounded rationality, and other well-known instances in which individuals are clearly violating the canons of "ideal" rationality. This is premature. The fact that the mostly strictly reductionist model of practical rationality on offer fails to explain several aspects of social interaction does not render the concept of rational action as a whole methodologically otiose. It merely suggests that a less psychologically austere model may have greater success.

2

Social Order

One of the hardest things to understand about humanity is how it is that we can be such *sociable* creatures and, at the same time, so prone to destructive and antisocial forms of behavior. Our sociability extends far beyond the obvious fact that we rely on complex forms of cooperation in order to secure our physical survival. Most of us spend our entire lives embedded in a dense web of social relations, which we depend on both psychologically and emotionally. When we get lonely, we go looking for company and conversation, deriving pleasure from the simple act of talking with another person. But at the same time that we are so powerfully bonded to one another, we also routinely engage in activities that benefit us at the direct expense of others. The problem is not just with overtly aggressive behavior. People can be extremely uncooperative in very routine affairs, often refusing to set aside their own interests even when it makes everyone worse off in the end.

Immanuel Kant suggested that understanding the nature of this latent antagonism—what he called our "unsocial sociability"—was the key to understanding the development of human society.[1] This tension between our social and antisocial tendencies has, for subsequent generations of philosophers and social theorists, given rise to a number of extremely difficult technical questions. For centuries, they have been puzzled, not just by how social order in human societies is achieved, but by how it is even possible. In some ways, we know more about how the activities of ant colonies are organized and reproduced than we do about how human societies function.[2] People often engage in patterns of interaction that involve an amazing level of coordination, but our dependence on cultural transmission of these social structures suggests that we are not "hardwired," or programmed, to interact in these ways. Given this instinctual underdetermination of behavior, it is unclear how these stable patterns of social interaction are possible at all. According to sociologists Peter Berger and Thomas Luckmann:

> The human organism lacks the necessary biological means to provide stability for human conduct. Human existence, if it were thrown back on its organismic resources by themselves, would be existence in some sort of chaos. Such chaos is, however, empirically unavailable, even though one may theoretically conceive of it. Empirically, human existence takes place in a context of order, direction, stability. The question then arises: From what does the empirically existing stability of human order derive?[3]

But at the same time that human societies exhibit a greater level of order than our biology might lead one to predict, we are also capable of doing things that, while not producing total chaos, do involve catastrophic failures of cooperation or coordination. Often these failures are not induced by external events, but arise entirely as a consequence of actions taken by individuals within the society (with "crime waves" and civil wars being the most conspicuous examples). In human societies, elements of the social structure sometimes fall apart, and often no one is quite sure why (in part, this is because no one is sure what makes them hang together in the first place). When we refer knowingly to the "rise and fall" of empires, we are tacitly suggesting that every form of social organization, no matter how successful, eventually succumbs to its own inner tensions. There appear to be both centrifugal and centripetal forces at work in every society, but the nature of these forces is very poorly understood.

Many attempts have been made to explain the orderliness of social interaction in instrumental terms. The general strategy here has been to claim that there is some mechanism at work in certain social contexts that creates a harmony of interest among individuals. Social order, according to this view, is nothing other than a consequence of individually maximizing behavior under the correct set of institutional circumstances. The background image here is of course that of a market economy, which is widely thought to supply a system of incentives that seamlessly integrates the interests of instrumentally rational individuals in such a way as to produce mutually beneficial outcomes. The challenge is then to show that such mechanisms exist in other domains of social interaction, and that a set of agents, acting instrumentally, could be motivated to perform the sorts of actions needed to create or sustain social order.

In this respect, the various instrumentalist theories on offer have not been especially successful. Of course, there is no question that instrumental rationality is going to form an important *part* of any story that is to be told about social interaction. Social institutions clearly provide individuals with incentives, and individuals often respond to these incentives in a purely instrumental fashion. So the issue is not whether the instrumental conception of rationality is false, since there can be no doubt that it captures an extremely important *aspect* of our reasoning (and that it explains social phenomena like traffic gridlock or atmospheric pollution). The question is whether it provides the complete story, or whether there might not be something else going on as well. More specifically, there is no doubt that instrumental rationality does a good job of explaining the "unsociable" part of our "unsociable sociability." The question is whether it can also explain, or even accommodate, the "sociability."

The most popular alternative to the strictly instrumental view suggests that social order cannot be explained in terms of self-interest alone, but that it requires commitment to some set of shared *social norms*. Without such norms, agents simply lack the "glue" needed to hold together stable cooperative arrangements. We might refer to this view, for convenience, as the "sociological" perspective.[4] Of course, there are a variety of ways in which this claim can be formulated— not all of which are incompatible with instrumentalism. The version I will focus on here claims that norms are important insofar as they generate deontic constraints on the pursuit of self-interest. In other words, norms are relevant insofar as they provide nonconsequentialist reasons for or against a particular action. It is only when formulated this way that the "social norms" postulate adds something to the story beyond what the standard instrumentalist conception is able to provide.

The literature on this subject is very complex, and not always as sharply focused as it might be. I will offer a brief overview here, in order to bring out what I take to be the major theoretical insights. I begin by examining the limitations of instrumentalist theories, before going on to examine the "sociological" alternatives. However, my overview of instrumentalist theories in this chapter is somewhat selective, insofar as I examine only those theories that attempt to explain social order without modifying the standard decision-theoretic model outlined in chapter 1. It is only by seeing the limitations of this strategy that one can understand the motivation for the various attempts to modify decision theory in such a way as to incorporate norms (or more generally, to suspend the consequentialism hypothesis), which will be discussed in the following chapter.

2.1.   Instrumental Approaches

There is one respect in which the question of how social order is achieved in human societies is *not* mysterious. There is widespread agreement that *rules* play an extremely important role in securing cooperation. Take, for example, the collective action problem that generates traffic gridlock. In some parts of the world, we resolve this by making it illegal to block an intersection. Many big cities have a large crosshatched square painted in the middle of downtown intersections— anyone caught in the square when the light changes is subject to a fine. In other parts of the world (usually where the consequences of blocking an intersection are not as severe), we rely on moral restraint in order to resolve the problem. When learning to drive, people are taught not to enter the intersection prematurely, as a courtesy to other drivers. The rule is also enforced through informal social sanctions, such as honking at those who get stuck blocking the intersection, even though they are unable to move. In either case, it is fairly obvious not only that the existence of the rule is what resolves the underlying collective action problem, but that the rule exists *precisely in order to resolve this problem*.

Unfortunately, invoking rules as a solution to the problem of order has more the effect of *displacing* the theoretical puzzle than resolving it. This is because getting people to endorse a rule in the abstract, or ex ante, is not the same as getting them to comply with it at the point of decision. The mere introduction or invocation of a rule does not change the underlying incentive structure. It is still in the interest of drivers to enter an intersection on a green light, regardless of whether they will be able to clear it. Thus there remains some question about how the rules are rendered *motivationally effective*.

In considering this question, the first thing that most theorists of an instrumentalist persuasion have picked up on is the fact that the rules are *enforced*. Drivers are fined, or worse, for committing traffic violations. Discourteous drivers are honked and gestured at. Avoiding these sanctions provides drivers with an obvious incentive to obey the rules of the road. Hobbes turned this commonplace observation into a general theory about how social order is maintained. "Covenants," he said (somewhat dramatically), "without the sword, are but words."[5] He argued that people will obey the rules only if it is in their interest to do so, and the only way to make it in their interest to do so is to take away the benefits of free riding. This can be done by instituting a sanctioning system that punishes those who break the rules and rewards those who comply.

The advantage of this analysis, from Hobbes's point of view, is that the motivating force of external sanctions can be understood quite easily in instrumentalist terms. There is nothing mysterious about wanting to avoid a traffic ticket. Enforcement of the rules simply changes the environment in such a way that the "free rider" strategy is no longer utility-maximizing. The collective action problem disappears because the payoffs change. This analysis, however, while making the operations of the rule quite intelligible from the standpoint of the person being sanctioned, makes things somewhat mysterious from the standpoint of the person who is applying the sanctions. This question is one that Hobbes never adequately addressed. What motivates the individual doing the sanctioning? Most people, despite having some measure of retributivist sentiment, find the actual task of punishing other people to be a burden. But in order for the threatened sanction to work, the threat must be credible. This means that the sanctionee must believe that the sanctioner truly intends to carry out the action. Unfortunately, the same logic that prevents instrumentally rational agents from making credible promises to cooperate also prevents them from making credible threats to punish defectors. Consider figure 2.1.

The equilibrium of this game is (U,R). However, it would clearly be to player 2's advantage if she could in some way publicly *commit* herself to playing L in the event that she was called on to move. If player 1 believed that player 2 would choose L, then he would select D, which would be to player 2's advantage. Player 2 could perhaps threaten player 1 with the (0,0) payoff in order to force his hand. Unfortunately, this will not work. Player 2 could make such a threat, but would never actually carry it out if called on to do so. Thus player 1 will continue to play U, and player 2, faced with the choice between getting 0 and getting 1, will choose the payoff of 1.

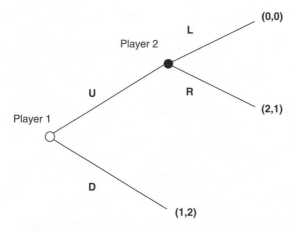

Figure 2.1 Empty threat.

When one person threatens another, he makes a claim of the sort "If you don't do *x*, I will perform mutually damaging action *y*." It is important to note that the action threatened must be *mutually* damaging. If it were not suboptimal for the threatener, then there would be no point in threatening it. For instance, when the police say to an armed suspect "Surrender or we'll shoot you," it is assumed that they would prefer *not* to shoot him. If the police wanted to shoot him, they would do it anyway (regardless of whether he surrendered), and so it would not be an effective threat. This means that in order to threaten, players have to be willing to engage in non-utility-maximizing actions. But since this is precisely what instrumentally rational agents are unwilling to do, there can be nothing but empty threats in strategic contexts. This illustrates a point long familiar to game theorists, which is that threats and promises have a similar action-theoretic structure, and that both are, from an instrumental perspective, irrational.[6] So it turns out that threats, without the sword, are but words as well. But since threats are supposed to *be* the sword, something of a regress problem looms large here.

Hobbes, in order to explain how individuals might be motivated to keep promises, suggests that they might create a sovereign power, which would punish them in the event that they defected. In so doing, he essentially appeals to threats in order to explain the binding force of promises—simply failing to notice that the former are just as problematic as the latter. As a result, he is not able to explain how an authority capable of punishing defectors could arise in the state of nature, that is, out of purely strategic interaction. The problem can be seen very clearly from the simple observation that punishing people usually involves costs for the person who is doing the punishing. The question, then, is what incentive anyone has to carry out the punishment. Certainly it can be somewhat uncomfortable having to complain or harass people who aren't pulling their weight. This gives rise to a new free-rider problem: everyone may put off punishing the person who isn't playing by the rules, in the hope that someone else will do it.

This happens all the time. Consider the familiar situation where someone brings too many items to the express checkout line in the grocery store. Everyone else in the line will typically say nothing, yet wish that someone *else* would confront her.[7] As a result, the wrongdoer is able to get away with it, because her actions are not sufficiently harmful to any one individual to make it worthwhile to sanction her. Punishing defectors and free riders is a kind of social service, since it generates a positive externality for all those who are harmed by the defection.[8] But because it usually must be carried out by one person, there is a problem motivating individuals to do the punishing. This means that people can get stuck in a suboptimal strategic equilibrium in which they make rules, but then no one punishes those who break them. (This is why evolutionary theorists refer to the type of sanctioning that one sees in human societies as "altruistic punishment," and regard it as just as mysterious as "altruistic cooperation.")[9]

Thus the *simple* Hobbesian solution to the problem of order is a nonstarter. There are, however, a number of more sophisticated ways to pursue the Hobbesian strategy. All of them depend to varying degrees on the observation that people are not just involved in "one-shot" interactions, but that they encounter one another—and stand poised to engage in mutually beneficial cooperation with one another—repeatedly over time. Cooperation may be beneficial if it increases the chances that others will behave cooperatively toward one in the future, that is, if the cooperative act is embedded in a system of reciprocity across time.

Of course, the reverse must also be true: defection must increase the chances that others will not behave cooperatively toward one in the future. So while future cooperation provides the "carrot" in this model, there must still be a "stick." The withdrawal of cooperation, however, appears to be a more credible punishment mechanism than the threat of mutually damaging action. It seems more sociologically plausible as well: people may not want to put themselves at risk in order to punish people who break the rules, but they will certainly be less inclined to trust that person in the future, and may even seek to avoid interacting with her. Many have felt that the "tit for tat" strategy made famous by Robert Axelrod articulates this sort of conditional cooperative strategy quite well: "cooperate with those who have cooperated in the past, defect on those who have defected."[10]

This intuition is what underlies the "folk theorem" (so called because the conclusion was widely believed by game theorists, long before it was formally proven) that implies that full cooperation is one of the equilibria of a repeated prisoner's dilemma game. However, what the folk theorem shows—in the various versions ultimately proven—is that conditional cooperation is a significantly less robust mechanism than initially assumed. It is no accident that "tit for tat" was the winning strategy in an *evolutionary* game, because it is actually not a subgame-perfect equilibrium strategy in a repeated prisoner's dilemma among rational agents—precisely because the simple one-turn withdrawal of cooperation that it uses as a punishment mechanism is not credible among rational agents.[11] In other words, the strategy only works when hardwired (or played by agents devoid of foresight). Whatever incentive rational agents have against defection as way of exploiting others will also, in general, serve as an incentive against defecting as a way of punishing others. The type of "revenge punishment" that tit-for-tat agents are programed to carry out is, as such, not available to the instrumentally rational agent.

Thus the folk theorem in its most general form requires either a total collapse of all cooperation in response to defection ("Nash reversion") or an escalating series of higher-order sanctions, so that people are punished for not punishing those who break the rules, and punished for not punishing those who do not punish those who break the rules, and so on.[12] The former is very simple, but sociologically implausible (it would be as though the law were enforced by having all of society revert to the state of nature in response to any criminality). The latter is very delicate. It is possible to construct a model in which individuals withdraw cooperation from those who have failed to cooperate, withdraw cooperation from those who fail to withdraw cooperation, and so forth. However, such a model turns out to be relatively nonrobust. It also suffers from sociological implausibility.[13] There are many circumstances in which collective action is sustained simply on the basis of the *trust* that exists among participants that everyone will cooperate. In these cases, the participants themselves often acknowledge that there are no credible threats of punishment, and so everyone has an incentive to defect.[14] The recent literature on "social capital" has drawn attention to the importance of such trust relations even in the economic sphere, where the instrumentalist account comes closest to providing a persuasive account of social order.[15] Not only does it strain credulity to imagine that the participants themselves are systematically confused about the true structure of their interaction, but the fact is that if the participants don't *perceive* there to be any sanctions, then in effect there are none. After all, sanctions work only if they constitute credible threats, and in order to be credible, participants must at very least be aware of them.

The most significant limitation of these models, however, is that the incentive to cooperate disappears as soon as the end point of the game is known (and thus the "folk theorem" results obtain only in infinitely repeated games). Since there can be no incentive to cooperate in the final round of a finitely repeated game, given that there will be no future cooperation, everyone can anticipate that everyone will defect in the penultimate round, because one will be "punished" in the final round regardless of what one does. This means that there is no incentive to cooperate in the third-to-last round, because one will be "punished" in the second-to-last round regardless of what one does, and so on. Backward induction (or "sequential rationality") leads to the unraveling of cooperation right back to the first round. Similarly, if individuals discount the future too heavily, or individuals change interaction partners frequently, or there is a high probability that the interaction will end, there will be no incentive to cooperate.

Finally, it should be noted that these models of reciprocity are an excellent example of cases where a two-person game does *not* generalize easily to the *n*-person case.[16] Withdrawal of cooperation is a very blunt instrument for enforcing cooperation, because it does not allow individuals to enact targeted punishment against a single defector (unlike retaliatory punishment, which usually does). Thus in a large-scale repeated collective action problem, the only way to enact punishment is for everyone to pull out of the entire cooperative scheme—a response that damages everyone involved, not just the defector. So even if it were possible to sustain cooperation among ideally rational agents, it only takes a small probability of irrational conduct or error to create a very high probability that large-scale cooperative projects will collapse.[17] Adding a communication system, or a reputation mechanism (to sustain a system of "indirect reciprocity"), does nothing to change this fundamental problem.[18]

Thus the core instrumentalist strategy, which focuses on the enforcement of cooperative arrangements as the key to understanding social order, is marred by the fact that, with the simple Hobbesian strategy, the selected *explanans* (punishment) is just as mysterious as the *explanandum* (cooperation), and with the more sophisticated strategy, the posited mechanism—reciprocal cooperation coupled with the threat of withdrawal of cooperation—is simply not a robust enough mechanism to explain the stability of social order, and the ease with which individuals enter into cooperative arrangements. There is a vast literature on the subject, and theorists motivated by the vision of a Hayekian "spontaneous order" continue to search for some purely strategic consideration that will transform the "race to the bottom" of the Hobbesian state of nature into the "race to the top" of the competitive marketplace. It would be impossible to survey all of these attempts here (not to mention those that are undoubtedly still to come). My goal has simply been to articulate the central conceptual difficulties, in order to show why the general research program is widely regarded as moribund.[19] There has been an enormous movement among social theorists away from rationality-based modeling techniques toward evolutionary game theory models, precisely because the latter are regarded as immune to many of these difficulties. This will be discussed further in chapter 6. For now, the focus will remain on instrumental theories of *rational* action.

2.2.   Revealed Preference Theory

There are other explanatory strategies available to the instrumentalist, but none with the same level of intuitive plausibility as the punishment model. It is possible, for instance, to suppose that collective action problems are simply not as common as a superficial analysis of social interaction would lead us to expect. There are no restrictions on the sorts of preferences that we ascribe to agents within the instrumental model. Thus it is quite possible, for instance, to suppose that people refrain from creating gridlock because they feel bad about blocking other drivers. The appearance of a collective action problem is created simply because the outcomes are being improperly specified—people care not only about how quickly they get home but also about the sorts of consequences their actions have for others. The assumption that they have a free-rider incentive arises only because of the assumption that their desires are self-interested in a narrower sense than the instrumental model necessarily requires.

There is no question that people do sometimes act cooperatively in order to avoid the consequences that defection would have for others (i.e., that they act from altruistic motives). The question is whether this mechanism is robust enough to provide a general account of social order. Here the argument needs to be handled with great caution. First, it should be noted that the instrumentalist need not be committed to any particular theory of how individuals wind up forming any of their preferences, including any "cooperative" ones they might have. This is really a question about where the individual's desires come from, which does not belong to the theory of practical rationality strictly construed. So, because the content of preferences is left unspecified, there is nothing to preclude "solving" the problem of order by simply instantiating preferences in such a way as to generate precisely the level of "orderliness" that social interaction in fact exhibits. The instrumentalist is free to suppose that agents acquire these sorts of cooperative preferences through socialization (although some instrumental account of why we choose to socialize people this way, and how we organize ourselves to carry it out, would then be owing). One might also suppose that sanctions are enforced because people—or at least enough people—simply have a preference for enforcing them (perhaps because they get upset, on observing a violation, and so derive pleasure from punishing the malefactor).[20]

The danger here is that the account of preference required by the theory will become a "just-so story"—rigged up in such a way as to avoid producing any outcomes that are embarrassing to the instrumental conception of rationality. Such an account of preference also suggests that not only have game theorists and philosophers been quite mistaken about the sort of preferences that people have, but that individuals themselves, engaged in routine social interactions, are also consistently mistaken.[21] For example, a certain amount of laziness is an almost constitutional feature of all human beings. Given a choice between doing some work (like, say, making dinner or cleaning up the house) and having someone else do it, most people, all things being equal, would prefer that someone else do it. When two people with these sorts of preferences interact with one another, it will almost automatically generate a collective action problem, as they both wait around a bit to see if the other will do the job. Thus we should expect collective action problems to be endemic in these sorts of social interactions. This makes it a bit too convenient to suppose that people's preferences just happen to be instantiated in such a way that they are able to avoid interactions with this structure. Furthermore, the individuals involved often *perceive* such interactions as having the structure of a collective action problem. Since the way they act is determined by these perceptions, some explanation needs to be provided for the systematic misalignment of perception and behavior posited by this account.

Many theorists have been tempted at this point to reformulate the instrumental model in such a way as to make it effectively unfalsifiable. "It may seem to be miraculous," they say, "if people just happen to enter these interactions with the sorts of preferences that allow them to avoid suboptimal outcomes. But obviously they do. The fact that they cooperate shows that the interaction was modeled incorrectly, and that it was not really a prisoner's dilemma." This is one way of stating the "revealed preference" version of utility theory, popular among some economists. According to this view, agents will always act in accordance with their von Neumann–Morgenstern utility functions, because the latter is simply a mathematical shorthand used to represent the way that they actually act. Preferences are "read off" of agent behavior—hence the idea that preference is revealed through choice. "It then becomes essentially a tautology that a rational person will fail to cooperate in the Prisoner's Dilemma," Ken Binmore writes.[22] If they do cooperate, it is because their preferences have been misrepresented, and they are in fact playing some other game.

Unfortunately, most theorists who are tempted by this view fail to appreciate its enormous disadvantages. Binmore, for example, insists that game theorists are merely "toying with tautologies." He compares the results of game theory to mathematical theorems, which are also, he claims, tautologies. "They cannot be false because they do not say anything substantive."[23] Of course, were this true, it would certainly come as a surprise to both mathematicians and logicians.[24] Thus game theorists, if they truly want to claim that their discipline is vacuous, should not take any solace from Binmore's false analogy to mathematics (or pin their hopes on the success of "neologicism"). Statements that are trivially true are just that, *trivially* true. Not only would such a theory lack explanatory or predictive value, it could not even be used to formulate explanations or predictions. Rational choice theory, on the other hand, has been the source of enormously fruitful research hypotheses in the social sciences. It does a great disservice to this body of work to trivialize the theory, merely to avoid having to deal in a forthright manner with the many anomalies it generates.

At any rate, there are much more serious problems with the doctrine of revealed preference. The most elementary is that preference is not in fact revealed through choice, even in nonsocial contexts. Because the instrumental view explains actions in terms of belief and preference, any particular ascription of intentional states will always be underdetermined by the available evidence. As Donald Davidson has observed, any action can be rendered consistent with any preference ordering, simply by varying the beliefs that are ascribed to the agent.[25] (I may drink the coffee because I like coffee, or I may drink it because I like tea, and think that it is tea.) If we take beliefs as fixed, then preferences are revealed through choice; and if we take preferences as fixed, then beliefs are revealed through choice. But they cannot both be revealed simultaneously. Revealed preference theorists simply failed to notice this, because they took the agent's beliefs for granted. Thus the only theory of action that could be grounded in observed behavior would be one that explains the agent's choice of *a* as a consequence of a preference to do *a*. There is nothing to stop the theorist from advancing such a theory, although in this case the absence of explanatory or predictive value is much closer to the surface. But insofar as we seek to explain this preference for *a* in terms of some more complex set of intentional states, we must abandon the hope that the theory could have such direct empirical foundations.[26]

Finally, it is sometimes suggested that the instrumental view can explain social order more easily if, instead of using the highly idealized conception of deliberative rationality expressed in the utility-maximization theory, one adopted a more realistic account of how people actually go about making decisions. Agents seldom have the time or energy to consider all of their options, and to figure out which of their strategies is the very best one. Usually they just look for a solution that is "good enough," according to some fairly rough criteria. This is the idea underlying "bounded" conceptions of practical rationality.[27] According to this sort of view, agents might choose to adopt a very general policy that calls for cooperating in prisoner's dilemmas, and then simply stick to this policy without calculating whether it is the very best in all circumstances.

Such a move, unfortunately, does not really help things. There is no question that once we have a satisfactory account of how a fully rational agent would deliberate under ideal conditions, we will have to produce a scaled-down version of it in order to capture how people actually reason under real-life conditions. But in order to get the right conception of bounded rationality, we need to start with the right theory of idealized rationality, and whether the instrumental conception of rationality counts as such is precisely what the problem of order throws into question. In any case, introducing bounded rationality doesn't help solve the problem of order, since even epistemically or computationally challenged agents would not choose to cooperate in a prisoner's dilemma. Playing strongly dominated strategies *never* benefits the agent, and so is no more attractive as a general rule of thumb than it is as a particular game strategy. Thus, no matter how bounded the rationality of agents may be, one of the first things they are going to figure out is that they always benefit from defecting in prisoner's dilemmas.

2.3. Rule Instrumentalism

A slightly more radical response to the problem of order, among theorists of a broadly instrumental persuasion, has been to go back and reexamine the process of generalization that led from decision theory to game theory. Recall that the problems with the instrumental conception of rationally begin to show up only when a second rational actor is introduced into the frame of reference. Utility-maximizing actions taken in nonsocial contexts never lead to suboptimal outcomes, and the process of deliberation is never indeterminate. It is only when decision-theoretic reasoning is applied to social interaction that the difficulties begin. This has led several theorists to reconsider some of the orthodox ideas that underlie the transition from decision theory to game theory. In particular, many have suggested that rule-following can be explained by reconceptualizing the structure of strategic reasoning, and the associated set of equilibrium solution concepts. According to this view, decision theory could be retained as an accurate characterization of instrumental choice in nonsocial contexts; only the account of social choice would need to be modified.[28]

Most of these theories have now converged on a position that we can refer to as a "planning theory."[29] The idea, roughly, is that agents do not choose particular actions. Instead they choose plans (which are basically temporally ordered sets of actions). Their choice remains instrumental, insofar as the value of a plan is a function of the outcome or outcomes that it achieves. The difference is that choice of a plan implies a type of commitment, or *resoluteness*, that is lacking in standard game theory. Agents who choose a plan will also stick to it, unless given some very specific reason not to. This is what explains, according to such views, the stability and orderliness of social interaction.[30]

An example will help to illustrate the intuition that informs this approach. Consider the game shown in figure 2.2.[31] The only equilibrium of this game is for player 1 to play Down immediately, resulting in an outcome of (2,2). This outcome is evidently Pareto-inferior (i.e., worse for both players), since if player 1 chose Across, player 2 chose Across, and player 1 then chose Cooperate, they would get (4,4). The problem is that player 1 has an obvious incentive to play Defect at the last stage. Since player 2 can easily anticipate this, she can be expected to choose Down. This leaves player 1 with a choice between (1,3) and (2,2). So evidently the best thing to do here is simply to play Down, and end the game before it even begins.

But playing Down must be quite frustrating for player 1. After all, this action eliminates any chance of cooperation. Furthermore, the problem is not player 2. If player 2 believed that player 1 would cooperate in the final stage, she would happily choose Across. The problem is that she has no reason to believe that player 1 will actually do so. Thus, it is player 1's *own anticipated future defection* that makes cooperation impossible, and therefore leads him to make the non-cooperative choice at the beginning of the game. The problem is not that he cannot trust player 2, but that he himself cannot be trusted.

Contemplating interactions of this sort has led many theorists to the conclusion that there simply *must* be some instrumental rationale for player 1 to choose [Across, Cooperate] rather than [Down].[32] After all, how could it be rational to choose an outcome with a payoff of 2, when it is within one's means to choose an action that would generate a payoff of 4? Thus if orthodox game theory recommends choosing Down at the very beginning as the only rational strategy, there must be something wrong with orthodox game theory.

The process of reasoning that leads player 1 to act noncooperatively is called backward induction (the same process that leads to universal defection in a finitely repeated prisoner's dilemma). In working out a solution to an extended game, one starts out at the end of the game and determines what the last player will do. One then takes the outcome of this choice, and substitutes it for that player's choice node, in order to determine what the second-to-last player to move should do. In figure 2.2, this process allows one to characterize player 2's choice as one between Down, which gives (1,3), and Across, which gives (5,2). One then repeats the process until the game is resolved. (The spirit of this procedure is codified as the principle of "sequential rationality," which states simply that a rational strategy must contain only actions that are utility-maximizing at the point at which they are to be played. In other words, the player must never have an incentive to defect from his or her own strategy.)

In this example, it would appear to be the sequential rationality principle that makes cooperation impossible (and not instrumental rationality per se). So perhaps the "solution" to the problem of cooperation is to preserve decision theory as an account of nonsocial choice, but to rethink sequential rationality

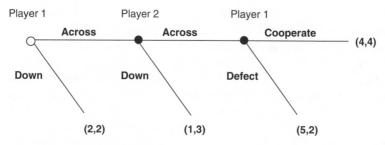

Figure 2.2 Caterpillar game.

as a constraint on strategic reasoning. If player 1 were able to choose actions as a "package," then he could plan to do [Across, Cooperate], which would make it advantageous for player 2 to select Across as well. Thus cooperation could be sustained, it is supposed, without anyone *really* acting noninstrumentally. The primary difference between this model and standard game theory seems to be only in the way time is treated. Sequential rationality implies that agents must always reoptimize their strategies, whenever they have an opportunity to do so. The planning approach says that agents need only reoptimize their strategies when some new information comes along, or some unexpected event occurs. Absent such an occurrence, it is rational for agents simply to stick to their plans. If player 1 adopts [Across, Cooperate] as a plan, and forms an intention to cooperate at the final choice node, then there is no reason for him to reconsider this intention when the time to act rolls around. After all, when he arrives at his final choice node, nothing new or unexpected has occurred. The plan is unfolding precisely as anticipated.[33]

Thus the goal of this sort of planning theory is not to make any fundamental revisions in the instrumental conception of rationality, or to change the way that utility is defined at the decision-theoretic level, but simply to eliminate sequential rationality as a constraint on equilibrium selection. Unfortunately, planning theorists have said very little about what broader consequences the elimination of this principle would have for game theory. Instead, they have focused all of their energy on trying to rationalize cooperation. Yet if agents were able to privately adopt plans that took them off the so-called equilibrium path, this is bound to exacerbate the problem of indeterminacy. Not only would it lead to a proliferation of equilibria, but it would become much more difficult for any agent to anticipate what any other intends to do. Game-theoretic equilibria depend crucially on the ability of individuals to "mirror" one another's reasoning. The introduction of plans creates an important impediment to this process. How is anyone supposed to know whether, at time t, player x will be optimizing or simply carrying out a previously adopted plan? It is worth keeping in mind that planning theory offers no account of communication, and so one cannot assume that agents are able to announce their plans before embarking on them. Such announcements would need to be modeled as a preplay segment of the game, an account of linguistic meaning would need to be provided, and the complex problem of deciding when these announcements are credible would need to be addressed. Unfortunately, planning theorists have focused their attention on a very narrow class of games—largely prisoner's dilemmas—and so have not addressed any of these important concerns.

However, even in the interactions that have been closely studied, such as the assurance game above, there is still a sticking point in the argument. Our everyday experience tells us that agents are not capable of suspending their capacity for rational choice at will. One could vow, for instance, never to pay ransom to a kidnapper. But faced with the kidnapping of one's own child, it is inevitable that one would rethink this commitment (even if only to reaffirm it). Thus in a prisoner's dilemma we should assume that player 1 is not able to start out the game by literally depriving himself of the capacity to choose Defect. All of his choices remain live options. The question is whether, when the time comes to choose, player 1 still has a reason to select Cooperate. Thus it all comes down to the integrity of the argument that supports choosing Cooperate.

The idea that player 1 should "stick to the plan" at his second node depends on the observation that he has been given no reason to revise his intention, given that nothing new or unexpected has occurred. Yet it is apparent that something important does happen between player 1's first choice node and his second. By the time he arrives at his second choice node, player 2 has passed the point of no return. Her cooperation is no longer conditional, as it was when the initial choice of strategies was made. This represents a significant change in the strategic situation, since it gives player 1 an opportunity to defect with impunity. In fact, forcing one's opponent to commit to an action, then quickly reoptimizing, is an extremely common and important feature of many strategic interactions. One need only think of the number of (actual) games, like tennis, hockey, or basketball, where this ability is often the key to success. And everyone can recall dozens of cases of having done one's share of a cooperative enterprise, only to find the gesture unreciprocated. The phrase "So long, sucker" entered the vernacular precisely as a way of flagging these key moments.

So given that agents clearly have the ability to reoptimize, if they refrain from doing so, it must be because they have chosen not to *at the point in time at which the option of reoptimizing presents itself. But choosing* not to reoptimize is, *ex hypothesi*, non-utility-maximizing.[34] Thus it is simply not rational for player 2 to believe that player 1, qua instrumentally rational agent, will choose Cooperate once the option of defecting with impunity arises (keeping in mind that the utility functions constitute an accurate representation of the relevant preferences). As a result, it is irrational for player 1 to believe that player 2 will cooperate, and thus irrational for him to choose Across. Thus, if he does select the plan [Across, Cooperate], and he does find himself at his second decision node, he can now infer that player 2 has also acted irrationally. But his original plan is still irrational, and there is no more reason to carry it out now than there was to select it in the first place. It is always rational to abandon an irrational plan, especially when that plan is about to lead you to perform a non-utility-maximizing action.

The basic problem here, as Michael Bratman has pointed out, is the same as the one that continues to plague the various versions of rule-utilitarianism.[35]

There are in fact very close parallels between rule-utilitarianism and planning theory (the latter can be thought of as a sort of "rule-instrumentalism"). The problem, simply put, is that when some purely consequentialist criterion is initially used to justify a particular rule, then there appears to be no reason to adhere to the rule in cases where the rule happens not to serve the original ends in terms of which it was justified. The rule of the road that dictates "right of way," for instance, has a purely consequentialist justification—avoiding traffic collisions, easing traffic flow, and so on. But certain situations may arise in which the rule impedes this end. An example of this occurs in traffic circles—ceding priority to cars on the right would give traffic entering the circle priority over traffic already inside. As a result, the right-of-way rule is ignored by drivers in traffic circles (in most countries). This seems like the natural course of action. More dramatically, when a car comes barreling toward you on the highway in the wrong lane, it makes no sense to continue driving as you have been, on the grounds that "on the whole," staying in your lane reduces accidents. Maintaining adherence to the rule, in cases where it is clearly not serving its intended purpose, would be empty "rule worship." Thus simply saying "Well that's the rule" does not constitute an adequate justification. Similarly, in the cases dealt with here, saying "That's the plan," is not adequate, especially when the plan is supposedly subject to purely consequentialist justification.

Finally, the planning theory approach does run the risk of proving *too much*. If one were to show that the rational course of action in a prisoner's dilemma is simply to cooperate, then it would be difficult to explain the very extensive range of cases in which individuals do not cooperate in interactions that have this structure. David Gauthier makes the unintentionally humorous suggestion that people who cheat on their taxes may not in fact be free riding—since that would be irrational, in his view—but protesting the way their tax dollars are spent.[36] More dramatically, if planning theory were correct, then market economies would not function very well. Price competition between firms is a collective action problem—suppliers would all be better off if they refrained from lowering their prices, just as buyers would be better off if they refrained from bidding against one another. However, achieving "cooperation" in this domain usually requires some form of explicit collusion and enforcement. Antitrust law is designed precisely to prevent firms from putting such mechanisms in place. But if the planning theory approach is correct, then it would be irrational for firms to engage in such competition, and antitrust law would be unenforceable. Rational managers simply wouldn't engage in price competition, any more than they would impose production inefficiencies on their own firm.[37]

Thus any solution to the problem of order must carry out a delicate balancing act. We need to explain why agents *sometimes* act cooperatively, but also sometimes do not. The external sanctions approach has the merit of at least in principle being able to explain this—agents cooperate when they fear the punishment associated with defection, but not otherwise. Resolute planning theory, on the other hand, tips the balance too far in the direction of "sociability," making it difficult to see why failures of cooperation are so common, even in the absence of asymmetric information or assurance problems.

Planning theory does, however, identify a very important internal connection between the *cooperative norms* that govern human behavior, the *commitments* individuals adopt in social interaction, and the *intentional states* in terms of which they deliberate. The explanatory power of the theory trades on the observation that all three of these have a normative structure, and thus in some sense are able to bind the agent. What planning theory proposes is an order of explanation in which the normativity of intentional states can be used to explain the force of adopted intentions, which in turn can explain the force of commitments, and ultimately the force of social norms. The coherence of this order of explanation ultimately rests on the account of intentional states, and the way the agent's beliefs and desires are thought to acquire this ability to bind the agent—in this case to his or her own plans. This is a much deeper question, which I will discuss in greater detail in chapter 4, where I will attempt to show that planning theory correctly identifies the important conceptual connections, but proposes an order of explanation that is exactly backward.

2.4. Conventions

The discussion so far has touched on only one aspect of the problem of order, namely, the problem of securing cooperation. Nothing has been said so far about coordination. Here the picture is somewhat brighter for the instrumentalist. There is a single, generally accepted solution to this problem, namely, the theory of conventions developed by Thomas Schelling and elaborated by David Lewis.[38] However, I will attempt to show that this theory, while no doubt correct in some respects, still leaves a significant amount to be explained. It provides a mechanism that can be used to resolve coordination problems, but it fails to explain how this mechanism interacts with the intentional states posited by standard decision theory. It also provides no traction when it comes to explaining cooperation.

Schelling's analysis takes as its point of departure the observation that individuals, when placed in an interaction that is genuinely indeterminate, are often able to coordinate by selecting strategies that are somehow "salient" or "focal."[39] Schelling reports the results of a series of experiments in which people were given coordination problems and asked to select strategies. For example, two people were told to meet in New York City on a certain day, but the time and the place were left unspecified. A surprising number chose to meet at 12 noon at Grand Central Station. Similarly, people were shown a map and told that they were parachutists who had become separated during the jump. Where would they meet? Large numbers chose the one bridge over the river.[40]

There appears to be something about round numbers, equal shares, bright colors, and other such aesthetic qualities that attracts attention, and therefore allows outcomes exhibiting such properties to serve as solutions to coordination problems. Similarly, as Lewis observed, a history of having been played before can also make a particular outcome focal. Thus, when faced with a coordination problem, agents may initially flounder a bit, and have to guess what the other will do. But once they hit on a particular arrangement, they will keep playing it, because their expectations will have become focused on that outcome. An equilibrium in a coordination problem that is sustained in this way is referred to by Lewis as a convention.[41]

Most people can relate to these sorts of examples, so the theory has enjoyed widespread popularity. However, there has been some tendency to overlook the fact that the analysis explains very little—it does not so much *resolve* the mystery as simply *name* it. Schelling says nothing about how a particular equilibrium becomes focal—he argues that the task of developing such a theory should be farmed out to "psychologists." Even more important, however, is the fact that the theory he presents does not license the ascription of any intentional states to the agents; or if it does, the nature and content of these states is left unspecified. Schelling says nothing about what sort of *beliefs* focal point reasoning generates, or what sort of inferences it warrants. As a result, it is difficult to see how this theory is to be integrated into a theory of rational action. (Indeed, one suspects that the theory remains plausible only insofar as it remains unintegrated. Once the intentional states generated by the focal point are specified, one would need to reformulate the decision problem, and chances are this reformulated problem would harbor higher-order indeterminacy.)

Finally, it is worth mentioning that the theory of convention provides, at best, only a solution to the problem of coordination.[42] Focal point solutions, at least of the type that Schelling and Lewis consider, have absolutely no bite when it comes to resolving cooperation problems. With collective action problems, the question is how agents manage so often to achieve outcomes that appear to be out of equilibrium. The focal point mechanism is just an equilibrium-selection mechanism, and so it is of no use in such circumstances. This may seem obvious, but there is a surprising amount of literature that attempts to apply this analysis of conventions to provide an analysis of legal or social norms—completely ignoring the fact that these sorts of norms often sustain out-of-equilibrium behavior. Certain legal norms—like the law that specifies which side of the street people are to drive on—clearly enforce conventions. But the vast majority of laws—for example, the system of property rights, most of the criminal law—are designed to enforce rules that people have a clear incentive to violate.[43]

The responsibility for this confusion must no doubt be laid at the doorstep of David Hume. In his analysis of the "artificial virtues," Hume resolutely insists that collective action problems be treated as though they were just coordination problems. With respect to property, for instance, Hume characterizes the interaction as follows: "I observe, that it will be for my interest to leave another in the possession of his goods, provided he will act in the same manner with regard to me. He is sensible of a like interest in the regulation of his conduct. When this common sense of interest is mutually express'd, and is known to both, it produces a suitable resolution and behaviour."[44] Hume is claiming, in effect, that the mere recognition among two individuals that their interaction has the structure of a prisoner's dilemma is enough to resolve it, without any need for enforcement. The mere "expression" of a common interest is supposed to generate the relevant trust. The only remaining problem, then, is the coordination one: which of the various cooperative outcomes to select.

He makes a similar argument with respect to upholding promises.[45] There, however, he is forced to deal with the trust problem more seriously, because he imagines an interaction in which one party must perform first, then trust the second to uphold his promise. He handles this by tacitly transforming the "one-shot" game into a repeated game: "I learn to do a service to another, without bearing him any real kindness; because I foresee, that he will return my service, in expectation of another of the same kind, and in order to maintain the same correspondence of good offices with me or with others."[46] Thus it is no longer merely the common sense of interest in producing an optimal outcome in the one-shot interaction that produces "suitable resolution and behaviour," but rather the desire to maintain "good offices" in the future. This tacitly transforms the analysis back into an instrumentalist account of the sort discussed in section 2.2, by suggesting that the anticipated withdrawal of future cooperation is in fact the important deterrent of defection. Reciprocity, however, is an extremely weak mechanism for maintaining cooperation, and withdrawal of cooperation is an equally blunt instrument for imposing punishment.

Hume's view is that people's "self-interest" will lead them to cooperate in collective action problems. As a result, the rules of justice are nothing but a set of conventions, which help individuals to pin down the precise modalities of their joint endeavors. The reason individuals sometimes defect, therefore, cannot be that they are acting rationally. In Hume's view, it is because people often assign priority to their short-term over their long-term interests. Thus the function of government, in Hume's view, is not to control collective action problems, but simply to act as a commitment mechanism. We know that we suffer from temptation, and so we create an authority capable of forcing us to perform the actions that are in our long-term self-interest. According to this view, there is really no such thing as free riding, just shortsightedness.

These arguments all rest on a compositional fallacy. Hume for the most part assumes that if something is in the "common interest" of a group, it must also be in the "self-interest" of each member of the group. Yet it is clearly false to maintain that lying, stealing, and other free-rider strategies are never in anyone's interest. Unfortunately, Hume's arguments continue to exert influence, despite the fact that they rest on such an elementary confusion. Thus many theorists simply fail to perceive that a theory of conventions does nothing to explain the possibility of cooperation. And insofar as they do perceive the problem, and appeal to a system of reciprocity as a mechanism to sustain cooperation, then they are tacitly transforming "conventionalism" into little more than an equilibrium-selection mechanism for the folk theorem (with the folk theorem doing all the work, when it comes to explaining cooperation).[47]

2.5. Experimental Game Theory

Finally, it should be noted that instrumentalist accounts of social order—to the extent that they rest on falsifiable versions of the rational choice model—have been the subject of overwhelming empirical falsification. Experimental game theorists have found not only many interactions in which there is significant deviation from the predictions of the canonical rational choice model but also interactions where *not one single agent* behaves in the predicted manner.[48] "Experiment evidence is baffling," as one commentator notes. "Results systematically disconfirm not only predictions based on rationality, but also reasonable expectations from simple psychological theories."[49]

It is well known, for instance, that experimental subjects exhibit much greater cooperation in collective action problems than standard rational choice theory predicts. The most widely studied interaction is the "public goods game."[50] In a typical experiment of this type, four individuals are grouped together under conditions of strict anonymity. At the beginning of each round, they are each assigned 20 points, which they can place in either a "public" or a "private" account. Points in the private account are simply retained by the individual. The public account "pays out" into each player's private account a sum equal to 40 percent of the total number of points contributed by all players to the public account. The game continues for a certain number of rounds, after which players can cash in all the points accumulated in their private account for real money.

This game is a classic collective action problem. If all four players put all of their points into the public account, they would each receive 32 points in their private accounts each round. However, a player who "defected" from this arrangement by putting all 20 points in her private account would receive a payoff that round of 44. In general, each point placed in the public account is worth only 0.4 to the player who invests it there, but 1.2 to the other players. Since it is worth 1 when placed in the private account, investing in the public account is strictly dominated. Thus rational choice theory predicts zero contribution to the public account as the sole equilibrium of this game. What happens in fact is that individuals typically contribute between 40 and 60 percent of their holding to the public account.[51]

This deviation from the equilibrium strategy is not an isolated anomaly either—contribution rates in the 40–60 percent range remain stable under a wide variety of conditions: across a range of different cultures, among subjects playing for the first time and among those with previous experience, in groups ranging from 4 to 80 members, and with a variety of different monetary rewards.[52] The only significant exception to be reported in North America was when the game was played among economics graduate students. There the contribution rate fell to only 20 percent.[53] While the latter finding was the source of some amusement, it is actually quite revealing. It is possible that some sort of adverse selection is at work in recruitment to the economics profession. The more likely hypothesis is that economics students are inclined to disregard non-instrumental considerations in their deliberations, precisely because they are committed (in keeping with the norms of their profession) to a conception of practical rationality that classifies such concerns as irrational. Thus the anomaly suggests that cooperation is not the product of individuals having special preferences, but rather of their having brought different sorts of norms to bear on the choice problem.

It is important to note that individuals cooperate in "one-shot," anonymous versions of these public goods games, when they are perfectly well aware that there is no possibility of punishment, reward, or reciprocity. Contrary to the expectations of rational choice theorists, the introduction of an opportunity for repeated play tended to *decrease*, rather than increase, the level of cooperation.[54] This constitutes striking disconfirmation of the "reciprocity" account of cooperation. Meanwhile, all sorts of things that, according to standard rational choice models, should have had absolutely no impact on levels of cooperation—such as the opportunity for participants to engage in "cheap talk" (i.e., non-payoff–relevant communication) before the game, or even framing effects introduced by the experimenters—had dramatic effects. (In one example, calling the public goods game "the community game" rather than "the Wall Street game" doubled the level of cooperation.)[55]

The other game that has been widely studied in experimental settings is the "ultimatum game." Here, one player is given a fixed sum of money. This individual must propose some division of the money between himself and one other person. The second player can then either accept this proposal, in which case the money is divided up as per the offer, or reject the proposal, in which case both players receive nothing. Of course, the second player never has any positive incentive to reject any offer, since no proposed division is worse than receiving nothing. Thus rejecting the offer is a punitive action—and the threat to carry it out should not be credible (as in figure 2.1). As a result, standard rational choice theory suggests that the proposer should select a division that gives the second player as little as possible, and that this proposal should always be accepted.

In reality, not only do players tend to offer much more than rational choice theory would predict, but proposals also tend to be rejected if they fall too low. In industrialized societies, mean offers tend to be around 44 percent, while offers below 20 percent are rejected about half the time. Experimental evidence from nonindustrialized societies reflects greater variability—including examples of mean offer rates above 50 percent, combined with frequent rejection of such offers. But in general, none of the experiments come even close to conforming to the expectations of "canonical" rational choice theory.

The authors of one major international study explain these findings by observing that "the degree of cooperation, sharing, and punishment exhibited by experimental subjects closely corresponds to templates for these behaviors in the subjects' daily life." In other words, "when faced with a novel situation (the experiment) they looked for analogues in their daily experience, asking 'what familiar situation is this game like?' and then acted in a way appropriate for the analogous situation."[56] In Western societies, the ultimatum game is normally interpreted as a division problem (of the cake-cutting variety), and so is taken to be governed by norms of fairness. The modal offer is exactly one-half the money, presumably because this is what the norm prescribes in this case (the mean is slightly skewed toward the one who makes the offer, as a modest concession to that person's evidently superior position).[57] Individuals who offer less, and hence violate the fairness norm, are often punished with a rejection of their offer.

Things are quite different in various parts of New Guinea, where offers of over 50 percent were often made, and routinely rejected. Here there are very strong norms pertaining to the giving of gifts. "Among these groups, like many in New Guinea, accepting gifts, even unsolicited ones, commits one to reciprocate at some future time to be determined by the giver. Receipt of large gifts also establishes one in a subordinate position. Consequently, excessively large gifts, especially unsolicited ones, will frequently be refused because of the anxiety about the unspecific strings attached."[58] Because the proposer's offer was interpreted as a gift, the norms of gift giving were applied to the experimental situation, leading to large offers and high rates of rejection.

Similarly, behavior in the public goods game often depended on subjects' interpretation of the interaction. For example, "Orma experimental subjects quickly dubbed the public goods experiment a *harambee* game, referring to the widespread institution of village-level voluntary contributions for public goods projects such as schools or roads. Not surprisingly, they contributed generously (58 percent of the stake), somewhat higher than most U.S. subjects contribute in similar experiments."[59]

What makes this so significant is that the nature of the experimental setting—especially the strict anonymity of the interaction—immunizes the subjects from the consequences of their decisions. Thus the sort of guidance people are looking to their "cultural templates" for cannot be simply beliefs about likely consequences. On the contrary, experiments have shown that subjects can easily be biased toward either cooperation or defection, merely through the suggestion that *others* have been cooperating or defecting.[60] The most plausible hypothesis is that they look to either cultural norms or behavioral regularities to decide what sort of action is *appropriate* under the circumstances. They are seeking to conform to the prevailing set of norms. The fact that "cheap talk" and promising in public goods games has been shown to increase rates of cooperation also suggests that actions aimed at creating normative salience can have important consequences.[61]

Experimental game theory reveals a pattern of choice in these interactions that could best be described as deontically constrained. Agents adhere to norms, even when the conduct prescribed by these rules runs counter to their interests, defined in consequentialist terms. This is exhibited in two primary ways. First, agents are often willing to follow norms, even when this leaves them open to exploitation by others, and requires that they abstain from advantageous opportunities for defection. Second, agents are willing to impose sanctions on those who have violated the norms, even when it means depriving themselves of some benefit. Furthermore, when asked to explain their choices, experimental subjects do so in precisely these terms, and with reference to the relevant set of norms. There is no evidence that false beliefs or post hoc rationalizations play any role in their thinking. Thus the suggestion that norm-conformity represents a pattern of rational action has been gaining widespread acceptance. There is, however, still no consensus when it comes to strategies for incorporating such constraints into a formal model of rational action.

2.6. Conclusion

None of the findings canvassed in the previous section constitutes a decisive refutation of the orthodox rational choice model, simply because the model itself
is nothing but an ideal type. Thus it is possible to dismiss the findings of experiment game theory by supposing that the subjects involved acted irrationally,
or that their preferences differed from those that were ascribed to them as part
of the experimental design. And there is still the option of producing increasingly baroque models, to reveal the supposedly "hidden" instrumental incentives underlying what appears to be straightforward rule-following behavior.
Nevertheless, there is reason to hope that the era in which this sort of contrari-
anism (or naïve cynicism) was professionally rewarded is over.[62] It is perhaps a
sign of this broader change in the intellectual climate that a game theorist like
Herbert Gintis, in an article calling for the development of a "unified" theory of
action for the social sciences, could express "surprise" at the thought that norm-
conformity, "perhaps the most singularly characteristic feature of the human
mind, and central to understanding cooperation and conflict in human society,"
has been either "ignored or misrepresented" throughout the social sciences
(with the exception of "anthropology and social psychology").[63]

In this context, it is perhaps worth recalling the original purpose of developing a
formal model of practical rationality along the lines of rational choice theory. The
whole project starts out from what is often referred to as "folk psychology"— that
is, the sort of psychological theory we use in everyday life to describe each others'
reasons for action.[64] When someone asks "Why did she go to bed so early?" we say
"She wanted to be well rested for her interview tomorrow," and when someone
says "Why is he digging that hole?" we say "He believes treasure is buried there."
In other words, we routinely point to people's desires and their beliefs as a way of
understanding and explaining their actions. Similarly, when we deliberate, we do
so in terms of our beliefs and desires. When people ask us for advice, we say "What
do you really want?" or "How do you think he will react if you say that?" Rational
choice theory is best thought of as a *regimentation* of this sort of folk-psychological
framework. It simply states more precisely what the intentional states relevant to
deliberation are, and then tries to work out more carefully how these should be
brought to bear on choices under conditions of uncertainty.

Thus rational choice theory serves first and foremost an expressive role.[65]
It allows us to state more clearly the structure of practical deliberation, along
with the commitments we implicitly undertake when we bring certain beliefs
and desires to bear on a choice problem. This is ultimately what the theory must
be held accountable to. The question is one of expressive adequacy—does it permit a more or a less perspicuous articulation of these implicit commitments?
As we have seen, there is good reason to believe that rational choice theory permits greater perspicacity when it comes to articulating the structure of decision
in nonsocial contexts, but that it fails to offer comparable illumination when
it comes to analyzing social interaction. Indeed, many of the arguments that
have been used to immunize rational choice theory against the sort of anomalies

detected by experimental game theorists have the effect of obscuring, rather than elucidating, the intentional structure of social interactions.

In folk psychology, it is common for agents to distinguish between means and ends, between the goals they have and the sorts of means they are prepared to employ in order to achieve them. In nonsocial choices, this distinction is not terribly important, and most people are willing to endorse purely instrumental modes of reasoning. For example, when dealing with rocks and trees, most of us are happy to endorse the principle that "the end justifies the means." In social interactions, on the other hand, things are quite different. Here, the distinction between means and ends becomes quite salient. This is reflected in our folk-psychological vocabulary, primarily in the distinction we often draw between the goals that we seek and the principles that govern our actions. This distinction gets built into the intentional structure of the interaction, because agents not only draw on it with respect to their own options but also apply it to others in order to determine *their* likely courses of action. If the objective of developing a model of practical rationality is greater expressive adequacy, then it is essential that any theory of social interaction be able to model the relevant set of intentional states, along with the set of expectations that develop when agents mutually ascribe these states to one another.

3

Deontic Constraint

Anyone who has ever lived with housemates understands the Hobbesian state of nature implicitly. People sharing accommodations quickly discover that buying groceries, doing the dishes, sweeping the floor, and a thousand other household tasks are all prisoner's dilemmas waiting to happen. For instance, if food is purchased communally, it gives everyone an incentive to overconsume (because the majority of the cost of anything anyone eats is born by the others). Individuals also have an incentive to buy expensive items that the others are unlikely to want. As a result, everyone's food bill will be higher than it would be if everyone did their own shopping. Things are not much better when it comes to other aspects of household organization. Cleaning is a common sticking point. Once there are a certain number of people living in a house, cleanliness becomes a quasi-public good. If everyone "pitched in" to clean up, then everyone would be happier. But there is a free-rider incentive—before cleaning, it's best to wait around a bit to see if someone else will do it. As a result, the dishes will stack up in the sink, the carpet will not get vacuumed, and so on. Things may get cleaned less frequently than *anyone* would like, resulting in a suboptimal outcome for all.

But anyone who has lived with housemates also knows that the "state of nature" is not so hard to escape. People can counteract their tendency to fall into suboptimal interaction patterns in a variety of ways. The most common is to *make rules*. Thus the usual solution to the problems of cohabitation is to draw up a list of household chores, and then assign responsibility for them to individuals. Setting rules allows people to decide what outcome they would like to achieve, then simply instruct individuals to perform the actions needed to bring it about. Of course, everyone also knows that just telling people to do things does not automatically translate into a willingness on their part to do them. There is still an incentive problem that needs to be addressed.

This is where the most important conundrum in contemporary action theory has arisen. The problem stems from a tension between the motivational psychology of rule-following and the instrumental conception of rationality. Rules prescribe actions, not outcomes. Yet "an almost unquestioned hypothesis of modern normative decision theory is that acts are valued by their consequences."[1] So how can a rule confer value on an action? Confronted with this prima facie tension, many theorists have been inclined to look harder, hoping to uncover some indirect or hidden instrumental rationale for the rule. In effect, they have tried show that concern for rules is just a subset of concern for consequences, misleadingly described. The major motivation for these efforts has been a rather diffuse sense that expanding the conception of practical rationality to include noninstrumental reasons for action would involve introducing a range of mysterious (not to mention mathematically intractable) mental states. In this chapter, I will try to show that reasons for action derived from shared rules can be integrated directly into a formal model of practical deliberation without any of these adverse consequences. The mechanism for doing so has been overlooked, I will argue, because the usual von Neumann–Morgenstern derivation of utility functions significantly obscures the motivational psychology underlying the instrumental conception of rationality. When the basic structure of this psychology is kept in view, it can easily be seen how rule-following considerations can be introduced into the model of deliberation without positing any dubious intentional states.

3.1.   Social Norms

The major reason that instrumentalists have struggled to explain the role that rules play in regulating social interaction is that most social norms have an overtly deontic structure. They constrain agents by imposing specific duties on them. Rules usually classify *actions* as permissible or impermissible; they do not specify which outcomes are more or less desirable. They take the form "You must do x," and not "If you want y, do x" or "You should want y."[2] For example, children are taught that they must share their toys, regardless of how little they may want to do so, or that they must suffer having the last piece of cake offered to guests, regardless of how much they might like to eat it. All of these rules have at least superficially a nonconsequentialist structure. They have the form of what Kant called categorical imperatives, not hypothetical imperatives. This sort of deontic structure is difficult to account for in instrumental terms. After all, according to the instrumental view, all actions are supposed to be chosen merely as means to the realization of some further end. Rules appear to give the agent reason to perform an action directly, without reference to any further end. This is why instrumentalists have had a strong tendency to look to the downstream consequences of rule-following for some sort of instrumental justification. Punishment and reward seemed promising, precisely because they constitute *consequences* of rule-following, and so might provide an instrumental reason for following the rule.

What the theories that focus on punishment and reward fail to account for is the phenomenon Talcott Parsons referred to as the "voluntaristic" character of social order—the fact that individuals do not merely adapt themselves to the circumstances they find themselves in, but often choose, in an unforced way, to follow the prevailing set of social norms.[3] If external sanctions were doing all the work, we would expect to see a lot more violations of the rules when others aren't looking. Instead, what we see time and time again is agents conforming to rules even when they could easily get away with defecting.[4] Hence the near-impossibility of finding a "rational choice" criminologist.[5] Of course, there is no question that external sanctions play *some* role in keeping agents motivated. But there is good reason to believe that they cannot be the *only* mechanism, since there seems to be a great deal of willing cooperation involved in the production of social order.

Many social theorists have taken these sorts of observations as evidence that some kind of internal control mechanism is at work in much of the rule-following that we see in everyday life. The most common view is that people are *socialized* in a way that leads them to acquire a disposition to comply with social expectations, or to conform to the dominant mode of group behavior.[6] The simplest version of such a theory is the one that is often referred to in the literature as the Durkheim-Parsons theory of social action.[7] This is the familiar idea that individuals, over the course of their socialization, come to *internalize* the prevailing set of social norms.[8] In its crudest form, this theory can be given a behaviorist formulation. According to this view, external sanctions would be inadequate to maintain social order, save for the fact that these sanctions have a conditioning effect on agents. Through internalization of the sanction, agents begin to associate a negative cathexis with actions that are negatively sanctioned, and a positive cathexis with ones that are positively sanctioned. This makes them favorably disposed toward actions that are in conformity with the rules, and averse to ones that violate them. Thus, as Viktor Vanberg puts it, following rules involves "a kind of preprogrammed behaviour."[9]

This view helps to explain why sanctions are so infrequently applied, and why they often have merely symbolic significance. After having been sanctioned a few times, the agent will begin to conform to norms of her own volition, because failure to do so triggers feelings of guilt, shame, or remorse. As a result, when fully socialized agents fail to respect the normative order, the sanctions applied against them can be largely symbolic in nature, because the sanctions are used only to activate these underlying feelings. According to this view, sanctions exist initially to punish, but punishment has a socializing effect by virtue of our capacity for internalization (or even just conditioned learning). As a result, social order is maintained through a complex combination of internal and external control. (The term "social norm" is then used to refer to rules that are maintained through a hybrid motive of this type.)[10]

The important thing about this theory—what distinguishes it from the instrumental account—is that the process of socialization does not result merely in the formation of preferences over states of affairs. It also gives the agent a concrete disposition to perform a particular type of action, regardless of its consequences. Thus the theory treats rule-following as a sui generis phenomenon—in effect, a direct preference for a particular type of action, which can be propagated as a cultural pattern. This introduces considerations that extend beyond what can be represented in the standard instrumental theory of action. Socialization, according to this conception, while capable of reproducing conventions (in the game-theoretic sense), can also generate out-of-equilibrium behavior, insofar as agents just do what they have been trained to do without considering the consequences.

Regardless of how the details are worked out, it is easy to see how a behaviorist theory along these lines could be used to solve the problem of order. Consider the case of two siblings who insist on fighting over their toys. If this fighting results in damage to the toys, or the children, then the interaction has the structure of a classic prisoner's dilemma. How is this resolved? The parent steps in, threatening to take the toys away entirely unless the two share. After this threat has been carried out a few times, the children take the bad feelings associated with having no toys, and begin to associate it with the act of fighting over toys. They begin to feel bad about fighting. Thus they acquire a disposition to share their toys by internalizing the parent's negative sanction. Each would still *prefer* to have all the toys to himself, but has simply become averse to the means that must be employed in order to secure this outcome.

Very few people would deny that there is *something* right about this sort of theory. There are problems, however, with the cruder formulation of it. The behaviorist version clearly conflicts with certain observations about the kind of competencies that agents acquire through socialization. The primary difficulty is that it makes the relevant sorts of action dispositions extremely particular. According to the behaviorist view, what agents acquire through socialization is a commitment to a very specific type of behavior. As a result, if they come across some new social norm—one that they have not encountered before, or been socialized to uphold—they would have absolutely no disposition to conform to it. Yet what we usually observe is something quite different. Agents have much more flexible dispositions when it comes to norm-conformity. When they come across some new practice, they usually fall into line rather quickly, without having to be beaten into submission (or, less hyperbolically, without having to undergo an entirely new process of socialization). There also seems to be a significant cognitive element in the way that agents integrate into new social contexts. They actively observe the actions and reactions of others, then adapt their routines accordingly. This is why psychologists and sociologists usually distinguish between primary socialization (wherein agents acquire or develop the fundamental dispositions required to conform to social norms) and secondary socialization (wherein agents learn the specific norms of a particular cultural environment). The general point is that primary socialization occurs only once, whereas secondary socialization can occur whenever an agent spends long enough in a new social milieu.[11]

Social theorists have tried to capture these two "levels" of socialization with the distinction, introduced in its canonical form by Parsons, between values and norms. According to this view, what individuals acquire through socialization is not a specific disposition to perform a particular type of action, but rather a more generalized disposition to uphold the "values" that underlie the set of social norms. The general claim is that while children initially experience the sanctions associated with norm-violation as merely punishments and rewards, they gradually displace their emotional cathexis from the specific sanction to the more general attitude of the person who is doing the sanctioning. This generates an incentive not just to perform the correct sort of actions but also to secure the approval of the cultural parent.

This process of generalization continues, over the course of primary socialization, so that children acquire a set of increasingly diffuse "value-orientations," for example, a desire to be a "good boy" or a "nice girl," to "get along with others," to "fit in," and so on. Of course, as these dispositions become more general, they must be supplemented with knowledge of the particular expectations in the relevant social contexts. This is what generates the two levels: the difference between the agent's particular cultural knowledge and the more abstract norm-conformative disposition that develops through socialization.

This theory has two primary advantages over the cruder behaviorist theory. First, it does much greater justice to what we know about the psychological development and socialization of human infants. In particular, Parsons is able to explain why it is important that children form strong, stable emotional attachments to their primary cultural parents, and why children who do not establish supportive, loving relations with these parents often suffer from a general failure of socialization. It is precisely the role that these relationships play in *generalizing* the cathexis associated with norm-conformity—displacing it from actions to attitudes—that explains the crucial role that they play in the development of the child.

The other major attraction of Parsons's approach is that it is able to explain the *reflexivity* exhibited by agents in their norm-conformative acts.[12] Even when following rules, people generally know what they are doing, as they are doing it.[13] The behaviorist theory, in its simplest form, treats norm-conformity as little more than a conditioned reflex. It is a pattern of behavior that agents conform to because they have been trained to do so. One can see the influence of this perspective in Jon Elster's assertion that "the operation of norms is to a large extent blind, compulsive, mechanical or even unconscious."[14] (This naturally encourages the charge that norm-conformity is nothing but backward-looking "rule worship" or irrationality). But even though agents who are following rules may act with a certain disregard for consequences, this does not mean that they are unaware of what they are doing. First of all, agents may refuse to conform to norms if they don't believe that others will reciprocate. They may also be more likely to conform if they feel that doing so will improve the chances of reciprocation. This is why Ernest Fehr and Joseph Henrich, two scientists who have done considerable empirical work studying the role of social norms in sustaining cooperation, categorically reject the explanation in terms of subintentional factors:

> If indeed unconscious mechanisms are the reason for helping and punishing responses, why do subjects respond so *quickly* to changes in the cost of helping or punishing? Likewise, why do subjects *instantaneously* change their behavior when repeated interactions or the possibility of reputation formation are introduced? These quick behavioral changes are almost certainly mediated by sophisticated evaluations of the costs and benefits of different courses of action that are available to them. We find it hard to reconcile subjects' quick responses to treatment changes, which almost surely are mediated by sophisticated, conscious, cognitive actions, with the view that a cognitively inaccessible mechanism drives the base line pattern of reciprocal responses.[15]

Even when following rules, the agent's motive is clearly tied up with a certain structure of expectations. Furthermore, many norm-conformative actions are successful precisely because of these expectations. It is often important not only that agents know what they are doing when they follow a rule but also that their knowledge of what they are doing be common knowledge among everyone involved. A ritualized greeting, for example, is carried out not just because the person doing it wants to but also because this person expects that everyone else will recognize it for what it is.

Furthermore, it is quite common for agents to selectively violate social norms, knowing that this action will be understood and interpreted as an intentional norm-violation by others. For instance, people often communicate displeasure to one another by violating small norms of civility—such as not saying "Hello" when passing in the hall.[16] This works only because the norm is common knowledge, and because the sanctionee knows that the sanctioner knows that the sanctioner is *supposed* to say "Hello." There is of course a strategic dimension to all this, but not entirely so. Important aspects of the interaction are obscured unless the relevant set of social norms is represented through some sort of intentional mechanism, which can then be integrated with the belief-desire states used to model the strategic aspect of the action. Treating the norms as grounded merely in dispositions (or some other type of subintentional state) will not do the trick.

The major problems with Parsons's work lie in his use of the term "value." In the first place, it suggests that agents conform to norms as a *means* to achieving certain values (and thus that norm-conformative action is just a more abstract form of instrumental action, aimed at achieving "symbolic" outcomes.)[17] If this were the case, then there would be no reason not to integrate symbolic value into instrumental value, treating them all as merely different determinants of the agent's "all-things-considered" preference ordering over outcomes. The second problem is that values are too concrete. Philosophers are accustomed to using the term "value" to refer to second-order preferences, or "conceptions of the good." And it is well known that values, in this sense of the term, are not widely shared in a pluralistic liberal society. Christians and Buddhists may have very different values, but they are still able to interact with one another in a perfectly orderly fashion. Thus what primary socialization appears to cultivate is a much more general disposition toward norm-conformity.

It is more useful to think of primary socialization as a process that instills a "normative control system."[18] The limitations of Parsons's theory have led many social theorists to develop a theory of socialization according to which agents do not acquire a set of specific dispositions to perform particular actions, or even a more general commitment to specific values, but rather an entirely formal disposition to assign a certain deliberative weight to normative constraints. According to this view, agents are not punished for failing to conform to a particular pattern of behavior per se, but only insofar as their actions reflect a failure to assign sufficient deliberative weight to social norms. Socialization designates the process through which *these* sanctions are internalized. Parsons used the word "deviance" as a technical term to refer to cases in which agents adopt an inappropriate "action-orientation" (such as acting instrumentally when they should be conforming to norms).[19] So according to this Parsonian conception, sanctions secure social order not by punishing simple violation of the rules, but by punishing *motivated* violation of the rules (i.e., deviance, not mere nonconformity). This means that sanctions provide agents with an instrumental reason to follow the rules, but they also, when internalized, help to cultivate a disposition to assign social norms greater deliberative weight relative to one's desires.

According to this view, social order requires at least some agents who are disposed to assign social norms deliberative priority, and for those agents who are not so disposed, an effective system of sanctions to give them instrumental reasons for conforming to the normative pattern. These sanctions, when implemented through a norm-conformative orientation, function simultaneously as a mechanism of *socialization* and *social control*. Social control refers to their instrumental significance—sanctions make deviance unattractive, from an instrumental point of view. Socialization refers to their psychological effects—through their expression of disapproval and the internalization mechanism, sanctions generate the disposition to assign normative reasons for action greater deliberative weight. When the internal and external incentives are appropriately aligned, it produces what Parsons referred to as the *institutionalization* of a norm.

3.2. Principles

There is nothing especially mysterious about this theory of socialization and norm-conformative action, and no reason to think that it cannot be accommodated within a formal model of rational action. To ask what *reason* a person has for acting in a particular way is to ask for an explanation of a certain form, namely, one that explains the action in terms of some set of underlying intentional states. The instrumental conception of rationality explains action through reference to two such states: beliefs and desires. A *reductive* account of social norms attempts to explain rule-following in terms of these two states, while a nonreductive account would attempt to do so by positing some new type of state. We have seen in the previous chapter that the reductive account encounters serious difficulties. The question now is whether a *nonreductive* account of rule-following can be constructed that satisfies the standards of conceptual clarity set by rational choice theory.

What is it about rules that makes them so difficult to account for from an instrumental perspective? As we have seen, the key characteristic is that they are directly associated with actions. Yet this observation suggests a very simple way of integrating social norms into the decision framework. Desires are intentional states associated with outcomes, beliefs are intentional states associated with states. Norms, or rule-following considerations more generally, can be accommodated simply by positing an intentional state associated directly with actions.

There may be a temptation to use the Kantian term "maxim" in order to refer to an action-prescribing intentional state, although in the interests of keeping the folk-psychological motivation for the theory close to the surface it is perhaps better to use the term "principle." In this context, it is helpful to remember that beliefs and desires acquired their contemporary philosophical meaning through an attempt to develop a regimentation of folk psychology. In everyday talk about action, we routinely explain behavior in terms of what outcome the agent hoped to attain and how he thought his action would conduce to that end. But we also routinely characterize agents as exercising restraint in their pursuit of such outcomes. We describe an individual as desiring an outcome, but not pursuing it "as a matter of principle," or because of a "principled" reservation concerning the means needed to bring it about. This is how we would normally talk about the employee who could achieve promotion through lying or deception, or the impatient motorist tempted to cut off another driver. The attempt to reduce this sort of talk to an oblique form of talk about desires and outcomes has been a failure. As a result, there is good reason to think that a perspicuous regimentation of folk psychology would preserve reference to these sorts of principles as independent deliberative considerations. If we follow this suggestion, then it is natural to think of desires as a set of preferences over outcomes, and principles as a set of preferences over actions.

Although this may seem like an obvious move, most theorists who have been tempted by this line of reasoning fail to take it. Instead, there is a widespread tendency to commit what might be referred to as "the error of premature concreteness." Rather than introducing norms in a way that formally parallels the existing structure of beliefs and desires—taking principles as given, in the same way the decision theorists take preferences as given—they try to enumerate a set of particular norms and then incorporate them directly into the theory of action through a substantive modification of the agent's utility function. As a result, they wind up burdening the theory of practical rationality with structural elements that should really be farmed out to the theory that explains the origin and content of the agent's intentional states.

Cristina Bicchieri, for instance, recognizes that norms cannot simply be subsumed into the agent's outcome-based utility function, but that they represent sui generis constraints on the actions chosen. Thus she undertakes to develop a system of representation for "a general utility function based on norms."[20] Yet what she winds up proposing is conspicuously lacking in generality. For a prisoner's dilemma, she suggests that the utility functions be transformed, in order to deduct from each individual's payoff some (appropriately weighted) concern for the loss of utility to any player caused by deviation from a norm of cooperation. While it may be possible that such a modified utility function does provide an accurate representation of how some individuals deliberate in collective action problems, it captures only a very particular sort of normative concern (since it translates the agent's "concern for the norm" into a "concern for the worst consequences, in terms of forgone utility, of any failure to respect the norm"), which may not be universally, or even widely, shared. Similarly, Matthew Rabin, in his attempt to "incorporate fairness into game theory," builds in a direct concern for the norm of fairness into each individual's utility function. He does so by modifying the utility functions, so that individuals experience an increase in satisfaction from reciprocated "kindness" and a decrease in satisfaction from unreciprocated kindness.[21] Ernest Fehr and Klaus Schmidt do something quite similar, by building "inequality aversion" into the individual's utility function—subtracting from the individual's satisfaction a certain measure of dissatisfaction, reflecting the *difference* in satisfaction level between himself and others.[22] Bruno Verbeek argues that utility functions should be modified into order to incorporate a set of "cooperative virtues" that generate process-oriented preferences for cooperation.[23] He describes these preferences as "second-order reasons of a dispositional character with regards to first-order reasons directed to self-interest, broadly conceived" or more colloquially, "attitudes towards our own interests."[24] Again, "concern for the norm" is represented as a function of concern for the consequences, in terms of payoffs, of general compliance or violation.[25]

In all four cases, an attempt is made to cash out "concern for the norm" as some sort of "concern for the payoffs to the various parties to the interaction." Yet this reflects a set of highly welfarist preoccupations, which are simply not relevant in a wide range of cultural contexts, and with respect to a large number of norms. One need only consider the case of highly ritualistic religious obligations. Even something as straightforward as the gift-giving norm, which produced such intriguing ultimatum game results in New Guinea, defies representation using any of these modified utility functions. For example, the sort of "kindness" that Rabin treats as a source of increased satisfaction was typically punished in New Guinea, simply because gift-giving norms are quite different from fairness norms (giving too much is not regarded as supererogatory, but rather hubristic).

Why not represent concern for the norm as just that, concern for the norm? People follow the rules because they want to follow the rules. In order to produce a truly *general* theory of action, the best approach is to introduce norms into the utility function in a way that is completely vacuous with respect to the content of these norms (in the same way that "preferences" are introduced into the utility function in a way that is vacuous with respect to the content of the agent's desires). What is needed, in other words, is something like what Herbert Gintis calls a "beliefs, preferences and constraints" model of action.[26] In chapter 1, beliefs and desires were introduced through a pruning of the agent's decision tree. Under conditions of epistemic certainty, they could be used to cut the decision tree back until only one branch remained. Normative constraints have often been characterized in very similar terms.[27] Thus principles can be thought of as deontic constraints that are imposed in a manner quite similar to that of their doxastic and desiderative cousins. We may start out by looking at the options that are *actually* available to us. This amounts to a doxastic pruning of the decision tree. We then consider which among these options are *normatively* permissible, that is, we eliminate all the options that violate the prevailing set of social norms. This amounts to a *deontic pruning* of the decision tree. Once this is finished, we can select the action that gives us the most desired outcome (this is the desiderative pruning of the tree).

The analogy between doxastic and deontic constraints can be elaborated in the following way. Under conditions of epistemic certainty and strict obligation, we can think of the agent as qualifying a set of propositions according to a set of modalities:[28]

Doxastic Modalities	Deontic Modalities
M = possible	P = permitted
N = necessary	O = obligatory
I = impossible	F = forbidden

The analogy between these modalities has been widely noted in the literature. For example, these doxastic and deontic modalities are interdefinable in exactly the same way: $Mp =_{df} \sim N\sim p =_{df} \sim Ip$, and $Pp =_{df} \sim O\sim p =_{df} \sim Fp$. (In words: "it is possible that p means that it is not necessary that not p, and that it is not impossible that p." In the same way, "it is permissible to do p means that it is not obligatory to not do p, and that it is not forbidden to do p.") In practical deliberation, the agent may begin by determining which of her actions are *possible* ways of attaining a desired outcome. She then decides which of her actions represent *permissible* ways of attaining the same outcome.[29] She then makes a decision among the options that remain (if there are any), looking at which is the most *desirable*. This procedure corresponds fairly closely to the way Kant thought practical reasoning should unfold. It is, of course, rather simplified (and need not proceed in the order specified). It assumes that states are known with certainty, and that actions are absolutely prohibited. But just as states can be known with varying probabilities, actions can be more or less frowned on. Breaking a promise, for example, is contrary to duty, but the norm can be overridden in many circumstances. For this reason, permissible actions can be ranked as more or less *appropriate*, in the same way that possible states are ranked as more or less *probable*. A forbidden action, according to this view, could be represented as having an appropriateness of, say, zero, and an obligatory action as having some high positive value.[30] All other actions can be assigned some intermediate value that specifies their appropriateness, relative to the others (using, for the moment, a scale that reflects the significance that the agent assigns to these constraints, relative to the desirability of the consequences). These values can then be integrated into the agent's utility function, so that they act as a kind of "filter" that reduces the value of normatively inappropriate actions relative to more appropriate ones. These normative considerations can be added to the decision tree

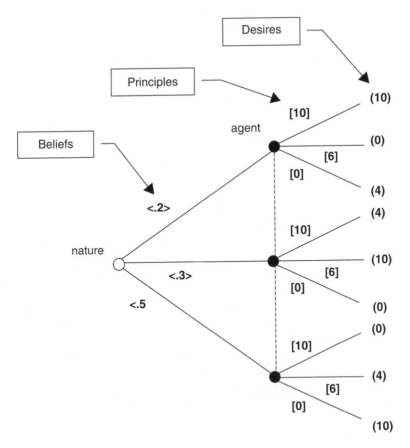

Figure 3.1 Decision tree with norms.

in the way shown in figure 3.1. (Appropriateness factors are shown between square brackets, [x], given here on a scale between 0 and 10.)

We now have a complete decision tree: beliefs associated with states, principles associated with actions, and desires associated with outcomes. From the standpoint of practical rationality, each of these intentional states can be treated as "subjective." Thus beliefs stand to facts as principles stand to norms, and, perhaps, as desires stand to goods. The nature of these relationships will be explored later. For the moment, the goal is just to show how principled constraints on the pursuit of a goal can be integrated into the agent's decision function. The simplest way of doing this is simply to add the normative appropriateness of each action, indicated as $n(a)$, to the expected utility of that action (which is a function of the consequences of that action). To avoid confusion, we can call the utility function that results from the introduction of deontic constraints a *value function*, represented $v(a)$:

$$v(a) = n(a) + \sum_o p(o \mid a)u(o) \qquad (1)$$

In the example shown in figure 3.1, this gives:

$$v(a_1) = 10 + [(0.2 \cdot 10) + (0.3 \cdot 4) + (0.5 \cdot 0)]$$
$$= 13.2$$
$$v(a_2) = 6 + [(0.2 \cdot 0) + (0.3 \cdot 10) + (0.5 \cdot 4)]$$
$$= 11$$
$$v(a_3) = 0 + [(0.2 \cdot 4) + (0.3 \cdot 0) + (0.5 \cdot 10)]$$
$$= 5.8$$

Thus a_3, despite being utility-maximizing, is bumped down through the introduction of deontic constraints. It should be noted that the appropriateness of principles and the priority level of desires in this example are both represented on a scale of 0 to 10. Just as in the case of desires, the precise scale that is used to represent appropriateness is merely notational. What matters is only that the numbers reflect the significance of the agent's principles relative to one another, and to the agent's desires. If the appropriateness factors range from 0 to 100, and desires only from 0 to 10, this suggests that the agent considers "doing the right thing" to be ten times more important than "getting the best outcome."

In principle, commensurability between the scale used to represent the agent's principles and her desires can be established in much the same way that a von Neumann–Morgenstern utility function is conventionally constructed. In order to determine the relative strength of desires, one offers the agent a hypothetical choice between a particular outcome and a lottery over the extremes. In the case of actions, one can do the same sort of thing, by offering the agent a hypothetical choice and trying to find a point at which the agent becomes indifferent between some particular action and, for example, some other less appropriate action that has a higher utility payoff. By determining how much utility must be added in order to compensate for a given decrease in appropriateness, it will be possible to determine how much the agent considers utility to be worth relative to appropriateness.

The procedure is one that should be familiar. The way to ascertain someone's level of commitment is to offer her some temptation, and see how much it takes to weaken her resolve. Of course, there may be some people who assign absolute (or "lexical") priority to their normative obligations—so that the wrongness of the action completely overshadows the desirability of the outcome. This is not really a problem, since it can be handled in the same way as agents with "lexicographic preferences" over outcomes.[31] There is a school of thought that claims that moral constraints should always constitute absolute prohibitions, such that they "blank out" any utility associated with their violation. This seems fanatical to me, but there is no need to settle the question here. Since appropriateness factors are being used to represent the role that any social norm plays in deliberation, including rules of etiquette and so on, which can legitimately be abrogated when the consequences are serious, it is natural to assume that agents will be willing to countenance trade-offs between appropriateness and utility. The issue of whether or when absolute prohibitions are justified belongs then to the theory of principle rationality, not the theory of practical rationality strictly construed.

In the end, the conception of practical rationality that is represented in equation (1) is a version of what Jean Hampton calls *weight consequentialism*, "a view that permits a person to factor into her decision both how she feels about the consequences of an action and how she feels about the action itself."[32] It is not clear, however, why she thinks of this as a form of consequentialism, as opposed to nonconsequentialism, since no one in his right mind (not even Kant) has ever suggested that rationality might *preclude* the consideration of consequences across the board. Critics of consequentialism have never aspired to show that consequences don't matter at all, they have simply been trying to show that consequences are not the *only* thing that matters.

3.3.   World Bayesianism

The proposal outlined above is guided by an effort to keep the theory as close as possible to its roots in folk psychology. The distinction between principles, desires, and beliefs corresponds to the common-sense distinction—introduced into decision theory in its canonical form by Leonard Savage—between actions, outcomes, and states. Deontic constraints are accommodated simply by integrating direct preferences over the set of actions with the expected utility derived from their anticipated outcomes.

Yet once preferences over actions are introduced in this way, it eliminates one of the major reasons for distinguishing between actions and outcomes in the first place. The von Neumann–Morgenstern procedure, for example, treats actions as simply lotteries over possible outcomes, with no intrinsic merit (hence the "reduction of compound lotteries" axiom). Once we grant that the agent may care about these actions, one way or the other, then they begin to look a lot more like outcomes. So how can we retrace the distinction, or should we even do so? The discussion has proceeded thus far as though actions and outcomes were distinct events (with propositions representing these events forming the content of the associated intentional states). But since any sequence of events can easily be treated as just one big long event, there is some question as to where the action stops and the outcome begins. When I hit a golf ball, it would be normal to say that my hitting the ball is the action, and that where it lands is the outcome. But where does the action stop? When I make up my mind about how to strike it? Or when I initiate the swing? Or when the club makes contact? Or sometime when the ball is in the air?

The common-sense answer to this question would be to say that the action is the segment of the sequence of events that is under the agent's direct control. After a certain point, the way events unfold becomes hostage to fortune. The golf ball may be caught by a gust of wind, so that just hitting it in a particular way will not guarantee that it lands where it is supposed to. One way of distinguishing between actions and outcomes is therefore to imagine the intervention of some random event between the two that puts the outcome outside the direct control of the agent, and makes it depend on the results of some natural "lottery." The significance of this lottery is that it forces the agent to factor some probabilistic belief into his calculation of the desirability of various alternative actions. The action, according to this view, is an event that the agent is *certain* he will be able to bring about, while the outcomes represent the set of events whose occurrence is tinged by *uncertainty*.

Yet this way of thinking of actions is still too concrete. As Isaac Levi points out, an action and an outcome can be the same event under different descriptions. Consider, for instance, the case of an individual who owes money to either Paul or Jane, but can't remember which one. He has two actions available to him, "send $100 to Paul" or "send $100 to Jane," with two possible outcomes, "Repay my debt" or "Fail to repay my debt." If he sends the $100 to Paul, and it turns out that he did owe the money to Paul, then he will succeed in repaying his debt. But the action of sending the money to Paul *constitutes* the repayment of the debt—the outcome is simply the action under a different description. The only difference is that the agent is certain that he will be able to bring about the action if he decides to, but uncertain about his ability to bring about one or the other outcome (because of his uncertainty as to who the debt is owed to). Thus the distinction between actions and outcomes becomes a purely epistemic one—actions are those propositions to which the agent assigns a "credal probability" of 1.[33] As a result, it seems clearly arbitrary to insist that the agent's preferences range only over consequences (especially since a mere change in the agent's beliefs could transform an action into a consequence). In Levi's example, the debtor may happen to like Paul more than Jane, and so have an intrinsic preference for sending the money to him. There is simply no reason to insist that preference for the action be based exclusively on the desire to repay the debt. Given its subjectivism with respect to preference, decision theory is simply too formal a model of practical rationality to entail a commitment to a restrictive doctrine like consequentialism.

The recognition that there is no principled distinction between actions and outcomes is one of the factors that motivated the move toward what Jordan Howard Sobel calls "world Bayesian" formulations of decision theory among philosophers.[34] Instead of defining actions and outcomes in terms of particular events, one can define "a consequence" in terms of possible worlds (where a possible world is identified with a set of sentences describing a total state of the world). Speaking very roughly, a consequence such as "the glass breaks" can be defined as a subset of the total set of possible worlds, one in which the sentence "the glass breaks" (suitably indexed) is true. The agent's preferences can then be represented as simply a weak ordering of the set of possible worlds. This permits a rather elegant mathematical formulation of decision theory, because it allows one to dispense with states, and simply define the agent's beliefs as a set of conditional probabilities over the same set of possible worlds.

The other major advantage of world Bayesianism is that it dissolves the entire debate over the distinction between actions and outcomes, by essentially defining consequences broadly enough to include the actions that brought them about. If action *a* makes it the case that possible world *w* becomes the actual world at time *t*, and *w* is the complete set of sentences true at *t*, then *w* will presumably include a sentence specifying that action *a* was performed. Since a possible world in which action a_1 was performed is clearly different from one in which a_2 was performed, and since preferences in this view are regarded as rankings of possible worlds, it is automatic that the agent's utility function will incorporate whatever preferences the agent may have over her own actions. Thus, where *a* is an action, *w* is some possible world, and $p(w \mid a)$ is the probability of *w* becoming actual given *a*, the desirability (or expected utility) of the action *a* will be the sum of the utility associated with the possible worlds that it might bring about, weighted by the probability that it will do so:[35]

$$des(a) = \sum_w p(w \mid a)u(w) \qquad (2)$$

Since *a* is one of the propositions true in *w*, *u(w)* will incorporate whatever feelings the agent happens to have about that action. As Levi and others have observed, this essentially makes consequentialism—understood as the claim that "actions are valued only for the sake of consequences"—tautological. Actions are valued only for their consequences simply because a consequence has been defined as the total world that results from an action, up to and including the action itself. (Or as Sobel writes, "what are consequences or worlds for a particular agent will be logically independent of paths to them only in so far as he is indifferent to these paths.")[36] Levi suggests that this formulation be referred to as "weak consequentialism," in recognition of the fact that it winds up classifying everyone, "even Kant and Bernard Williams," as a consequentialist. Thus critics of instrumental rationality, he observes, "cannot be complaining about weak consequentialism since it is sufficiently flexible to accommodate any mode of nonconsequentialist evaluation they care to consider."[37]

Yet far from being a vindication of consequentialism, what Levi presents is much closer to being an abandonment. His own analysis suggests that world Bayesianism should be regarded as a form of "nonconsequentialist" decision theory, since it permits agents to select actions on the basis of their intrinsic merits, whatever these may be, rather than for their consequences. Again, critics of consequentialism in action theory have never claimed that *only* actions count, and that consequences are irrelevant—they have argued that both the nature of an action and the value of its consequences are factors that enter into rational decision, and that the former is not always simply derived from the latter.[38]

Like the value function developed in section 3.2, world Bayesianism therefore represents a way of modifying decision theory in recognition of the fact that individuals often care not only about the outcomes of their actions but also how those outcomes are achieved. In fact, applying the "desirability" function (2) to the decision problem shown in figure 3.1 would generate exactly the same numbers as the value function (1). Thus the difference between them is purely

notational—the value function removes the action from the scope of the probabilistic weighting, whereas the desirability function keeps it in, but tacitly assigns
it probability of 1. The latter strategy has been challenged by several theorists
on technical grounds, since it has several very unattractive properties when
it comes to representing the dynamics of deliberation (roughly speaking, the
problems arise from the fact that the agent must be represented as entertaining beliefs about the probability that he will perform action a while deliberat-
ing about whether or not to perform a—thus the desirability function *changes*
as the agent deliberates).[39] But even apart from these difficulties, there are good
reasons to avoid assimilating actions to consequences. This becomes especially
obvious when it comes to representing social interaction—which is something
that world Bayesians typically are not interested in doing.

3.4. Social Interaction

The world Bayesian model provides one example of how a direct concern for
norms can be represented in an agent's utility function. What distinguishes
it from the standard instrumental model is its rejection of the consequentialism hypothesis in its strict form. The "desirability" function presented above
acknowledges that an agent may value an action for its own sake, as well as for
the sake of any further outcomes that it may promote. It achieves this by bun-
dling the two together and treating them as a global "consequence"—a possible
world that is complete with respect to everything that the agent cares about. Yet
while these sorts of world Bayesian views are popular among philosophers, they
have not been widely adopted by game theorists. The reasons for this are not
hard to find. The value function outlined in section 3.2 is designed to address
these concerns, and to provide a nonconsequentialist version of decision theory
that is more suitable for use in modeling social interaction.

World Bayesianism trades on the fact that, in decision theory, the distinction
between an action and an outcome can be drawn somewhat arbitrarily. But in
game theory, the intervention of uncertainty, which serves as the point of demar-
cation between the two, is not caused by the presence of an unknown natural
state (corresponding to a probabilistic belief) but rather by the *decision* taken by
another player. Thus game theorists use the distinction between actions and outcomes not just as a way of stating how confident the agent is that certain effects
can be achieved but also as a way of distinguishing strategic from nonstrategic
elements of a choice problem. As a result, there are important structural differences in game theory between reasoning about outcomes and reasoning about
actions. Furthermore, because the sequence in which moves are made can be
crucial to the equilibrium of a game, it is not a matter of indifference to the game
theorist how actions and outcomes are classified.

This is why game theorists generally presuppose the "Savage trichotomy" of
actions, states, and outcomes when modeling social interactions, and usually
think of both actions and outcomes as concrete events. This is also why they
continue to define expected utility over the space of outcomes, not global conse-

quences. Yet because of this, they remain tacitly committed to consequentialism in its strict (and implausible) form. They assume that the only preferences agents have over actions are those that are derived from preferences over outcomes. Yet they also treat actions as concrete events, which occur in temporal sequence, and are often observed by other players. Thus the consequentialism hypothesis, which is relatively trivial when introduced in decision-theoretic contexts, becomes inadvertently transformed into a substantive, controversial, and essentially unmotivated claim when the move is made from decision theory to game theory. (This becomes even more evident when the move is made from mathematical to experimental game theory, and the inference is drawn that individuals should be indifferent toward all characteristics of the choices that they make, and be concerned exclusively with the monetary payoff.) This has been a source of considerable mischief.

Consider, for example, a standard "public goods" game. From the standpoint of the agent's desires, the free-rider strategy of investing in the private account strongly dominates the cooperative strategy of investing in the public account. Yet most subjects invest only half of their income there. The most natural way of analyzing this finding is simply to suppose that, despite wanting the money, individuals are also somewhat averse to engaging in selfish or uncooperative behavior. It is not that they like the money any less, it is that they are not indifferent to the means through which the money is acquired. Thus their reasoning incorporates a nonconsequentialist element. The most natural way of representing this is simply to determine how strong this aversion is, then write it into the game in a way that associates it directly with the action.

Unfortunately, when confronted with a situation like this, the dominant impulse among game theorists has been to go the opposite direction, and rewrite the notation in such a way as to make the action a part of the consequences (thereby "sucking the alleged value into what we might call the consequentialist vacuum cleaner," as David McNaughton and Piers Rawling put it.)[40] So, if we have an agent who would like to make $10, but also doesn't want to take advantage of other people, we can simply treat "made $10 by free riding" as a different outcome from "made $10 by cooperating." The fact that agents do not uniformly defect then just goes to show that some people value cooperation more than the $10.[41]

This strategy, however, is in tension with the commitment among game theorists to the Savage trichotomy, and creates a lot of confusions further down the line. Because the distinction between actions and outcomes also serves to demarcate the strategic from the nonstrategic component of the interaction, writing the value of actions into the consequences makes it seem as though everything that matters to the agent depends on what the other player chooses, when often this is not so.[42] This makes it impossible for either agent to calculate the merits of any action without first resolving the regress of anticipations that constitutes the strategic dimension of the problem. Obviously this generates a technical violation of the thought that an action is an outcome to which the agent assigns a "credal probability of 1." More troublesome is the fact that it generates a straightforwardly false representation of the choice situation in games with multiple equilibria, where the probabilities associated with the other player's actions cannot be pinned down. The lack of a unique equilibrium renders the entire choice problem indeterminate, when in fact only a portion of it is problematic. Thus writing actions into the consequences makes it *seem* as if everything hinges upon strategic elements of the interaction, even when this is not the case.

Consider the simple coordination game shown in figure 3.2. Two people would like to meet at a café, but neither can remember which one they agreed to go to. Here the regress of anticipations is irresolvable. If player 2 is going to choose café x, then player 1 would like to choose x, but if player 2 is going to choose y, then player 1 would like to choose y, and vice versa. (There is also a mixed strategy equilibrium, in which both players go to either café with probability 0.5.) It is important not to underestimate the seriousness of this indeterminacy problem. The expected utility of going to café x or café y remains undetermined for both players, that is, there is no such thing as a utility-maximizing course of action. This is because neither player is able to assign any probability to the actions of the other. They cannot even fall back on Laplace's principle of insufficient reason (treat all events as equiprobable unless given reason not to) since the use of this principle amounts to the ascription of a mixed strategy to the other player. This strategy will in turn be either a part of one of the equilibrium strategy profiles (in which case it is question-begging to privilege it) or else not a part of one (in which case it would be demonstrably irrational to believe that the other player would choose it). Thus, from a strictly instrumental perspective, players have no grounds for favoring one action over the other.

Suppose, however, that we add to this problem the information that player 1 likes café x a lot more than café y. The natural way of representing this—adhering to the Savage trichotomy, along with the representation of the choice problem adopted in figure 3.2—would be to say that he now prefers one *action* over the other (since going to café x is something that he can do all by himself, unlike meeting player 2, which is clearly contingent on that person's decision). This seems intuitive. Unfortunately, most rational choice theorists have been tempted to handle this sort of situation by writing this preference for café x into the outcome, treating "meeting at café x" as a different, more preferable, outcome than "meeting at café y."[43] This strategy—what Jean Hampton refers to as "load-

Player 2

		café x	café y
	café x	they meet (2,2)	they miss (0,0)
Player 1			
	café y	they miss (0,0)	they meet (2,2)

Figure 3.2 Coordination problem.

Player 2

		café x	café y
Player 1	**café x**	they meet **(3,2)**	they miss **(1,0)**
	café y	they miss **(0,0)**	they meet **(2,2)**

Figure 3.3 Asymmetric coordination problem.

ing up the consequences"[44]—generates the reformulation of the payoff matrix shown in figure 3.3.

Here we can see the problem with this sort of dogmatic consequentialism: while one equilibrium may now be Pareto-superior to the other, the expected utility of both players' actions is still undetermined. Adding the piece of information about which café player 1 prefers has done absolutely nothing to make the problem more tractable. It is still a game with two pure-strategy Nash equilibria, and no grounds for choosing one over the other. The mixed strategy equilibrium shifts to ($[0.5x, .05y], [0.25x, 0.75y]$), but this is of no consequence (other than the weird fact that it makes it positively irrational, not just arbitrary, for player 1 to believe that player 2 might toss a fair coin in order to decide what to do).

The fact that this new information leaves the choice problem indeterminate seems unreasonable. We can easily imagine player 1 thinking "well I have no idea where player 2 is going, so it will be just a matter of luck if I succeed in meeting up with her. And if I am going to be sitting alone in a café, it might as well be the one that I like. So I will go to café x." We can also imagine that if player 2 is aware of player 1's preference for this action, she will also go to café x, knowing that this is where he will go when he *gives up* trying to coordinate. With the type of value function introduced in section 3.2, it is easy to represent this line of reasoning. Since $u(x)$ and $u(y)$ are unknown, they can be represented as some variable ζ. Player 1 then has a choice between $v(x) = 1 + \zeta$ and $v(y) = \zeta$. So x is clearly the dominant strategy. Thus a better way of representing the coordination problem, in this case, is to keep the payoffs associated with the actions outside of the outcomes matrix. Figure 3.4 shows how the café problem can be represented, in both extensive and normal form. Each action has an associated appropriateness factor, shown in square brackets. Outcomes are given, as usual, as a vector of utility payoffs (showing how much player 1 desires that outcome, how much player 2 desires it, etc.).

We can then see how, when player 1 gives up on instrumental reasoning (because of the indeterminacy of the choice problem), he is not at a complete loss. The instrumental component of his motive simply drops out, leaving him with a direct preference over actions. The reason this is possible is that *not everything he cares about depends on the choice made by the other player*. Writing preferences over actions into the outcomes misrepresents the choice problem, by making it seem

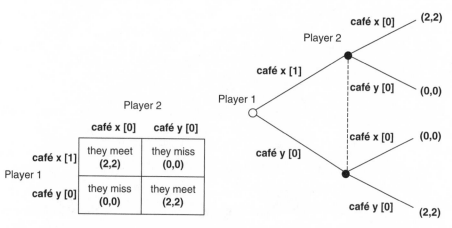

Figure 3.4 Resolving the coordination problem.

as if it all does. It obscures the fact that he still has a reason to perform one of the actions available to him, because of a direct preference.[45]

Naturally, the way that player 1 is reasoning will be transparent to player 2, assuming common knowledge of preferences. This allows the two of them to resolve the coordination problem more fully. Player 2 can rationally infer that when player 1 gives up on trying to coordinate, he will go to café x. This gives player 2 a rational belief that player 1 will choose this action, and this in turn allows her to calculate a utility-maximizing course of action. And, of course, player 1 will be able to figure all this out as well, which will give him a reason to expect player 2 to choose x, and hence will allow him to calculate the expected utility of his own action. Thus player 1's preference for café x gets converted into a strong strategic equilibrium when it is common knowledge among the players. It is able to serve this role because it supplies a reason for action that is not caught up in the cycle of interdependent expectations that renders the strategic problem indeterminate. Thus the introduction of principles provides the basis for a very simple mechanism to generate Thomas Schelling's psychological solution to the problem of coordination, one that fully specifies the nature and content of the intentional states that generate the solution. (The agent's direct preference for the action can be thought of as generating a "focal point" effect.)

It is worth noting that the mechanism presented in figure 3.4 is extremely "low powered," insofar as it will fail to generate a focal equilibrium in many circumstances. For example, if player 2 happens to prefer café y, then the two of them are right back where they started. Thus, in order to provide a "pure" focal point solution, principles of action must be derived from very widely shared psychological propensities (which is why many of Schelling's examples appeal to features of objects that would have been highly salient in the "environment of evolutionary adaptation.")[46] However, it is quite easy to generate an artificial focal point through the introduction of a social norm. Such a norm, insofar as it is coherent, will prescribe a set of complementary actions. For example, when two people approach a doorway simultaneously, there is often a coordination problem determining who will pass through first. There is a widely respected gender norm specifying that if one person is a man and the other a woman, the man should let the woman go through first. Of course, generating such a norm and getting everyone to accept it is a complicated process, one that will be discussed at greater length further on. For the moment, it is sufficient to note that many social norms have a coordinating role, by virtue of their capacity to prescribe a set of complementary actions to agents involved in an interaction.

In summary, agents are understood to enter into practical deliberation with a global preference ordering, which ranks both actions (via their principles) and outcomes (via their desires). There is no hard-and-fast metaphysical distinction between actions and outcomes, and so there are many ways in which choice problems can be represented. In the café example, one could choose to model the interaction as a multistage game: with the first stage a game against nature, in which the agents choose a café, and then enjoy the payoff associated with that café, and the second stage a game against each other where, after having chosen a café, they then discover whether they have succeeded in coordinating (the fact that these two games are simultaneous would then be represented by linking both players' nodes at each stage into a single information set). Again, this would allow one to avoid positing preferences over actions (by redescribing the agent's action as a consequence in the first stage of a multistage game). On the other hand, one could do as I have suggested: break down the global preference ordering into its components and represent explicitly in the game the weight that the agents' preference orderings assign to the actions and the consequences available to them. There is no uniquely correct way of proceeding here, since these are all just notational variants. The question is simply how well they articulate the logic of the decision, and the structure of the agent's deliberation. From this expressive perspective, it seems to me clear that the latter option is the superior one.

3.5.   Normative Control

It is important to recognize that the notation developed here is still extremely formal. The content of the agent's "principles" is completely unspecified, as is the content of the agent's "desires." Both are simply preferences. Furthermore, the way that the agent weighs one set of preferences against the other is also not specified, it is merely implicit in the way that the scales used to represent appropriateness and desirability are calibrated. In order to represent something like the "normative control system" described in section 3.1, it is necessary to add a bit of meat to these bones.

Normative control, in this view, is simply a preference that assigns reasons for action that arise from social norms a certain deliberative weight relative to one's desires. In this respect, it is a metapreference, which determines how much weight is to be assigned certain other first-order preferences. When it comes to modeling such a metapreference, it is helpful to consider the way that economists have dealt with a very similar issue, involving the representation of the agent's *time preference* in decision problems. The idea that agents have a time preference is based on the observation that for any given desire, people seem to have a preference for seeing that desire satisfied sooner rather than later. Some of this attitude usually involves concern about risk, but another dimension seems to be a pure preference for present over future satisfaction (or an aversion to delay in the satisfaction of desire).

Metapreferences of this sort are a subspecies of what Harry Frankfurt calls "higher-order desires" (desires that take other desires as their object, rather than states of the world), although they are slightly more formal in structure than what Frankfurt had in mind, since they do not take any particular preference as their object, but rather apply equally to all preferences.[47] Yet they still need to be considered preferences, not structural features of practical reason, because they vary across individuals (e.g., different people have different attitudes toward delay, with some being very impatient and others not so impatient). When a utility function is constructed using the agent's attitudes toward hypothetical lotteries, the result is a completely atemporal ranking of alternatives. It will tell us that the agent prefers $100 to $50, and by how much. Yet if the agent also dislikes having to wait, she might prefer $50 now to $100 later. So when it comes to producing an all-things-considered ranking of possible outcomes, at the point of decision, these preferences will interact in such a way as to result in a lower priority level being assigned to the desire for $100. The standard way of articulating this is to say that agents *discount* future satisfaction.

When economists first began to introduce player discount rates into their models, the place they looked to for an analogy was the practice of paying *interest* on savings or loans.[48] Saving represents a way of deferring consumption, and generally speaking, people will only defer consumption if they are compensated for so doing. They must have some reason to believe that they will be able to consume *more* if they wait than if they consume now. I may choose to take the $100 today instead of tomorrow, but if instead I am offered $105 tomorrow, I may choose to wait. Since interest rates reflect the amount extra that people need to be given in order to persuade them to defer consumption (as well as the opportunity cost of present consumption), these rates are normally understood to reflect an underlying time preference.

The discount rate (r) can be defined as the extra fraction of a payoff needed to make an agent indifferent between satisfying some desire now and satisfying it one time period from now. The discount rate can be used to define a discount factor, $\delta = 1/(1 + r)$, which shows what the *present* value of future satisfaction is.[49] So if I am willing to save $1,000 once annual interest rates go as high as 7 percent, this means that I need to be paid an extra $70 in order to compensate for the hardship of deferring that much consumption for a year. Thus the present value to me of having $1,000 in a year's time is only $935 (which, when added to the *present* value of the $70 interest payment, comes to roughly $1,000).

Naturally, the same analysis can be generalized to cover time periods that are further removed in the future. Having $1,000 two years from now will be worth

$935 in one year, and therefore is worth $875 in the present. Thus if $u_k(a)$ represents the payoff that I will receive at period k, the value of some stream of future payoffs is worth the following to me in the present:

$$u(a) = u_1(a) + \delta^2 u(a) + \delta u_3(a)... + \delta^{n-1} u_n(a), \qquad (3)$$

Or more generally, where n is the total number of time periods:

$$u(a) = \sum_{k=1}^{n} \delta^{k-1} u_k(a) \qquad (4)$$

Economists and game theorists almost automatically add a discount factor to players' utility functions when dealing with a repeated game. Partly this is for the technical reason that it provides the easiest way to compare infinite payoff streams. Investing $1,000 at a 10 percent interest rate generates a revenue stream of $100 per year forever, just as investing it at 5 percent generates a revenue stream of $50 forever. Unfortunately, if you try to compare these two revenue streams by adding up the sum, you wind up with the same for both (∞), and thus, ridiculously, no reason for preferring the 10 percent return over the 5 percent. The easiest way to avoid this is simply to suppose that, while the potential revenue stream is infinitely large in both cases, the individual discounts future utility using some variant of (4).

The assumption that is being made here is of course that the agent's preferences over outcomes are relatively independent and stable across time.[50] In order to model repeated plays of a game, for instance, one normally just assumes that the payoff matrix remains the same each time the game is played, and that the value of the payoffs is discounted. So, to take a simple example, suppose that an agent, on entering a hospital for three days, is asked to choose what meals she would like to be served. Three meals are offered: p, q, and r; and suppose that the agent's preferences rank them in that order: $p > q > r$. The standard procedure for determining the agent's utility function is to assign p a value of 1 and r a value of 0. One can then determine the priority of the agent's desire for q by constructing a set of lotteries over p and r, and finding the lottery that renders her indifferent between q and that lottery. So if the agent is indifferent between q and a lottery that gives her a 60 percent chance of getting p, we would assign q a utility of 0.6. This represents the agent's atemporal preferences over meals. The next step is to determine the agent's discount rate. For the sake of illustration, suppose that it is 0.5 per day. Once we have all this information, then we can calculate the *present* value of each meal on each day. Table 3.1 shows the values in this case. The expected utility of any meal plan can then be calculated just by adding up the three values, so, for example, [p,q,p] would be worth (1 + 0.3 + 0.25), or 1.55.

This seems like a fairly natural way to model the decision, even though it does contain some substantive assumptions that will not be satisfied in all contexts. For example, use of a discount rate in a repeated game assumes that "decision

Table 3.1 Discounted Value of Three Meals

Meal	Value at time…		
	t_1	t_2	t_3
p	1	0.5	0.25
q	0.6	0.3	0.15
r	0	0	0

time," that is, the sequence in which choice nodes occur, bears some linear relationship to real time. Similarly, it assumes that first-order desires remain the same from one time to another, and that meal p at time t_1 and meal p at time t_2 can be treated as "the same meal," just at different times, when it comes to eliciting the agent's first-order preferences. Yet despite these limitations, the modeling strategy has certain clear advantages. For instance, suppose that this agent is offered a choice between the following two meal plans: $[p,q,r]$ and $[q,q,p]$. Despite the fact that from an atemporal perspective the second plan is the best, the agent will nevertheless choose the first. One simple way of explaining this is to say that she is *impatient*. Rather than waiting until the third night to get meal p, she chooses to get it right away, even though this means accepting a slightly less desirable meal later on.

Unfortunately, philosophers have been somewhat resistant to the idea of incorporating discount rates, or a time preference, into agents' utility functions. This gives rise to a number of pseudoproblems in the literature on practical rationality (to be discussed in chapter 8). It also generates a preference for choice models that are expressively impoverished. The inclination among world Bayesians, for instance, is to absorb a temporally extended sequence of outcomes into a single possible world. With the "choice of meals" problem, for instance, instead of treating the case as one of an individual making the *same* choice three times, the world Bayesian regards it as a single choice producing one total outcome. Thus $[p,p,p]$ represents one subset of the set of possible worlds (picking out the very large set of possible worlds in which it is true that those three meals are consumed, in that sequence) and $[q,p,r]$ simply another. A utility function can be constructed by offering the agent lotteries over the 27 global consequences. This might produce a utility function like the one shown in table 3.2.

There is absolutely nothing wrong with this utility function per se. In fact, it is nothing other than a "normalized" version of the utility function that could be constructed by taking each possible permutation of meals, looking up the value of each meal in table 3.1, and adding them up. However, while the utility function shown in table 3.2 can easily be derived from table 3.1, the reverse is not true. If one assumes that the agent's preferences over meals are invariant, then there is a discount rate implicit in the utility function. Extracting it, however, is no easy task. It is clear, however, from this example that nothing in the world Bayesian account precludes the possibility of agents discounting their future satisfaction. It is quite open to the world Bayesian to argue that all of the information about the agent's discount rate belongs in the theory of preference formation, not in

Table 3.2 Utility of 27 Consequences

World	Utility
p,p,p,	1
p,p,q,	0.94
p,p,r,	0.85
p,q,p,	0.88
p,q,q,	0.82
p,q,r,	0.74
p,r,p,	0.71
p,r,q,	0.65
p,r,r,	0.57
q,p,p,	0.77
q,p,q,	0.71
q,p,r,	0.62
q,q,p,	0.65
q,q,q,	0.6
q,q,r,	0.51
q,r,p,	0.48
q,r,q,	0.42
q,r,r,	0.34
r,p,p,	0.42
r,p,q,	0.37
r,p,r,	0.28
r,q,p,	0.31
r,q,q,	0.25
r,q,r,	0.17
r,r,p,	0.14
r,r,q,	0.08
r,r,r,	0

the model of practical rationality. For example, one could claim that the utility function given in table 3.2 is just what practical rationality takes as "input." It is derived, however, from a set of preferences that look just like table 3.1, plus a time preference. One of the rules of rational preference formation, then, might be one specifying that the utility of some total "world" is the discounted sum of the value of some world at time t_1, some world at time t_2, and so on.

The question then becomes one of choosing between two different notations. Is it better to represent the agent's discount rate as part of the theory of practical rationality, or should it be bundled up as part of the total "outcome" of an act, and farmed out to the part of the theory that specifies how the agent decides which consequences are more or less desirable? From a purely formal point of view, it makes no difference. The only way of deciding the question is to look at it from an expressive point of view.

The question of whether the agent's concern for principles should be represented explicitly in a "value function" or subsumed as a part of the consequences has exactly the same structure. In order to provide an explicit representation of the normative control system we may choose to introduce some factor γ, in order to represent explicitly the weight that the agent assigns to principles, relative to utility.[51] We may refer to this as the agent's "fundamental choice disposition."[52] Putting all this together, the agent's value function can be represented as follows. Where $n(a)$ represents the agent's principles, and $u_t(a)$ represents the agent's expected utility at time t from action a, we can express the agent's value function as:

$$v(a) = \gamma n(a) + \sum_{k=1}^{n} (\delta)^{k-1} u_k(a) \tag{5}$$

Again, this notation contains certain substantive assumptions and conventional elements. In the same way that the discount factor can be used to represent more than just pure time preference (e.g., it can be used to represent uncertainty as well, or the probability that a repeated game will end), the fundamental choice disposition can be used to represent more than just the normative control system. Thus the two should not be thought of as equivalent; the fundamental choice disposition is much more formal. Furthermore, the assumptions underlying both the discount rate and the fundamental choice disposition may remain controversial. Not all game theorists accept the idea that agents should maximize the *sum* of time-discounted expected utility.[53] The important point is simply that a normative control system can be introduced into the representation of the agent's value function without requiring any sort of technical apparatus that is not already used in standard game theory, and that the proposal to add appropriateness to expected utility is no more controversial than the existing game-theoretic strategy for handling repeated games. The value of the notation lies in its expressive role—the way that it provides an intuitively compelling formal representation of the most significant structural features of particular practical deliberations.

In a decision-theoretic context, it really makes no difference how the discount rate gets handled—as part of the theory of practical rationality, or as part of the theory of preference-formation. It only starts to matter when the attempt is made to model social interactions. In particular, when a group of agents are faced with a series of interactions that will be repeated over time, it is extremely unhelpful to have only total preferences over total sequences of play, with each permutation treated as a separate outcome. For example, consider a two-person prisoner's dilemma that will be played 10 times. In games of this type, the players' discount rates may be extremely important in determining whether cooperation will be sustainable. But if the discount rate is handled in the theory of preference-formation, then this game will have to be modeled as one very large game in which each player has preferences over 1,048,576 different outcomes. It makes a lot more sense to think of it as a game with just four outcomes, played 10 times, where strategies can be conditional on past play. Thus explicit incorporation of a discount rate into the theory of practical rationality provides a more expressively adequate regimentation of our folk psychology.

The argument favoring an explicit representation of the agent's fundamental choice disposition follows a logic similar to that favoring an explicit representation of the discount rate. Impatience is a familiar element in the phenomenology of choice. The same can be said for normative control. Not only do agents themselves often conceive of their own choices in terms of a tension between deontic constraints and desirable outcomes, but their partners in interaction are likely to use a similar framework to interpret and anticipate these actions. This is particularly apparent in cases where there is some question as to whether they are able to trust one another. It is possible to subsume the principle/desire distinction into the theory of preference-formation, and simply represent the agent as having a set of global preferences (over, say, complete possible worlds including both actions and future consequences). But the resulting gain in formal elegance is offset by a loss of expressive adequacy.

3.6. Social Integration

In order to see the expressive power of the notation that renders the agent's fundamental choice disposition explicit, consider the case of the ultimatum game (described in chapter 2). No matter where you go in the world, actual human behavior in this game *always* deviates from the standard model of instrumental rationality, and does so in a number of very stereotypical ways. As we have seen, several game theorists have tried to explain these anomalous results by developing more complicated utility functions that include multiple sources of utility, such as a "material payoff" and a "fairness function."[54] Apart from committing the "error of premature concreteness," these theorists also make the dubious choice of lumping the concern over fairness in with the payoff, thereby obscuring the deontic component of the agent's motive. As a result, they are unable to explain clearly one significant feature of the interaction. In the typical North American trial, it is actually only the pattern of rejection that is mysterious. *Offers* are largely consistent with utility-maximization, given the pattern of rejections. In other words, the individual making the offer usually tries to keep as much of the money as possible, but knows that "low-ball" offers are likely to be rejected. Thus a common strategy for this player is to make an offer that is low, but not *too* low. Many theorists have felt this to be somewhat odd, given the peculiar combination of maximizing behavior on the part of the player making the offer and nonmaximizing behavior on the part of the player deciding whether to accept.[55] (By contrast, in the "dictator" game, in which one person is simply given the money and asked to specify a division, offers are much lower than in the ultimatum game—typically about 20 percent of the stake on average. Here one can see the impact that the norm of fair division has when all strategic considerations are factored out.)

The best way to clarify all of this is to separate out the deontic from the consequential features of the decision problem, and then show how the two can be reintegrated. First, consider the situation of the individual faced with the choice of how much money to offer his opponent. He wants to keep as much of it as possible. Yet he knows that the norm of fairness applies to this situation, and thus that the appropriate action is to split the money 50-50. How should all this be represented? The type of structured value function presented in equation (1) suggests that we should find a way of representing how each agent feels about the money, and how each feels about the fairness norm, keeping the two separate. Let us suppose, for the sake of simplicity, that both agents are risk neutral and that their utility is a linear function of their monetary payoff. Then we can set the utility of $100 at 1, $50 at 0.5, and so on. This much is pretty standard. Now consider how the players' attitudes toward the norm should be represented. Suppose that for the first player, perfect conformity with the norm has an appropriateness of 1, while complete violation of the norm is worth 0. Suppose further that offers are considered better the closer they are to the ideal of even division, so that "more fair" is better than "less fair" in a linear fashion. Thus an offer of $50 will be worth 1, an offer of $30 worth 0.6, an offer of $10 worth 0.2, and so on. (Offers above $50, along with any possible "supererogatory" valuation, will be set aside here.)

For the second player, we can imagine a perfectly symmetric scale, except that it will be the action of *rejecting* unfair offers that is positively valued (and both agents consider the normative dimension of the situation to be about half as important as the monetary stake). Thus rejecting an offer of $0 will be worth 1, rejecting an offer of $10 will be worth 0.8, rejecting an offer of $40 will be worth 0.2, and so on again. Suppose finally that $\gamma_1 = \gamma_2 = 0.4$.

If we grant that this model provides an adequate representation of the interaction, it is now easy to see why individuals select the types of actions that have been observed. Under these circumstances, the player making the offer suffers from some loss of value in making unfair offers, but this is easily outweighed by the monetary advantage. As a result, we can expect this player's actions to conform to the utility-maximization hypothesis (i.e., he will offer the other player as little as possible). However, the second player is in a different situation. For the person making the offer, the more unfair the offer, the more lucrative it is. But for the second player, the more unfair the offer, the less lucrative it is. As a result, while the second player has a financial incentive to accept offers that are only somewhat unfair, there will be a point at which the desire to accept will be outweighed by the desire to punish the other for making a low-ball offer. In other words, the cost of punishing unfair offers decreases as the offers become more unfair. Thus value-maximization leads her to engage in non-utility-maximizing behavior. The value of player 2's options is shown in figure 3.5. Rejecting overtakes accepting at around $22. At this point, the satisfaction that player 2 gets from enforcing the norm begins to outweigh her desire to get the money.

Thus player 1, anticipating this, will try to maximize his own value by making an offer just high enough that player 2 will not reject it. This analysis of the problem clearly explains the asymmetry between the two players' behavior—the fact that one appears to be maximizing payoffs while the other is not. It can be seen to arise from structural features of the interaction, not from any asymmetry in the orientation of either player toward either the social norm or the money. This helps to explain why the same pattern of behavior persists even when the roles of the two players are reversed.

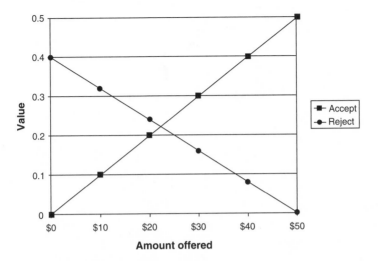

Figure 3.5 Ultimatum game.

In the actual experiments, the mean offer is much higher—closer to the 50-50 division. Apart from simple modeling and calibration issues, one can imagine a number of other factors that would contribute a higher mean offer than the one suggested by figure 3.5. First, some individuals making offers feel strongly enough about the fairness norm that they immediately select the 50-50 split, without making any calculations about what their opponent is likely to do. There is also considerable uncertainty in the actual experiments, so fundamental choice dispositions are not common knowledge. Since "playing it safe" in this game means making a higher offer, we can expect to see a mean in actual trials that is much higher than would obtain under perfect information.

The same type of representation can be used to model cooperation in public goods games. Figure 3.6 shows a classic prisoner's dilemma, but in this case between actors who both accept a norm that prohibits defecting. (For the sake of illustration, defection is assigned an appropriateness of −2.)

In order to resolve the decision problem, each player must calculate the expected value of each available action. In this case, however, because each agent's principles conflict with her desires, it is important to pay attention to how the two are being weighted against one another. In fact, the solution differs depending on what sort of weight the two players assign to the social norm that prohibits defection. Suppose both players assign relatively little deliberative weight to norms, such that $\gamma_1 = \gamma_2 = 0.25$. In this case, action d strongly dominates c for both players, and so the norm does nothing to resolve the prisoner's dilemma.

The picture changes if players assign greater weight to normative constraints. If $\gamma_1 = \gamma_2 = 1$, then dominance reasoning generates a different equilibrium. The inappropriateness of defection now outweighs the desirability of the

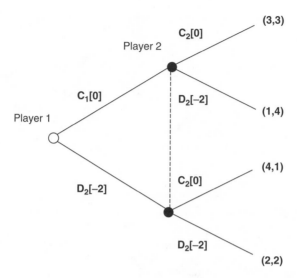

Figure 3.6 Cooperative norm.

associated outcome, and so both players are better off cooperating, regardless of what the other does.[56] Again, this gives them each grounds to believe that the other will choose c, and so grounds for calculating the expected value of their actions. Each will then choose c, resulting in an outcome with a payoff of 3 for both players. (Naturally, the players need not have the same value for γ. If $\gamma_1 = 0.25$, and $\gamma_2 = 1$, player 1 will in fact be able to exploit player 2 with impunity. Player 2 will cooperate, regardless of player 1's anticipated defection, simply because he is unwilling to "stoop to the same level." Of course, he may still take punitive action in the future.)

This example shows how normative constraint can provide a "moral" solution to the prisoner's dilemma. Of course, theorists like Ken Binmore would be right to observe, at this point, that such a "solution" merely shows that the interaction was not really a prisoner's dilemma in the first place. It was simply an interaction that had been modeled incorrectly, through omission of a salient factor, namely, the agents' preferences over their own actions. This is technically correct, but jejune. The important point is that this "solution" allows us to preserve the intuition that, in this interaction, both players have a strong *desire* to defect, and that there is a clear sense in which it is in their individual *interest* to do so. (Furthermore, it allows us to represent in the model the way individuals themselves typically interpret such interactions.) Individuals act against their self-interest (in at least one important sense of the term) when they allow deontic constraints to outweigh their concern for the consequences of their actions. This is how social integration is achieved—not through a preordained harmony of individual interest, but through norms that override individual interests in various contexts.

Examples of norms that secure cooperation in this way abound in everyday life. The norm that prohibits cutting into line is a typical example. Waiting to get through a grocery checkout, or a fire exit, is a classic multiplayer prisoner's dilemma—everyone wants to rush up front, but if everyone does that, the disorder will result in everyone getting through more slowly. The queuing norm corrects this simply by proscribing going through before those who arrived earlier. The norm doesn't change how much people want to escape the burning building, or how desperately they want to get home from the grocery store; it simply imposes constraints on the range of actions that they are willing to perform in order to achieve these outcomes.

Thus the analysis developed here provides a formal model of action that shows how, in principle, agents are able to use rules to work themselves out of the "state of nature." In practice, however, things are a bit more complicated. In order for the sort of equilibrium solutions outlined here to work, players must start out with a lot of knowledge about each other. In standard game theory, it is assumed that all players' beliefs and desires are common knowledge at the start of the game (and in repeated games, that all players' discount rates are common knowledge). If one simply adds common knowledge of principles and of fundamental dispositions to this, then interactions with value functions can be handled using variations of the standard game-theoretic solution concepts (Nash equilibrium, subgame perfection, etc.). Cases where there is some uncertainty about any of these intentional states or dispositions can be handled using a standard "Bayesian" transformation of the game.[57] In such a game, asymmetric information is represented by having nature first make a random move that determines player 2's "type." For example, suppose that player 1 must interact in a prisoner's dilemma-type interaction with an agent who is known only to have a γ_2 of either 0.25 or 1 (and $\gamma_1 = 1$). Player 1 can start out by assigning a prior probability to each value of γ_2 (based, perhaps, on the number of agents with γ values of 0.25 and of 1 in the population). The interaction can then be modeled as one in which nature moves first, "deciding" whether γ_2 is equal to 0.25 or 1 on the basis of this prior probability (shown in fig. 3.7, with some abuse of notation). So if nature goes "left," player 2 has a fundamental choice disposition of only 0.25, whereas if nature plays "right," $\gamma_2 = 1$. (In order to simplify the diagram, the value of actions is shown as the appropriateness weighted by the agent's fundamental choice disposition.) Player 2 observes this move (i.e., knows her own disposition) while player 1 does not. Thus when player 1 chooses, he does not know whether he is playing against an individual who assigns a weight of –0.5 to the act of defecting, or –2. However, his belief about the probability that player 2 is of one type or the other allows him to calculate the expected value of each of his actions. For instance, if $\gamma_2 = 1$ with probability 0.5, this suggests that there is a 0.5 probability player 2 will choose d, and a 0.5 probability she will choose c. This gives cooperating an expected value for player 1 of 2, and defecting an expected value of only 1. Thus player 1 will cooperate, even if he believes there is only a 50 percent chance that player 2 will do the same.

If the players are involved in a sequence of interactions (i.e., a multistage game), this framework can be used to model the development of *trust*. Trust can be defined as simply a state in which everyone believes that everyone has a broadly norm-compliant disposition (i.e., assigns a sufficiently high value to γ

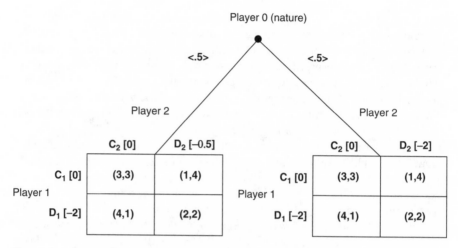

Figure 3.7 Game of incomplete information.

that their normative constraints outweigh their desires).[58] The best way to achieve this state is if the parties are able to somehow reveal to each other that they have such a disposition. This can be done, for example, by establishing a *known history* of having forgone opportunities for utility-maximizing defection. For instance, if player 2 does select *c*, this gives player 1 reason to "update his prior," that is, to reevaluate his belief that the probability of $\gamma_2 = 1$ is 0.5, in light of this new information. Agents who start out without knowledge of each others' fundamental dispositions may therefore be able to reveal these to one another by performing actions that provide evidence for specific hypotheses.

Such an analysis helps to explain the common practice of using exercises in reciprocity to "build up" trust. People will often start out conducting small experiments to see if they are able to trust one another. They will create opportunities for defection, where the cost of being suckered is relatively small, in order to see how the other responds. If everyone passes this first test, they will move on to a second cooperative project, this one with higher stakes. Eventually, they may build up to the point where they are engaging in cooperative projects in which the risks associated with being exploited are so great that no one would undertake them unless they had a history of past interaction with the individuals involved.

Of course, the sort of reasoning that leads to the development of trust in these contexts will generally be obscure from a strictly instrumental point of view.[59] Insofar as the interaction has an incremental structure, it should be obvious that anyone acting strategically would cooperate in the initial stages merely to secure opportunities for more advantageous defection later on. Thus instrumentally rational agents would never cooperate, even in the initial stages. But rather than diagnosing the widespread practice of building up trust as merely the result of a false induction, it is preferable to consider the possibility that it has a rational basis. If the norms of honesty and trustworthy behavior are common knowledge (or at least shared among the relevant set of individuals) and agents are endowed with a fundamental disposition that assigns a certain weight to these normative considerations, then the entire exercise starts to make much more sense. Reciprocity is often important, not because of the incentive structure it creates, but because of the way it allows individuals to "reveal their type" to one another.

This analysis suggests that social integration can be achieved through internal control alone only under specific information conditions, that is, among agents who know one another well, or who interact in a "high-trust" social milieu. This in turn provides an explanation for the role of external control—sanctions—in stabilizing cooperative interactions. In the absence of trust, people can generate confidence that they will comply with the prevailing set of norms by agreeing to be punished in the event that they defect. This is the central insight in Hobbes's view. People want to be able to trust one another, because they can benefit from avoiding collective action problems. This makes it in their interest to submit to some authority who will sanction them in the event of noncompliance. Hobbes's mistake was simply to think that this kind of a sanctioning system rendered trust superfluous. Trust, however, is still required in order to maintain the integrity of the punishment mechanism. Thus if two individuals do not trust one another, but both trust some third party, they may arrange with that party to impose the sanctions. In this way, sanctions can be used to extend cooperative behavior beyond the immediate circle of people who trust one another, by giving individuals the confidence to enter into cooperative arrangements that they might otherwise avoid for fear of being "suckered."

This observation allows us to specify more clearly the role sanctions play in social interaction. Typically people are punished not because they have performed the wrong action but because they have violated the *trust* of others. This trust is grounded in the expectation that agents have a fundamental disposition to accord deontic constraints a certain weight against desiderative constraints in their practical deliberations. It is this disposition that, at root, enables them to adopt rules to govern their conduct, which in turn allows them to avoid suboptimal interaction patterns. When the distinction between deontic, doxastic, and desiderative constraints is sharply drawn, the way these rules are integrated into the agent's deliberations, along with the role of internal and external control in social integration, can be clearly specified. The theory that results is one that points to the same *phenomena* the instrumentalist account identified as the key to social order—sanctions and reciprocity—but provides a different interpretation of them. The supplementation of the instrumentalist account with a conception of normative control generates a much more robust account of social integration, one that explains how people are able to enter into cooperative relations with one another despite being in a situation of fundamentally conflicting interests.

This analysis also serves to explain why so many theorists initially found instrumental theories far more compelling than they eventually turned out to be. As Peter Richerson, Robert Boyd, and Joseph Henrich observe, "the intuition that cheap talk, symbolic rewards, and clever institutions are in themselves sufficient to explain human cooperation probably comes from the common experience that people do find it rather easy to use such devices to cooperate."[60] The reason, however, that people find these "instrumental" devices effective is that they use them only to *supplement* the generalized presumption of trust that serves as the background to everyday social interaction.[61] It is because most people voluntarily follow the rules, most of the time, that a system of external incentives as weak as the one we generally deploy can be successful at maintaining social order.

3.7. Conclusion

An enormous amount of effort has been expended over the years in an attempt to show that instrumentally rational agents can adopt commitments, special choice dispositions, or some other mechanism that will allow them to work their way out of collective action problems (and more generally, to resolve the problem of order). The underlying motivation has been to explain how it is that we are able to avoid the extremes of uncooperative behavior that simple instrumental theories of rationality consistently predict. Over the years, the arguments advanced have become increasingly baroque.[62] The model presented here is comparatively simple. It shows how agents are able to cooperate with one another, even when more desirable outcomes can be achieved through defection. By integrating preferences for actions into the agent's overall utility function, without thereby obscuring the distinction between preferences for actions and preferences for outcomes, the model is able to provide an extremely straightforward representation of the way norms might function as deontic constraints in social choice. The fact that the model is also able to supply deliberative microfoundations for a "focal point" –style solution to coordination problems is an unexpected bonus. It functions as indirect support for the proposed analysis, however, insofar as it fulfills the traditional expectation, among sociological theorists, that a solution to the "problem of order" will require an account of both cooperation and coordination.

More generally, the model proposed here shows that the natural alliance that was once assumed between decision and game theory on the one hand and consequentialist or instrumental theories of rationality on the other has largely been the result of a confusion. Insofar as one wants to adhere to the Savage trichotomy, and treat actions, states, and outcomes as three analytically distinct classes of events, then the prohibition of preferences over actions is simply unmotivated. If one responds by reading consequences more broadly, in order to incorporate any concern over actions into the agent's preference ordering, then one tacitly introduces nonconsequentialist elements into the theory of practical rationality—while at the same time obscuring many of the important conceptual distinctions that structure our everyday management of social interactions. The model I have proposed aims to provide a more expressively robust notation, by maintaining the Savage trichotomy (as game theorists are wont to do), while introducing nonconsequentialist elements (i.e., principles) explicitly into the representation of the choice problem. The result is a theory of action that renders mathematically tractable the sui generis force of deontic constraint in practical deliberation.

4

Intentional States

The discussion so far has been focused quite narrowly on the question of how the various intentional states related to decision can be combined in order to yield a particular practical recommendation. It explains why people follow the rules, but not why they care about the rules. This reflects the general intuition that it is possible to act rationally, even if one's beliefs turn out to be false, one's preferences unreasonable, or one's principles empty "rule worship." The theory of practical rationality, narrowly construed, simply specifies what it is rational to do, *given* one's beliefs, desires, and principles. Naturally, such a narrowing of the field leaves many traditional philosophical questions untouched. In order to develop a more robust theory of practical deliberation, it is necessary to pull back the curtain a bit further, and consider the question of where the agent's beliefs, desires, and principles come from.

But this enterprise turns out to require much more subtlety than many of the early proponents of the instrumental conception of rationality ever imagined. The reasons for this are deeply connected with some of the major movements of philosophical thought in the past century, in particular, the development of the so-called linguistic turn. Initially, it was simply assumed (by Hobbes among others) that agents came equipped with a full set of beliefs and desires, prior to any social interaction. Or to express the same point methodologically, the assumption was that one could work out a complete psychology for the agent *prior* to working out a theory of social action. However, on closer examination it became apparent that many of the beliefs and desires we hold are ones we can only ever have by virtue of our mastery of a language. And it is not so obvious that our grasp of language can be explained prior to an account of social interaction.

Standard decision and game theory sets all of these problems aside by treating beliefs as "subjective probabilities" and preferences as "exogenously determined."[1] Thus decision theory assumes that agents assign some probability to all states, but refrains from endorsing any particular account of how these probabilities are related to either objective probabilities or the available evidence. Similarly, decision theory takes the agent's preference ordering as given, without imposing any commitments regarding the origin or nature of those preferences (although in practice, the view that preferences are "given" is often interpreted to mean that preferences are arbitrary, or beyond the scope of rational deliberation).

This strategy of avoidance is adequate if the goal is simply to use action theory as a tool for developing social-scientific models. But it is clearly inadequate for an inquiry into moral philosophy structured by action-theoretic concerns. As we have seen, there are two components to Hobbes's instrumentalism: the first is his *consequentialism*—the view that actions have value only as means—the second is his *noncognitivism* about desire—the claim that there is no deliberation about ends. So far, we have seen that there is very little to recommend the first of these two views. In order to evaluate the second, it is necessary to develop in greater detail a theory of desire. And in order to work this out, we need a more general theory about what intentional states are.

4.1. The Linguistic Turn

The core conceptual revolution at the heart of the so-called linguistic turn is extremely simple. Beliefs, desires, and principles are all intentional states. The use of the term "intentional" is aimed at identifying the central characteristic they all share: they are all "about" something; they possess "content." This "aboutness" is often taken to be the distinguishing mark of thought, setting it apart from mere sensation. In other words, it is often claimed that what makes a particular series of events count as a process of reasoning, rather than, say, nervous agitation, is precisely that the relevant states possess this sort of content. This view forms the cornerstone of Edmund Husserl's philosophical work, but it can be traced back quite easily through most of modern philosophy.

It has also been widely noted that this sort of aboutness is shared by two sorts of entities.[2] Our thoughts clearly have an intentional structure—to think is to think about something. Thought always has an object. But *language* also has the same structure. To say something is necessarily to say something about something. This much is imposed by the subject-predicate structure of our sentences. The question, then, is what sort of relationship obtains between mental and semantic intentionality.[3] Until the late nineteenth century, it was almost universally assumed that the intentionality of our thoughts was to be accorded explanatory priority. According to this view, mental intentionality reflects the fundamental structure of consciousness. We wake up, we see objects in our environment, and we experience perceptions of them. The aboutness of our thoughts reflects the way information is transmitted to us from the world, through our senses. Semantic intentionality is then treated as derivative. Language is regarded as a "code" we use, in order to communicate thoughts from one person to another—thoughts that are fully formed prior to their linguistic articulation.[4]

All of this seems quite plausible at first glance. But this view of the world generates a series of quite significant puzzles—Cartesian skepticism and solipsism being the best-known examples. The central problems all revolve around the difficulty philosophers have had finding some primitive structure of consciousness that would provide a noncircular and nonregressive explanation of the intentionality of our thoughts. Visual perception provides the most plausible basis, hence the common philosophical idea that our thoughts must be pictures of the world. But this is subject to notorious difficulties. Husserl's work—particularly the fifth of his *Cartesian Meditations*—is widely regarded as a reductio ad absurdum of this conceptual strategy (Wittgenstein's *Tractatus Logico-Philosophicus* is also often cited in this way).[5] The problem, roughly, is that it is hard to see how we ever get a secure link to anything outside our own minds. How do we know that our thoughts hook on to the world, as opposed to something more proximate, such as our perceptions of the world?

The linguistic turn represents a radical break with this tradition. The basic idea is simple. Rather than treating the intentionality of consciousness as primitive, philosophers began to consider the possibility that semantic intentionality might be more fundamental (or perhaps equiprimordial). After all, insofar as our thoughts have content, they can also be given linguistic expression. Thus the set of intentional states is also a set of states with *propositional* content. The suggestion at the heart of the linguistic perspective is that the intentionality of these mental states may be inherited from the propositions that give them their content. This would explain why, as Michael Dummett put it, "thought is communicable without residue."[6]

It is not difficult to imagine the mechanism that might be responsible for such an order of explanation. People who talk to themselves as they try to resolve a problem are often described as "thinking out loud." It is possible that the opposite is true—that thinking (in the sense of rational, analytic thought) is really a form of silent talking.[7] In the same way that we first learn to read out loud, then gradually acquire the ability to internalize this practice and read to ourselves, philosophers (and psychologists) have suggested that we first acquire the ability to talk, and then acquire the ability to think by internalizing this practice. In the process, the language becomes compressed and abbreviated. Similar phenomena can be observed with a variety of different cognitive skills. For example, one can see older merchants and accountants in China do extremely complex arithmetic calculations "in their heads" while at the same time making slight movements of their fingers. The reason is that they have been trained using an abacus. After a certain period of time, abacus users become so accustomed to the feel of the beads that they no longer need to look at the apparatus in order to determine the outcome of their calculations; they can visualize it perfectly in their minds. After a while, the more experienced among them no longer need the machine at all. The slight movement of the fingers is a vestigial trace of the external apparatus they used to acquire the cognitive skill. There are no doubt many who have eliminated even that, so that they are able to run a fully "virtual" abacus, giving them a capacity to do mental arithmetic far exceeding that of the average individual.

Of course, running a fully internalized device of this type requires a very high level of attention. Experienced chess players, for instance, no longer need to play on a chessboard; they can simply call out their moves. Nevertheless, they may break out a chessboard and set up the game at a certain point as an aid to memory, if their ability to concentrate is impaired. We notice similar phenomena in the case of reading and speaking. Many people will read a passage out loud if they find that they are having trouble making sense of it. Similarly, people forced to follow complex instructions, or trying to summon greater concentration, will often begin to talk out loud to themselves. One study of children between the ages of 5 and 10 found that "most of the children's private speech (speech not addressed to some other listener) seemed keyed to the direction and control of the child's own actions, and that the incidence of such speech increased when the child was alone and trying to perform some difficult task."[8]

According to this "external" view, language is a tool that, like the abacus, starts out as an element of our environment. Individuals first master the tool in that external form, as a way of making interventions in the world—in the case of language, as a tool for interacting with other people, or for planning complex actions. They then internalize that tool, so that they can perform virtual manipulations, using linguistic markers as a device for planning out complex interventions. Thus they acquire an *intentional planning system*. (And of course, as language learning becomes increasingly important for human survival, evolutionary adaptation begins to favor learning biases and heuristics in children that facilitate this learning and internalization process.)[9] This would explain why human beliefs bear such a striking similarity to assertions, and reasoning bears such a striking similarity to argumentation. It is because they are both *in foro interno* versions of those *in foro externo* practices.[10]

This is a radical inversion of the usual explanatory order, and is clearly motivated by philosophical considerations that extend far beyond the scope of this work. There is one issue, however, that is of quite direct relevance. The linguistic turn creates enormous doubts about what we might call the autonomy of the mental. From the standpoint of the philosophy of consciousness, each individual is regarded as a pretty much self-sufficient reasoning machine, capable of forming beliefs, making inferences, and acting rationally, with absolutely no input from his or her fellow creatures. However, if mental states depend crucially on language for their content, and language arises out of social practices, then the individual's own intentional planning abilities—precisely those abilities that various conceptions of practical rationality seek to model—would appear to depend in very important ways on aspects of the agent's social environment.

Early instrumentalists all assumed that intentional states were states of consciousness. This is very clear in the sort of mechanistic views of mind one finds in Hobbes and Hume. These theorists took such states as given in a very concrete way (especially desires, which they referred to with such terms as "springs of action" or "vital motions"). If, however, one chooses to regard these states as at least in part a product of social interaction, then one cannot imagine that people come equipped with them prior to any such interaction. More specifically, one cannot follow Hobbes's recommendation and "consider men as if but even now sprung out of the earth, and suddainly (like Mushromes) come to full maturity without all kind of engagement to each other."[11] Intentional states cannot be taken as "input" into a comprehensive theory of practical rationality, since one of the features of social interaction will be precisely that it serves to create agents endowed with such states. Thus the elaboration of the theory of practical rationality must proceed with much greater caution, and take much less for granted. The potential rewards, however, are great. In the same way the linguistic turn promises to cut the Gordian knot when it comes to the traditional problems of Cartesian skepticism, it also promises a way out of the sterile impasse of moral noncognitivism that dominated Western philosophy in the twentieth century.

4.2.   The Priority of Language and Consciousness

The central conceptual revolution underlying the linguistic turn—what Dummett calls "the extrusion of thoughts from the mind"—still strikes many people as implausible.[12] It is therefore necessary, before beginning a more serious inquiry into the nature of our intentional states, to consider some of the reasons the older "philosophy of consciousness" view, which was an unspoken assumption of Western philosophy from Descartes through Husserl, came to be regarded as problematic.

There are two central distinctions that structure this entire discussion. First, there are different ways of conceiving of intentional states. The older view, often referred to as *psychological imagism*, treats beliefs as a kind of picture or image of the world. This is the theory of mind one can find in Hobbes, Descartes, Locke, and Hume, among others. The dominant view in contemporary philosophy, on the other hand, is known as *psychological sentimentalism*.[13] According to this view, beliefs are fundamentally sentence-like in structure, governed by natural-language-like syntax and semantics. The contents of beliefs are propositions, not pictures.

The second major distinction concerns the status theorists assign to natural language. As we have seen, early modern philosophers thought that beliefs developed in a completely autonomous manner within the individual, and that language was a type of code used merely to *communicate* these beliefs to other people. According to such a view, it is conceivable that an agent could have a fully developed cognitive system without any ability to communicate. In contrast to this communicative view, many philosophers have argued that natural language plays a *constitutive* role in cognition. Language is regarded not just as a tool that we use to communicate, but rather as a tool that we use to think. Language is, as Dummett puts it, the "vehicle of thought." Beliefs and desires, according to this view, have a language-like structure because they are the internal correlate of external speech acts.

There is a certain neatness of fit between psychological sentimentalism and the constitutive view of natural language. However, there are many who defend both sententialism and the communicative conception of natural language, by arguing that our intentional states are formulated in a "language of thought" that exists prior to natural-language acquisition.[14] Thus it is helpful to begin by looking at the arguments that have been advanced for sententialism, before moving on to consider the question of where these sentences come from.

The problems with imagism are sufficiently obvious that it is often hard to see how they could have been ignored for so long. Apart from the case of completely elementary fact-stating sentences, there is simply no image that corresponds to most of our beliefs. It is difficult even to know where to begin, for instance, giving an account of all but a few of the sentences in this book. Fundamental problems show up even in easier cases, such as elementary descriptive sentences that are tensed, modalized, or negated. Which element of a picture represents the fact that "it will rain *tomorrow*" as opposed to "it will rain *next Tuesday*"? What about "it *might* have rained," or "it has *not* rained"? There is also the well-known problem that people seem to be able to think about a "triangle" without thinking of any particular type of triangle, of a "speckled hen" without thinking of a hen with any specific number of spots, and so on.[15]

There are many other respects in which entertaining a belief is quite different from imagining a picture. Much of the logic of our ordinary belief-talk precludes thinking of beliefs as nonlinguistic. First, when we ascribe one belief to an individual, we are also generally entitled to ascribe to that individual belief in the logical consequences of that belief. A person who believes that the ball is red must also believe that it is not blue. This means that beliefs are the sort of thing that can play the role of premises or conclusions in inferences. Yet there is reason to think that only sentences or sentence-like objects can play this role (for example, many people think that valid inference must be defined truth-functionally, and only sentences are capable of truth or falsity).

There are also a number of considerations arising from the way that we individuate beliefs. For example, substituting coreferential expressions within a belief does not preserve its identity: "Bill left fingerprints at the crime scene" is not the same as "The thief left fingerprints at the crime scene," even if Bill and "the thief" are the same person, and even if the individual holding the belief believes that Bill is the thief. Among other things, the two beliefs license different counterfactual inferences. There are even cases where substitution of synonymous expressions does not preserve identity of belief.[16] This suggests that the linguistic form in which a belief is expressed strongly determines the identity of that belief.

Finally, there is the observation that individuals are able to hold beliefs in two different ways, one of which seems to imply a stronger epistemic tie to the world than the other. We may say that John believes that the thief escaped, or that John believes, of the thief, that he escaped. The latter (known as belief *de re*) is epistemically stronger than the former (*de dicto*), since it implies that there was in fact a thief, whereas the former does not.[17] But this sort of discrimination is very difficult to explain if we do not assume that beliefs have a sentence-like structure. For example, it doesn't make much to sense to ask of a dog whether he believes that his owner is about to feed him, or whether he believes, of his owner, that she is about to feed him.

These observations have several immediate consequences. The first is that mental pictures cannot provide an appropriate model of belief. Beliefs have an internal structure that pictures lack, and are inferentially articulated in a way pictures cannot be. We have some sense of how the belief that "the ball is red" could be a picture. But what does the picture of "the ball is not blue" look like? Or imagine two individuals watching security camera footage of a crime. One of them recognizes the thief as Bill, the other does not. They have the same picture of the events in their minds, but their beliefs have radically different content.

Thus it is largely taken for granted in contemporary discussion that beliefs have a linguistic structure. Of course, there can be no doubt that certain forms of thinking do involve the manipulation of images in our minds (as when we rotate an object in "the mind's eye," in order to analyze it from different perspectives). Furthermore, no one doubts that our cognitive-linguistic system is integrated with this perceptual system, so that, for example, we can associate names with faces, in order to better remember them, or associate images with concepts, in order to better grasp their relations. The point is that this perceptual imaging system does not provide a set of explanatory primitives that is sufficient to explain belief, or any other contentful intentional state. The intentionality of thought is not reducible to the "aboutness" of our perceptions. So when we try to explain beliefs and desires, or any of the other intentional states that figure in our practical reasoning, we need to understand the role of language in cognition.

These considerations help to explain why many philosophers are loathe to ascribe beliefs to animals. To a certain extent, this is a terminological dispute, since almost everyone is prepared to grant that dogs and cats have some kind of protobelief that is functionally similar to beliefs in humans.[18] The question is really how much sense it makes to ascribe beliefs to an organism when that organism is incapable of accepting or rejecting any of the inferential consequences of that belief, and where most of the standard criteria we use to individuate belief cannot be applied. In other words, since the vast majority of conclusions that follow from the claim "x believes that p" simply do not follow when x is a dog, rather than a person, there is something very misleading about using the term "belief" in this context.[19]

This would be just a terminological quibble, were it not for the fact that ascribing beliefs to animals is an invitation to commit a certain type of fallacy. There is still a tendency to imagine the animal kingdom organized in much the way that Aristotle conceived of it. According to this view, the soul has various parts, and all living things are organized into a hierarchy, structured by possession of these parts. Thus plants have a soul that includes only a nutritive part, animals have both a nutritive and an appetitive part, while humans have nutritive, appetitive, and rational parts. This view gives rise to the tendency to regard humans as "animals-plus," that is, as creatures with all the parts possessed by the lower forms, *plus* the capacity to use language, or to reason. Thinking this way invites the following fallacious inference: "It must be possible for humans to have beliefs without language, because dogs have beliefs, and we all know they can't talk."

The problem here is that humans are not dogs with some extra capabilities added in. We are two separate species, which branched off from a common ancestor well over a half billion years ago. Furthermore, humans have specifically evolved as a language-dependent species. In other words, our biology has undergone significant adaptation since the time we began to use language. In the same way that our larynx is adapted for speaking, our brains are adapted for linguistic processing (after all, having a brain that allows one to learn language faster improves one's fitness, when one develops in a community of language-users). Chimpanzees have a cognitive system that is fully functional without language, so that when they are taught to sign they receive a kind of cognitive bonus. Humans are not like that. Our cognitive systems are adapted to operate using linguistic resources, and are not fully functional without them. Thus the question of whether animals have beliefs is not merely terminological, since many people affirm the claim on the basis of conceptual confusion.

The more powerful arguments against psychological sententialism arise, therefore, not from observation of animals, but rather from consideration of the cognitive performance of human infants. Here there is no danger of slipping into anthropomorphism. Human infants, it is argued, are clearly capable of performing a variety of cognitive tasks prior to the acquisition of language. They are able to engage in goal-directed activities, to plan their behavior, to use tools, to anticipate the trajectories of moving objects, and so forth. Thus the basic apparatus of practical rationality, it is argued, including beliefs and desires, must be in place before the acquisition of language. This is the argument advanced by, among others, Jerry Fodor, who claims that thinking occurs in "mentalese," an innate "language of thought" that is prior to natural language. Language is developed as a way of *expressing* ideas that are developed in mentalese.[20]

Of course, no one doubts that infants have some kind of cognitive machinery in place that allows them to perform goal-directed tasks. More specifically, they have an entire set of innate evolutionarily adapted mechanisms, each of which specializes in certain processing tasks. Keith Stanovich refers to these as "the autonomous set of systems" (TASS).[21] They allow infants (and, of course, adults) to perform a variety of sophisticated computational tasks, such as calculating trajectories, remembering faces, and determining the gender of other persons. These systems are characterized by certain highly specific features: the processing is very fast, computationally undemanding, unconscious, heuristic, domain-specific, and functionally rigid.[22] Furthermore, these mechanisms typically bear the hallmarks of evolutionary adaptation, since the type of competencies we exhibit seem very closely tailored to solving problems that would have arisen in the environment of evolutionary adaptation. (For example, our intuitive grasp of trajectories generates the right anticipations in the air, but the wrong anticipations underwater.) For this reason, Timothy Wilson refers to this level of processing as "the adaptive unconscious,"[23] in order to distinguish it from the more explicitly language-dependent intentional planning system (or what Stanovich calls the "analytical system"), which is slow, computationally demanding, rule-based, highly flexible, and normally conscious.[24]

The question is whether language is a "module" at the level of the adaptive unconscious or, more generally, whether the resources provided at that level are sufficient to explain the content of expressions formulated in natural language.[25]

In other words, the question is whether mentalese (or whatever other computational "language" or system the adaptive unconscious runs on) is governed by a natural-language-like syntax and semantics. Fodor maintains that when a child sees a brown dog, this experience causes the child to have thoughts, in mentalese, that include terms that refer to "dogs" and "brown."[26] Thus a child might formulate a self-standing mentalese belief with the content "there is a brown dog." The child will later learn how to translate this thought into one or another natural language, so that she can express it in English, Chinese, or what have you.

This thesis, incidentally, should not be confused with the Chomskian hypothesis that *grammar* is an innate structure residing at the level of the adaptive unconscious. The distinction sometimes gets blurred, when people talk about a "language instinct" or the "innateness" of language.[27] Fodor is making what might be thought of as the maximal innateness claim—that people come with both the meaning of words and the rules of grammar built in. This should be distinguished from the more moderate view that individuals come equipped with certain innate grammatical rules, but that they learn their lexicon of meaningful terms from the (natural language) linguistic environment. Finally, there is the minimal view that individuals learn both the syntax and semantics of their language from the environment, but have an innate language-acquisition mechanism (at the level of the adaptive unconscious) that explains both the ease and rapidity of language learning and the characteristic structural constraints that the grammars of human languages all respect.

If either of the latter two views were correct, then it would clearly be illegitimate for decision theorists to take beliefs and desires as given, prior to any practical deliberation or social interaction. The basic Hobbesian explanatory strategy—of characterizing individual psychology first, then generalizing the account to cover social interaction—depends on the correctness of the "maximal" innateness claim. Of course, Hobbes thought such a claim was correct because he treated beliefs as images, and thus as independent states of the individual's consciousness (in the same way our perceptions of the world are independent states of our consciousness). According to this view, we could have a belief that there is a tree in front of us, even if the rest of humanity had never existed, for the same reason that we would be able to *see* the tree in front of us, even if the rest of humanity had never existed.

The suggestion that beliefs must be sentential in form, rather than pictorial, threatens to undermine this independence. If language (or even just semantic content) is learned through social interaction, and beliefs are linguistically formulated, then belief cannot be an explanatory primitive in the theory of practical rationality. An explanation of the nature of belief will have to emerge out of our account of social interaction. Thus Fodor's proposal offers to rescue the Hobbesian explanatory strategy, by suggesting that beliefs, despite being linguistic, can still be explained in a purely individualistic fashion. They are formulated in an innate mentalese, not a language learned through social interaction. In fact, languages learned through social interaction can only be made sense of against a background grasp of mentalese, according to Fodor. Thus we could have a mentalese belief that there is a tree in front of us, even if we had neither the means nor the occasion to express this belief.

The question, then, is whether this concept of mentalese is plausible. Unfortunately, most of the debate over the innateness of language is quite confusing on this point. Stephen Pinker, for instance, despite saying that "language" is innate, only really marshals evidence to show that certain structures underlying natural language *syntax* are innate.[28] The concept of mentalese involves the claim that there is not just an innate syntax underlying all natural languages but also an innate semantics. There is no empirical reason to believe this claim, which is why it needs to be assessed on its philosophical rather than its scientific merits. The relevant philosophical question is whether it is coherent to think that a purely individualistic language of this type could have *content*, such that it could explain the intentionality of our beliefs and desires. There is a very influential line of argument, stemming from the later work of Ludwig Wittgenstein, that claims that it cannot. This is, of course, the famous "private language argument."[29] Despite the tendency among subsequent generations of philosophers to interpret this argument to mean pretty much whatever they would like it to mean, one can nevertheless see how the more powerful objections to Fodor's hypothesis are all variations on this basic line of thought.

4.3. The Private Language Argument

The interest in beliefs and desires here stems from the central role they play in practical reasoning. One of the central features of reasoning is that it is, by its very nature, something that can be done correctly or incorrectly. That is what distinguishes a rational conclusion from a conclusion that simply happens to have been reached. Reason is an intrinsically normative concept. This normativity is shared by all of the elements that go into a given sequence of reasoning. Reasoning involves inference, which can be either valid or invalid. These inferences operate on beliefs, which seek to represent states of affairs, and can be either true or false. These beliefs are in turn formed out of concepts, which seek to refer to some object or property, and do so either successfully or unsuccessfully. Thus there are three orders of semantic value: reference, truth, and validity, which articulate the normative criteria we use to evaluate subsentential, sentential, and intersentential operations, respectively.[30] Grasping a concept means applying it correctly, for example, applying the word "dog" to dogs and only dogs. Understanding a sentence means using it correctly, for example, saying "it's going to rain" only when it is going to rain. And grasping an inference means drawing the correct conclusion from the correct premises, for example, concluding that someone is going outside when he announces "I'm going for a walk."

The important point here is that all three of these forms of normativity are interdependent. Thus the "normativity" of reason does not just involve the conclusions we draw from our beliefs. It extends down all the way to the level of the concepts we use. Grasping the meaning of a word means understanding how to

use it correctly. Thus in seeking to understand language, and linguistic meaning, we need to provide some account of this normativity. It is here that Fodor's
account of mentalese, along with the communicative conception of language,
runs into trouble.[31] The upshot of Wittgenstein's private language argument
is precisely that normativity cannot be explained as a purely private relation
between the individual and the world.[32] It follows from this that the adaptive
unconscious does not have the resources, all by itself, to confer semantic content
on terms, because no individual has the resources, all by herself, to distinguish
correct from incorrect uses of these terms.

Wittgenstein frames his investigation in terms of what it means to follow a
rule. He argues that purely private rule-following is incoherent. In order to say
that one is following a rule, there must be a difference between thinking that one
is following it and actually following it. However, an individual all by himself
is unable to draw this distinction. As Wittgenstein put it, if "whatever is going
to seem right to me is right...that only means that here we can't talk about
'right.' "[33]

To strip the argument down somewhat, consider the following scenario.[34]
Imagine a man shipwrecked on a desert island. He decides to keep track of how
many days he has been on the island by carving notches on a tree every morning on awakening. However, he finds that later in the day, he is often unable to
remember clearly whether he made the notch for that day or not. So he decides
to implement a second mechanism, which will allow him to check to make sure
that he hasn't forgotten. Perhaps he resolves to put a pebble in a jar, to show that
he has made his check for the day. But obviously this is no help, since it is vulnerable to the same problem. Later in the day, he may find that he cannot remember
whether he has made the notch or added the pebble.[35] He may also be unable to
remember whether the plan was to add a pebble every day, or every other day.[36]

Thus there is a sense in which the shipwreck survivor is unable to regulate his
conduct by a rule, simply because there is no difference between following the
rule and just doing whatever it is that he happens to do and thinking that he is
following the rule. Inventing a second rule to act as a check on the first rule is,
to use another of Wittgenstein's analogies, like the man who, finding it hard to
believe the morning's headlines, goes out and buys a second copy of the same
newspaper. The practice of keeping track of the days that pass only acquires the
character of a rule when more than one person does it, so that they can check
against one another. (So it is only the possibility of rescue that could give the
survivor's practice of tracking the days a rule-like character.) Rules are the way
individuals coordinate behavior among themselves; it is precisely this interpersonal dimension that makes the normative concept of *error* meaningful.

One can see quite easily how this argument can be applied to the case of
private language. The idea that there might be a "language of thought" has
traditionally run into trouble when it comes to characterizing the reference relationship that exists between a concept in someone's mind and the actual objects
in the world to which it refers. A mere causal connection (or "nomic covari-
ance") will not suffice, because it cannot account for the possibility of error.[37] A
child can be caused to think "dog" in response to a dog, but can also be caused to

think "dog" in response to a wolf or a coyote, or even a pile of laundry sitting in the shadows. But the word "dog" nevertheless only refers to the first.[38] A private sensation will not suffice either. If we apply names to our inner sensations, such as dog-like patterns of retinal irradiation, how do we know that we are doing so correctly? When one sees another dog, how is one to know that *this* sensation is of the same type as the previous sensation? In other words, how are we to know if we are using words consistently or erratically?

If the private language argument is correct, then the answer must depend on whether other people can understand us. Individuals do not have the ability to determine, all by themselves, whether what they say (or think) makes sense. Language makes sense when people are able to use it to understand one another, to bring about "agreement in forms of life."[39] Of course, once individuals have learned a language and internalized the apparatus of conversational exchange, they can run virtualized discussions in order to test the correctness of their assertions, or their arguments. Thus the private language argument does not imply that individuals are unable to retain language in isolation, or that people begin to babble the moment that they find themselves shipwrecked on desert islands. It simply shows that the idea of an individual who comes fully equipped with a language prior to all social interaction is incoherent, because the type of rule-following that governs language is impossible in the absence of an external check on the individual's conduct.[40] This is what makes correction possible, which in turn is what makes it possible for linguistic representations to be misrepresentations.

The private language argument suggests that language (as a social practice) has priority over consciousness when it comes to explaining our intentional states. Human infants have all sorts of cognitive abilities and behavioral dispositions. What the private language argument shows is that this innate psychological machinery, despite providing most of the building blocks necessary to the development of linguistic competence, does not provide *all* of the resources required for an account of contentful mental states such as beliefs and desires. Infants, like all animals, have an environment with which they interact. They have an extremely rich perceptual-motor system that allows them to distinguish between various states of this environment, and to conduct themselves in various ways with respect to it. The mistake is simply to describe these operations in terms that presuppose a structure that is a part of the intentional frame of reference. So, for instance, it would be a mistake to suppose that the significance of color vision is that it allows infants to form *beliefs* that dogs, and other creatures that lack color vision, are unable to form (such as "these are red peppers" and "those are green peppers"). The significance of color vision is that it allows infants to react differentially in ways that covary with certain features of the environment (e.g., to eat only green peppers and not red peppers).[41] It is therefore helpful to distinguish, when talking about cognition, between sentience and sapience—where the latter term refers to those operations that involve intentional states, and hence are language-dependent.[42]

This analysis suggests that a fully developed theory of rational action is going to be quite complicated, since it cannot simply take intentional states as given.

We will need to start out with a proto–action theory, which will not presuppose such states. At this point, it might help to introduce a terminological distinction between a theory of human *behavior*, which does not explain conduct in terms of intentional states, and a theory of *action*, which does. Our theory of action will therefore need to begin with a theory of behavior. Such a theory can ascribe a wide range of cognitive abilities to human agents, just not ones that depend on language or rationality. We will then need to explain how language could arise, within such a behavioral framework, and then how the practice of language use could give rise to intentional states. Only then will the foundations have been provided for a theory of rational action, of the type sketched out in chapter 3.

The payoff of this lengthy enterprise will be that it helps us to further determine the structure that the theory of practical rationality should have. It is no accident that standard instrumental theories of rational action have difficulty accommodating rule-following, and explaining social order. As we have seen, the standard imagistic theory of intentional states that underlies classic instrumentalist theories of action is also unable to provide an account of rule-following. The entire paradigm has a blind spot for normativity, from its psychological microfoundations all the way to its macrosociological modeling.[43] The solution, as we shall see, is to build normativity and rule-following in on the ground floor of the theory of action, right into our characterization of the agent's intentional states. It will then be much easier to see why they play out as they do at higher levels of the theory.

4.4. The Sources of Normativity

In order to understand language we need an account of normativity grounded in a theory of behavior. In other words, we need to explain, in a way that does not presuppose intentionality, how it might come to be the case that certain actions are right and others wrong (or correct and incorrect). Naturally, such an account will not initially account for how agents are able to *say*, or to *believe*, that certain actions are either right or wrong. It will only explain what it is for agents to *treat* certain actions as right or wrong, in their conduct. It will be an account of what Robert Brandom calls "norms implicit in practice."[44]

Brandom's way of setting up the problem is instructive. His discussion of social norms is structured by his attempt to avoid two explanatory strategies that he considers to be unsuccessful. The first of these views, which he calls *regulism*, identifies norms with some explicit formulation of a rule. According to this view, a social norm is to be understood on analogy with, say, a sign on the beach that says "no swimming." Normative assessment of action is possible because we can take a particular action, compare it against some rule that specifies how the action is to be performed, and determine whether it was done correctly or incorrectly. This view fails, according to Brandom, because the relevant species of normativity is merely subsidiary, or derived. "Proprieties of performance that are governed by explicit rules do not form an autonomous stratum of normative statuses, one that could exist though no other did."[45] In this case, the normativity of the rule is simply derived from the normativity of the intentional state that represents the rule. This is clearly not what we are looking for. What we need, as Brandom puts it, is a "pragmatist conception of norms—a notion of primitive correctnesses of performance implicit in practice that precede and are presupposed by their explicit formulation in rules and principles."[46]

These considerations remind us that any attempt to explain rules through our explicit, or ideational, formulations of them is bound to be question-begging. But while this reminder is helpful, it is possible to take the implied anti-intellectualism too far, and to assume that the rules can be identified in a way that completely disregards our attitudes toward them. One such approach would be to identify social norms with simple regularities in conduct. This is the idea at the heart of the second type of explanatory strategy, which Brandom refers to as *regularism*.

The problem with regularism, according to Brandom, is that it loses sight of the distinction between what *is* done and what *ought* to be done. In other words, it loses sight of the properly normative dimension of social norms. One symptom of this difficulty—and a crucial objection to regularism—is the problem of gerrymandering. For any finite batch of behavior, one can dream up an arbitrarily large number of rules of which that behavior would be an instantiation. As a result, when presented with a form of behavior that appears to deviate from a rule, it is always possible to generate some other rule, with which that behavior would be consistent.

The regularist's mistake is to think that just because norms do not consist in our explicit representations of them, our attitudes should be completely eliminated from the account. Thus the regularist hopes to discern the presence of norms simply by looking at behavioral regularities, while ignoring entirely the question of what agents take themselves to be doing. This is ultimately what generates the gerrymandering problem. Without some attention to what agents take themselves to be doing, there are simply too many rules that "fit" the data. Furthermore, everything is an instance of *some* rule. Thus the distinction between correct and incorrect performance collapses. According to Brandom:

> For the simple regularist's identification of impropriety with irregularity to get a grip, it must be supplemented with some way of picking out, as somehow *privileged*, some out of all the regularities exhibited. To say this is to say that some regularities must be picked out as the ones that *ought* to be conformed to, some patterns as the ones that *ought* to be continued. The simple regularity view offers no suggestion as to how this might be done and therefore does not solve, but merely puts off, the question of how to understand the normative distinction between what is done and what ought to be done.[47]

Thus the trick is to find some form of behavior that can be appropriately understood as an instance of "taking something to be correct"—and thus expresses the right sort of normative attitude—but is not itself an explicit formulation of the idea that something or other is correct, and does not presuppose any such formulation. In order to find norms implicit in practice, we must first find normative *assessments* of behavior implicit in practice.

The most obvious candidate for a type of behavior that manifests normative assessment is the *sanction*. We respond to acts that are correct with positive sanctions, acts that are incorrect with negative ones. A positive sanction can be understood in the standard sociological sense as anything that has positive gratificatory status for the agent acted on, and hence reinforces the behavior—a reward. A negative sanction is anything that has negative gratificatory significance, and hence encourages the agent not to repeat the behavior—a punishment. (Needless to say, a sanction need not be produced with the intention of bringing about this reinforcing or inhibiting effect.) It is easy to imagine the implementation of such a sanctioning system in a way that does not presuppose intentional states in any question-begging way.

The most straightforward way of trying to generate an account of social norms out of this conception of sanctioning would be simply to define a norm as a sanctioned regularity in conduct. Brandom ascribes a theory of this sort to John Haugeland.[48] According to such a view, agents conform to particular patterns because the pattern is positively sanctioned, or because any deviation from the pattern is negatively sanctioned, or both. Thus the agent's behavior is implicitly subject to normative assessment—an act is implicitly deemed to be correct when it is responded to with a positive sanction, and incorrect when it is responded to with a negative one. This sanction is what privileges a particular pattern, elevating it above the level of a mere regularity.

There is something attractive about this account, since the sanction in question can be understood without presupposing other normative concepts, and yet clearly counts as a type of implicit normative assessment. Nevertheless, Brandom takes it to be inadequate. His central concern is that it is still a type of regularist theory, and so "merely puts off the issue of gerrymandering." The introduction of sanctions allows one to pick out a privileged pattern at the base level of behavior. But the sanctioning itself is just another pattern of behavior, and so can be understood as "enforcing" an arbitrary number of different rules. "Just as there is no such thing as *the* regularity of performance evinced by some actual course of conduct...so there is no such thing as *the* regularity that is being reinforced by a certain set of responses to responses, or even dispositions to respond to responses. The issue of gerrymandering, of how to privilege one specification of a regularity over equally qualified competitors, arises once more at the level of the reinforcing regularity."[49]

One way of putting the problem would be to say that, according to the simple sanctioning view, there is no way of telling whether the person doing the sanctioning is doing a "proper job" of it. The actions of the sanctioner are just a behavior pattern, which can always be understood as an instance of some rule. Thus the distinction between "what ought to be done" and "what is done" disappears at this higher level.

One way of trying to fix this would be to add on another level of sanctions—to treat the sanctioning behavior as itself subject to further sanctions. This would be to recognize that "assessing, sanctioning, is itself something that can be done correctly or incorrectly."[50] This strategy, however, seems to merely put off the gerrymandering issue a bit further, and ultimately generate a regress. No matter how many levels of sanctioning are introduced, there will always be arbitrariness in the pattern at the highest level. Thus, according to Brandom, "if actual reinforcement of dispositional regularities is all that is available to appeal to in making sense of this regress, it might still be claimed that what is instituted by this hierarchy of regularities of responses to regularities of responses ought not to count as genuinely normative."[51] (The account, incidentally, cannot be patched up just by turning to regularities of communal assessment either.[52] Brandom observes that whether one person or some group of people is involved in making the assessment, the gerrymandering problem persists.)[53]

In the end, Brandom refrains from offering a clear resolution to these difficulties, arguing instead that the constitution of normative statuses may be "norms all the way down."[54] Thus he claims that there may be no way of explaining normative statuses in terms of "nonnormatively specifiable dispositions."[55] (He has his own reasons for thinking that this prima facie difficulty may not be that damaging to his project.[56]) He does, however, overlook one promising strategy for resolving the regress problem. The best way to eliminate the regress is to close the circle after the first iteration of higher-order sanctions. Suppose one person acts. In order to say that this action is norm-conformative, we must introduce a second person, who will sanction the first. And in order to say that this sanctioning is norm-conformative, we must introduce a third person, who will sanction the second, and so on. Or so it would seem. But do we need to introduce the third person? Instead of introducing a third person to sanction the second, we might simply stipulate that the *first* person sanctions the second. The second agent has what might be called an "expectation of behavior"—she expects the first to behave in a certain way. If the first person anticipates these expectations, he may develop what we can call an "expectation of recognition"—he expects her to respond correctly to his actions, to punish him only when it is appropriate to do so, or to reward him when he is entitled to it.[57] Whenever either expectation is disappointed, sanctions are imposed. In this way, the second person's sanctioning efforts become subject to sanctions by the first, just as the actions of the first are subject to sanctions by the second.

Of course, this structure of reciprocal sanctions and expectations generates its own form of regress. The way the first sanctions the sanctioning efforts of the second must also be sanctioned by the second. But this regress is clearly harmless in cases where all of these expectations and sanctions converge on a single pattern of behavior—when everyone enforces a particular pattern of behavior, but also sanctions deviant patterns of sanctioning with respect to this pattern of behavior. And these are precisely the cases in which we would want to say that there is a norm implicit in the practice. When the second expects the first to do x, the first expects the second to expect the first to do x, the second expects the first to expect the second to expect the first to do x, and so on, and all of these expectations are backed by sanctions, then only one action can satisfy all these expectations, namely, x. And so x is the *correct* action. Thus the regress, far from being vicious, generates something very much like the set of mutually reinforcing expectations that sustain game-theoretic equilibria.

As a result, when sanctioning is reciprocal, two agents can each act in a way that confers normativity on the actions of the other, and this, by extension, confers normativity back on their own actions. There is nothing left in the interaction that could count as "mere behavior." In particular, because everyone engages in a normative assessment of everyone's conduct, everyone has no choice but to adopt such an assessment of his or her own conduct (at least implicitly). Thus it is plausible to suggest that "original normativity" inheres in the practices of a community in which everyone sanctions everyone else, and sanctioning conduct is itself sanctionable conduct. Furthermore, there is no reason to think that this account presupposes cognitive abilities that are beyond the reach of prelinguistic hominids. The sanctioning behavior can be described as a set of responsive dispositions—it need not at any point involve any contentful *representation* of what the other has done, or will do.

4.5.   The Fall of Semiotics

This account of norms implicit in practice may appear to leave us still quite far away from an account of language and intentionality. But the distance is not nearly as great as it might at first seem. In order to see why, there is one more piece of the puzzle that needs to be put in place. The past century has seen an enormous conceptual revolution in the dominant approach to the understanding of language. In the past, it was widely assumed that the primary bearers of meaning were individual signs. Thus the dominant explanatory strategy in the philosophy of language was to explain how words acquired meaning. Once this explanation was in place, it was thought, it would then be possible to derive the meaning of all other units of semantic significance, such as sentences or arguments, from looking at how these words got combined. This approach can be broadly described as semiotic, since it takes the sign, along with the reference relationship, to be the explanatory primitive in the theory of meaning. The problem is that no one has ever been able to give a convincing account of how individual words could get meanings, independent of the sentences in which they occur. The dramatic conceptual revolution initiated by Kant's *Critique of Pure Reason* begins with the suggestion that words and concepts may not be the appropriate explanatory primitive. It may be that whole sentences (i.e., judgments) are the primary bearers of meaning, and that the meaning of words is derived from the contribution they make to the meaning of sentences in which they occur. This idea was later codified in the form of Gottlob Frege's "context principle," which states that "it is only in the context of a sentence that a word has a meaning."[58]

It seems clear that to learn a language is to learn the rules for the use of its expressions. However, if the expressions in question are *words*, then the account of rule-governed action developed in the previous section may not seem to provide many useful resources. But if the point of departure for the development of a theory of meaning is not the question of how words acquire meaning, but rather how whole sentences get their meaning, then the picture changes quite dramatically. Sentences are, after all, the basic unit we use in order to *do* something with language—to make an assertion, give an order, or ask a question. It is not hard to see how social practices could provide rules for the use of expressions in this way (and thus, how the norms implicit in these practices could confer meaning on such expressions). Thus an account of why sentences might be regarded as the primary unit of semantic significance would go a long way toward closing the gap between the behavioral account of norms articulated so far and the account of linguistic meaning that we need to develop.

Although there is no single widely accepted "theory of meaning" for natural languages, there is widespread agreement about many of the characteristics that a successful theory would have to exhibit. First and foremost among these is *compositionality*.[59] The vast majority of sentences that people encounter in their daily life are ones that they have never heard before. Thus their grasp of language cannot consist of simply a memorized list of all the sentences, along with some recollection of what elements of the environment they covary with. Such a list would be infinitely long. Furthermore, since the grammar of natural languages clearly provides a set of rules for constructing more complex sentences out of less complex elements, the natural supposition is that our understanding of language must consist of a grasp of the meaning of various subsentential elements, along with mastery of the combinatorial rules that can be applied to these elements in order to generate more complex constructions. Put crudely, the thought is that we understand sentences because we know the meaning of the words and we grasp the rules through which they are combined. This will sound familiar to anyone who has learned a foreign language, since there are two primary elements to this task: learning the grammatical rules and memorizing vocabulary.

Thus the compositional structure of language has encouraged a "bottom up" approach to the understanding of meaning and thought. A simple declarative sentence, such as "the table is brown," contains two important elements—a reference to a particular object, and the attribution of some property to that object. This is what gave rise to the classic "Aristotelian" analysis of thought into two elements: the universal and the particular. Within this framework, the secret to understanding knowledge and thought is first to explain the nature of universals and particulars.[60] Once this is done, it should be possible to specify how these two types of concepts get conjoined in order to form complete judgments. This is the task assigned to the theory of categories. Finally, once complete judgments are formed, a theory of syllogisms can be introduced in order to explain how these judgments get linked together to form chains of reasoning. Thus according to the classic explanatory architectonic, universals and particulars are explanatory primitives, subject to two orders of "logical" transformations: they are subsumed under a *category* to produce judgments, which are then incorporated into a *syllogism* to produce reasoning.

The problem with this venerable construction is that no one has ever been able to explain in a satisfactory way where universals get their content from.[61] The particular seems, at least in principle, somewhat easier to understand, since it often refers to a concrete object. It is not hard to imagine that "the table" might get its content, in some way, from the table to which it refers. But it is hard to see how universals can be subjected to the same analysis. "Brown" does not pick out an object in the same way that "the table" does. Plato reasoned, on these grounds, that if the particular gets its content through some kind of relationship to a material object, then the universal must get its content from a relationship to an abstract object. Hence his notorious claim that there must be an "intelligible" realm that parallels the physical one. More ontologically parsimonious philosophers have tried to show that the universal gets its content from some characteristic of particulars, such as a property that they all share. The "nominalist" tradition developed out of precisely this idea—that universals might be just "names," with only particulars having real existence. But without getting into all the details, suffice it to say that no account of how this would work has ever attracted widespread conviction. For centuries, the debate has swung back and forth between nominalism and Platonism. (The popularity of realism about properties or natural kinds in contemporary philosophy signals the return of the platonic impulse to ontologize universals.)

There is, however, one dramatic way of making "the problem of universals" go away. The basic ambition has always been to understand the relationship between particulars, universals, and judgments. The classical strategy is to explain the content of particulars and universals, then use this to derive the content of judgments. Kant observed, however, that one can turn the same trick by explaining the content of particulars *and judgments*, then using this to derive the content of universals.[62] There is no reason why universals must be explanatory primitives—philosophers generally just assumed that they were. But given a three-level theoretical structure, containing concepts, judgments, and inferences, it should in principle be possible to take content at any level as primitive, and derive from it content at the other two.

There is some danger here of simply substituting a mystery for an enigma. Where does the content of a judgment come from, if not from its constituent parts? It is in response to this problem that Kant initiated the current of thought that has come to be known as philosophical pragmatism. It was always assumed that the content of universals would turn out to be some kind of *representation*, on analogy with the particular. Underlying this assumption was a commitment to psychological imagism. Naturally, if one adheres to this representationalist paradigm, then the content of judgments will appear equally mysterious. One will be forced to choose between an implausible ontology of facts and a story like the one Wittgenstein told in the *Tractatus*, which treats facts as "configurations" of objects.[63] Kant, however, suggests that judgments are not representations at all. Judgments, in his view, are *actions*. Judging is something that we *do*. Thus in Kant's view, we receive input from our senses ("the faculty of intuition"), which gives us the particulars. We then perform judgments (various forms of "synthesis" and "unification"). Concepts, or universals, are simply functions that map these particulars onto the relevant set of judgments.

Of course, Kant is still operating within the framework of "the philosophy of consciousness." Thus for him the kinds of actions that one might perform, in the act of judgment, are quite limited. They are all basically acts of individual will and imagination—acts of spirit. It was never terribly clear what the *point* of this sort of judgment is, why the action is performed, if it is just an act of consciousness. Kant eventually claims that these operations of successive synthesis and unification are what produce the unity of the individual ego. Thus judgment is an act of self-constitution. It is this idea that steers Kant's fundamentally pragmatist insight in the direction that would lead to German idealism. Its implications are captured perfectly in the title of Schopenhauer's work *The World as Will and Representation.*[64] Judgment is an act of will, while perception is a form of representation. The world emerges at the intersection of the two; hence the falsity of both empiricism and rationalism.

With the linguistic turn, however, and the rejection of psychological imagism, Kant's suggestion acquires a completely different character. Kant conceived of judgment as a type of inner act of consciousness. In this respect, it is difficult to see what sort of content would be contributed to cognition by the act of judgment. But if we choose instead to treat judgment as an interiorized version of assertion, then the horizon of possibilities expands quite significantly. The content contributed by an assertion is precisely the pragmatic implications of the speech act, as a move in the relevant language-game. In other words, the content is given by what one can *do* with a given utterance in a particular social practice (i.e., a pattern of behavior structured by implicit norms).

It has therefore become increasingly common for philosophers to regard whole sentences—not words—as the primitive bearers of linguistic meaning. Donald Davidson, for instance, argues that our point of entry into a language, in a situation of "radical interpretation," is to figure out first the *sentences* that speakers of a language hold true.[65] Once we have grasped a sufficient (but finite) number of these sentences, along with the occasions on which they are used, we can begin to find patterns in the subsentential expressions, and infer the contribution that these expressions make to the truth-conditions of the sentences in which they appear. We will posit reference relationships between singular terms and objects, satisfaction relationships between properties and sets of objects, and so forth. The important point is that these relationships will be posited as part of a theory, used to make sense of people's speech behavior, to be adjusted as necessary "on the fly." Thus Davidson's theory appropriates the fundamental Kantian insight, by taking sentences as the point of entry into the theory of meaning, rather than words (which is equivalent, in Kant's terms, to starting with judgments rather than concepts).

It is inevitable that a theory of meaning of this type will have a somewhat more complex structure than the older semiotic theories. The suggestion is that people begin with a finite linguistic capacity, mastering a set of holophrastic signs and simple composite sentences by rote. They then infer the meaning of individual words and expressions, along with the combinatorial rules, from patterns that occur among the composite sentences. It is only once this is accomplished that they are able to go on to construct new sentences, using novel combinations. This explains why, for instance, when asked the meaning of a word, people will often look for an example of its use in a sentence (and why we often feel that we understand a word when used in certain sentences, even though we would be at a loss to give a "dictionary" definition of it).

Of course, once people have acquired a language and are able to use it correctly, their grasp seems to have an atomistic structure, since they are able to combine words in new and original ways. The importance of the sentence in the explanatory order can still be observed, however, in the type of mistakes people make. For example, people often understand the use of expressions without knowing the meaning of the constituent words. Mistakes *within* expressions or figures or speech also often go uncorrected. It is quite common, for example, for students to write "for all intensive purposes" in essays, when they mean to say "for all intents and purposes." This suggests that their grasp of the meaning of the expression is not "built up" from a grasp of its constituent words, but is rather "inferred down" from the contribution it makes to sentences.[66] Because the words always occur together in the phrase, and the two versions sound alike, the mistake never shows up until it is written. It is only by producing mistakes significant enough to turn true sentences into false ones, or vice versa, that we learn how we should and should not be using words.[67]

Incidentally, the priority of the sentence over the word in the theory of meaning provides a simple explanation for the phenomenon—often appealed to as an argument in favor of the language of thought hypothesis—of having a thought, but not being able to come up with the right word to express it. In this case, the speaker knows the "move" she would like to make with the sentence as a whole; she is simply having difficulty assembling the right constituent elements. It also explains why words can have several meanings (again, it has to do with the inferential properties of sentences in which they occur), along with other facts that are routinely appealed to by those who think that the existence of a language of thought can be established through introspection.[68]

I began these reflections with the observation that meaning is normative, and thus with an attempt to provide an account of the sources of normativity that did not presuppose either meaning or intentionality. This gave us a conception of norms implicit in practice, an account that is able to explain how behavior could acquire normative status—how it could come to be correct or incorrect. We have now seen that the normativity associated with meaning may also inhere originally in speech acts. But in order to connect these two insights, we need to determine what kind of practice could confer meaning on a pattern of linguistic behavior. Naturally, Wittgenstein's conception of a language game will provide the template here. This theory, however, fails to provide the systematicity that a compositional theory requires.[69] For a more promising suggestion, we must turn to the work of Wilfrid Sellars.

4.6. The Game of Giving and Asking for Reasons

The idea that language use should be understood through an analogy with games has been extremely influential in contemporary philosophy. In a game of chess, for instance, the pieces have no intrinsic significance; they are generally just pieces of wood, stone or plastic. What gives them their significance is the set of game rules that specifies how they can be moved. In this way, they are like the sounds that we use to communicate, none of which has any intrinsic meaning, but which are governed by rules specifying their appropriate use.

Each position in a chess game can be thought of as a type of normative status. The rules determine when one is entitled to occupy any given position, and what other positions such a position entitles one to move to. Take, for example, the "status" of having a bishop at QN4. There are a finite set of antecedent positions of the bishop that entitle one to acquire that status. For example, one is entitled to move the bishop there from QB2. Once the status is acquired, it in turn generates a set of entitlements to a set of other positions. One is now allowed to move to QB6. The identity of each piece can be thought of as the set of entitlements that govern it. What it "means" to be a bishop is precisely to be the piece that can attack QB6 from QN4, as opposed to the knight, which can attack QB7 and Q5. And, of course, understanding the game means having a practical mastery of the pieces, knowing what one can and cannot do with them.

There is something about all this that is strikingly parallel to certain types of linguistic exchanges. The practice of argument, inference, and justification is similarly structured. In this case, we make assertions, which correspond to a type of normative status. We must be entitled to make them, and they, in turn, license us to take up further positions. Thus inferences can be thought of as akin to moves in chess. They allow us to move from one position in the language game of assertion to another. (This structure is especially obvious in "natural deduction" systems of logic, used to model inference.)[70]

The primary difference between chess and the assertion game, however, is that one can acquire entitlement to make an assertion by a state of affairs that is itself not a part of the game. Thus the game of language includes what Sellars calls language-entry and language-exit moves.[71] For simplicity, imagine a language that consists of holophrastic signals (i.e., that has no compositional structure). Saying something like "smoke" amounts to making a move in this game, which will in turn license a number of other intragame moves, such as saying "fire." However, one's entitlement to say "smoke" need not flow from some other state of the game. It could be the presence of smoke in the vicinity that entitles one to say it (and thus reflects one's capacity to respond differentially to features of the environment). Similarly, "fire" may license a series of moves external to the game, such as the action of pulling back one's hand, or running away.

The other rather peculiar feature of the assertion game is that once a position is taken up by one person, anyone else is entitled to it as well. Assertoric warrant is interpersonally transferable. Thus if my neighbor says "smoke," this entitles me to say "fire," which may then entitle someone else to run away. We have a whole set of rules governing the shared use of the utterance "fire." Some of these are observational—specifying the nonlinguistic conditions under which one is entitled to say it. Others are inferential—specifying the other utterances that entitle one to say it. And many others are behavioral—specifying what we are either entitled or supposed to do in the presence of fire. When someone fails to grasp these rules, for example, fails to suspect fire in the presence of smoke, or fails to heed a warning and is burned, we may doubt that he understands the meaning of the term. Furthermore, when someone exhibits clear mastery of all these rules, including the ones that govern connections between utterances, it is difficult to imagine what *else* a grasp of the meaning of the expression could consist in.

Brandom argues, on these grounds, that our primitive understanding of the meaning of expressions consists of a grasp of the role that they play in the language game of assertion. This is what gives them their *semantic content* (not the reference relationship that obtains between their individual components and the world—that comes later, and is a derived relation). Assertion is privileged in this analysis because assertion is the form that utterances are placed in when used in inferences, and it is inferences that constitute the intralinguistic language game moves one is entitled to make with a given expression. As Brandom puts it:

> *Assertions* are fundamentally fodder for inferences. Uttering a sentence with assertional force or significance is putting it forward *as* a potential reason. Asserting is giving reasons—not necessarily reasons addressed to some particular question or issue, or to a particular individual, but making claims whose availability as reasons for others is essential to their assertional force. Assertions are essentially *fit* to be reasons. The function of assertion is making sentences available for use as premises in inferences. For performances to play this role or have this significance requires that assertional commitments and entitlements to such commitments consist in the ways in which they are *heritable*; their heritability is the form taken by the *inferential* articulation in virtue of which they count as semantically contentful.[72]

The meaning of subsentential elements is determined, in this analysis, through the contribution they make to the inferential properties of sentences in which they appear (in much the same way that the meaning of subsentential expressions is determined by their contribution to the truth-conditions of sentences in theories of meaning that privilege truth, rather than inference). The core distinction between universal and particular flows from the type of substitution relations that govern the relevant sentence components. Take, for example, the sentence "Fido is a dog." From this, we are entitled to infer various other sentences by substituting for a subsentential component. Thus we are entitled to infer "Fido is a mammal." We are also entitled to infer "My pet is a dog." The difference is that the latter inference is reversible, while the former is not. From "Fido is a mammal" we are not entitled to infer that "Fido is a dog," whereas we can infer "Fido is a dog" from "My pet is a dog" (given an appropriate instantiation of the indexical). The particular, in other words, is that segment of the sentence that has symmetric substitution relations, while the universal is the one that does not. It is this symmetry that gives us the notion of different particulars being "coreferential," and out of that, the very idea that there is an object to which singular terms refer.

Thus the idea that the world contains particular and universals, or objects and their properties, is a distinction that is imposed thanks to the internal structure of our language. (If we continued to use only holophrastic signals, we would have no such a distinction, and so would conceive of ourselves as simply interacting with an "environment," not a world of objects with properties.) Our language has these two distinct subsentential roles, according to Brandom, because of the expressive power that is provided by the combination of the two. Having one symmetric and one asymmetric component is essentially what makes our language inferentially productive, while still allowing us to predict the inferential behavior of "new" sentences from an understanding of the inferential properties of their subsentential elements.[73]

This analysis is intended to show how a pragmatist account of language can provide a compositional semantics for natural language, and can explain the concept of representation that is implicit in the notion that singular terms refer to objects. Prior to the conceptual revolution inaugurated by Kant's *Critique of Pure Reason*, it was assumed that representation must be taken as a primitive (or at least as an *explanans*) in any theoretical account of mental content. This is a major reason perception has so often been taken as a model for the explanation of belief, which has in turn led philosophers to think that beliefs are a component of the brain's innate computational resources (simply because so much of our visual processing is done at the level of the adaptive unconscious).[74] This analysis has encouraged the view that agents enter into social interaction already equipped with a full set of beliefs and desires, which in turn provides aid and comfort to both Hobbesian atomism and the instrumental conception of rationality. Thus the pragmatist turn in the philosophy of language, by treating both language and, by extension, the intentional planning system as primarily *social* in origin, fundamentally changes our approach to action theory.

4.7. Intentional States

From a pragmatist perspective, language develops not as a device for communicating privately formed thoughts, but rather as an external social practice. Such a practice has several obviously useful functions, first and foremost its ability to help agents coordinate social interactions. Even in its most basic form, it allows participants to signal one another, and therefore to communicate information (on the language-entry side), to announce intentions, and to give orders (on the language-exit side).[75] The most important contributions of language, however, may lie not with these interpersonal functions, but rather with its ability to amplify the cognitive power of the individual language-user. In the same way an abacus, as an external artifact, significantly amplifies the computational ability of our biological brains, language, as a system of external signs and tokens, increases our cognitive abilities in several different dimensions.

As Andy Clark puts it, public language "is a species of external artifact whose current adaptive value is partially constituted by its role in re-shaping the kinds of computational space that our biological brains must negotiate in order to solve certain types of problems, or to carry out certain complex projects."[76] Most obviously, even in nonwritten form, language use significantly augments memory. Clark argues that language also improves computational power in at least five other ways: environmental simplification, preplanning (and thus reduction of "on-line" deliberation), reduction of path-dependency of learning, improved attention and resource allocation, and enhanced data manipulation.[77] If our brain were a computer, then language would be the "ultimate upgrade."[78]

One observation that renders this sort of pragmatist order of explanation plausible is the fact that people perform very poorly on abstract tests of logical reasoning, but do much better when the same problems are reformulated in practical or deontic terms. When solving particular problems, there is ample evidence that people do not apply "content-free, syntactic rules of inference comparable to those in formal logic."[79] Instead, they apply what Patricia Cheng and Keith Holyoak call "pragmatic reasoning schemas," which constitute generalized patterns of reasoning abstracted from particular classes of problems that are solved routinely. This explains, for example, the counterintuitive finding that people are much better at applying rules formulated in deontic terms, such as $O(p \rightarrow q)$, than those formulated in terms of an unqualified material conditional, $p \rightarrow q$.[80] They solve these problems by applying a "permission schema," namely, "a type of regulation in which taking a particular action requires satisfaction of a certain precondition."[81] As a result, they do not get confused by the fact that the falsity of the antecedent renders the conditional true (i.e., if the action has not been taken, then the rule has not been violated). Indeed, it is the superior facility that people exhibit with deontic, as opposed to indicative, reasoning that has led many psychologists (somewhat impetuously) to the conclusion that there is an innate "deontic reasoning" or "cheater detection module" in the brain.[82] Yet the difference in performance—namely, the fact that "in contrast to the sparse (or absent) reasoning strategies evoked by indicative reasoning tasks, deontic reasoning tasks evoke strategies that are sophisticated and conceptually rich"[83]—might just as well be a consequence of the cognitive architecture postulated by the pragmatist order of explanation. It is precisely because people master the art of reasoning first as a social practice that they are better at solving problems that are formulated in these terms.

The external origin of language also serves to explain the differences in the *style* of reasoning that explicitly conceptual thought exhibits, compared to the adaptive unconscious. Daniel Dennett sums up this idea nicely with his suggestion that language permits the implementation of a serial virtual machine "inefficiently—on the parallel hardware that evolution has provided for us."[84] This is a view known as the "dual process" theory of mind, which is characterized by the distinction that is drawn between the parallel processing style of the adaptive unconscious and the serial, or linear style of conscious, intentional thought.[85] Our ability to focus on a single sustained line of reasoning stems from our essentially linguistic ability to chain together strings of assertions, and to winnow away the "noise" generated by our other cognitive systems. Furthermore, language allows us to produce arbitrarily long chains of inference.[86] The fact that assertion is neutral with respect to content means also that the domain of problems to which it can be applied is open. Finally, the substitution operations that confer meaning on subsentential elements, which give rise to the hierarchical phrase structure characteristic of natural languages, are believed by many to be essential to the human capacity to process recursive functions (which may be in turn foundational for mathematical reasoning).[87]

Initially, the states of this computational system are purely external, with words used as "markers." People literally reason out loud. Through a process of increased internalization, speech eventually became the "vehicle" for a style of cognitive processing that is quite distinctive, relative to the native architecture of the brain. And because of the advantages language provides, it is natural that it would become increasingly integrated into our planning processes, and that our behavior would come to be increasingly under the control of linguistically formulated plans. There is certainly ample evidence that language does play such a role.[88] For example, cognitive psychologists have studied extensively the way individuals will rehearse planned actions before performing them, by running through a series of sentences that describe what is to be done. This ability to linguistically rehearse the steps has a very direct impact on behavior, and has been shown in many cases to dramatically improve performance of the task.[89]

Furthermore, language allows us to deal more effectively with states of affairs that are not immediately present to consciousness. It thereby improves our foresight and recollection, allowing us to develop long-term plans or strategies. It also allows us to calculate more effectively, and thus to correct many of the biases that compromise our "natural heuristics." The work of psychologists like Daniel Kahneman and Amos Tversky shows precisely the gap that can exist between the intuitions that arise from the adaptive unconscious and our considered judgments.[90] It is no accident that we arrive at these considered judgments through an explicit symbolic representation of the choice problem. The adaptive unconscious is notoriously fickle when it comes to reasoning about hypothetical or counterfactual states of affairs, very low probability events, and events that occur over very long periods of time (unsurprisingly, since the ability to plan for such scenarios was not especially salient in the environment of evolutionary adaptation). Thus it is only through deployment of the "language upgrade" that we are able to develop plans that take into account such scenarios.[91]

In the classic psychological model proposed by Donald Norman and Tim Shallice, the "supervisory attentional system"—which we can interpret here as a product of the "language upgrade"—has five central functions: planning and decision making; troubleshooting; novel or ill-learned action sequences; dangerous or technically difficult actions; and overcoming strong habitual responses.[92] Of course, when we look at these sorts of capabilities, we can see that these are precisely the sort of cognitive processes that decision theory seeks to model. In other words, maximizing expected utility is the kind of capacity that is unique to language-users, and more specifically, is an exercise of our language-processing capacity. One can see the contrast quite vividly by comparing the capacity for utility-maximization with something like the capacity for facial recognition. We have the ability to recognize people we have seen before, often despite major changes in their appearance. This ability is clearly a part of our biological inheritance. It has all the characteristics of an evolutionarily adapted cognitive mechanism (part of the adaptive unconscious) and is probably shared with many other animal species. This is reflected in the fact that none of us really knows how it is that we do what we do. When we recognize someone we haven't seen for many years, most of us would be unable to say precisely what it was about his or her appearance that triggered the identification. Similarly, most of us are unable to say what characteristics allow us to determine gender by looking at someone's face.

Compare that to the case of utility-maximization. Here it is not just that we happen to be able to say what we are doing, when we make a utility-maximizing decision, it is *essential* that we be able to say it. If we cannot articulate the preferences that we are maximizing with respect to, there would no grounds for claiming that we are acting rationally (assuming, of course, the falsity of revealed preference theory). Furthermore, as Kahneman and Tversky have amply demonstrated, people do not do a particularly good job at utility-maximization when reasoning in an intuitive way. Strategic reasoning, in particular, requires the use of counterfactuals, hypotheticals, and probabilistic judgments, along with the ability to hold long chains of intermediate conclusions in working memory. All of these cognitive operations bear the hallmark of the "analytical system," not the adaptive unconscious (which is why it is easy to develop a computer program that will maximize utility, but has so far proven impossible to develop one that can perform more than rudimentary facial recognition).[93] The process is very slow, linear, makes intensive use of cognitive resources (i.e., requires concentration), and is functionally flexible. Thus we have good reason to believe that the style of reasoning that is modeled in decision theory, the kind of cognitive skills that are deployed, is part of the language "upgrade" that we get from social interaction, and not part of our innate psychological machinery. It is an exaptation, or as Dennett put it, "a *very* recent and rushed add-on, no doubt an exploitation of earlier sequencing circuitry."[94]

It is essential to this view that language (or the intentional planning system) *not* be regarded as simply "one more module" added to the heap, but that its introduction be understood as a colonization and "repurposing" of cognitive capacities that we share, not only with other primates, but with many other animals. Leda Cosmides and John Tooby, leading proponents of the "one more module" approach to understanding the analytical system, describe the brain as "an intricate network of functionally dedicated computers, each activated by different classes of content or problem, with some more general-purpose computers embedded in the architecture as well."[95] The problem with their hypothesis is evident from the "tacked-on" feeling one gets from the final clause of this sentence. Modularity is attractive as an explanatory concept, not only because of its introspective plausibility, but because modularity (or more generally, a system of parallel processing that draws on a multitude of domain-specific, encapsulated, fast problem solving heuristics) seems like the kind of structure that natural selection could produce through incremental change. Yet why would natural selection produce, in addition to all these dedicated computers, aimed at solving highly specific problems that arose on the African savannah, some "general purpose computers" as well (one for language, one for mathematics, one for "mind reading," etc.)? And why in only one species? This account, despite carrying the label of "evolutionary psychology," is actually lacking in evolutionary plausibility. As Derek Bickerton writes,

> if there is no single development that accounts for all human-specific traits, then separate evolutionary histories have to be discovered for each and every one of those traits: for language, for our particular brand of consciousness, for the ability to plan ahead, for mathematical and artistic capacities, and so on. Moreover, since the nature of the fossil record...suggests that, with regard to all of these characteristics, all of our ancestral species were closer to modern apes than to modern humans, then each of these human-specific traits must have evolved independently within a period of at most two to three hundred thousand years. The evolutionary plausibility of such developments must be close to zero. The only alternative approach is...to hypothesize a single polyfunctional mechanism that could have somehow transformed pre-existing hominid capacities in an extremely short period of time.[96]

For example, it appears that human infants share with other primates (and animals) two basic heuristics for handling numerosity: the first a "subitizing" system for making judgments involving very small numbers of objects, and the second a "large number" system for making approximate judgments ("guesstimates") concerning large collections of objects. Perhaps surprisingly, human infants do not perform much better than other primates when it comes to these heuristic judgments.[97] Yet using linguistic resources, humans acquire the ability (at about age four) to count, not just to 50 or 100, but as high as they like. Chimpanzees who have learned numbers, on the other hand, never reach the "now I can go on" moment. They interpret 2 to mean "more than 1," and so teaching them the difference between 3 and 2 is a long, arduous task. What they learn, however, is that 3 is "more than 2," and so the whole process must be repeated when it comes to introducing the number 4. Thus what one sees in human infants is a qualitative, not merely a quantitative, improvement in performance, one that suggests a completely different style of cognitive processing.[98] It is also very difficult to explain this difference as an adaptation, or some type of new cognitive module. (After all, what would be the purpose?) It is far easier to explain it as a byproduct of the "upgrade" that our brains receive from the social practice of language use.

Beliefs and desires (or preferences) should be understood as part of this language upgrade. If psychological sententialism is correct, then they are not part of the native architecture of the brain (in fact, they do not even fully reside in the brain). According to this view, intentional states arise because of our ability to talk about our own linguistic performances. It has often been noted that language, by introducing external markers for our thoughts, facilitates the development of reflexivity. In other words, it makes it easier for us to take one of our own thoughts or concepts as the object of a further thought. One can see this even among chimpanzees.[99] Chimpanzees who have not been taught to sign are able to sort objects into groups according to similarities that these objects exhibit. However, they cannot sort pairs of similar objects from pairs of dissimilar ones. In other words, they can group together red objects, or blue objects, but they cannot form the group of all "similar" pairs of objects. Thus they are able to visually detect the relation of "similarity" between objects, in order to sort them, but they cannot accomplish the higher-order task of taking the relation itself, "similarity," as the object of such an exercise. Chimpanzees who have been taught to sign, however, are able to accomplish this task. First-order sorting is used to teach the sign for "same" and "different." Once this is done, and the symbol for "same" is identified with all of the pairs in a group, the chimpanzee is able to sort them using this criterion.

A comparable phenomenon occurs with the developing of *semantic vocabulary* in human languages. When a thought is expressed linguistically, it becomes much easier to take this thought as an object of further thought. The simplest form is perhaps linguistic reporting, where we talk about speech behavior that we have observed. "Bill said that he is going to the store." The central characteristic of semantic vocabulary is that it creates an opaque context—coreferential expressions are no longer substitutable *salva veritate*. Even if the store in question is the 7-Eleven, it is not correct to say "Bill said that he is going to the 7-Eleven," since that isn't what he said. This reflects that fact that the object of the reporting sentence is a piece of language, not a piece of the world.

Prior to the development of semantic vocabulary, it is only possible for language users to take up deontic statuses in practice. With the development of semantic vocabulary, they can not only take up such statuses, they also can say *that* they have taken up such statuses. Similarly, they are able to ascribe such statuses to others.

As we have seen, producing an utterance has certain normative implications. To use one of Brandom's examples, both humans and parrots have the ability to react to red objects in the environment by saying "this is red." The reason that the human's reaction counts as a judgment, or as the application of a concept, is that this utterance generates a series of commitments to *other* utterances, such as "this is not blue." Each utterance comes with a set of commitments and entitlements (both to other utterances and to observations and actions). These commitments and entitlements are kept track of as part of an exercise Brandom calls deontic scorekeeping. People keep a running tab on each others' statuses, just as they try to keep track of their own. This is comparable to the way chess players keep track of the position of their opponent's pieces, and which squares they are able to attack from where they are.

In a perfect world, where the rules were clear and everyone's memory infallible, there would never be a difference of opinion among the participants in a practice as to the status of the game. However, such is often not the case. As a result, there often develops an "internal" and an "external" perspective concerning deontic statuses— for example, where an agent does not acknowledge a commitment or entitlement that others think she is under. (I have had the experience of an opponent challenging one of my chess moves when playing without the board: "That would be a great move, except you don't have a rook there." The situation is similar to the one we often encounter in discourse: "That would be a good argument, except the premises are false.") In the absence of semantic vocabulary, there is not much we can do in such cases. However, with semantic vocabulary, it is possible for everyone involved to state what commitments and entitlements each one is positing, and to track the inferential connections forward or backward in order to uncover the source of the discrepancy.

One of the central pieces of semantic vocabulary is belief. Unlike the expressions "said" or "claims," which ascribe the actual utterance of an assertion to an agent, along with its associated commitments, the expressions "believes" or "thinks" ascribe only the commitments (leaving open the question of whether the actual assertion has ever been uttered). This is especially useful for explicating the sequence of entitlements that precede a given speech act, or an action. Sometimes people will shout out "fire," and then run away. At other times, they will simply run away. Under such circumstances, it may be helpful for onlookers to know that they are running away because they believe that there is a fire. These sorts of explanations are especially useful when there is a disagreement between the agents and the onlookers as to the "score" (i.e., when there is an error). In a world in which such disagreements never arose, there would be very little use for the "believes that" locution.

Something quite similar can be said in the case of desire. People will often explicitly articulate their goal when they are trying to decide which course of action to take. Announcements of this type play a crucial role in not only interpersonal coordination but also, as we have seen, individual planning. As has often been remarked, these announcements generate commitments, even in the weak case in which the action is being selected on purely instrumental grounds. This provides a general template for explaining action as a confluence of belief and desire. These explanations are, of course, also most useful with failed attempts, since they allow us to explain what the person was *trying* to do.

One of the primary advantages of this scorekeeping account of belief and desire is that it resists the tendency to reify intentional states.[100] The way we use folk-psychological vocabulary encourages us to imagine that agents actually walk around with a set of "beliefs" and "desires" in their heads. This generates a number of well-known problems. The most obvious is that we naïvely ascribe what turn out to be infinitely large sets of beliefs and desires to individuals. As Dennett has observed, we would not hesitate, when asked, to declare that we believe 7,000,002 to be greater than 7,000,001, or that zebras in the wild do not wear overcoats, do not read Shakespeare, and so forth. At the same time, none of these questions are ones that we are likely to have thought about prior to reading Dennett. Thus the beliefs in question cannot be in our heads; they are simply consequences of other things that we believe. This squares nicely with the view that "belief-talk" is a way of articulating our commitments.

Theorists who think beliefs have psychological reality generally respond to these objections by positing a "core" set of beliefs that are actually in the agent's brain, followed by a finite set of "dispositions," which generate assent to claims that are obvious inferential consequences of these core beliefs. But it is difficult to believe that there could be any psychological reality to this distinction. In any case, the appeal to dispositions, in order not to run afoul of private-language difficulties, is forced to appeal to one type of modal claim (what the agent "would" assent to) as a way of explaining the belief, as opposed to another (what the agent "should" assent to). It is not clear that the former, alethic modality is any more transparent, or naturalistically respectable, than the latter, deontic one (especially given the purely behavioral account of norms-implicit-in-practice provided in section 4.4).[101]

To see the psychological implausibility of the dispositional account, compare the case of belief to that of facial recognition. There is good reason to think that when we see someone, their image is stored in something like a mental data bank where it can later be searched and retrieved. The more we see that person, the greater the prominence of that image, and the easier recognition becomes. There are several characteristics of facial recognition that might lead us to think that these images actually are "stored" in the brain. The first is that our capacity for this sort of recognition is clearly finite. This may seem obvious, but it bears emphasizing. We cannot recognize people we have never seen before. And even with this finite structure, our capacity for facial recognition is clearly subject to storage constraints. We don't remember the vast majority of people we have seen, and we tend to forget people as time goes by.

But despite these evident disanalogies, philosophers have long tried to explain belief on the same model as visual recognition. They treat beliefs as though they were memories. One can see the analogy at work most clearly in Hume's view that beliefs are simply "lively ideas." Yet the cognitive processes involved in determining what we believe are completely different. When asked whether I remember what my grandfather looks like, I have to do a bit of a mental search, to see if I can summon up the image from a photograph that I once saw. But when asked whether I still believe something I wrote 10 years ago, I do not do a mental search to see if the belief is still in storage somewhere. Despite the fact that the belief has been explicitly formulated, and thus should belong to the "core" of my convictions, my approach to retrieval is completely inferential. I check to see whether a commitment to what I wrote is precluded by any of the changes I have made in my theoretical commitments since that time.

There is also the fact that we grant individuals only limited first-person authority when it comes to beliefs. If someone claims not to recognize someone, I have little choice but to accept this claim (even if it seems to me that this person *should* remember him). When someone claims to believe something, I am inclined to give her the benefit of the doubt. But if the belief she claims to hold is flatly inconsistent with a number of other beliefs she holds, I may be inclined to say that she doesn't really believe it, or that she only thinks that she believes it. This limit on first-person authority would be mysterious if the belief were really in the person's brain, but it is precisely what one would expect if one adopts a deontic scorekeeping perspective. We assume that the person making a claim about her own commitments is the best positioned to do so, because under normal circumstances she is most likely to be the one doing the best job of keeping track of her own commitments. Similarly, sports officials tend to defer to the judgment of the referee who was closest to the play. But this presumption is defeasible, if everyone else thinks that the call should have been different.

Thus intentional states are not, first and foremost, mental states. They are "markers" that are put down in the game of giving and asking for reasons. This game is initially a public practice that we master—it is only later that we acquire, through internalization, the ability to run "virtual" simulations of moves in this game, and thus acquire the capacity to use this game to amplify our own planning abilities. This is why "planning theorists" are right to point to the implicit normativity of our intentional states (chapter 2, section 3). The mistake they make is to believe that the normativity of these states could be used to *explain* our capacity to make commitments, or to respect the rules of a social practice, when it is in fact the latter that must be appealed to in order to make sense of the former.

4.8. Conclusion

The presentation of this argument has been quite complex, but the account that emerges in the end is straightforward. The complexity in the exposition is imposed by the need to shake off the mistaken ideas and misleading images that have until recently dominated philosophical thinking, and still enjoy widespread currency in other circles. Most of these stem from the attempt to explain intentional states as a type of mental picture. There may have been a time at which protohominids planned their actions using cognitive resources of this type. But the development of language changes everything. It gives us a tool to use in planning our actions that not only massively augments our computational ability but also provides many of the cognitive skills needed to define long-term goals, contemplate hypothetical scenarios, calculate probabilities, and rehearse plans. In short, language allows us to act more successfully. We might think of it as providing the agent with an intentional planning system, one that massively upgrades the innate ability of what Clark calls "our biological brains."[102]

It is precisely the set of skills contributed by our linguistic ability that decision theory seeks to model. Talking about decision in terms of beliefs and desires is a "psychologistic" way of describing deontic statuses, or positions taken in the game of giving and asking for reasons. Decision theory is a vocabulary designed to make explicit the commitments implicit in these statuses. It allows us to say that an individual who believes that it is going to rain, and who wants to stay dry, *should* bring his umbrella to work. Hence the psychological implausibility of the theory. Rational choice theorists have never claimed that people actually have probability assignments in their mind, or complete preference orderings over sets of possible worlds, or that they perform the computations needed to determine the rational course of action in a given situation. This would have been self-evidently absurd.[103] The point is simply that, given a particular set of beliefs and desires, there is only one way of acting that is consistent with these commitments. Decision theory allows us to articulate the implications of these commitments.

In practical contexts, agents use explicit articulation of their beliefs and desires as a way of planning their actions. When this planning is conducted *in foro interno*, beliefs and desires provide us with a framework for our practical deliberations. When ascribed to others, beliefs and desires provide us with a framework for the explanation of action in terms of intentional states. It is the use of this cognitive structure that qualifies our actions as *rational*. Of course, there is no doubt that we have an enormous number of behavioral dispositions acquired during earlier stages in our evolutionary history, prior to the acquisition of the "language upgrade." Yet it is important not to confuse concepts that belong at the level of behavior (sentience) with those that belong at the level of action theory (sapience). The latter are characterized by a form of normativity and intentionality that the former entirely lack. Confusion of these two levels is responsible for a number of different philosophical errors, not just psychological realism about belief but also, as I shall attempt to show, noncognitivism about desire.

5

Preference Noncognitivism

There is a long-standing tradition in Western philosophy that treats human desire as somehow outside the sphere of rational control. Of course, few people think that hunger and thirst can simply be willed away. The controversy emerges only with the claim that these basic bodily functions should be taken as a model for all our motivational states (preferences, desires, emotions, sentiments, etc.). According to this view, since it is these motivational states that prescribe what ends we seek to obtain through our actions, it follows that all of our human goals and aspirations are essentially *given* to us; they are not chosen. Our rational deliberation can at best channel our underlying impulses; it cannot fundamentally revise or alter them. And under no circumstances can a desire arise de novo through a process of rational deliberation. As Hume put it, "we can naturally no more change our own sentiments, than the motions of the heavens."[1] It is because of this widespread *noncognitivism about desire* that philosophers have traditionally had so much more to say about belief than about desire.

The decision theorist's methodological injunction to "treat preferences as given" is, in itself, nothing more than a harmless attempt to partition a certain set of problems, so that the genesis of preferences can be treated as exogenous to the theory of practical rationality, strictly construed. However, in practice, the view that preferences are simply "given" is often taken to mean that preferences are "arbitrary" or "irrational." In other words, decision theorists often take the old saying "De gustibus non disputandum est" (There is no arguing over taste) and apply it to *all* preferences. This is unmotivated—especially when one understands this preference ordering in terms of a set of intentional states with propositional content (and even more so when one interprets these intentional states as merely positions in the game of giving and asking for reasons). However, the noncognitivist view of preference is sufficiently widespread that it is worth examining in greater detail, in order to root out the habits of mind that have lent it aid and comfort over the years.

The claim that desires are entirely outside the sphere of rational deliberation and control is strikingly at odds with everyday intuition. The more common-sense view of the matter is that we struggle with our motivations. This struggle is often experienced as a conflict between what we *want* to do and what we *know* to be best. Sometimes the struggle goes one way, sometimes the other. Some impulses are extremely recalcitrant to the will, and we eventually succumb to them. On other occasions, we are able to squelch unwelcome impulses with a minimum of fuss. (In fact, a reasonable degree of self-mastery of this sort is one of the characteristics that we normally take to distinguish adults from children.) Thus it is prima facie implausible to say that our sentiments are completely outside the scope of rational deliberation and control.

Historically, however, it is not difficult to see where this sense of helplessness in the face of desire comes from. The Christian tradition has always been characterized by a powerful dualism between body and soul, with desire typically being identified with the body and belief with the soul. Since Augustine, loss of control over the body, paradigmatically in the case of sexual arousal, was regarded as the primary consequence and mark of original sin.[2] But this historical backdrop does not explain why the noncognitive conception of desire should continue to enjoy such widespread popularity. In particular, it does not explain why theorists who subscribe to monistic theories of mind—and thus consider beliefs and desires to have a comparable ontological status—should continue to place desires outside the sphere of rational deliberation. The fact that they are sometimes involuntary is neither here nor there, since many of our beliefs are also involuntary.[3] The noncognitivism thesis becomes even more problematic once it is acknowledged that desires have propositional content. In early materialist theories of mind, beliefs were conceived of as a type of picture, while desires were thought of as forces (or springs, or hydraulics). These mechanical metaphors helped to obscure the fact that desires, like beliefs, have representational content. And given the internal connection between representation, concept use, and rationality, it becomes increasingly difficult to sustain the noncognitivism thesis.

In contemporary philosophical terms, it is often granted that desires exhibit *surface cognitivism*.[4] In other words, desires stand in inferential relations to one another in much the same way that beliefs do. We also impose logical consistency constraints on our desires, in much the same way that we do with beliefs. It is well known, for instance, that decision theory presupposes that preference orderings are transitive. It is also well known that people's actual preferences often violate this principle.[5] It is not nearly as well known, however, that in many psychological studies in which individuals are shown to have intransitive preferences, they immediately revise their preferences in order to eliminate the intransitivity as soon as it is pointed out to them. They react to intransitive preferences in much the same way that ordinary reasoners react to inconsistent beliefs.[6]

Thus desires look and behave very much like beliefs in our everyday practices of argumentation and deliberation. The only way to sustain the noncognitivism thesis, therefore, has been to argue that there is some deeper level at which desires are cognitively defective, and thus somehow less rational than belief. This is the position that has been most actively defended by proponents of the so-called Humean theory of motivation.

5.1. Skepticism about Practical Reason

There are a variety of different ways of formulating the noncognitivism thesis with respect to desire. Many are quite closely tied to problematic theories about the nature of intentional states, or rationality. For example, the claim that desires are not cognitive states is often expressed as the thesis that desires are neither true nor false. But this is not so helpful, since it has no real significance unless supplemented with a theory of truth, along with some account of how truth is related to other epistemically important notions, such as validity and justification. These supplementary theories are often just as problematic as the conception of desire at play.

These sorts of theories also tend to distract from what really animates the debate, which is a concern over rational argumentation.[7] The issue between the cognitivist and the noncognitivist is over what we can do in cases where we are trying to convince some person that he should do x, and he responds by saying that he does not *want* to. What argumentative resources are at our disposal? Is this the end of the discussion, or should it be possible to convince this person to do x regardless of what he happens to want? This question obviously becomes most pressing in cases where x is some moral obligation, and the agent does not want to perform the action because it conflicts with his self-interest.

The noncognitivist position takes as its point of departure the observation that in many cases, these sorts of arguments seem to go nowhere. You can argue until you're blue in the face, and you will still not convince someone who likes vanilla to prefer chocolate. The noncognitivist extends this observation to include, in principle, *all* preferences. Put in decision-theoretic terms, each agent has a preference ordering that ranks the set of possible worlds (including both actions and consequences) from best to worst. These preferences are not the conclusion of any process of reasoning, according to the starkest form of the noncognitivist position; they are a brute datum. So if a person really does not want to perform an action, there is nothing that can be done about it from the standpoint of rationality.

This picture has a few twists, however. The noncognitivist view of desire generally does not deny that there is instrumental deliberation, and that this form of deliberation has the capacity to generate "new" desires. The claim is that anything that appears to be deliberation about *what* to desire is really just deliberation about *how* best to satisfy some antecedently given desire. Thus Hume argued that reason does not set ends for us, it only channels our existing desires. It does so in one of two ways: "either when it excites a passion by informing us of the existence of something which is a proper object of it; or when it discovers that connexion of causes and effects so as to afford us means of exerting any passion."[8] An example of the former would be when I want to buy a reliable car, and a friend tells me which model has the best record. An example of the latter would be when I want to find my way to the car dealership, and my friend tells me which bus to take. Naturally, there is no sharp distinction between the two. The point is that the contribution made by "reason" in both cases is purely factual. Both forms of advice work by supplying me with a belief that allows me to satisfy my desires. So when trying to convince someone to do x, when she does not want to, we may be able to engage in rational debate for a while. However, if it turns out that this person is not laboring under any false beliefs, and has not made any errors in connecting these beliefs up with her desires, then eventually we will run out of arguments.

Bernard Williams, in a widely discussed article, stated this thesis in the following way.[9] He argued that each individual has some core set of preferences S (which he referred to as a "subjective motivational set," in order to emphasize that the *content* of these preference is completely open). In order to persuade this person that she has reason to do x, we must show how the performance of action x in some way conduces to the satisfaction of some element of S. If we are unable to hook x in to the agent's subjective motivational set in some way, then we can still apply psychological or social pressure to that person, but we cannot really argue any further with her.

This view is often referred to now, more or less following Williams, as the Humean theory of motivation. The debate that followed the publication of Williams's article generated some clarification of the issues. In particular, it became apparent that there were two components to the Humean theory. The first is the claim that every action needs to be justified through reference to some desire or preference—that a belief alone is never enough to motivate the agent to act. The argument that purports to establish this conclusion is referred to as "the teleological argument." The second thesis is that desires themselves can only be justified through reference to further desires. This is called the "desire-in desire-out" principle. It has been suggested that these two arguments are all that is needed to establish the noncognitivist thesis about desire.

The teleological argument is intended to rebut the suggestion that, when trying to convince someone to do x, we might choose simply to ignore that person's desires, and argue that the commitment to do x follows from her beliefs. The teleological argument attempts to show that, in principle, our reasons for performing some action must always include both a belief and a desire. Of course, there is little doubt that our reasons for action *usually* include both. But there do appear to be some significant exceptions. In particular, Thomas Nagel has observed that we often act, not on the basis of our current desires, but rather on the anticipation of our future desires.[10] An agent may not be hungry right now, but may start to prepare dinner because he *believes* that he will soon be hungry. Furthermore, it would appear that a prudent agent may assign beliefs that are based on the anticipation of future desires motivational priority over present desires. She may override her current desire to sleep in order to go search for food. In both cases, it is misleading to say that she acts on the basis of a desire, since it is precisely the absence of a present desire to eat that makes the action prudent.

Of course, it is always possible to cook up an explanation in these cases that does involve some kind of desire. One could argue, for instance, that the agent has a desire to satisfy his future desires.[11] This desire then gets hooked up with the belief that she will soon desire to eat, in order to generate a desire to prepare dinner. The most obvious problem with this strategy is that we would hesitate to call an agent who lacked such a "desire" rational, and yet it is far from obvious that we should want to associate practical rationality with the possession of certain substantive desires. The more serious problem, however, with this response is the ad hoc way that such desires can be posited. Rather than demonstrating the existence of an underlying desire, it tends to suggest that our talk of desires in this case is trivial.

The teleological argument seeks to remedy this difficulty by showing that there is something intrinsic to the idea of having a goal, or a purpose, that requires us to posit a desire in the explanation of an agent's conduct. This argument was given its first clear formulation by Michael Smith, although it can be found lurking in the background of much previous discussion. It runs something like this:

1. Intentional action is explained teleologically, in terms of the goal that the agent intends to bring about.

2. An intentional explanation of this type must be framed in terms of some *goal-directed psychological state* of the agent.

3. *Beliefs* are psychological states that aim to represent the world, and thus do not qualify as goal-directed.

4. *Desires* are goal-directed psychological states.

5. Therefore, intentional explanations cannot be framed strictly in terms of belief; they must also include reference to a desire.

Yet whatever the success of this argument in demonstrating the need for desires in any explanation of action, it is now generally accepted that the teleological argument does not itself have any noncognitivist implications. This is because the notion of desire invoked is purely formal. As Smith says, since desires are simply defined as goal-directed intentional states, "it follows that having a goal just *is* desiring."[12] This amounts to treating statement (4) as a definition of desire. Thus the teleological argument does not show that action needs to be explained in terms of some substantive desire, like hunger or thirst. It just means that the explanation has to feature a desire in it somewhere. Nothing stops us from simply making up a desire that is an oblique redescription of the goal sought.

Nagel, among others, has therefore argued that the teleological argument is perfectly compatible with a purely cognitive theory of motivation. He is inclined to think that an evaluative belief of the type "x is good" is sufficient to explain why an agent might seek to perform an action that leads to x. However, if a proponent of the Humean theory of motivation were to come along and say "that explanation is defective, you still haven't told us why the agent wants x," there is no real problem for the cognitivist. It is open to Nagel to offer the following response: "if you insist on having a desire in the explanation, we can say that the agent's belief that x is good gives him a desire to make it the case that x, and this desire then provides him with the necessary 'motivation.'" The point is that the desire is an extra gear in this explanation. It turns, but it does no work.

This makes it clear that the substance of the Humean view lies not in a theory about how actions are to be planned, executed, or explained, but rather in a thesis about the origins of our desires. The teleological argument is neither here nor there. The key to Williams's position is the "desire-in desire-out" principle. According to this view, any deliberative process that produces a desire as output must have another desire as input (not just a belief).[13] This is what precludes the possibility of a rationalist theory like Nagel's. Furthermore, since all deliberation must take some desire as "input," not all desires can be a product of deliberation. There must be some that are simply given, to serve as a basis for the production of all the rest.

So even though the Humean view is often described as a type of "skepticism about practical reason,"[14] this turns out to be quite misleading. The Humean does not claim that practical reason is defective, or is unable to generate adequately justified recommendations. The thesis is really one about the origins of our desires (i.e., that some of them must be simply given, and thus must not be open to rational or cognitive evaluation). According to Jay Wallace, this observation results in an important redirection of the debate: "we see that the real burden on the Humean is to defend a claim about the rationalizing explanation of desires, the claim I have called the desire-in desire-out principle. It is because the teleological argument by itself lends no support to this crucial principle that it fails to settle the issue between the Humean and the rationalist."[15]

Smith initially thought that the desire-in desire-out thesis could be established through simple iteration of his version of the teleological argument.[16] After the first application, in which an action is explained in terms of a desire (or a belief and a desire), an attempt is made to explain this desire. Since this desire is also a goal-directed psychological state, it must be explained in terms of a further goal-directed state, and so on. A number of critics of the Humean view have focused on this argument, in an attempt to show that desires can arise through some other process (such as the application of an evaluative belief, or through the exercise of pure practical reason).[17] But while these arguments create problems for the Humean, they are also fundamentally misguided. The critics all accept that an adequate defense of the desire-in desire-out thesis would constitute a defense of traditional Humean noncognitivism. I would like to suggest that the desire-in desire-out thesis, like the teleological argument, is not decisive. Taken by itself, the desire-in desire-out thesis has no skeptical implications, and can be readily accepted by a rationalist or cognitivist. It is only when *combined with a foundationalist conception of justification* that it starts to generate problems.

5.2. The Desire-in Desire-out Principle

To show that the "desire-in desire-out" principle is not sufficient to provide an argument for noncognitivism about desire, it suffices to note that many philosophers subscribe to a comparable thesis with respect to belief, without taking it to have any skeptical implications.[18] It is widely thought that the only thing that can justify a belief is another belief. This amounts to saying that there is a "belief-in belief-out" principle governing the derivation of our beliefs, just as the Humean says there is in the case of desire. But this should not be a surprise. Justification is an inferential relationship. The only thing that can be slotted into the "premise position" of an inference is some kind of sentence or assertion. Thus it is not unusual to find that justification relations exist only *between* intentional states.

This characteristic of justificatory relations does give rise to a well-known skeptical argument, the "epistemic regress problem." And it is possible to use this argument to defend noncognitivism about desire. However, having made such use of the argument, it then becomes very difficult to see why noncognitivism about belief should not follow as an immediate consequence as well. Many Humeans have unfortunately fallen into this trap—trying to use *general* skepticism in support of a *particular* theoretical position. They use what amounts to a skeptical argument to attack their opponents' views, without noticing that these arguments cut the ground out from under their own feet just as well.

What is the regress argument? Suppose that some agent *a* holds a belief that p. In order to determine whether *a* is justified in holding this belief, we might ask her to provide us with the reasons for which she believes that p. The skeptic then observes that the agent will be unable, in principle, to provide a satisfactory response to this request. If she presents some new belief, *q*, as grounds for believing that *p*, then she succeeds only in deferring the problem. In order for *q* to serve as good grounds for *p*, there must in turn be some grounds for believing that *q*. However, when asked to explain what grounds she has for believing *q*, the agent is faced with a trilemma. If she continues with the strategy of introducing a new belief, this time as grounds for *q*, then she has clearly embarked on an infinite regress. But the only other options appear to be to circle back on some belief that has already been mentioned, or else simply cease to provide further reasons. Since neither of the three options presents a course of action that is capable of redeeming the claim that the belief is justified, it appears that the agent cannot have any justified beliefs. The chain of inferences that supports any belief must be infinite, or else be circular, or else have an arbitrary stopping point.

The structure of this argument should be familiar. It is similar to the causal regress argument that has animated philosophical speculation about the origins of the universe and existence of God since Aristotle.[19] According to the most influential version, since all motion in an object must be communicated to it from some object that is already in motion, there is a problem explaining where all this motion could come from. If the chain is infinite, then there is no first mover, and hence there can be no motion at all. Thus there must be an unmoved mover somewhere that gets the whole process going.

People have argued, using a similar structure of reasoning, that there must be "unmoved movers" in the realm of belief. If we assume, along with the skeptic, that inferential chains should not be circular and cannot be infinite, then we are left with the conclusion that all justification must eventually terminate at some point. These "foundational" beliefs will be the unmoved movers of the epistemic realm. The same argument can just as easily be made in the case of desire. Thus when Williams talks about the agent's "subjective motivational set" or Smith about the agent's "unmotivated desires," what they are really talking about are the unmoved movers of the practical domain.[20] Both tacitly rely on regress arguments to establish the existence of such entities. In order to determine whether agent a has a good reason to perform action p, we must ask her for an explanation. According to the teleological argument, this will take the form of a desire for p. If we inquire further into why the agent desires p, then according to the desire-in desire-out thesis, the rationalizing explanation must cite some antecedent desire as the grounds for p, for example, a desire for q (along with some belief about the probability of q given p). However, in order for the desire for q to serve as a good reason for p, there must in turn be some reason for desiring q. The same trilemma appears: either an infinite chain of rationalizing desires must be advanced, or the chain of reasons must circle back on itself, or it must simply end with a desire that is not subject to further rationalizing explanation.

Taken at face value, the skeptical regress argument suggests the very radical conclusion that these unmoved movers are *arbitrary*.[21] Such a view would imply a genuinely noncognitivist stance toward desire. For example, one might suggest that the justifications we provide for our desires are simply rationalizations, in the Freudian sense of the term. According to such a view, our desires are a product of purely irrational processes, but we become quite adept at telling "justificatory" stories about where they come from, what licenses them, and how they are related to one another. These stories are never satisfactory, and in principle never can be, because the justificatory chains would go on forever if we didn't choose to stop them at some arbitrary point.

This view is a fair bit more extreme than what most Humeans have in mind. The more common use of the regress argument has not been to establish the thoroughgoing skeptical conclusion, but rather to suggest a certain form of subjectivism. Take, for instance, Hume's use of it:

> It appears evident that the ultimate ends of human actions can never, in any case, be accounted for by *reason*, but recommend themselves entirely to the sentiments and affections of mankind, without any dependence on the intellectual faculties. Ask a man *why he uses exercise*; he will answer, *because he desires to keep his health*. If you then enquire, *why he desires health*, he will readily reply, *because sickness is painful*. If you push your enquiries farther, and desire a reason *why he hates pain*, it is impossible he can ever give any. This is an ultimate end, and is never referred to any other object.[22]

What Hume suggests here is not that the regress must end at some arbitrary point, but rather that it must end at a very specific point, namely, in a desire that is "given," such as the desire to avoid pain. Thus the regress argument is not used to establish a skeptical position, but rather a foundationalist one (and thus the Humean position is better described as a form of "foundationalism about practical reason" rather than "skepticism about practical reason"). The foundationalist strategy for responding to the regress argument involves two major points of agreement with the skeptic.[23] First, the foundationalist agrees that infinite chains of justification are unacceptable, and that it is either false or pointless to ascribe an infinite chain of supporting beliefs to an agent. Second, the foundationalist agrees with the skeptic that circular reasoning is unacceptable, and that insofar as the agent's belief system is rational, it does not exhibit a circular structure. As a result, the foundationalist grabs hold of the third horn of the trilemma, and accepts that justifications do at some point simply run out.

Where the foundationalist disagrees with the skeptic is over the significance of the last point. The epistemological foundationalist argues that the agent can be justified in holding certain beliefs by virtue of some property that these beliefs possess, other than their inferential dependence on other beliefs. For instance, certain beliefs might be intrinsically justified by virtue of their content, or causally connected to an empirical state of affairs, or known through some quality of the subject's experience. Thus the foundationalist divides the agent's beliefs into two types, those that are justified inferentially and those that are known directly. The latter are often referred to as "basic beliefs." The regress argument does not threaten the claim that the agent has justified beliefs, so long as her inferential beliefs occur in justificatory chains that terminate with some set of basic beliefs.

In this view, the regress argument is important because it tells us something about the structure of the agent's belief system. Since the skeptical conclusion is manifestly unacceptable, what the regress argument shows is that every rational belief must, in the end, be justified by some basic belief that is itself not capable of further justification. This means that any rationalizing explanation of a belief must at some point end with a basic belief that provides, in some sense, the "ultimate" explanation for an agent's holding the other beliefs in the associated inferential chain. In the empiricist tradition, it is common to imagine that these "basic beliefs" are simple observational sentences. "The table is brown," according to this view, is a basic belief, because it cannot be inferentially justified; it can only be confirmed through direct confrontation with experience—looking at the table.

Thus foundationalist views tend to be characterized not only by the claim that our beliefs are stratified into two classes—basic beliefs and theoretical beliefs—but also by the idea that there is some characteristic that all of these basic beliefs share, by virtue of which they possess this status. The standard empiricist view is that the set of basic beliefs are those formed directly through the exercise of our senses. (During the medieval period, the more common view was that divine revelation gave us the essential set of premises from which we could then work.)

What Hume does, in the passage cited above, is adapt this argument to the case of desire. According to this view, our desires are stratified into two classes—motivated and unmotivated. What do the unmotivated desires have in common? Here the subjectivist argues that the unmotivated desires come to us not through our external senses, but rather through our internal ones. They come from our immediate experience of our own bodily states—our thirst, our hunger, our anger, and in some more reductive versions, simply our own pleasure and pain. Hume groups these together under the general category of the "passions." These passions constitute the set of intrinsic desires, and all other motives are, in some way or other, derived from one of these primitive passions.

It sometimes escapes notice that this sort of subjectivism still stands in need of philosophical motivation. Hume does not really offer any argument to show that the chain of explanations must end in one of our bodily states (as opposed to something else). And not everyone sympathetic to the account agrees with Hume's identification of unmotivated desires with "the passions."[24] What these theorists take away from the argument is the conclusion that each agent's actions are in the end motivated by a core set of desires that are themselves not the product of deliberation, and hence not open to rational revision.[25] But the fact that they are not open to further deliberation does not mean that they are subjective. Aristotle used an almost identical regress argument in the *Nichomachean Ethics* in order to demonstrate the existence of a single "best good," which must be the same for all persons. Thomas Aquinas adapted this argument only slightly in order to show that the "unmoved mover" of the practical realm must be the same as the "unmoved mover" of the physical realm, that is, God.[26] In fact, the foundationalist conception of practical justification continues to enjoy enormous popularity among Christian theologians, precisely because it shows the contingency of all human ends. This is the philosophical basis for the doctrine that the exercise of human reason must always be supplemented by divine *authority*.

In contemporary philosophy, foundationalists like Christine Korsgaard continue to use the same sort of regress arguments in defense of objectivist metaethical views. Korsgaard argues:

> Justification, like explanation, seems to give rise to an infinite regress: for any reason offered, we can always ask why. If complete justification of an end is to be possible, something must bring this regress to a stop; there must be something about which it is impossible or unnecessary to ask why. This will be something unconditionally good. Since what is unconditionally good will serve as the condition of the value of other good things, it will be the source of value. Practical reason, then, has the noninstrumental task of establishing what is unconditionally good.[27]

This style of argument is surprisingly pervasive. Nagel employs the same line of reasoning to establish the need to ground practical reasoning in an ultimate "interpretation" of agency that transcends any particular justification:

> For if we justify a requirement, it is in terms of a principle from which that requirement follows, perhaps with the aid of further conditions. But that principle must itself represent a requirement, or else what it is adduced to justify will not be one. Therefore any requirement which we set out to justify will not be ultimate. Something beyond justification is required.[28]

Thus the mere fact that there must be some set of unmoved movers in the practical realm does not mean that they must be physiologically based. Humeans are subjectivists, insofar as they believe that the set of basic motives can vary from person to person, or from time to time. Nagel and Korsgaard on the other hand are objectivists, insofar as they believe that the point at which justification is exhausted will be one that is the same for all persons, and will thus command convergence of practical judgment. It has become a common strategy among objectivists to argue that the type of unmoved movers appealed to by subjectivists (e.g., somatic states like hunger) fail to provide genuine "reasons" for action, since the mere fact that one feels this or that does not in itself give one grounds for acting in one way rather than another. The same sort of regress can be pursued: "Why should you want to satisfy your hunger?" or "Why should you want to experience pleasure?" or more radically, "Why should you want to satisfy your desires?"[29] The claim, essentially, is that the subjectivist position collapses into the radical skeptical position, and so we wind up, according to that conception, having no reason to do anything. This is thought to push one in the direction of objectivism (although it represents, in the end, simply another attempt to use general skepticism as a strategy for refuting a particular philosophical position). In any case, nothing in the teleological argument, the desire-in desire-out principle, or the foundationalist response to the regress argument helps to mediate this dispute.

The fact that all parties to this debate share a foundationalist conception of justification does tend to generate a presumption in favor of the Humean view (and may thus represent a tactical error on the part of the objectivist). The reason is simply that once the passions, sentiments, and other somatic states are taken out of the picture, the remaining candidates for "unmoved mover" are all extremely abstruse. Both Nagel and Korsgaard wind up claiming that all our motives ultimately stem from a certain conception of our own agency. Taken literally, this generates a sort of preposterous intellectualism, simply because any end sufficiently general to be shared by all persons is destined to be exceedingly abstract. The ultimate motives of our acts tend to become nth order desires (or else desires with conceptual content that only people with advanced university degrees might be thought to possess). And no matter how normative it may be, the theory is still supposed to provide something like a recognizable reconstruction of our actual deliberative processes. So these theorists wind up committing themselves to the claim that, ultimately, we drink coffee in the morning not because we want to feel more alert, but because we want to maintain the integrity of our rational agency. Given a choice between Hume's account of "the passions" and this sort of intellectualism, I'm sure most people would be inclined to accept the passions as the best candidate for unmoved mover.

But this is a false dilemma. It is important to remember that the various candidates for unmoved mover are all purely theoretical posits. It is not as though the presence of "unmotivated desires" or a "subjective motivational set" was an empirical discovery, made by psychologists in a lab somewhere. These entities were posited by philosophers, in order to put forward a foundationalist response to the regress problem. The theory that necessitates them is the same theory that requires us to posit basic beliefs in epistemology. However, outside the context of debates in moral philosophy, foundationalism is regarded as a deeply troubled philosophical doctrine. The problem stems mainly from a widespread inability to make any sense out of the idea of a basic belief. (Indeed, both "unmotivated desires" and "basic beliefs" are clear instances of what Wilfrid Sellars referred to as "the given," when talking about "the Myth of the Given.")[30] A recent resurgence of interest in coherentist and contextualist models of justification stems directly from the perceived failure of the foundationalist project. Thus before going on to evaluate the merits of subjectivist and objectivist theories of motivation, it is worth examining the foundationalist theory of justification more closely, in order to see how it fails to provide an adequate response to the regress problem.

5.3.   Problems with Foundationalism

To recap briefly: the type of radical noncognitivism about desire that dominated early modern philosophy of mind has largely been set aside in contemporary philosophical discussion. While agents no doubt have a wide range of behavioral dispositions that are devoid of cognitive content, when we talk about preferences or desires we are dealing with intentional states. It is very difficult to sustain a noncognitivism thesis when desire is conceived of as an intentional state, since desires behave in very much the same way that beliefs do in inferential contexts. As a result, subjectivism has become more persuasive than noncognitivism as a theory of desire. What the subjectivist argues is that despite having certain similarities, there is a fundamental asymmetry between belief and desire. While beliefs can be expected to command convergence, we cannot expect agreement when it comes to questions of desire.[31] The regress argument is drawn on to show that there must be some class of noninferentially grounded "basic beliefs" and "unmotivated desires" to serve as a foundation for the rest. The reason for the asymmetry is that while beliefs are "ultimately" grounded in our experience of the external world, desires are ultimately grounded in an experience of our own bodily states. The agent derives an entitlement to believe that the ball is red through simple observation of the red ball, just as she derives an entitlement to the desire for a drink through the direct experience of feeling thirsty. Because the world is shared, but feelings are not, there is reason to expect agreement among persons in the former case but not the latter.

Both of these theories derive a measure of plausibility from the absence of attractive alternatives. If one accepts the need for a set of basic beliefs to serve as a foundation for all the rest, then simple empirical observation reports seem to be the best candidate. Similarly, if one accepts the need for a set of unmotivated desires, then our basic bodily urges seem to fit the bill. And it is true that if our desires were all ultimately based on an immediate experience of bodily states, then at some level there would be no arguing over taste. The question is whether our intentional states have this sort of fixed hierarchical structure. After all, if the foundationalist picture were correct, then it would be difficult to have any sort of productive argument over beliefs either. Just as all of our desires would be grounded in our bodily states, all of our beliefs would be ultimately grounded in a direct experience of brute facts. In cases of disagreement, one could look over the inferential sequences that led to the divergent conclusions, checking for errors. But absent such obvious flaws, there would be nothing that could be done, short of confronting one's opponent with the brute facts that led to one's own conclusion.

Real arguments, however, are seldom settled simply by putting our beliefs before the tribunal of experience (something that philosophers, more than anyone, should know). Since W. V. O. Quine's "Two Dogmas of Empiricism," it has become a commonplace observation that the confirmation of our beliefs by experience is not punctual, but at least moderately holistic.[32] In other words, we cannot take one single belief and directly compare it to the world, to see whether it is true or false. The experience confirms the belief only when combined with a large set of complementary beliefs. Seeing that the ball is red entitles us to claim that "the ball is red" only if it is observed under standard lighting conditions, by a competent observer, and so forth. In other words, the belief must not only "fit" the experience, it must also "fit" with a whole set of other beliefs. If the latter type of fit is not there, then we tend to doubt the integrity of the experience. Furthermore, it is possible to preserve any particular belief, despite some recalcitrant experience, if we are willing to make sufficient adjustments elsewhere in our system of belief.

Susan Haack introduced a useful way of thinking about the character of our belief system by comparing it to a crossword puzzle.[33] There are two elements that support any given solution to a crossword: the clues, which give us punctual evidence concerning the correctness of particular words; and the "crossings" of the entries, which provide holistic and incremental support for sets of words. In a good crossword, the solution tends to be underdetermined by the clues alone. In many cases, there will be several different words that satisfy certain clues equally well. One has to build the case for one of the options by filling in some letters from other words. Sometimes one has to go back and undo a bunch of entries, because they fail to "fit" with the others. Sometimes words get entered purely as a consequence of other entries, while the clue remains uninterpretable. So if someone asks "why is this word here?" the answer may refer to the clue, or it may refer to the fit with other words, or both.

The importance of this analogy is that it helps us to state quite clearly why the idea of a basic belief is problematic. Even though there is a clue for every entry, we generally cannot solve a crossword simply by going through the list of clues. What we tend to do instead is pick some clues that seem reasonably determinate, then use these to build inferential support for the other entries. However, no entry is immune from subsequent revision, if it turns out not to fit with the other constraints. Even the most obvious answer to an easy clue may turn out to be incorrect. Thus the distinction between those entries one takes to be the "foundation" of one's solution and those one takes to be "derived" is extremely ad hoc, and liable to change.

Furthermore, consider how someone who proposes a solution to a particular crossword puzzle would respond to a regress-style argument. When asked to justify a particular entry, she would probably start by referring to the clue. But the questioner might not find this clue decisive, and might propose some other word of equal length. At this point, the author of the solution would have to make an inferential move, appealing to the correctness of some other entry that intersects that word. If asked to justify that entry, she might refer again to the relevant clue. But the questioner might not find that clue decisive either, forcing the author to appeal again to another intersecting word, and a third inference. This process can go on and on, and will eventually have to cycle back on itself. There is no reason to think that there should be one ultimate regress-stopper. It is always possible that there is a clue somewhere that admits of only one solution, but this need not be the case. Furthermore, the absence of such a decisive clue would not stop us from saying that a particular solution, taken as a whole, is correct.

Our belief system appears to have very much the same structure. The clues in a crossword puzzle are like the empirical observations that underlie our beliefs. Of course, our belief system is vastly more indeterminate, because unlike a crossword, where there is a clue for every entry, the vast majority of our beliefs have only the most tenuous connection to any empirical experience. However, even those that do relate directly to experience have no fixed role. They can serve as evidence for other beliefs, but they can also stand in need of justification. The distinction is ad hoc, and may vary from context to context. As Michael Williams observes:

> Consider Wittgenstein's remark that "My having two hands is, in normal circumstances, as certain as anything that I could produce in evidence for it." Entered in the right setting, a claim to have two hands might function like a foundationalist's basic statement, providing a stopping place for requests for evidence or justification.... But in other circumstances *the very same claim* might be contestable and so might stand in need of evidential support. The content of what is claimed does not guarantee a claim some particular epistemic standing.[34]

It is a general feature of the game of giving and asking for reasons that it contains a set of language-entry moves. For instance, one is entitled to say "the ball is red" on observing a red ball. It is what Robert Brandom calls a "default entitlement," attached to a commitment "in virtue of the circumstances in which it is tokened," namely, the fact that it "is elicited through the exercise of a reliable differential responsive reporting disposition."[35] However, this content is still not interpersonally available. My seeing a red ball does not, as such, entitle others who have not seen it to claim that there is a red ball nearby. Their entitlement to this assertion is inferential, and depends, in standard cases, on a reliability inference (as Brandom has observed).[36] A second person may infer the presence of a red ball from the fact that I am a competent observer of red balls, that I speak English correctly, and that I claim to have seen a red ball. This reliability inference is also available to the speaker, if I am challenged to show that the ball is indeed red. The fact that I, a competent observer, am inclined to describe the object as a red ball constitutes prima facie evidence that it is indeed a red ball. So as in the case of the crossword, I can attempt a direct justification ("Look, there it is!"), or an inferential one that appeals to my own reliability ("I've seen a lot of red balls in my day").[37]

It is also possible to elaborate somewhat more the theoretical steps "between" the observation report and the object of experience. As Brandom observes, the entitlement to make a language-entry move differs from person to person, depending on that person's competence at both observation and inference. Following Quine, he gives the example of physicists using a bubble chamber to detect the presence of mu-mesons.[38] Initially, we would want to say that they infer the presence of mu-mesons from the hooked vapor trail that these particles leave in the chamber. However, as the process of observation becomes more routine, and everyone has thoroughly mastered the theory that explains why mu-mesons and only mu-mesons leave this particular type of trail, we should not hesitate to say that the scientists simply "see" mu-mesons in the bubble chamber. After all, we do not really "see" regular physical objects either, but only light that has bounced off them. And we don't really see that either, just a certain retinal image of that light. The regress problem here is obvious. What we can and cannot see is therefore not decided by our perceptual system; it is decided by the entry moves we are entitled to make into our language games. Thus "what is observable varies from community to community."[39] The question of *what* we can see is determined by the position in the language game that we are entitled to take up on the basis of some state of the environment. Some people under some circumstances are entitled to take up a position "deeper" into the game, a position that others are only entitled to arrive at through inference.

This means that when our entitlement to a particular observation is challenged, we can always come up with some inference that supports it, which takes as its premise some language-entry move that has broader entitlement-conditions. We almost always jump over several steps that, under some conditions, we may need to make explicit. If the scientist is asked "How do you know there is a mu-meson?" she can say "Because mu-mesons leave a hooked vapor trail, thanks to the superheated liquid within the chamber." Similarly, the observer of the ball could say "Well I saw this red thing go by, and I figured it was the ball that those kids were playing with." Observation reports can in principle always be "unpacked" in this way, although we have no need to do so in the standard run of cases. Furthermore, the fact that these reports can be further unpacked does not mean that these elaborating inferences "really" (in the realist sense of the term) underlie either our capacity to make the observation or our entitlement to it.

What all of these features of our justificatory practices suggest is that there is no simple answer to the question whether a particular belief is justified. Foundationalism has made us accustomed to the idea that "being justified" is some kind of property belonging to beliefs, independent of their discursive context. But what we really are asking, when we pose such questions, is whether a particular agent is *entitled* to a particular claim. Entitlement is fixed by the game of giving and asking for reasons, which is a social practice. Thus securing entitlement is a matter of satisfying the normative assessments of the participants in this practice (which is what accounts for the "externalist" observation that agents can be entitled to claims without knowing that they are).[40] So when asked to defend a particular entitlement, there is no natural end point to the discussion. As in the case of the crossword puzzle, the explanation ends when a consideration is reached that is decisive for everyone involved.

5.4.   Practical Reasoning without Foundations

Supposing that all this is true, what does it imply for our understanding of desire? Most obviously, it shows that the epistemic regress argument needs to be approached with considerable caution. One could easily use this argument to show that a crossword puzzle is unsolvable, even when this is clearly not the case. Thus the sort of casual deployment of regress arguments that one finds in the literature on practical reason is unacceptable. Anyone who is at all skeptical about foundationalism should be immediately suspicious of the claim that agents come equipped with some single set of "unmotivated desires," or a "subjective motivational set." There is no question that we have all sorts of desires, and that these desires are caught up in a web of inferential relations with one another, but the idea that these desires must "ultimately" be grounded in some set of primitive states is a highly contentious philosophical claim.

To say this is not to deny that there are a set of simple language-entry moves available in the case of desires. These are in some cases quite similar to those governing observation reports. Under standard circumstances, feeling a pang of hunger entitles an individual to assert "I would like to eat," or to acquire the desire to eat. The important point is that somatic bodily states of the type Humeans appeal to in their account of the passions are not themselves desires, any more than patterns of retinal irradiation are beliefs. The somatic state simply constitutes stimulus that may form the basis for a reliable responsive disposition, and thus serve as grounds for a legitimate language-entry move, in this case the acquisition of a desire. Thus Hume's account of the passions is wrong *for exactly the same reason that his account of the impressions is wrong.*[41] It is a version of "the Myth of the Given."[42]

The Humean theory clearly sounds most plausible when applied to very basic desires, relating to the direct satisfaction of our bodily needs (as opposed to abstract preferences concerning states of the world that have no connection to our own person). However, even given this very restricted set of desires, the nonfoundationalist account is both conceptually and empirically more plausible. Rather than thinking of each basic physical desire as "punctually" related to some underlying somatic condition, we should think of the entire set as something like a *model* constructed by the agent of his own bodily needs. Even when we experience what we think of as very powerful, highly directed physical needs, most of the time what we are actually doing is providing an *interpretation* of an extremely diffuse and indeterminate state of physiological arousal. In this respect, Humeans massively overestimate both the specificity of our "passions" and the level of introspective access that we have to them.[43] Psychologists have shown that people can very easily be tricked into forming the "wrong" desire, by putting them in an environment that encourages them to misidentify the source of the somatic arousal they experience. In one particularly clever experiment, subjects were tricked into misidentifying a fear of heights as sexual attraction (proving that even sexual desire is not self-identifying).[44] People have to learn how to figure out what they want—and they rely heavily on cultural knowledge and environmental cues in order to do so. Furthermore, much of the cultural knowledge that they do employ is unreliable, which contributes to the widespread phenomenon that psychologists refer to as "miswanting."[45] This is particularly true in dynamic contexts, where people rely upon what Daniel Kahneman calls a "lay theory of hedonic changes" that exhibits only "mediocre accuracy."[46]

The type of systematic misalignment of people's official "wants" with their underlying affective and somatic states is very difficult to reconcile with the Humean account, which posits a straightforward identity of the two at the foundational level. Thus a better way to think about the agent's desires—even the ones we commonly regard as physiologically grounded—is as a theoretically informed model, an explicit representation constructed at the level of the intentional planning system of that person's own needs (which includes some conception of how to take care of one's own body).[47] From this perspective, whether or not someone "experiences" a particular desire is directly analogous to whether someone "sees" a particular object. We take it for granted, for instance, that most people are able to directly experience thirst. We have direct internal access to that somatic state, and can therefore use this as grounds for taking up the position, in the game of giving and asking for reasons, that constitutes a desire for a drink of water. Thus feeling thirst and then acquiring the desire to drink something is a language-entry move. It represents, as in the case of experience and belief, the exercise of a reliable responsive disposition—namely, the ability to act one way rather than another in response to different states of the environment.[48] Naturally, no language-entry move is self-licensing and uncontestable. In particular, our ability to detect the need for fluids is not entirely reliable. Thus we are able to use explicit reasoning to augment whatever innate capacities are available at the level of the adaptive unconscious. For example, we may not naturally identify having a headache while in the hot sun with needing water. However, when we learn to identify signs of heat exhaustion, we can start to take this as evidence of thirst. In effect, we can use our linguistic inferential capacity to train ourselves to become better detectors of a physiological need for water. One could argue that we are not really feeling thirsty in this case, we are merely inferring that our body needs water, on the basis of symptoms other than the feeling of thirst. But who is to say that there is only one way of feeling thirsty? And how do we know that as children, we weren't simply taught to infer that our bodies need water from other symptoms, like dryness in our mouths? What Brandom's example of the cloud chamber and the mu-mesons suggests is that we need not insist on a single "correct" answer here, either in the case of belief or desire.

To expand the analogy, consider the diabetic whose body needs an occasional shot of insulin. Clearly we have no innate ability to feel a need for insulin. Initially we have only a set of symptoms, and a scientific theory that hooks them all together. In other words, the diabetic starts with a purely cognitive model—that is, a representation—of what her body needs. But who is to say that, after years of injections, she does not simply experience the symptoms *as* a need for insulin? Or the asthmatic experiences the slight wheeze as a need to increase his intake of bronchiodilator? It is no different from the scientists in the lab learning to see mu-mesons. The medical analogies show that caring for our bodies is not something that comes automatically; it is something we learn to do. Our capacity to form representations—beliefs and desires—massively augments that capacity. However, because much of the learning is done in childhood, and thus is not something we can clearly remember having done, it is tempting to imagine that the standard set of basic desires is just given.

This is why "raw feels" provide only a defeasible license for desires, and why it is always possible to ask further questions, such as "Why should you care whether you feel thirsty?" But this should not mislead us into thinking that feeling thirsty does not, in the ordinary run of cases, give us a reason to drink something. The fact that one can initiate a regress does not mean that our ordinary judgments are not well founded, or that desires as such do not provide reasons for action without further supplementation by higher-order principles.[49] Desires, like beliefs, are deontic statuses, and so we do not need a reason to act on our desires; on the contrary, desire-talk is simply an oblique way of talking about reasons for action. The correct way of formulating the anti-Humean point is to observe that the mere experience of a somatic state does not provide nondefeasible grounds for adoption of a corresponding desire.

It is very important to recognize also that the model we construct of our own needs contains very significant theoretical elements.[50] Furthermore, the resources we use to construct it are largely acquired from the ambient culture. If this were not the case, then there would be no way to explain the massive cultural variation we see in the ways people conceive of their own inner states. Experiences of emotion provide a very clear-cut example. There is evidence that certain very basic states of arousal are culturally universal: fear, anger, startle, laughter, and so on. However, even in these cases, the type of "raw feel" generated by the emotional state is highly indeterminate, and individuals are not able to reliably determine which emotion they are experiencing through introspection.[51] And as we have seen, introspection generally gives them no capacity to determine which object in the environment provoked the state of arousal. Thus in the cases where emotions exhibit intentional structure, as in the case of someone who is "afraid of x," the idea that the state is provoked by x is typically an interpretive gloss contributed by the individual (and may be entirely a confabulation).[52]

Even more noteworthy are the enormous cultural differences in the range of emotional states that individuals are thought to experience.[53] Many of the states posited are powerfully structured by quite abstract theories about the human person. People often find themselves feeling restless and unhappy, for instance, without having the faintest idea what is causing this unhappiness. Their attempts to diagnose the problem draw heavily on theoretical constructs. Of course, to claim that our desires are a model of our own needs is not to say that they are simply made up (or that "thinking makes it so" in this domain). It is commonplace for philosophers to talk about the underdetermination of theory by evidence in the case of belief. Similarly, we might say that there is an underdetermination of desire by "feels." In most situations, there are all sorts of possible interpretations of what we're experiencing and feeling. However, this does not mean that there are not better and worse theories. It is quite obvious that some people have better models of their own needs than others, in part because they are more attentive to their bodies, or their behavioral dispositions. (Psychologist Timothy Wilson has suggested that, given the dramatic limitations of introspection, people can do a much better job at figuring out what they want by observing biases in their own actions, combined with their own "first impulses" when it comes to behavior.)[54] In many cases, the "official" desires and attitudes that people hold are entirely inconsistent with their subintentional behavioral dispositions (which psychologists elicit in various ways, typically through tasks that demand very fast responses, and so do not permit processing by the slower intentional planning system).[55]

As in the case of belief, when problems show up with an individual's system of desires, they tend not to be punctual. It is typically not the case that an agent "thinks" that he desires p, whereas "in fact" he desires q. Both confirmation and disconfirmation are holistic. Individuals with bad models of their needs tend to find themselves experiencing inchoate frustration, anxiety, regret, or some other highly diffuse condition. It often takes a lengthy trial-and-error process to determine what is needed to relieve a particular state of tension. Furthermore, the consequences of having a bad model at the level of desire is not that the body steps up and imposes some other desire, but that the individual suffers a more general loss of intentional control (acting impulsively, out of frustration, anger, or anxiety) and in the long term exhibits spontaneous behavioral trends that are in tension with his "official" plans (and thus behaves in a self-defeating manner).

Another complication routinely ignored by Humeans is that most of the desires we act on are not occurrent, in the sense that we are not "experiencing" them at the time of deliberation (i.e., there is no phenomenological correlate). Most of our current desires depend in important ways on guesswork about our future desires (known as "affective forecasting"). As it turns out, most of us are not particularly good at doing this sort of guesswork.[56] In many cases, predictions made by complete strangers are as reliable as "self-forecasting" on the part of individuals.[57] This raises serious questions about how large a role introspection plays in determining an individual's system of desires, which in turn casts doubt on the Humean view. After all, if the Humean account of desire were correct, shouldn't individuals enjoy some sort of *advantage* over strangers when it comes to figuring out how to generate satisfying experiences for themselves?

This literature points to an important yet often overlooked aspect of our system of desire, namely, the active role that the individual plays in scheduling or establishing priorities with respect to the satisfaction of these desires. Just as somatic stimulus is extremely diffuse, its intensity level is also quite indeterminate. Generally speaking, the intentional planning system is not afflicted by a paucity of stimulus. On the contrary, at any given time, dozens of different systems at the level of the adaptive unconscious will be clamoring for attention. Even pain does not have an automatic override, but has to compete with other systems for attention (which is why people who suffer an injury while engaging in a very intense activity may not feel pain until after they stop what they are doing). Thus a major activity of the intentional planning system involves taming this cacophony of impulses into an orderly system of desire, then scheduling them into a sequential plan (e.g., "first I'm going to eat breakfast, then I'm going to go over to the couch and read the newspaper, etc."). This is informed by a very general sense, developed through experience, of which needs can most easily be "put off" and for how long. Forming a desire to do x at time t always involves deferring the satisfaction of dozens of other impulses (some of which will simply be ignored, while others will be scheduled for later). The way an individual discounts future satisfaction can be seen to be based, in part, on her estimates of what can be put off and for how long. Again, failure to carry out this task effectively can lead to losses of intentional control, or else the need to rearrange one's plans in response to the unexpected persistence or intensity of a certain somatic stimulus.

This is why psychologists (i.e., those who study the mind empirically) typically include "inhibitory control" as one of the central functions of the intentional planning system. Consider the following (fairly standard) statement of the "executive function" of intentional planning: "The cognitive abilities subsumed within this construct include attentional control, previewing, strategic goal planning, temporal response sequencing, self- and social monitoring, abstract reasoning, cognitive flexibility, hypothesis generation, and the ability to organize and adaptively use information contained in working memory"[58] This sort of monitoring and control involves much more than simply weighing one desire against another. It involves fairly systematic "vetoing" of behavioral impulses. Yet this sort of function—absolutely essential to the control of aggressivity, in particular—has no correlate in Humean psychology (or sentimentalist moral theories more generally).

The fact that the intentional planning system exercises general executive control accounts for the importance of *values*, and other cultural influences, in our system of preference. Bodily states are simply too diffuse to provide us with a ranking of possible outcomes in the world, especially given the type of fine-grained partitioning of the set of possible outcomes that our intentional planning system is capable of working with. Hobbes thought that before acting, the faculty of the imagination presented the set of available options to the agent's consciousness. The agent then consulted his inner passions to see which state evoked the greatest attraction, or the least aversion. But this model is not realistic, even in the case of our very immediate bodily needs. It is fantastical when we consider more abstract preferences, such as our attitudes toward the actions of people we have never met, our preferences regarding political parties or public policy initiatives, or our concern for the welfare of future generations.[59] It is because of this indeterminacy that individuals turn to cultural templates in order to know what to want. One can think of values as a set of culturally transmitted rankings of states of the world relative to one another. They are, in other words, *culturally transmitted preference orderings*. The central vehicle through which this transmission occurs is role modeling and dramatic narrative. This is where we learn that family is important, life is precious, cruelty is a vice, there can be nobility in suffering, and so on. Sometimes these values reaffirm existing behavioral dispositions, but quite often they run contrary (e.g., many of the values governing sexuality run against the grain of our dispositions, sometimes unnecessarily so, other times quite usefully). Most narrative is fundamentally concerned with either reaffirming these rankings or exploring conflicts between the various criteria.

These values are often regarded as irredeemably subjective. According to one popular view of the matter, values all derive their authority from some background set of "ultimate values," which are themselves beyond further justification. They are, in Max Weber's famous phrase, like "rival gods and demons"—since disputes among them cannot be rationally mediated, only fought over. Yet the problem with this argument is that it relies on the same sort of epistemic regress argument that led Humeans to posit unmotivated desires (in fact, "ultimate values," according to this conception, just are a class of unmotivated desires). Yet there are very few systems of ethical conviction that start out positing a set of ultimate values, then proceed to deduce the rest. The kinds of everyday values that are reflected in our conduct are part of a theory that we adopt, designed to make sense out of our experience—both our inner experience and our experience of social life. It is a theory of what we should want. Where there are fundamental posits, or ultimate values, these tend to have been introduced post hoc, through abstraction from the more concrete preference patterns at play. For example, the role that happiness plays in various forms of *eudaemonistic* or virtue ethics is comparable to the role that utility plays in decision theory. It is not an underlying state; it is a piece of expressive vocabulary introduced in order to engage in higher-order talk about practical reason. Thus it is backward to say that "happiness" is an ultimate value, and that all the rest are deduced through constitutive and instrumental reasoning.

The idea that values are subjective and irrational has unfortunately become a dominant element in our "folk sociology," which therefore treats values as being primarily inculcated through early childhood socialization, or some other noncognitive process. This sometimes occurs. But individuals also integrate new values into their systems of desire through purely cognitive processes. There are a variety of highly elaborate value systems in circulation. Sometimes people are exposed to just one, and therefore adhere to it throughout life from force of habit, or through lack of a better alternative. But others may find that one or another system of values "chimes" with them more effectively, and therefore adopt some or all of it. Or they may experience a "crisis of meaning," through inability to decide in favor of one or another. Either way, it is difficult not to be impressed by how much cognition is involved in the entire process, and how much control and discretion individuals exercise over the outcome.

5.5. Cognitivism about Norms

The discussion so far has been aimed at showing that desires are a lot more cognitive, and a lot more similar to beliefs, than they are often taken to be. The fact that we sometimes turn back requests for justification of our desires by saying "that's just the way I feel" does not show that all of our desires are based on indefensible commitments, or that "ultimately" they are all immune to rational criticism and revision. It merely shows that, in evaluative discourse, there are certain argumentative moves that commonly function as regress-stoppers (in particular, claims that result from standard language-entry moves). Reports of occurrent "feelings" are normally taken to license desires, without the need for further justification, in the same ways that "seeings" are normally taken to license beliefs, without the need for further justification. This does not mean that they cannot in turn be questioned—especially if there is some reason to believe that normal conditions do not obtain.

The focus on desires has limited the discussion so far to one that concerns the way agents deliberate about the appropriateness of various "ends" of action. Yet as we have seen, agents also routinely adopt and respect constraints on the means that they are prepared to employ in pursuit of these ends. Their preferences take the form not only of desires to see particular outcomes achieved but also of principles that either prescribe or proscribe actions directly, independent of their consequences. Thus their overall preference orderings incorporate preferences over both actions and consequences.

The fact that principles constrain our choice of actions is such a ubiquitous feature of social interaction that it often escapes our attention. Game theorists usually incorporate it into their models simply by leaving out of their representation of a choice problem all of the options that, while physically possible, would never be performed, simply because the agents "would never dream of it." It is very common for us to preprune our decision trees this way, prior to any serious deliberation. Most people, for example, when getting on to a bus, would like to sit down. Even if all the seats are taken, it is still possible to sit on the floor, or on someone's lap. One could simply order another person out of his seat, or request that he move, or physically grab him and pull him out. Most people never even consider these options, simply because such behavior is inappropriate in the context.[60] Instead, they will often give up their seats to persons more in need of them. They will also hesitate before taking a newly vacated seat, to see if anyone else is moving for it, so that they may seem duly deferential to the needs of others. All of these constraints on the pursuit of one's objectives are a consequence of the set of social norms that govern social interactions on crowded buses (differentiated by age, gender, infirmity, and so on).

This sort of norm-conformity has traditionally been regarded, even among sociologists, as noncognitive, nonrational, and often nonintentional.[61] There are both sophisticated and unsophisticated motives for holding this position. The unsophisticated motive arises out of puzzlement over the fact that these reasons for action do not have an overtly instrumental form. Thus many theorists, impressed by the way that rules structure all of our social interactions, yet confused by the fact that conformity serves no overt purpose for the individual, have assumed that norm-conformity must be generated through some subintentional mechanism, such as habit or a conditioned response. Thus, for example, agents are thought to have been trained through socialization to act in certain ways in certain contexts, regardless of the consequences. If these agents stopped to reflect on what they were doing, it was assumed, they would find themselves with very little reason to continue acting as they had been.

The problem with this theory, as we have seen, is that it fails to explain the reflexivity that agents exhibit in norm-governed interactions.[62] By positing a subintentional mechanism to explain norm-conformity, the theory winds up treating agents as "cultural dopes," deprived of any insight or control over the motives for their own behavior—simply acting out scripts that have been instilled through socialization. Yet what one usually observes, in norm-governed interactions, is a high level of self-awareness on the part of all agents when questioned, combined with a willingness to violate the rules at will, in order to send "messages" to other agents involved in the interaction. The young man who sits on a crowded bus with his legs spread wide, straddling two seats, is not merely ignoring the needs of others so that he can sit more comfortably. He is engaging in a display of conspicuous social deviance, intentionally violating the rules in order to communicate to other passengers his lack of concern for their needs. In so doing, he also dares the other passengers to enforce the social norm, which they know that he knows that he is violating. This is what makes his behavior not just a way of sitting more comfortably, but a strategy of intimidation.

Thus the unsophisticated version of the noncognitive analysis of norm-conformity quickly runs into difficulty, simply because the respect people show for rules exhibits the same surface features that any other form of rational action exhibits: people are aware of what they are doing as they do it, their dispositions are reflectively stable, and they are able to provide an account of what they are doing, which will often involve explicit reference to the relevant rule. Social order is not a "spell" cast over us that begins to dissipate the moment that we adopt the objectivating attitude of the sociologist, or the practiced cynicism of the economist. It is extremely robust. Thus, in the absence of some kind of deeper philosophical argument, there are simply no empirical grounds for thinking that actions chosen on the basis of principles are any less rational than those chosen as a means to the satisfaction of our desires.

But what about the rationality of the principles? If a person thinks that following a rule is important, then it may be rational for that person to follow the rule. But how could anyone come to the rational conclusion that it is important to follow a rule? According to one influential line of reasoning in contemporary philosophy, one cannot. Being committed to a rule is irrational, unless this commitment at some level involves a desire. One can find a particularly clear instance of this argument in the work of John Mackie. However, on closer inspection, it turns out that this argument is just a variation of the same old foundationalist insistence that there be some set of unmoved movers in the practical realm.

Mackie starts out by granting that agents often explain their actions through appeal to "institutional reasons," and that these reasons often have a categorical form: they say "do x," not "if you want y, do x." He argues, however, that each institutional reason is a reason only for those who accept that institution.[63] But, he asks, what is the reason for the institution? It must be justified through reference to some other institution. What justifies that institution? Eventually the chain of reasons must give out. Then we will have no choice but to find some desire of the agent, "perhaps simply the desire to keep out of trouble," that explains the action. Since all of the intermediate reasons would then be contingent on this desire, they would all be reduced to hypothetical imperatives. Thus, Mackie concludes, every "categorical imperative" must eventually depend on a "hypothetical imperative," that is to say, every principled reason for action must "ultimately" depend on a desire.[64]

Another variation on this argument takes as its point of departure the observation that institutional reasons for action are "prescriptive," insofar as they specify what an agent *ought* to do. However, any argument that has a prescriptive conclusion must have, on pain of committing the naturalistic fallacy, some prescriptive statement among its premises.[65] That prescriptive premise must be licensed, in turn, by some further prescriptive statement. If one follows the justificatory chain back far enough, it is then claimed, the sequence of prescriptive premises must simply run out, and so end with an undefended assumption. (The same problem, it is assumed, does not undermine the status of descriptive statements, since the justificatory chains that support them can terminate with some brute fact, which corresponds directly to "reality.") This is simply foundationalism, presented as an argument for noncognitivism about norms.

In everyday life, of course, normative reasons for action are considered perfectly acceptable, and often serve as a stopping point for discussion. In fact, we would consider it quite odd for someone to say, on leaving a restaurant, "I know you are supposed to tip, but why did you *really* do it?" And even if someone challenges the norm, people will often appeal to further norms to justify it, without this setting off a further round of inquiry (e.g., "The minimum wage is lower for those who receive tips, so it's unfair not to tip them"). There is in fact something faintly obnoxious about the philosopher who feels entitled to opt out of any and all social institutions, simply because he or she does not feel like complying, or because the relevant social obligations are "merely institutional." This is a position that is much easier to maintain alone in the study than out in the world, where the very dense network of obligations arising from these institutions completely structures even the lowliest social interaction.

In the background of Mackie's regress argument is an image of the rational individual as one who can take a hypothetical attitude toward the entire set of norms that constitutes his or her form of life, and can thus demand that the system of social institutions as a whole be given some foundational justification. This image is, to put it mildly, sociologically naïve. It is no different in kind from the image of Descartes, alone in his study, adopting a hypothetical attitude toward his entire system of beliefs. A more appropriate image would be that of Neurath's boat—so often used to represent the way we must set about changing our system of beliefs—applied to our principles, and to the institutions that constitute our social world. Every action is taken against a massive background of social norms, which not only structures our interactions but also constitutes the matrix of intelligibility of these actions. (Parents, when socializing their children, spend a lot more time teaching them the right and wrong ways of going about things than they do teaching them facts about the physical world.) We may be able to adopt a hypothetical attitude toward particular norms, but we do so only against an enormous background of further norms, which remain taken for granted. These constitute the "regress-stoppers" in the majority of debates over the organization of social life. Thus the analysis presented here suggests that institutional reasons should be taken at face value, as reasons for action that are just as good as ones that appeal to desires or beliefs.

Of course, there is the further argument that because institutional reasons are categorical in form, they represent "external reasons" from the standpoint of the agent, and so not ones that she is necessarily committed to adopting in the form of principles. One could observe that a particular norm of politeness is observed in a society, and yet have no particular reason to respect it. I will have more to say about this problem later, but for now it is sufficient to observe that this argument in no way demonstrates the need to provide an incentive—in the ordinary sense of the term—for agents to respect institutional norms. My reason for adopting some external norm as a principle to govern my own conduct need not be a consequence of any particular desire that I have, or concern over the consequences of respecting it. I may accept the norm as a principle simply because it follows from, or coheres well with, other principles that I adhere to. Without the regress argument, there is no reason to think that this is problematic.

The more common reason for adopting a particular principle, however, arises simply from the observation that others are conforming to a norm. This is, I would argue, not a consequence of a desire to conform (any more than acquiring a desire to eat in response to a hunger pang arises from a desire to satisfy one's bodily needs). It is, rather, the exercise of a reliable responsive disposition, one that provides the basic language-entry move with respect to principles. In the same way that individuals develop certain responsive dispositions, which lead them to develop appropriate beliefs in the case of observations, or desires in the case of somatic stimulus, people also acquire rules to govern their conduct by *imitating* observed regularities of behavior in their immediate social environment. Imitation, in this respect, establishes what Ap Dijksterhuis and John Bargh refer to as "default social behavior."[66] Summarizing the relevant psychological literature, Dijksterhaus observes that imitation is absolutely ubiquitous and far more influential than we typically imagine:

> We adjust motor behavior and a range of interpersonal behaviors such as helpfulness or aggression; it affects mental performance in different ways; and it affects our attitudes. More concretely, relevant research has shown by now that imitation can make us slow, fast, smart, stupid, good at math, bad at math, helpful, rude, polite, long-winded, hostile, aggressive, cooperative, competitive, conforming, nonconforming, conservative, forgetful, careful, careless, neat, and sloppy.[67]

Conforming to the prevailing set of social norms, along with the prevailing set of normative expectations, is our default mode of social action, and thus the relevant principles (understood as the corresponding intentional states) constitute default entitlements. Yet just as in the case of desires, these default entitlement can be trumped by other considerations (such as a conflict between the prevailing norms and some more long-standing principles that the individual adheres to). Nevertheless, imitation remains the primary mechanism through which individuals acquire principles to govern their conduct (which is why the "spade turns" pretty quickly, when people are pressed to give an account of why they follow the rules that they follow).[68]

So why is this view a species of cognitivism about norms? We can represent the system of goals generated by the agent's intentional planning system as a global preference ordering of possible worlds. In practical contexts, especially in social interactions, this preference ordering will contain two analytically separable contents: desires pertaining to various outcomes, and a set of principles governing the available actions. Many of these desires and principles have their origins outside the game of giving and asking for reasons, and are acquired unreflectively, through the exercise of a disposition either in response to somatic states or patterns of social behavior. However, these "occurrent" desires and principles must be integrated, at the level of the intentional planning system, into the agent's more comprehensive (and atemporal) set of goals, projects, plans, and principles. The important point is that they are all "defeasible" at this level (i.e., they are not foundational). Thus the agent may choose to ignore a somatic stimulus, or reject a particular social practice, if she finds that it conflicts with her standing commitments. Agents exercise broad but not unlimited discretion at the level of intentional planning (as any study of the history of asceticism would suggest). Furthermore, the type of standing goals and principles that the agent subscribes to will be heavily structured by the corresponding cultural templates: values in the case of desires, social norms in the case of principles (which correspond roughly to culturally transmitted conceptions of the good and of the right, respectively). Thus there is room for productive argumentation among agents at every level, with no intentional state being entirely immune to revision. This is why people can, and do, engage in extremely profound reflection and debate, not only over what one should want but also over how one should behave.

Where noncognitive theories of motivation get it right is in drawing attention to the amount that is going on in our minds that is "encapsulated," unavailable to consciousness, or otherwise outside the purview of the intentional planning system. "Reason" is often not in the driver's seat when it comes to human behavior, yet we find it easy to fool ourselves into thinking that it is.[69] In this respect, noncognitivists point to an important feature of the mind (and expose a form of self-deception that rationalists may all too easily succumb to). The error of noncognitivists lies in thinking that this "irrational" element reaches right through *into* the intentional planning system—that there is a special class of *intentional states* (namely, desires) that are outside the scope of rational deliberation and control. This involves a category error—ascribing characteristics of the adaptive unconscious to states of the intentional planning system. Insofar as goals are linguistically formulated and subject to explicit cognitive representation, they have entered into the "space of reasons," and are subject to the same norms of rationality as any other intentional state.

5.6. Brandom on Practical Rationality

The theory of practical rationality that has been presented here is strongly influenced by Brandom's theory of meaning and his analysis of intentional states. However, Brandom takes a very different course when it comes to developing his theory of practical rationality. He begins by noting that the following are all perfectly respectable "material inferences" (i.e., moves that are available to an agent in the game of giving and asking for reasons): "Only opening my umbrella will keep me dry, so I shall open my umbrella," and "I am a bank employee going to work, so I shall wear a necktie."[70] These all start with a belief as a premise, and have an action as a conclusion (or an intention, in Brandom's view, which then licenses a language-exit move). Anyone who is impressed by the teleological argument (see section 5.1) will naturally insist that each of these inferences has a suppressed (or unstated) premise. In the first case, Brandom notes, this premise takes the form of a "desire," such as the desire to stay dry. In the second case, it takes the form of a rule, such as the dress code that governs bank employees. Brandom correctly notes that these can both be represented simply as preferences, or "pro-attitudes,"[71] with no difference in principle between them. The central question that he raises concerns the *status of these* proattitudes, and herein lies the peculiarity of Brandom's proposal.

What he argues, in effect, is that these proattitudes, which are introduced as supplementation of the material inference, are not intentional states—that is to say, are not *positions* one may take up in the game of giving and asking for reasons—but rather are a product of the expressive vocabulary that is introduced in order to articulate *moves that are available* to an agent within that game. They articulate, as Brandom puts it, "material proprieties of practical reasoning." The agent is entitled to move from the claim that opening his umbrella is the only way to stay dry to the action of opening it *because* the game of giving and asking for reasons contains a rule that allows such an agent to move from that belief to that action. The proattitude simply puts in "propositional form the endorsement of a *pattern* of inferences."[72] When questioning the accuracy of such an attribution, "the question is whether entitlement to the doxastic commitment serving as the premise is inferentially heritable by the practical commitment serving as the conclusion. To take it that it is, for a particular interlocutor, just is implicitly to attribute a desire or a preference for staying dry."[73]

This is a counterintuitive theory, but one that has considerable merit. It provides, first of all, a simple and nonregressive explanation for the fact that desires have normative authority (the elusive "source of normativity" sought by Korsgaard, among others). Desires (or proattitudes more generally) have authority not intrinsically but because they are elements of an expressive vocabulary designed specifically to articulate the content of norms-implicit-in-practice. Thus they are normative for exactly the same reason that logic is normative—because they are expressive shorthand for talking about our normative obligations.[74] The second attractive feature of Brandom's account is that it is able to explain why beliefs appear motivationally inert, whereas desires are somehow able to rouse the agent to action. (This latter, motivational aspect of desire is of course the primary intuition driving preference noncognitivism.) The asymmetry is entirely due to the fact that desires are expressive vocabulary introduced in order to articulate inferences, which are *moves* that individuals can make in the game of giving and asking for reasons. Beliefs, on the other hand, articulate *statuses* in the game, not moves, which is why they appear inert. Thus the idea that desires, as intentional states, are somehow more dynamic than beliefs arises as a consequence of a grammatical illusion (the fact that a proposition is used to describe a pattern of inference, rather than a doxastic status).

The easiest way to get an intuitive grasp of Brandom's position—and to understand the difficulties with it—is to see that it represents a simple reversal of Kant's analysis of instrumental reasoning. The primary difference between Kant's view and later formulations of the instrumental conception of rationality is that rather than talking about beliefs and desires, Kant talks about hypothetical imperatives and incentives. Hypothetical imperatives have the structure of an inference: "if you want x, then you should do y." This is what allows one to infer, on the basis of a desire for x, a practical commitment to do y. Of course, another way of expressing the hypothetical imperative would be in the form of a belief that some state obtains, such that doing y will bring about consequence x. This is precisely what contemporary decision theorists do, when treating beliefs as probability distributions over states. If one adopts the Kantian perspective, however, what decision theorists call a belief is actually just a piece of expressive vocabulary, introduced in order to articulate the inference that allows one move from a desire to an action. What Brandom has done, in his own theory, is flip this around. He treats the desire as the element that articulates the inference from a belief to an action.

Naturally, there is no simple fact of the matter that will enable us to decide whether it is the belief that "really" represents the material inference, or rather the desire. The question is one of expressive adequacy. And in this respect, it is worth noting that Brandom's proposal encounters the same difficulties that afflicted Kant's, those that eventually led decision theorists to abandon entirely the vocabulary of "ends" and "means." The problem is that treating either the belief or the desire as an oblique redescription of an inference license generates significant difficulties as soon as uncertainty is admitted into the choice problem. Once beliefs are assigned probabilities, then the agent can no longer make a rational decision with simply an ordinal ranking of possible outcomes; she must also assign priority levels to each of her desires (or preferences more generally). Yet hypothetical imperatives provide a very poor framework for the articulation of probabilistic beliefs. If one treats a belief as a doxastic status, it is easy to assign it a probability or confidence level. Treating it as an inference, on the other hand, gets more difficult. Similarly, Brandom's analysis of proattitudes as "material proprieties of practical reasoning" is very poorly suited for the articulation of desires with priority levels. Thus the need to treat practical rationality as utility-maximization (or value-maximization more generally) imposes the need to treat both beliefs and desires as distinct types of statuses in the game of giving and asking for reasons.

The problem, simply put, is that inferences of the type that Brandom describes have a truth-functional (or Boolean) logic. Assigning intensities to desires would require a Bayesian logic, in which the inference rule acted like a filter that allowed only a portion of the probability associated with the premise to be conferred on the conclusion. Thus if the agent had confidence of 0.8 that opening the umbrella is the only way to stay dry, and a moderate desire to stay dry (say, 0.6), the latter would have to be represented by saying that only a weak material inference obtains between "opening my umbrella will keep me dry" and "I shall open my umbrella," such that a 0.8 commitment in the premise generates only a 0.48 commitment to the conclusion. The advantage, on the other hand, of treating *both* beliefs and desires as premises in an inference is that one can retain a traditional Boolean logic to model the inference, and handle the probabilities/priorities as "internal" to the status that the agent has adopted.

Similarly, once preferences are assigned priority levels, it is no longer adequate for the agent simply to determine the one "top-ranked" consequence in order to make a decision. Each desire and principle generates a *pro tanto* reason in support of a particular ranking of the set of possible worlds, but determining a final preference ordering will require a weighing of all these considerations. Brandom's analysis suggests that in the absence of the expressive vocabulary of "desire," introduced in order to represent patterns of inference, the only way to engage in deliberation about what states of the world one should prefer would be to work through, hypothetically, a series of belief-to-action inferences of the form "If I thought such-and-such, then I would want to do the following, but on the other hand, I also believe something-else, so I would be somewhat more inclined to do this," and so on. This is a strikingly implausible reconstruction of the way we deliberate about our desires. The idea that there could be such an asymmetry between belief and desire therefore speaks against Brandom's theory.

5.7.   A Note on Intentions

The discussion so far has been carried out without any serious talk of *intentions*, despite the fact that much of the discussion of action theory in contemporary analytic philosophy is focused on the status of intentions. Part of the reason for this emphasis among such philosophers has been the hope that a more careful examination of these states will provide a solution to some of the classic dilemmas in game theory, such as why people cooperate in prisoners' dilemmas. The basic idea is as follows. Agents start out with beliefs and desires. These two states get hooked together through practical deliberation. However, the outcome of practical deliberation is not an action, but rather an *intention* to act. It is the intention that serves as the proximate cause of the action. With respect to the prisoner's dilemma, it has then been claimed that an agent might cooperate by virtue of a prior intention, despite the fact that reoptimization would give her a preference for defection.

The idea that practical deliberation issues in intentions is diametrically opposed to the view, which dates back to Aristotle, that the conclusion of practical reasoning is the action. Intentions get posited as an odd sort of intentional state interposed between actions and desires. What makes them unlike desires is that they do not provide independent reasons for action; they merely channel the agent's desires. Thus if the agent loses some desire, the "stranded" intention does not by itself provide any further reason to perform the action.[75] But then why posit them at all, if they do no independent work explaining action? The rationale for this prima facie violation of Occam's razor ("entities must not be multiplied without necessity") is the need to explain failed attempts.[76] Individuals often make a decision to carry out a particular action, yet are unable to carry it through. In such cases, we say that they *intended* to do it, but were prevented or unable. Thus interest in intentions has been highest among those interested in weakness of the will—since weakness of this type seems to characterize precisely the class of cases where intention and action come apart. The Aristotelian thesis is faulted for its inability to explain these failures. If our reasoning leads directly to action, how could it be that we sometimes know what is best, and yet do not do it?

This would be a somewhat weak rationale, were it not for one other aspect of the theory. The most interesting feature of intentions is that they seem quite clearly to incorporate a structure of *commitment*. An agent who intends to do x seems to be committed to doing x in a way that the agent who merely desires x is not. Thus theorists who view beliefs and desires as normatively inert states of the individual's consciousness can easily be misled into thinking that intentions represent the source of normativity. If one thinks that individuals in perfect isolation are able to have beliefs and desires, then it seems plausible to think that they can also adopt intentions in isolation. And if they can have intentions, it seems that they can make commitments.[77] Norms could then be explained as a sort of joint commitment (or a shared intention), adopted in social contexts.[78] Thus one would be able to provide the purely reductive account of social norms that has for so long eluded instrumentalist theories. The case for such an order of explanation has been developed most influentially by Michael Bratman.

Some critical attention has been focused on this last step, since we expect both cooperative and resolute behavior in many contexts where agents have had no chance to form an antecedent intention—sometimes choices get sprung on us.[79] And the previous two steps are clearly vulnerable to private-language type arguments (from the perspective that has been advanced here, any normativity enjoyed by intentions will merely be inherited from their relationship to desires). The more fundamental question, however, is whether or not our understanding of practical deliberation is enhanced through inclusion of intentions in the set of intentional states posited by the theory of action. There is no question that agents develop plans, and that there is a useful way of talking that refers to what the agent intends to do as part of one or another plan. One might also follow Donald Davidson in talking about the agent's "unconditional" or "all-out" practical judgment as her intention.[80] But neither of these ways of talking suggests that there is a distinct type of intentional state underlying these attributions, other than just beliefs and desires.

The other thing that should make us nervous about talk of intentions is the peculiar hybrid character of these states. This is not the first time that philosophers have felt the need to posit such entities. In fact, the entire discussion of intentions bears a suspicious similarly to an earlier episode in the history of philosophy, namely, the debate over sense impressions or qualia.[81] Structurally, it is easy to see that intentions perform the same function on the language-exit side, with respect to desires, that sense data were thought to perform on the language-entry side, with respect to beliefs. It is helpful, therefore, to remember why theorists considered it necessary to posit sense data, and why this sort of phe-nomenalism was ultimately abandoned.

When agents observe some state of affairs, and form a correct belief, there is no obvious "gap" between the observation and the intentional state. When an agent sees a red ball, and forms the belief "there is a red ball," there is no problem. It is only when the agent forms a false belief that we begin to suspect that there is something interposed between the object and the intentional state. When the agent sees a white ball, and forms the belief "there is a red ball," we begin to think that there is no direct connection between the belief and the object. We say that the ball *looked* red, but that it turned out not to be. This is all harmless. It becomes problematic, however, when philosophers move from this observation to the conclusion that what we *really* see are not the objects, but rather some inner state that represents them, such as an "appearance" or a "sense datum." The problem is not with the idea of an inner episode, it is with the idea that these inner episodes have propositional content (i.e., that they "rep-resent" something). Such a status would allow them to be inferentially related to the belief, yet causally connected to the state of the world.

According to the phenomenalist view, it is our knowledge of "appearances" that is fundamental. Our knowledge of the world is inferred from our contact with these "appearances." The reason for advancing such a theory is that it seems to offer support for a foundationalist account of justification. It is difficult to say that the belief "there is a red ball" is justified by the presence of the red ball, since this connection is not infallible. Agents often have mistaken percep-tions. The advantage of appearances is that they stand in incorrigible relations to the "full-blown" intentional states. The belief is always correctly related to the appearance; it is the appearance that may fail to adequately mirror the object. In other words, the breakdown will be on the causal side of the relation. The ball may be white, and look red. But if the ball looks red, then the agent will necessar-ily form the belief that it is red. Thus positing appearances seems to allow us to insulate the normativity of belief from the unreliability of our perceptions.[82]

One can see a similar pattern of thinking in recent work on intention. In ordi-nary cases, practical reasoning leads directly to action. In some cases, however, the agent fails to carry out plans that have been adopted. This suggests a gap between our intentional ~~states and our actions. So we posit a hy~~brid psycho-logical state—an inten~~tion—interposed between~~ the reasons and the world. Practical reason generates an intention, necessarily and infallibly, through an inferential mechanism. The intention then causes the agent to take action in the world. Weakness of the will arises through a breakdown on the causal side of this relation, between the intention and the action. Thus positing intentions allows us to insulate the normativity of decision from the unreliability of our actions.

The fundamental question is whether the relationship between belief and sense datum could be more fundamental than the relationship between beliefs and the world. Or as Sellars puts it, the question is whether "looks-red" could be conceptually prior to "is-red."[83] The comparable question in the case of inten-tion is whether intending to do x could be more fundamental than doing x. One way of testing our intuitions in this regard is to consider the possibility of systematic failure. If our beliefs are related to appearances, first and foremost, then it is possible for our beliefs to be systematically false. In the same way, the "priority of intention" view suggests that the agent could systematically intend to do various things, and yet never do any of them. Sellars, on the other hand, argues that both views are incoherent. If people were systematically mistaken in their use of the term "red," this would simply change the meaning of the word "red." For the same reason, "it is a necessary truth that people tend to do what they think they ought to do, for it is a necessary truth that people who occupy a linguistic position which means *I ought to do A now*, tend to do A. If they did not, the position they occupy could not mean *I ought to do A now*."[84]

Instead of getting into the full details of Sellars's critique, I would like to outline his alternative analysis (since this is, in my view, the more persuasive). Sellars's basic argument is against any sort of psychological realism about appearances and intentions, in favor of a pragmatist analysis. Our powers of observation and reporting involve the cultivation of certain responsive dispositions with respect to the environment. It is these responsive dispositions that give us the basic set of language entry moves. We say or think "there is a red ball" in reaction to red balls in the vicinity. However, the assertion that we make carries with it a whole series of commitments. One of these commitments is to our own reliability—this is what allows other people to use the assertion as a premise in their own chains of reasoning. The experience of error teaches us, however, that we are not always reliable. We may find ourselves disposed to report a red object, and yet also aware that this disposition may be falsely triggered by the presence of red lighting, and so forth. Thus we may sometimes want to report on our disposition, and yet not commit ourselves to the reliability of the report. This is what "looks" talk does. In other words, the correct analysis of "it looks to be the case that x" is "I judge that x, but don't take my word for it."

Consider now what happens on the language-exit side. Making a decision about what to do is not that different from making a decision about what to believe. In both cases, one takes up a certain commitment. The difference is that in the case of action, the conclusion of the process of deliberation is an action, not an assertion. It is, in other words, a move that takes a person out of the game of giving and asking for reasons. Such a move also carries with it commitments. In the same way that saying "the ball is red" entitles others to expect that the ball is red, saying "I shall go to the store" entitles others to expect that one will go to the store, to infer that one will be there at a certain time, and so on. However, as in the case of observation, there may be cases in which one does not want to commit oneself to this inference. For example, if one does not know what traffic will be like on the way to the store, one may want to caution people against assuming that one will be there. This is where intention-talk comes in. Saying "I intend to do x," or "I will try to do x" is equivalent to announcing "I shall do x," then adding "but I may not succeed." This is why intentions are such an important component of our talk about future plans. The more distant the anticipated actions are, the less certain we can be that we will be able to carry them out, and thus the less willing we should be to commit ourselves to the claim that they will take place. We talk about the distant future in terms of intentions for the same reason that we talk about the distant past in terms of recollections (rather than events).

There is no question that in the cases of both intention and observation, the agent has made a distinctive move in the game of giving and asking for reasons, one that is different from simply acquiring a belief or performing an action. Thus what I am proposing is not a reduction of intention to desire, or the elimination of the term "intention" from our vocabulary. The point is simply to suggest that there is no distinct psychological state corresponding to an appearance or an intention, having some special causal connection to the world. The incorrigibility of the relation between appearances and beliefs, or between practical deliberation and intentions, is not due to some special character of these states. Appearances and intentions are special types of deontic statuses in which the agent refrains from making one of the commitments that is typical of everyday language-entry and -exit moves. It is the absence of these commitments that makes them less corrigible than the "full-blown" versions. The idea that they might afford any special purchase on the problems of Cartesian skepticism, or the problem of weakness of the will, is a grammatical illusion generated by the expressive vocabulary that we have introduced in order to articulate these deontic statuses.

Thinking of an intention as a kind of deontic status, and not as a special sort of intentional state, helps to clear up a lot of the confusion surrounding the concept. For example, it helps us to see what is going on in Gregory Kavka's toxin puzzle. Kavka invites us to consider the following proposal:

> You have just been approached by an eccentric billionaire who has offered you the following deal. He places before you a vial of toxin that, if you drink it, will make you painfully ill for a day, but will not threaten your life or have any lasting effects.... The billionaire will pay you one million dollars tomorrow morning if, at midnight tonight, you *intend* to drink the toxin tomorrow afternoon. He emphasizes that you need not drink the toxin to receive the money; in fact, the money will be in your bank account hours before the time for drinking it arrives, if you succeed.... The presence or absence of the intention is to be determined by the latest 'mind-reading' brain scanner and computing device designed by the great Doctor X.[85]

Many people's reaction to this puzzle is governed by the intuition that it would be irrational to drink the toxin (given that the money is already in the bank at the time that one is called on to drink it), and therefore that one cannot form the intention to drink it. However, according to the "realist" view of intention, this is puzzling. According to the standard view, an agent chooses to perform an action on the grounds that it maximizes expected utility. The realist about intention claims that the agent does not literally decide to perform *the action*, she simply decides to form the intention. The intention then causes the action. But if this is the case, then it suggests that we decide to form intentions just in case it is utility-maximizing to do so. The toxin puzzle drives a wedge between the intention and the action, presenting a case in which it is utility-maximizing to form the intention, but not utility-maximizing to perform the action. Yet we have the intuition that the agent cannot form the intention, even though it would be utility-maximizing to do so. This seems puzzling.

The analysis of intentions in terms of deontic scorekeeping advanced here suggests that it is not psychologically impossible to form this intention, it is logically impossible. It doesn't matter how hard the agent tries. It's like accepting the validity of an argument, then trying to believe the premises and not the conclusion. Furthermore, there is no fact of the matter as to whether the agent has a particular intention or not (or certainly not the sort of fact that could be determined through use of a "brain scanner"). Who has what intention is determined by deontic scorekeeping—commitments and entitlements both ascribed and acknowledged. When an agent says "the ball is red," we may ascribe "the ball looks red" to that agent. The latter is simply a doxastically weaker version of the former. The mistake is to imagine that because the latter generates a weaker commitment than the former, the belief is somehow based on the appearance, not the object. Similarly, when an agent decides to do x, we can infer that she intends to do x. This does not mean that what she really decided to do was adopt the intention, and that the action follows from the intention.

What the toxin puzzle shows is that intentions are what Sellars calls, somewhat pejoratively, "mongrel" concepts. To assign such concepts psychological reality, and to give them a place in the theory of action, is to confuse the explanatory and the justificatory orders of explanation. The fact that some theorists, such as Gauthier and Bratman, have thought that intentions might hold the promise of providing the "source" of normativity is precisely a symptom of the "mongrel" character of these concepts. There are circumstances in which it may be helpful to use the related set of locutions in the explanation of an action, but to include such concepts in the theory of action as psychological posits is nothing but a recipe for confusion.

6

A Naturalistic Perspective

It will come as no surprise to many people to discover that the *homo economicus* model of rational agency is in trouble. Standard rational choice theory maintains a rigid adherence to the two central postulates of Hobbes's instrumentalism, namely, that practical reasoning is consequentialist, and that preferences are noncognitive. As we have seen, the former claim is unmotivated, while the latter is indefensible. Thus when the model is applied to real subjects, they turn out to have a much greater capacity to engage in collective and coordinated action than rational choice theory predicts, not only because they are capable of respecting deontic constraints but also because they are able to engage in joint deliberation and revision of preferences (both desires and norms). So despite the cries of "economic imperialism" associated with the spread of rational choice theory to other disciplines, the long-term effect has tended to be quite the opposite. The attempt to wrangle with nontraditional subject matter (such as crime, or family structure) has provided a wealth of examples revealing the limitations of the economic model. Thus not only did many of the imperialists "go native," some even brought foreign customs back to the metropole.

But if the *homo economicus* model is in trouble, it is still not clear what will emerge to take its place. Many economists have turned to experimental game theory for an answer to this question.[1] Several classic experiments show quite clearly that agents do not approach social interactions myopically, and do not view the actions of others as simply variables affecting their chances of attaining their preferred outcome. Their choices are governed by something like metapreferences that are linked to the structure of the social interaction. According to standard rational choice theory, people should not care whether the player making the offers in an ultimatum game is another person or a random-number–generating computer. But clearly they do.

These observations have not escaped the attention of moral philosophers. The prisoner's dilemma is often regarded as a clear-cut illustration of the conflict that can arise between self-interest and morality. In an interaction of this type, two individuals are in a position where they can engage in mutually beneficial cooperation, but where they can also exploit each other's willingness to cooperate. If they make an agreement to cooperate, they are normally taken to be under a moral obligation to respect that agreement, yet it is in their self-interest to defect. The *homo economicus* model suggests that defection is the only rational course of action in prisoner's dilemma situations. Moral philosophers, on the other hand, have long maintained that it is rational to cooperate. The problem is that moral philosophers have never been able to provide a convincing account of *why* it is rational to cooperate.

Experimental game theory has shown that people often do act morally in these contexts, and so are able to secure the cooperative outcome. As an empirical observation, this is neither here nor there. What makes the results of experimental game theory important is that the careful design of the experimental interaction has the potential to reveal interesting things about the structure of practical rationality. In other words, these experiments may offer us evidence as to *why* people are cooperating. Moral philosophers over the years have offered all sorts of different explanations: that people feel sympathy for one another, that they are committed to a shared conception of the good, that they are obeying principles, and so on. But most of this has been based on ad hoc observation and personal intuition. Before considering the normative question of whether and how such cooperative dispositions can be justified, it may be helpful to adopt a strictly naturalistic perspective, in order to *describe* the existing set of cooperative dispositions that human beings seem to all share, and consider how they might have come about.

6.1.   The Mystery of Altruism

The most useful place to begin, I will argue, is from the standpoint of evolutionary biology. The kind of spontaneous cooperation that one finds among human beings, which experimental game theorists have exhaustively detailed, is actually quite uncommon in nature. Human beings, along with colonial invertebrates and social insects, are what evolutionary biologists refer to as an *ultrasocial* species.[2] We sustain and reproduce life through unusually extensive and complex systems of cooperation. In fact, human beings have recently begun to overtake ants, termites, and bees as the most social species on the planet (in terms of the number of individuals and the degree of complexity of our societies).[3] This kind of cooperation is uncommon. Far more typical of natural patterns is the level of sociality exhibited by our closest primate relatives, who tend to congregate in tribes of no more than one hundred individuals, and who engage in very limited forms of cooperative behavior.

Apart from being uncommon, there is also something mysterious about the specific form that ultrasociality takes on in human societies. In the case of both colonial invertebrates and social insects, there is a very clear biological and genetic basis for the peculiarly high levels of sociality they exhibit. With social insects (ants, termites, bees, wasps), for example, it is due to the reproductive pattern known as "haplodiploidy," which increases the level of relatedness among members of the hive or colony. There seems to be nothing comparable in the reproductive biology of humans that could serve as an explanation for our ultrasociality. With respect to reproduction, and in many other aspects, we are not all that different from apes. This creates what Peter Richerson and Robert Boyd refer to as "an evolutionary puzzle."[4]

There are of course all sorts of candidates when it comes to explaining human ultrasociality, since there are many different things that are distinctive about our species. Humans have superior intelligence and planning abilities, make more extensive use of tools, communicate through language, rely heavily on cultural transmission for social learning, and have a prolonged juvenile phase that permits more extensive socialization. Furthermore, these characteristics are not unrelated to one another. In order to get a sense of which ones can provide more or less plausible explanations for the bases of ultrasociality, it is necessary to understand first what sort of constraints evolutionary theory imposes on such explanations.

We can begin by designating the term "altruism" to be used in a strictly naturalistic sense, to describe any behavior that benefits another organism, while being detrimental to the organism performing the behavior, where benefit and detriment are defined in terms of reproductive fitness.[5] (The relationship between human altruism, which is defined in terms of fitness, and human cooperation, which is defined in terms of self-interest, will be discussed later. The two overlap, but do not coincide.) There are many examples of altruistic behavior in the animal kingdom: a mother sacrifices herself to lead a predator away from the nest, worker ants sacrifice themselves to feed the colony, vervet monkeys emit alarm calls to warn each other of danger, and so on. It is worth noting as well that altruism can take both positive and negative forms. We normally think of altruism as involving "helping" behavior, but it can just as well take the form of *refraining* from engaging in damaging behavior, such as aggression, food competition, or infanticide.

It is only fairly recently that altruism has come to be seen as an evolutionary puzzle. In the early half of the twentieth century, there was a widespread tendency among evolutionary biologists to regard particular traits as adaptive merely because they were "good for the species," even though it was widely understood that individual-level selection would tend to work against the development of such traits.[6] For example, an individual (gopher, vervet monkey, etc.) who produced an alarm call on spotting a predator would also be likely to attract the attention of this predator, thus reducing his own fitness relative to others.[7] Nevertheless, it was felt that because groups that contained individuals exhibiting altruistic traits would do so much better than groups that lacked such individuals, natural selection would still tend to favor the development of altruism. This conviction rested in part on an unwillingness to countenance the possibility of massive suboptimality in the outcome of evolutionary systems.

These assurances were disrupted in 1966 by George Williams, who argued that group-level selection effects would almost always be weaker than those occurring at the individual level.[8] While groups that contained altruists might do better than groups that lacked them, a disproportionate share of these benefits would flow not to the altruists within the group, but to the nonaltruists. Thus what group-level selection tends to favor is not "being an altruist," but rather "being in the close company of an altruist." This has the structure of an evolutionary prisoner's dilemma, leading individually advantageous traits to be systematically favored, even when they are extremely damaging to the species as a whole. Thus altruism must be regarded as very much the exception, not the baseline.

Naturally, if silent monkeys are able to free ride successfully off the efforts of the alarm call monkeys, then they will gradually replace them, so that the population will eventually consist entirely of silent monkeys. This reduces the mean fitness of the species, but such reductions in fitness happen all the time in a natural context. The peacock's tail is an especially obvious example, but the phenomenon is ubiquitous. Short trees are, in general, more robust than tall trees. The energy expended pumping nutrients and water all the way up to the leaves reduces absolute fitness (not to mention making the tree more vulnerable to wind, lightning, and so on). The problem is that trees also compete against one another for sunlight. Being slightly taller than its neighbors improves the relative fitness of a tree, compared to its neighbors. Thus trees get locked into an evolutionary race to the bottom. Average height will tend to increase, until such time as the gain in relative fitness associated with increased height is outweighed by the loss of absolute fitness. The result is an evolutionary equilibrium that is suboptimal, from the standpoint of the species as a whole (e.g., in the competition against other species).

Sex ratios provide another very clear-cut example of a suboptimal equilibrium induced by evolutionary free riding.[9] From the standpoint of fecundity, what matters is the size of the female cohort. Eggs are costly, whereas sperm is cheap (by definition, as a matter of fact). So when it comes to reproductive fitness, the sex ratio that is best, from the standpoint of the *species*, might be 99:1 female to male. By contrast, a 1:1 ratio is extremely wasteful, from the standpoint of the species. It generates a huge population of "surplus" males, most of whom are not needed—and in many species, most of whom are not even used—for the reproduction of the species. At the same time, these males consume resources that would otherwise be available for members of the population involved in reproduction. Thus the 1:1 sex ratio is suboptimal, in the sense that it produces a much lower level of average fitness for members of the species than a ratio more skewed toward females. How could this be?

The answer lies in the fact that natural selection does not promote average fitness; it only promotes individual fitness. A 99:1 sex ratio is not evolutionarily stable. While it does promote a high degree of average fitness, it is also susceptible to deviation. The first male born with a tendency to produce two sperm containing Y chromosomes, rather than just one, out of every one hundred essentially doubles the number of grandchildren he can expect to have (and thus the number of offspring to possess this trait). Yet this is a race to the bottom. As more individuals acquire this trait, fecundity drops, and average fitness declines. Thus these individuals generate more male offspring, but at the same time, confer on each one a diminished probability of successfully reproducing. This continues until the number of males being born outnumbers females, in which case producing more female offspring becomes individually advantageous. So things settle out at around 1:1.

The example of sex ratio is useful, because it is massively suboptimal, yet ubiquitous. This shows, in turn, the power of the evolutionary forces that are lined up against the development of altruistic traits. Furthermore, it shows that human beings are not exempt from these general strictures at any deep biological level. If we were, there would be a lot more women around. Thus altruism needs to be understood as an exception, one that emerges against a background that systematically favors genetically selfish or "antisocial" behavior.

The problems that altruists encounter are not, of course, insurmountable, as witnessed by the number of clear instances of altruistic behavior patterns in many different animal species. Yet altruists are definitely swimming against the current, since the default tendency of natural selection within a sexually reproducing species will be to eliminate it. So in cases where altruism does persist, it requires some very specific mechanism to sustain it. One can sense the severity of the free-rider problem by looking at the ubiquity of parasites and "Batesian" mimics in nature. Cuckoos and cowbirds are "brood parasites" who free ride off the parental investment of other bird species by laying eggs in their nests. Viceroy butterflies copy the poisonous monarch butterfly by imitating the appearance of their wings (which in turn reduces the value of that pattern as a deterrent to predators). The list could easily be extended. Thus the concern that altruism will be undermined by free riders is not merely an abstract possibility; there are many examples of organisms whose entire survival strategy involves free riding off others. There is, unfortunately, still a tendency among philosophers to think that humans might have some specific adaptation, such as a "moral sense," or a "moral reasoning module," precisely because its presence promotes cooperation. This is a fallacious inference, one that arises from a failure to appreciate the magnitude of the free-rider problems that arise in evolutionary systems.

6.2. Inclusive Fitness

As a point of reference, is it helpful to begin by considering the two most uncontroversial mechanisms known to produce and sustain altruistic behavior in the animal kingdom. Many theorists have thought that they are adequate to explain human altruism as well, but as we shall see, they fall well short of the mark. The first and most well-known mechanism is what W. D. Hamilton referred to as "inclusive fitness," or "kin selection."[10] It is, perhaps ironically, a fairly direct consequence of so-called selfish gene theory.[11] Not only do the "interests" of the individual not always align with the "interests" of the group, but the "interests" of the gene do not always align with the "interests" of the individual.[12] Every gene reproduces in an environment that contains multiple copies of the same gene, housed in other individuals. Genes are fundamentally indifferent between reproducing themselves and reproducing the copies of themselves found in others. Thus a trait that reduces the fitness of one individual but provides a greater increase in fitness for some other individual who possesses that trait (or provides a lesser increase to a greater number of such individuals) will be favored by natural selection. In other words, selfish genes do not always benefit from selfish behavior on the part of the organism. (If our bodies are, as Richard Dawkins put it, "lumbering robots" constructed to advance the interests of our genes, the fact is that our genes can sometimes benefit themselves by programing the robot to sacrifice itself.)[13] Selfish genes can therefore generate altruistic behavior at the level of the organism.

The clearest example of this is parental investment in offspring. Imagine a species of bird that has no tendency to feed or care for its young, but simply lays the eggs and leaves. If a mutation occurs that makes the parent more inclined to stick around and feed its young, this mutation should spread quite rapidly in the population. Even though the presence of this gene will decrease the fitness of the parent (by increasing its energy expenditure while decreasing its food intake), there is a 50 percent chance that each of the offspring has that gene, and since each will have its fitness dramatically improved through the parent's efforts, the gene will prosper. In a sense, the gene sacrifices the copy of itself found in the parent, in order to promote the multiple copies of itself that are found in the offspring. When the notion of "individual fitness" is expanded in order to take these indirect effects into account, it yields the notion of "inclusive fitness."

In this respect, Dawkins's book *The Selfish Gene* is rife with rhetorically misleading passages. The title is often misread as implying that there is a "gene for selfishness." What it really means is that natural selection promotes selfishness only at the level of the gene, *not* at the level of the individual (or only indirectly at the level of the individual). The fact that the "interests" of a gene will typically be promoted by the individual pursuing his own interests is merely an empirical generalization, not a claim about the inner dynamic of evolutionary systems. Dawkins does state this in various ways, yet it still takes considerable mental effort to read sentences such as the following without misunderstanding: "Like successful Chicago gangsters, our genes have survived, in some cases for millions of years, in a highly competitive world. This entitles us to expect certain qualities in our genes. I shall argue that a predominant quality to be expected in a successful gene is ruthless selfishness. This gene selfishness will usually give rise to selfishness in individual behavior."[14] The hard part is to remember that the tenderness and compassion with which mothers to care for their young counts as an example of "ruthless selfishness" at the level of the gene (where the mother is essentially cast aside as a used husk, in order to promote the fitness of her parasitic brood). Thus the way Dawkins uses the word "selfish" bears only a tenuous connection to the ordinary English sense of the term.

Inclusive fitness can also explain why siblings and relatives in various species often help one another. While the chances that one shares a particular gene with one's child is 50 percent, the chances of sharing it with one's brother or sister is also 50 percent, and thus the chances of sharing it with one's nephew or niece is 25 percent. Because of this, saving four of one's brother's children is equivalent, from an inclusive fitness point of view, to saving two of one's own, which is equivalent to saving oneself. Of course, the sort of altruism that can be sustained in this way is limited. In general, the benefit at the receiving end of the altruistic act must be at least twice as great, in terms of fitness, as the cost to the individual performing it. Furthermore, if individuals have no way of discriminating between kin and nonkin, the pattern may not be sustainable. (Thus magpies, in order to defend themselves against the great spotted cuckoo, will destroy any egg that they do not recognize as their own. Since their ability to distinguish one from the other is limited, this requirement results in a reduction in fitness—but less so than being suckered by the cuckoo.)[15]

Thus kin selection is, in general, not sufficient to promote ultrasociality. Kin selection may occasionally produce "open-ended" dispositions that result in advantages being conferred on those outside the immediate family circle, but there are very powerful evolutionary forces working to either eliminate or circumscribe such dispositions. Chimpanzees, for instance, engage in a variety of altruistic acts toward kin, but are for the most part "indifferent to the welfare of unrelated group members,"[16] and thus engage in very limited cooperation. In species that behave differently, it is usually because their reproductive biology increases the size of the family circle, or the coefficient of relatedness.

Sexual reproduction, from this perspective, represents the primary obstacle to the development of altruism—because it reduces the probability of a particular gene being shared between the most closely related individuals to only 50 percent. A society of clones would be one in which natural selection favored unlimited altruism, and unlimited individual sacrifice for others. For confirmation, one need only look at the level of cooperation exhibited among cells in a body (since a multicellular organism is essentially a society of clones). Every somatic (or nongermline) cell in a body is essentially sacrificing itself for the sake of the gametes. If one looks at the division of labor within the body, for example, between liver cells and neurons, and compares it to the level of differentiation at the social level within a typical mammalian species, it provides some indication of the formidable obstacles that sexual reproduction creates for the evolution of altruism. From this perspective, what inclusive fitness represents is simply a partial attenuation of these obstacles.

In the case of humans, who have an unremarkable reproductive biology, kin selection cannot possibly explain the extent of social cooperation. That being said, it should still be noted that the effects of kin selection can still be seen quite clearly in human social behavior. One need only observe how people behave in the presence of infants. In many different animal species, there is a set of distinguishing "neotenous" or juvenile characteristics. This includes fur of a different color, distinctively proportioned facial and body features (e.g., large eyes, small nose, large head-to-body size ratio), and "a staggering 'infantile' gait."[17] In colloquial terms, infants "look cute." These characteristics in turn bring out distinctive responses in adults, including caring behavior and protection, a suspension of aggressive behavior, and much greater tolerance of impropriety in social interaction (e.g., violations of personal space, or the dominance hierarchy).[18] Among humans, not only are most of the characteristics that are considered "cute" culturally universal, but so are many of the behaviors they provoke, such as "baby talk," which most adults produce spontaneously in the presence of infants, and has similar intonation patterns around the world.[19] Thus it is widely believed to be an altruistic adaptation, designed to make language more learnable—or at least verbal communication more intelligible—for the young.

Examples such as these suggest that the way adults identify neoteny, and are disposed to respond to such characteristics, is a product of an evolutionarily adapted set of cognitive mechanism selected for reasons of inclusive fitness. The "cute" reaction is, of course, quite general, evoked not only by most human infants, but by the infants of many other mammalian species. Thus there may be some question as to how such a nondiscriminating mechanism could evolve through the kin mechanism. There are several possible responses: first, the extent to which it is shared with other species suggests that it is extremely archaic, and thus predates the development of more sophisticated discriminatory abilities; second, individuals are more likely to be in the company of their own infants, and so the latter are most likely to be the ones who benefit from a more general disposition (in the same way that anyone can hear an alarm call, and yet in many species these calls are thought to have evolved through kin selection);[20] finally, there is evidence that parents are inclined to regard their own children as more attractive than those of others, and that the identification of "family resemblance" is an important aspect of parental bonding.[21] This suggests that there may be some element of kin discrimination built into the mechanism.

One does not need to be a sociobiologist to acknowledge that humans are still powerfully affected by altruistic impulses whose probable origin lies in kin selection (in the same way that there are no sociobiological commitments associated with the claim that human behavior is strongly influenced by the impulse to reproduce). Indeed, there is good reason to think that the sort of spontaneous sympathy people feel when they see others in distress is a product of kin selection. First and foremost, there is the fact that it is a largely involuntary and unconscious response, usually narrowly limited in scope, and mediated through a mechanism of identification such as visual similarity.[22] Second, a basis in kin selection suggests that it may rely on very archaic psychological structures, which would explain why even very young children exhibit spontaneous empathy or caring behavior, prior to the development of more advanced cognitive skills such as instrumental reasoning or role-taking.[23] Finally, it would explain why there are (small, but statistically significant) sex differences in the nature and intensity of these reactions—given that the optimal level of parental investment is unlikely to be the same for males and females.[24]

There is a reason, however, that all of this occurs at the level of the adaptive unconscious. The moment that organisms acquire the sophistication required to learn new forms of behavior, they have an incentive to "unlearn" all of the behavior patterns that benefit their "selfish genes" at the expense of their own organism. For example, chimpanzees emit a specific call when they discover a food source. This behavior is altruistic, since it often results in the individual who made the discovery being denied access to the food by others further up the dominance hierarchy. Chimpanzees are smart enough to realize this, but they lack the cortical brain structures required to exercise direct control over these vocalizations. Thus Jane Goodall observed one chimpanzee, who had recently come across a cache of bananas at the Gombe reserve, emitting the standard vocalization associated with food discovery, while at the same time putting his hand over his mouth in an effort to muffle his own cry.[25] We can see here the earliest stage of what Keith Stanovich calls "the robot's rebellion" against the selfish gene.[26]

Thus one might expect that kin selection would explain many of the primitive altruistic responses exhibited by children, along with a certain range of behavioral dispositions among adults. But it is highly unlikely that kin selection operates directly to produce stable patterns of cooperation once more sophisticated cognitive resources have been developed. This is because cognitive reflection and calculation seem just as likely to "veto" altruistic behavior of this type as to promote it. Thus the influence of kin selection is likely to be found only in unconscious or spontaneous responses (such as the way people react to a puppy), through preference formation (via such mechanisms as empathic identification), or through very indirect biases (such as the elevated risk of abuse posed by stepparents to their partner's offspring).

6.3.   Reciprocal Altruism

The second primary mechanism known to promote altruistic behavior is referred to, following Robert Trivers, as reciprocal altruism.[27] This form of altruism has a "you scratch my back, I'll scratch yours" structure. If the altruist can somehow provoke the beneficiary of his actions to return the gesture, or to produce some other sort of benefit, then the net effect will be an improvement in fitness. Reciprocal altruism differs from inclusive fitness in that with the latter, it is the copy of the individual's gene found in the beneficiary that benefits, whereas with the former, it is the individual's own copy that benefits, via the actions of the beneficiary of the initial act. The beneficiary, however, need not possess the same gene. This is most obvious in the case of altruistic interspecies symbioses (as with gobies, a species of "cleaner fish" who remove ectoparasites from the gills of grouper, while the grouper, in turn, refrain from eating them). When altruistic behavior benefits individuals belonging to another species, it is impossible for the gene to be benefiting some other copy of itself. It must be that the benefits of the behavior somehow redound to the individual who performed it (and thus that the copy of the gene underlying the behavior improves its own chances of reproducing).

Thus systems of reciprocal altruism may be adaptive insofar as they enable individuals to cooperate in fitness-enhancing ways. Yet this connection between altruism and cooperation has the potential to generate some confusion. After all, with inclusive fitness, the individual genuinely sacrifices himself in order to benefit another. With reciprocal altruism on the other hand the individual who performs the action ultimately benefits from it (making the strategy seem more like "clever selfishness" than genuine altruism). What makes it count as altruistic is the availability of a free-rider strategy that the individual forgoes. The grouper could wait until the gobie was finished removing ectoparasites, then eat it, yet refrains from doing so. Thus cooperation involves a *failure* to enhance one's own fitness at the expense of another, which is what makes it altruistic.

Reciprocity is the form of altruism underlying the well-known "tit-for-tat" strategy in evolutionary game theory.[28] Tit-for-tat, as we have seen, essentially instructs a player confronting a repeated prisoner's dilemma game with a single opponent to act cooperatively on the first round, and in each subsequent round to do whatever the opponent did in the previous round (cooperate if the other cooperated, defect if the other defected). Thus two tit-for-tat players who encounter one another will be able to sustain cooperation, which in turn will confer significant benefits. Free riders, on the other hand, will get the "one shot" benefit of defection, but will have to pay for it by having others defect on them in future rounds. Thus they get limited benefits from free riding, and are denied access to the fruits of cooperation. Robert Axelrod found that not only was tit-for-tat a more successful strategy than defection, it was also superior to other, more complex conditional strategies.

Is it widely believed that this sort of conditional reciprocity underlies a range of altruistic behaviors among animals, such as food sharing, mutual grooming, and some alarm calls.[29] Nonhuman primates, for instance, spend significant amounts of time (up to 20 percent of the day) and energy grooming themselves and others. Although much of this occurs among kin, unrelated individuals also establish grooming relationships, which they often maintain over long periods of time. Since primates are quite capable of distinguishing kin from nonkin, it is widely thought that reciprocal altruism, and not kin selection, is responsible for this behavior. An individual may engage in "experimental" grooming of an unrelated individual. Reciprocation of the gesture increases the propensity to return to that individual and groom him or her again.

It should be noted that an altruistic disposition based on reciprocity, in order to be sustainable, must include not only a disposition to assist those who have assisted one in the past, but also a disposition *not* to assist those who have failed to assist one in the past. Altruists must not only want to be associated with other altruists, they must want to dissociate from selfish agents. There must, in other words, be some *correlation* of strategies in the way that interactions occur, so that altruists are more likely to interact with other altruists, and selfish agents more likely to interact with other selfish agents.[30] An unconditional altruistic strategy is not evolutionarily robust, even if there is some mechanism that increases the chances that it will be reciprocated, because the presence of such unconditional cooperators in the population enhances the fitness of the free riders more than it does the other altruists. Unless there is some mechanism that deprives the free riders of these benefits, they will steadily increase their share of the population at the expense of altruists. (This is the primary reason that group selection promotes altruism only in cases where some of the groups contain *only* altruists. If all the groups are mixed, then the free riders always do best.)[31]

Incidentally, there is no reason that reciprocal altruism needs to involve the *same* individuals interacting with one another over time. Since correlation of strategies is all that is required, one can still sustain altruism in a repeated game in which partners are "reshuffled" at the end of each round, so long as the tit-for-tat players "do whatever the opponent did in the previous round," *regardless* of whom that opponent was playing against. If adequate information is communicated at the end of each round about what each player has chosen, then individuals can develop "reputations" for being cooperators, and thus elicit greater cooperation from others. This was generally taken to be obvious by rationality-based game theorists, but was received as something of a discovery by evolutionary theorists.[32] The latter, following Richard Alexander, gave it the special name of "indirect reciprocity."[33] It is important to keep in mind, however, that indirect reciprocity does not involve any fundamental change in the mechanism that sustains cooperation; it basically just changes the assumptions made about information transmission in the game.

It is sometimes felt that reciprocal altruism is not true altruism, because the behavior in question ultimately increases the individual's own fitness, and thus is really just selfishness, understood more broadly, or over a longer time-horizon. This conflation of reciprocal altruism with selfishness is based on a confusion. Naturally, the organism that is performing the altruistic action will, in general and over the long run, derive some benefit from so doing (if it didn't, then selection would necessarily eliminate any propensity to behave in this way). The key point is that when the organism engages in altruistic behavior of this type, the behavior *itself* does not benefit the individual. The behavior itself reduces fitness. It only proves beneficial if and when it is reciprocated by someone else. One can see this in two aspects of the tit-for-tat strategy. First, tit-for-tat always starts out with playing "nice," by cooperating unconditionally in the first round. Because of this, the strategy is vulnerable to exploitation by free riders, who may move from player to player, taking advantage of this initial willingness to cooperate. In order to be evolutionarily stable, tit-for-tat agents must therefore be engaged in repeated interactions with the same individual, so that the benefits of sustained cooperation begin to outweigh the potential gains from multiple one-shot defections. Second, tit-for-tat agents play "blindly"—they do not consider what the other person will do in future rounds; they simply imitate whatever they saw in the previous round. This means that they will continue to cooperate right through to the final round of a repeated interaction, even though they could benefit by defecting at this last stage.

This "blindness" is not an accidental feature of the tit-for-tat strategy. In a rationality-based repeated prisoner's dilemma game, where agents act on the basis of their beliefs about their opponents' future play, cooperation among tit-for-tat players is not a subgame-perfect equilibrium (because the punishment of defectors is not credible). Thus while reciprocal altruism does require a higher level of cognitive sophistication and behavioral flexibility than kin selection altruism, insofar as the altruist must be able to recognize free riders and discontinue interactions with them, too much cognitive sophistication may in the end undermine the altruistic impulse. Individuals who acquire the ability to distinguish between one-shot and repeated interactions, or who learn to identify the final round of an interaction, will begin to defect. Furthermore, if they learn the lesson "once burned, twice shy," they may discontinue the initial altruistic move required to get systems of reciprocity off the ground. Thus we should not assume that an improved ability to calculate self-interest, or to adopt a longer planning horizon, should necessarily increase the prevailing levels of reciprocal altruism (any more than it should be thought to enhance kin selection). The type of behavioral dispositions that arise out of structures of reciprocal altruism can easily conflict with an individual's calculated self-interest. Nor should we generalize from evolutionary game theory models, in which agents are modeled as being blind to the anticipated moves of their interaction partners, to human agents, who suffer from no such handicaps.[34]

This kind of generalization is, unfortunately, extremely common in the literature. Trivers, for example, in his original article, used grooming symbioses, alarm calls among birds, and "the psychological system underlying human altruism" as his three primary examples of reciprocal altruism. Philip Kitcher does something very similar in "The Evolution of Human Altruism"[35] (which he later acknowledged to be an "oversimplification").[36] And Brian Skyrms, in *The Evolution of the Social Contract*, uses the fact that asking for a 50-50 split is one of the evolutionary stable strategies of a cutting-the-cake problem as grounds for speculating about the origins of the concept of fairness and justice. In so doing, he takes strategies that are equilibria of evolutionary games, *yet clearly not equilibria of comparable rationality-based games*, and presents them as explanations of the origins of particular patterns of human social behavior.[37] This is invalid, because the success of the strategy in an evolutionary context often *depends* on the fact that players have no foresight regarding future interactions.

Of course, all of these writers recognize that the case of human social interaction is complicated by a number of different factors, not the least of which is the plasticity of our behavioral dispositions. Yet they all assume that these other factors will extend the scope of reciprocal altruism, rather than limiting it. This leads them quite naturally to assume that reciprocal altruism can serve as an explanation for the existence of ultrasociality among humans. This is deeply implausible. In this context, it is perhaps worth observing that most of the capacities required to sustain reciprocal altruism are present not just among humans but also among our closest primate relatives. Yet chimpanzees, bonobos, baboons, and gorillas are able to sustain only very limited forms of cooperation using these resources. Indeed, the primary function of reciprocal altruism in our closest primate relatives seems to be merely to support the formation of friendships, coalitions and alliances.[38] As Richerson, Boyd, and Joseph Henrich observe:

> If a mechanism like indirect reciprocity works, why have not many social species used it to extend their range of cooperation? If finding self-reinforcing solutions to coordination games is mostly what human societies are about, why do not other animals have massive coordination-based social systems? If reputations for pairwise cooperators are easy to observe and signal (but unexploitable by deceptive defectors), why have we found no other complex

animal societies based on this principle? By contrast, we do find plenty of complex animal societies built on the principle of inclusive fitness.[39]

Reciprocal altruism seems to be adequate as a mechanism for sustaining networks of dyadic relations, but it seems completely unsuitable as a basis for sustaining altruism in groups. The reason for this is not difficult to find. Cooperative activities that involve many individuals are problematic, because as the group becomes larger, the probability that at least one person will defect, even due to error, becomes extremely high. Since the only punishment mechanism is withdrawal of cooperation, in large groups these systems of cooperation simply fall apart almost as soon as they are initiated.[40] This is why chimpanzees, despite being very good at reciprocity, are very bad at cooperation.

Thus reciprocal altruism provides very little purchase on the puzzle of human cooperation. The central characteristic of human sociality is not our capacity to develop cooperative relationships over time, but rather our peculiar tendency to cooperate in "one-shot" anonymous interactions, in which we know that there is no potential for future cooperation.[41] Thus the more probable hypothesis is that reciprocal altruism, like inclusive fitness, is responsible for various "archaic" aspects of sociality among humans. (It explains why "chimpanzee politics" resemble human politics, but fails to explain how humans sustain large-scale societies *despite* these factional tendencies.)[42] In particular, it may explain the seemingly universal human propensity to categorize individuals that we meet into "friend" and "foe" (or those whom we "like" and "dislike"), along with the "in-group" biases that people routinely exhibit in cooperative tasks.[43]

Among chimpanzees, bonobos, and some baboon species, an "animal's chances of securing food, receiving care and protection, exercising mate choice, and other important determinants of fitness depend on which other members of the troop will come to their aid."[44] Furthermore, there is evidence that in some species, including chimpanzees, the existence of one altruistic "relationship" increases the likelihood that others will be established, and even that some forms of altruistic service will be exchanged against others.[45] This explains the asymmetries that sometimes exist in the exchange of grooming services. For example, chimpanzees are more likely to share food with those who have groomed them in the past. Experimental studies have also suggested that in agonistic interactions, vervets and macaques are more likely to intervene in support of individuals who have groomed them in the past.[46] In other words, the type of relationships developed through reciprocal altruism bear a close resemblance to what we call "friendship." In this context, it is important to remain clear on the distinction between conditional cooperation as a rational strategy and the type of dispositions produced by evolution. The latter may generate genuine, unconditional altruism. The function of reciprocity is simply to shield this disposition from being eliminated by the forces of natural selection. Thus the development of feelings of friendship toward those who have helped us in the past may create on our part a genuine disposition to act altruistically toward them (based perhaps on a "warm" feeling we have when thinking of them), even if at the intentional level we come to anticipate that this action will go unreciprocated. Indeed, some have observed that when individuals explicitly keep track of the "favors" others have done for them, it tends to undermine the emergence of friendly feelings.[47] This does not imply, however, that friendship is not a product of reciprocal altruism. What it suggests is that the emergence of friendship relations occurs at the level of the adaptive unconscious, not the intentional planning system. As Frans de Waal writes:

> Whether what is involved is the returning of a favor or the seeking of revenge, the principle remains one of exchange; and, most importantly, this principle requires that social interactions be remembered. Much of the time the process may take place in the subconscious, but we all know from experience that things come bubbling up to the surface when the difference between costs and benefits becomes too great. It is then that we voice our feelings. By and large, however, reciprocity is something that takes place silently.[48]

Thus reciprocal altruism seems well suited to explain (in some broad sense) the universal human propensity to form a small number of sustained friendships. Yet it falls far short of what would be required to explain large-scale cooperation. Since reciprocity sustains primarily relationships, and not large-scale cooperative projects, many of the inclinations that can be persuasively traced back to such a mechanism are extremely parochial, and serve to limit the extent of cooperation. Most obviously, the "in-group" bias is a tendency that individuals engaged in large-scale cooperative projects must constantly guard against. Thus, far from explaining human ultrasociality, the existence of these instincts in many ways just deepens the mystery of what separates us from our nearest primate relatives.

6.4. Implausible Hypotheses

The effects of kin selection and reciprocal altruism can be seen quite clearly in human social interaction, and both mechanisms have obvious explanatory power when it comes to certain circumstances. They can help us to understand why people are naturally disposed to care about their families and friends. But neither is able to explain why humans are able to sustain large-scale societies, or why we are so much more cooperative than other primates. After all, chimpanzees exhibit altruism toward kin, and are extremely intelligent when it comes to managing relationships based on reciprocal altruism. The fact that they are unable to maintain "societies" of more than one hundred individuals therefore lends credence to the suggestion that human social organization must be achieved through some *other* mechanism. Evolutionary theorists, however, have been extremely reluctant to acknowledge this.[49] Many still take great pleasure in emphasizing the continuity that exists between humans and other animals, insofar as it allows them to score rhetorical points against those whom they take to be the enemies of science. As a result, they often end up downplaying the uniqueness of human social organization.[50]

A more balanced view would acknowledge that some other mechanism must be at work in human society, yet pay due respect to the fact that there is only a small distance, in evolutionary terms, between ourselves and our nearest primate relatives. A good theory, in other words, would recognize the fact that we are different, but keep in mind that we are not *too* different. Boyd and Richerson describe these competing considerations as follows:

> Humans are, arguably, a new page in the natural history of animal cooperation. Our reproductive biology is similar to the other social mammals. Among our close relatives, the apes and monkeys, genetic relatedness and reciprocal altruism support a diverse array of small-scale societies, but no other spectacular ones. Humans have built extremely complex societies by some mechanism or mechanisms different from any other known highly social species. At the same time, there are remarkable parallels between human and ape social behavior and material culture, not to mention many convergences between humans and other social and tool-using species. Consistent with classical comparative anatomy and modern molecular studies, human behavior is clearly recently derived from ape behavior. There is room for only relatively few modifications of the behavior of the last common ancestor of chimpanzees and humans.[51]

Many theorists have failed to appreciate the qualitative difference in sociability that distinguishes us from our other primates. Thus they propose explanations for human ultrasociality that represent only slight extensions of mechanisms that are known to function in other species. For example, Eliot Sober and David Sloan Wilson have argued that group selection, correctly understood, can be used to explain the psychological system underlying human altruism.[52] Yet the problem with their hypothesis is that while the group selection mechanism is real, it is not especially robust. When populations are partitioned into groups, who must then interact with one another repeatedly before recombining, groups that contain altruistic agents may expand at a much greater rate than those that contain selfish agents. However, in order for the group selection effect to occur, there must be much lower levels of variation *within* groups than *between* groups. Sober and Wilson build a set of rather optimistic assumptions into their model, by assuming a bias in the formation of groups, so that altruists will be more likely to be grouped together with other altruists.[53] This blurs the distinction between correlation and group selection, leading them to overestimate the robustness of the group selection effect when it comes to promoting and sustaining altruism.

The most damning criticism of the group selection effect, however, lies in its failure to explain how human social interactions are different from those of other species. In order for the effect to be present, the population must be split up into groups, who must then breed endogamously for several generations before recombination. Yet this pattern is far more common in nonhuman primates than in humans. Among humans, exogamy is a much more frequent pattern than endogamy, and as Boyd and Richerson point out, "wife capture" and rape is a common outcome of tribal warfare among humans.[54] All of this is incompatible with the hypothesis that genetic group selection underlies human altruism.

It simply doesn't fit with what we know about human reproductive behavior and tribal social organization.

It has also often been suggested that human sociality is simply a product of our superior intelligence.[55] In many cases, such arguments are based on a failure to grasp the Hobbesian structure of social interaction (i.e., to recognize that social organization requires a solution to free-rider problems, not merely coordination problems or assurance games). As a result, theorists ignore the fact that mere intelligence, in the form of calculative and predictive ability (i.e., the capacity to engage in instrumental reasoning), is just as likely to make us "nasty" as "nice."[56] It is not an accident that many forms of altruistic behavior are based on involuntary responses. Goodall's story of the chimpanzee trying to muffle his own vocalizations provides an excellent example. He was smart enough to realize that his altruistic impulses did not coincide with his self-interest. Thus intelligence, far from amplifying altruistic behavior, will often trump it. Similarly, tool use is just as likely to promote conflict as cooperation. There are many documented cases of chimpanzees using newly discovered tools to move up the dominance hierarchy. The history of armaments and warfare among humans gives no reason to think that we are much different in this regard.

Robin Dunbar has advanced a more subtle hypothesis, arguing that the size of the neocortex in primates limits the size or the cooperative group, by determining the number of social relationships that the individual can keep track of.[57] Complex social relations stimulate further increases in cognitive sophistication, which in turn permit more complex forms of social organization. The problem with this hypothesis, as an account of human ultrasociality, is that the amount of processing required to manage social relationships increases exponentially as group size increases, since it is necessary to track not only the relationship between oneself and each other person but also all of the relationships between these others. Thus it is extremely doubtful that an increase in raw processing power could ever account for the extent of human social cooperation. Increased social intelligence may explain why our capacity for informal management of social relations allows for the formation of tribes of up to about 150 individuals (larger than what one finds among chimpanzees), but it cannot explain the formation of large-scale societies—at least not as long as reciprocal altruism is the only mechanism posited to explain cooperation among unrelated individuals. It doesn't matter how smart people become, reciprocal altruism does not provide the right sort of tools for managing large-scale cooperation.

Finally, it has been suggested (by Robert Frank, among others)[58] that humans may have developed a particular set of emotional reactions that not only make us more likely to do our part in cooperative relations but also signal to others our willingness to do so. In effect, we humans "wear our hearts on our sleeves," and so project a willingness to cooperate. The problem with this hypothesis is that it, too, underestimates the severity of the free-rider problem. If there is an advantage to be had from experiencing and projecting such sentiments, there is an even greater advantage to be had from projecting such sentiments *without* truly experiencing them, and then not following them up with altruistic behavior. Frank specifies that these emotions must be hard to fake, but this is question-begging.

The fact—if it is a fact—that they are hard to fake *for us* does not explain why we do not find ourselves being exploited by a race of mutants who find them easy to fake. Thus the proposal tries to explain altruistic social behavior by positing a second, essentially altruistic disposition, one that is just as vulnerable to being undermined by free riders as the first.

The more general problem with these hypotheses is that they posit merely quantitative extensions of capacities and dispositions that we share with other primates. Thus they wind up being implausible, simply because the scale of the posited changes in the individual do not account for the magnitude of the effects that occur at the level of human society. They either fail to explain the scope of prosocial behavior among humans or fail to explain the prevalence of antisocial behavior among other primates. There is of course the possibility of a "tweak" that would change the qualitative character of some mechanism in such a way as to permit the emergence of large-scale cooperation. The example of haplodiploidy among social insects provides the model here, since it represents a relatively small change at the level of the individual organism that has had massive effects at the level of social organization. The haplodiploidy tweak, however, amplifies the effects of kin altruism, something that is clearly not relevant in the case of human ultrasociality. Thus many theorists have set out looking for a comparable tweak that might amplify the effects of reciprocal altruism. Of course, there is still the possibility that some *other* mechanism exists, one that is not simply an extension of reciprocal altruism. I will consider this in the next section. For the moment, I will focus on so-called strong reciprocity models, which claim that human ultrasociality is based on a strengthened form of reciprocal altruism.

The strong reciprocity model takes as its point of departure the unique role punishment plays in human social interactions. While nonhuman primates use aggressive and punitive behavior to impose their will, and to maintain the dominance hierarchy, there is little or no evidence of any connection between such punitive behavior and any of the actions associated with systems of reciprocal altruism. Chimpanzees, for example, may refrain from engaging in altruistic behavior that will benefit those who have failed to reciprocate such behavior in the past, but they will not go out of their way to punish that individual.[59] Humans, on the other hand, will often incur costs in order to punish those who have failed to reciprocate altruistic gestures. Even more singular is the fact that among humans, noninvolved third parties will often intervene in order to punish those who act noncooperatively.

Samuel Bowles and Herbert Gintis have argued that this connection between punishment and reciprocity is the "tweak" that explains human ultrasociality.[60] A strategy like tit-for-tat is based on weak reciprocity, since it relies entirely on the withdrawal of cooperation as a punishment mechanism. Individuals "punish" those who fail to act cooperatively by defecting on them in the future, but they do not incur any costs in order to carry out this punishment; they simply revert to the noncooperative baseline. Humans, on the other hand, exhibit a much stronger reaction to defection. As Gintis puts it, the human individual "comes to new social situations with a propensity to cooperate, responds to prosocial behavior on the part of others by maintaining or increasing his level of cooperation, and responds to selfish, free-riding behavior on the part of others by retaliating against the offenders, even at a cost to himself, and even when he could not reasonably expect future personal gains from such retaliation."[61] It is this willingness to incur costs, in order to punish defectors, that distinguishes the strong reciprocity disposition.

Of course, there is a sense in which a weak reciprocator who refuses to cooperate in a prisoner's dilemma with someone who has proven unreliable is incurring a cost. She is forgoing the benefits of possible cooperation, in order to deny them to the other person. But there is also a sense in which refusing to cooperate in a prisoner's dilemma is not really incurring a cost, it is just reverting to the baseline. It may be suboptimal, but it is nevertheless individually maximizing behavior. There are ways of punishing people, by contrast, that involve concrete sacrifices on the part of the person doing the punishing (recall figure 2.1, and the symmetry between promises and threats). Ignoring a person who is drowning, instead of risking death yourself by hopping in to save him, is an example of noncooperative behavior. Hopping in and pushing his head under water is an example of genuinely punitive behavior.

The difference is quite significant, though it is seldom clearly articulated. One way of formulating the cooperative disposition would be to say that a weak reciprocity disposition first "clicks in" when the opportunity for mutually beneficial cooperation presents itself but "clicks out" when one encounters defection. Thus the individual simply reverts to selfish behavior in response to failures of cooperation. A strong reciprocity disposition, on the other hand, is a disposition that "clicks in" when a cooperative situation is encountered, and continues to govern in cases of both cooperation and defection, prescribing potentially fitness-reducing action in both cases. Thus theorists refer to the type of punishment meted out by strong reciprocators as "altruistic punishment."

Altruistic punishment helps to explain a number of peculiarities of human behavior. The most significant is the fact that individuals routinely cooperate in one-shot prisoner's dilemmas, even though they understand clearly that there is no chance of future benefit through reciprocity. Considerable time and energy has been dedicated to the task of showing that this is a maladaptation—a disposition that evolved in order to promote cooperation under conditions of reciprocity, being blindly applied by individuals who fail to adapt their behavior to the differing circumstances of one-shot interactions. For example, the tit-for-tat rule recommends cooperation as an opening gambit in all interactions. Perhaps cooperation in one-shot games is just a mistaken application of this rule? Yet this thesis has very little evidence to back it up. Apart from the fact that no other animal species seems vulnerable to such misapplications of the reciprocal altruism mechanism, there is also the fact that the prospects of future cooperation exert a measurable, but quite distinct, influence on the propensity to cooperate among humans.[62]

Proponents of the strong reciprocity model argue that people cooperate in one-shot prisoner's dilemmas because they have a disposition to do so. They are not cooperating because they mistakenly fear punishment, but rather because of an open-ended cooperative disposition. The role of punishment in the model is more indirect—the presence of altruistic punishers in the population is what shelters the more open-ended cooperative disposition from the pressures of natural selection, making it more attractive than free riding. (The fact that individuals who are exploited will seek out retribution against those who have exploited them means that, by and large, it will be better to cooperate than to defect, even when the chances of future interaction are slim.) Of course, this just pushes the evolutionary puzzle back one step. Given that this form of punishment is altruistic—or at least in some cases not obviously fitness enhancing—the question is how and why it might evolve. The most common suggestion has been that it developed precisely *because* it expands the scope of possible cooperation. Of course, some additional mechanism will be required here, in order to avoid the "good for the species" fallacy. Thus Gintis and Bowles have presented a model that shows how group selection might have given rise to such a disposition.[63]

Prima facie, the strong reciprocity hypothesis has a lot to recommend it. It starts with two forms of behavior—reciprocal altruism and retaliation—that are exhibited by all primates, and yet appear to be merged into one behavioral complex only among humans. Retaliating against defectors represents a relatively minor "tweak" to the reciprocal altruism system, but it can have very powerful systemic effects. Most important, it makes cooperation possible in one-shot interactions. This is equivalent to saying that it makes cooperation possible among strangers, which is in turn equivalent to saying that it extends the boundaries of human sociality indefinitely. Thus strong reciprocity, unlike most of the other mechanisms that have been advanced in the literature, is at least a candidate for explaining human *ultra*sociality. It also has the potential to explain how large-scale cooperation develops, since it allows individuals to respond to defection not just by withdrawing from future cooperation, but by singling out the defectors for targeted punishment. Thus it can explain the use of punishments ranging from application of force to isolation of the offender to banishment from the group.

The weakness of the hypothesis lies not in the evolutionary models that have been developed to explain its origins, but in the descriptive adequacy of the disposition itself. In their definition, Gintis and Bowles mention that strong reciprocators have "a propensity to cooperate and share." They make special mention of sharing because the model was developed not just to explain why so many experimental game theory subjects cooperate in public goods games but also to explain why so many refuse to accept lowball offers in ultimatum games. The problem, from a theoretical standpoint, is that the ultimatum game is not a collective action problem—regardless of how much is offered, acceptance of the offer takes both players to a Pareto-optimal strategic equilibrium. Thus cooperation and altruism are not at issue, the question is simply whether the second player is going to be willfully obstructionist. And in cases where offers are being refused, the first player is not being punished for free riding, but merely for acting in a self-interested fashion. Gintis and Bowles finesse the issue by specifying that the strong reciprocity disposition is one that punishes those who engage in "selfish, free-riding behavior"—which in this case we must take to mean selfish *or* free-riding behavior, since the person who makes a lowball ultimatum offer is not free riding. But if we truly believe that the punishment disposition is one that is triggered whenever individuals pursue their self-interest in zero-sum interactions, then it is more likely to provoke counterproductive feuding than it is harmonious cooperation.

The most natural interpretation of this situation is to say that in the case of the ultimatum game, what individuals are enforcing is a *norm* of fairness, rather than a *norm* of cooperation, and that the disposition to punish is in fact a disposition to punish those who violate social norms, regardless of their content. Such an interpretation suggests that Gintis and Bowles are still too strongly influenced by reciprocal altruism models, and so formulate their favored choice disposition at too low a level of abstraction. They commit an evolutionary version of the "error of premature concreteness," by suggesting that individuals are being punished for a failure to cooperate, rather than for failure to respect a social norm that prescribes cooperation in that context. As a result, when it comes to explaining the fact that the punishment is triggered in many other circumstances, they are forced to start adding disjuncts to their formulation of the strong reciprocity disposition. Yet once this process begins, it is difficult to know when it will stop. For example, experimental evidence suggests that North Americans punish unfair offers in the ultimatum game because they interpret the interaction as a cutting-the-cake division problem, and thus identify "fairness" as the salient norm. The pattern changes completely once the suggestion is made that the first player is somehow "entitled" to the full amount.[64] When that happens, North American behavior becomes more similar to what is observed in New Guinea, where the interaction is interpreted from the outset as an instance of gift giving. Furthermore, from an anthropological perspective, gift-giving relationships are often far more important than those organized through norms of fairness. So should the strong reciprocity disposition be respecified, in order to include a concern for "cooperation, or fairness, or gift-exchange?"[65] What about respecting eating taboos? Greeting rituals? Funeral rites?

It seems clear in these cases that it is conformity to norms that is being enforced, not cooperation. In fact, there are many cases in which individuals do not appear to be terribly concerned about cooperation per se. There are an enormous number of prisoner's dilemmas in our society that are unresolved, which people feel no obligation whatsoever to eliminate. To take a very concrete example, many people waste tap water, because they pay a flat tax for it, rather than paying through a metered account. Similarly, many North Americans waste an enormous amount of time talking on the phone, because they do not have to pay for local calls by the minute. These are both collective action problems, since they result in everyone paying more for both water and local phone service. It was only through concerted public awareness by conservation groups that anyone began to think that personal water consumption should be reduced. And so far, no one has suggested that we should refrain from spending so much time talking on the phone. Certainly no one feels compelled to punish those who do—on the contrary, sanctioning someone who did would itself be a sanctionable offense.

The difference shows up even more dramatically when a collective action problem is itself *normatively enforced*. The basic structure of a competition, for example, is a prisoner's dilemma. The runners in the movie *Chariots of Fire* recognized this.[66] In an athletic competition, the person with the most natural ability generally wins. However, it is possible for people with less ability to improve their chances of winning by training. So as soon as one person begins to train, then all of the others must follow suit, just to retain position. But when they do so, everyone is back where they started—the person with the most natural ability will win. The difference is that they will all be spending a lot more time and energy achieving this result. Furthermore, this just gives the others an incentive to train even more, forcing everyone else to train more, and so forth. It is a classic race to the bottom.[67]

This is why the runners in *Chariots of Fire* had developed an informal agreement that they would *not* train. It was a strong reciprocity–style cooperative agreement. Everything was fine, until a "new kid" arrived, who refused to respect this pact. He adopted the free-rider strategy of training. This failure of reciprocity forced all of the "lazy" runners to follow suit, and so cooperation unraveled in the familiar manner. The movie, however, glorified the actions of this new arrival. He was the "good guy" of the story. Rather than adopting a punitive attitude in response to his noncooperative behavior, audiences hailed him as a hero. This is difficult to explain from a strong reciprocity perspective, but makes perfect sense if one interprets punishment in terms of social norms. Athletic competition is governed by a framework set of social norms, many of which are designed to prevent any solution to the underlying collective action problem. In other words, we think that athletes *should* compete with one another, and that when there is a conspiracy to violate this expectation, the one who breaks ranks does the right thing. (Similar reasoning underlies antitrust laws, as we have seen, since price competition is an interfirm prisoner's dilemma.) In these sorts of cases, we have norms that prescribe noncooperative behavior, enforced through exactly the same type of sanctions that support cooperation in other contexts. Thus it is a mistake to conclude that people have a direct concern with either cooperation or fairness in their interactions. They appear to be concerned above all with social norms. The concern with cooperation and fairness comes from the *content* of these norms, not the disposition that motivates their conformity. Thus the question that we should be asking is not how humans came to be disposed to cooperate, but rather how they became norm-conformists. Once the question is reoriented in this way, interesting avenues of inquiry open up.

6.5. Norm Conformity

The discussion of strong reciprocity takes as its point of departure the observation that human beings are the only social animals who appear willing to take costly punitive measures against individuals who fail to do their part in cooperative arrangements. But this is not the only unique feature of human social interaction. Considerable attention has been lavished, in recent years, on another characteristic feature of human beings: the extraordinarily heavy reliance that human infants have on *imitative learning*. This imitativeness is taken to be the basis for the cultural transmission of learned behavior. Cultural transmission, in turn, frees human behavior from the narrow constraints imposed by natural selection, allowing behavior that is genetically maladaptive—such as religiously inspired celibacy—to persist and even flourish. As long as the gains to the individual from culture-dependence outweigh the losses imposed by these maladaptive behaviors, we can expect the latter to persist.

If this analysis is correct, then the altruism that underlies human ultra-sociality might turn out to be one of these genetically maladaptive, culturally transmitted patterns of behavior. Furthermore, culture-dependence would represent a genuinely novel mechanism for sustaining altruistic conduct. Unlike systems based on reciprocity, where on average and in the long run the altruistic behavior enhances the fitness of the individual who performs it, culturally based altruism may have no such benefits. The specifically altruistic behavioral patterns that are sustained through culture-dependence could be genuinely maladaptive, so long as they are outweighed on average by other, more directly advantageous behavior patterns that are transmitted in this way.[68] To take an analogy, consider the human larynx. There is a general consensus among evolutionary theorists that the low position of the human larynx is an evolutionary adaptation favored because it facilitates speech. At the same time, it also makes it much easier for humans to choke while eating. The latter represents a genuine maladaptation (of the sort that is actually quite common, due to the path-dependency of biological evolution).[69] It persists because it is a maladaptive side effect of an adaptation that, on the whole, increases fitness.

According to this perspective, our capacity for altruistic conduct may be a mistake, from the standpoint of our selfish genes, like our capacity to invent and use contraceptives, or to commit suicide. These all represent culturally transmitted patterns of behavior that may reduce our genetic fitness. They persist because culture-dependence is a single adaptation, and so these "negative" side effects come bundled together with a large number of culturally transmitted patterns of behavior that increase genetic fitness, starting with agriculture and animal husbandry, extending to modern medicine and industrial production.

This argument, however, is one that must be approached with considerable caution. Many scholars in the social sciences treat "culture" as a "get out of jail free" card, one that instantly dissolves the obligation to reconcile their account of altruism with the constraints of human biology and Darwinian evolution. In reality, the relationship between culture, biology, and natural selection is much more complex, and the idea that altruism among humans is culturally sustained raises as many questions as it answers. Does culture-dependence have a substantive bias that favors the emergence of altruism in the cultural sphere, or does it simply shelter it from the forces of natural selection? And if it merely shelters it, then how does altruism get started in the cultural sphere, and what prevents forces of selection similar to those that eliminate it from the biological sphere from removing it from our repertoire of culturally transmitted behavior patterns? Is cultural transmission somehow more propitious for the development of altruistic behavior patterns than genetic transmission?

The first step toward an answer to these questions lies in an examination of the sort of biological structures that must be in place in order for human cultural transmission to occur, along with consideration of how these might have arisen. (Indeed, the very suggestion that culture-dependence represents a single adaptation, rather than a set of loosely related "modules," subject to independent selection pressures, is a claim that is controversial and must be defended.) Only when the biological substratum has been specified will it be possible to state clearly what culture is, how its patterns of transmission differ from those that occur in the genetic sphere, and the extent to which forces of selection will act on cultural patterns.

There is of course considerable controversy over the question of whether culture is unique to human beings. There are several celebrated examples of "traditions" developing among certain animals (such as songbirds) such that unrelated individuals brought into the group will pick up on a pattern of behavior. This is not surprising, since cultural transmission is based on a number of fairly obvious innovations that one can find throughout the natural world. What is distinctive about humans is that we exhibit cumulative cultural transmission, and hence our culture constitutes its own inheritance system.[70] We appear also to be the only species that exhibits domain-general cultural transmission (i.e., with respect to any sort of behavior).

The first step in this direction is simply developmental plasticity. In cases where an organism's environment is stable, natural selection will tend to favor a developmental trajectory that is "canalized," and thus invariably results in the trait that is the best (local) adaptation to that environment. In cases where the environment varies, between state x and y, selection will favor a developmental trajectory that is "plastic," and thus results in some trait a under conditions x, but trait b under conditions y (where each trait represents the best adaptation to those conditions). One of the most dramatic examples of this is the desert locust, which develops as a solitary, wingless, brown grasshopper when regional conditions are favorable for reproduction, but develops as a gregarious (i.e., "swarming"), winged, yellow, migratory locust when conditions are unfavorable. It wasn't discovered that the two shared the same genetic substratum (i.e., belonged to the same species) until 1921.[71]

The second major step is learning, which in its most primitive form is simply a feedback relationship between the environment and the developmental process, such that traits or behavior that are successful will be reinforced, while those that are unsuccessful will be extinguished. A fairly obvious extension of this is trial-and-error learning, in which the individual engages in some variation of the behavior, in order to discover the best form. Finally, there is social learning, where the individual looks to the behavior of conspecifics for clues as to which variant will be best. This is also a fairly obvious adaptation, since it allows individuals to economize significantly on learning costs. It is in fact a free-rider strategy—someone else pays the price associated with failed attempts in trial-and-error learning, while the individual who copies him derives all the benefits associated with any success that he has obtained.

Human beings possess these two characteristics—developmental plasticity and social learning—to an exceptional degree. The juvenile phase among human infants is extremely long, even by comparison to our closest primate relatives. As Stephen Jay Gould writes:

> Human evolution has emphasized one feature of this common primate heritage—delayed development, particularly as expressed in late maturation and extended childhood. This retardation has reacted synergistically with other hallmarks of hominization—with intelligence (by enlarging the brain through prolongation of fetal growth tendencies and by providing a longer period of childhood learning) and with socialization (by cementing family units through increased parental care of slowly developing offspring). It is hard to imagine how the distinctive suite of human characters could have emerged outside the context of delayed development. This is what Morris Cohen, the distinguished philosopher and historian, had in mind when he wrote that prolonged infancy was "more important, perhaps, than any of the anatomical facts which distinguish *homo sapiens* from the rest of the animal kingdom."[72]

This suggests that "our system of social learning is merely a hypertrophied version of a common mammalian system based substantially on the synergy between individual learning and simple systems of social learning" (as Boyd and Richerson put it).[73] There is, however, one important difference. Human infants rely far more heavily on imitative learning than members of any other species.[74] Rather than using the social environment as a source of useful suggestions, and then using their own intelligence to solve problems (a process sometimes referred to as "socially facilitated" learning), humans directly copy one another's behavior, in a way that involves much greater suspension of the capacity for teleological thinking. Michael Tomasello, for instance, argues that social learning among chimpanzees takes the form of what he calls "emulative learning," which differs from true imitation. He and his colleagues conducted an experiment in which they demonstrated, for both chimpanzees and human infants, the use of a tool to obtain an out-of-reach object.[75] The tool could be used in two ways, with one method being clearly more effective than the other. They found that the chimpanzees tended to use the tool in either of these ways, regardless of which method had been demonstrated. Human infants, on the other hand, used the tool in exactly the way that had been demonstrated (even when the inferior method was used). Thus what chimpanzees learned from the demonstration was simply *that* the tool could be used to obtain the food. They used their own intelligence to determine how to use the tool (and in this sense, reinvented the wheel). Human infants, on the other hand, learned not simply *that* the tool could be used, but *how* it was used as well. And this they imitated, even if their own intelligence might have led them to a better solution. Reviewing the evidence, Tomasello argues that "the overall conclusion is thus that during the period from one to three years old, young children are virtual 'imitation machines' as they seek to appropriate the cultural skills and behaviors of the mature members of their social groups."[76]

True imitation creates the possibility of cumulative cultural transmission, because it removes the "filter" that the individual organism's own intelligence (and objectives) imposes on the behavior patterns that are to be transmitted. Thus humans have what Boyd and Richerson refer to as a "dual inheritance" system, where infants benefit from a fund of both genetically favored and culturally transmitted behavioral patterns. It is extremely important to realize, however, that the mere fact that a cultural inheritance system of this type arises does not mean that there will be any divergence between culture and biology (and thus does not mean that there will be any room for the cultural transmission of genetically maladaptive behavior). It all depends on how cultural traits are inherited. If children engage in imitative learning only from caregivers, and for inclusive fitness reasons only parents and relatives act as caregivers, then culture will necessarily evolve in lockstep with biology. A particular pattern of learned behavior will be passed along only if it increases the individual's chances of becoming a "role model" or "cultural parent" to a child. And since only biological parents become cultural parents, the spread of a particular form of learned behavior will be determined entirely by its contribution to the reproductive fitness of the individual who learns it. Under such circumstances, the difference between culture and biology would be nugatory. (And thus, culture of this type would add nothing new to the story on altruism.)

Somewhat more surprisingly, if infants select a cultural parent at random (i.e., through an unbiased sampling procedure) from the population, then there will also be no difference between biological and cultural evolution. This point is often overlooked by critics of sociobiology. With unbiased transmission, a learned behavior pattern will only be able to propagate if it increases its representation in the population, which means increasing the longevity or fecundity of any individual who adopts it. While cultural evolution will be *faster* than biological evolution, due to its Lamarckian structure, there will be no culturally sustained profile of behavior in a population that could not *also* be sustained as the equilibrium of a purely biological system. By implication, all of the constraints that natural selection in the biological domain imposes on altruistic behavior would apply with equal force in the cultural domain.

In order for culture and biology to diverge in interesting ways, there must be some *bias* in the way the cultural variants are acquired. If, for example, the structure of the individuals' attention patterns makes them more likely to notice, and thus adopt, certain types of behavior rather than others, then the cultural fitness of a behavior pattern may diverge from the contribution it makes to the biological fitness of the individual. And when this occurs, it is possible for cultural and biological selection to begin working at cross-purposes. The classic example of this, noted by Dawkins, is the pattern of behavior we call martyrdom.[77] The prestige hierarchy in human society serves as one source of bias—high-prestige individuals are more likely to be imitated than low-prestige individuals. If sacrificing one's life or liberty for a cause serves as a source of prestige, then this pattern of behavior will tend to propagate in the population through cultural transmission, even as it reduces the opportunities for reproduction of those individuals who choose to imitate it. More generally, if performing altruistic acts serves as a source of prestige—and it is not difficult to think of circumstances under which it does—then altruism would have a high level of cultural fitness, despite reducing genetic fitness (of course, one would still need to tell an evolutionary story to explain how or why a prestige-biased learning system would be adaptive, relative to an unbiased one).

Social psychologists have documented a number of very interesting biases in the way cultural transmission occurs among humans. There is, for example, an important conformist bias in the way humans imitate behavior. Faced with multiple options, individuals will select the behavioral variant that is most common in the population. One can see this bias at work quite clearly in language acquisition. Children will initially adopt the dialect and pronunciation used by their parents, but at a certain age almost always switch to the one favored by their peer group.[78] Furthermore, rather than selecting one individual from the peer group to model themselves on, what they adopt represents something more like the majority behavior of the group. In this and many other areas, human learning has a "when in Rome, do as the Romans" bias. It is not difficult to see how this could be adaptive.[79]

This bias has important consequences for the character of cultural transmission. If everyone selects a cultural parent at random, then the majority behavior will be adopted by a majority of imitators. But if there is a strong enough conformist bias, the majority behavior will be adopted by *everyone*. This means that cultural transmission will be subject to tipping point effects far more extreme than those seen in biological evolution. While this does not directly favor the reproduction of any particular cultural pattern, it does change the dynamics. As Boyd and Richerson observe, for instance, it has the potential to make group selection a much more powerful force in the domain of culture. This in turn makes altruistic behavior much more robust as a cultural pattern. As mentioned earlier, in biological evolution, group selection has a very limited impact on the sustainability of altruism, because the chances that a group will be "contaminated" by selfish individuals increases along with both group size and migration rates. And if there are selfish individuals in the group, then the group selection effect will benefit the selfish individuals more than it will the altruists. Thus group selection favors altruism only when groups are very small, and recombination of groups is infrequent. In cultural transmission on the other hand, with a conformist bias, groups need not be composed entirely of individuals who are disposed to act altruistically. As long as enough of them start out disposed to act altruistically, this will be enough to convert the rest to altruism, as they seek to imitate the majority. Thus the level of variation within groups will be much lower than the level of variation between groups. New individuals introduced to the group will also have a tendency to change their behavior in order to fit in, thus neutralizing the disruptive effects of migration. Boyd and Richerson therefore describe cultural evolution as "potentiating" group selection. As a result, some of the explanations for human ultrasociality that are unconvincing when formulated as biological models become far more persuasive when formulated in terms of cultural evolution.

Similar arguments have been used to show that altruistic punishment associated with failures of cooperation can be sustained as a cultural pattern by group selection.[80] Yet these claims are vulnerable to the same objections that were leveled against Bowles and Gintis's formulation of the strong reciprocity disposition. It is important that punishment be associated with the failure to respect social practices, not the failure to cooperate. Thus Boyd and Richerson make a far more plausible claim when they suggest that "moralistic punishment"—that is, altruistic punishment that is itself altruistically enforced—becomes tied to our propensity for conformist imitation, such that agents are disposed to do what the majority does, and to punish those who do not. Boyd and Richerson speculate that moralistic punishment of this type arises because it augments the efficacy of conformist imitation (and also amplifies the tipping point effect that makes group selection a powerful force in cultural transmission).[81]

There are a number of different evolutionary models that provide plausible underpinnings for an account of the cultural evolution of cooperation. But whatever the ultimate story, it is important to note that the disposition that arises out of Boyd and Richerson's account—"conformist social learning" combined with "moralistic enforcement of norms"—is precisely what sociological theorists have posited for decades as the "norm-conformative" disposition at the heart of human sociality. Thus Boyd and Richerson's model provides a striking point of convergence between evolutionary biology and sociological theory. It explains why cultural transmission in human societies takes the form of shared rules of conduct, or social norms.

The explanation Boyd and Richerson provide for human ultrasociality is in the end quite subtle. The first thing to recognize is that, unlike altruistic tendencies that arise through kin selection or reciprocal altruism, here there is no genetically based disposition to perform altruistic acts. What biological evolution provides is simply a norm-conformative disposition—a disposition that itself is neutral with respect to altruistic and selfish behavior. As Boyd and Richerson put it (in the title of an article), "punishment allows the evolution of cooperation (or anything else) in sizable groups." Individuals simply have a disposition to conform to the dominant behavior pattern of the group, a disposition that is reinforced through punishment of nonconformative behavior. This disposition is acquired because of the enormous advantages it confers on the individual, primarily in the form of enhanced learning abilities. But it also permits the development of all sorts of maladaptive behaviors; even, as Boyd and Richerson point out, ones as ridiculous as the norm that prescribes wearing neckties in the workplace.[82] This is as it should be, since, as we all know, wearing neckties in the workplace *was* the norm in our society for a very long time.

Thus the reason that a norm-conformative disposition favors altruism is not that it instills any direct bias in its favor. It promotes altruism only indirectly, by serving as a platform for the beginnings of cultural evolution, which in turn provides both an evolutionary environment and a selection mechanism that is more propitious for the emergence of altruism. Thus the norm-conformative disposition favors altruism only because it is easier for altruism to emerge and prosper as a cultural pattern than as a biological one. The norm-conformative disposition serves only to insulate the altruistic phenotype from the pressures of biological selection, which would otherwise favor its elimination. (This also explains why ultrasociality has arisen only recently, in the last ten thousand years.)

They summarize the argument as follows:

> Theoretical models show that the specific structural features of cultural systems, such as conformist transmission, have ordinary adaptive advantages. We imagine that these adaptive advantages favored the capacity for a system that could respond rapidly and flexibly to environmental variation in an ancestral creature that was not particularly cooperative. As a by-product, cultural evolution happened to favor large-scale cooperation.[83]

This first component of the hypothesis should be kept conceptually distinct from the second, which involves the specific mechanism that Boyd and Richerson posit to explain why altruism does better in the cultural sphere. They claim that it is because norm-conformity amplifies the effects of group selection (the benefits of which, in turn, reinforce the norm-conformative disposition). However, there is no exclusivity in this hypothesis. For example, it could turn out that cultural evolution favors reciprocal altruism as well.

In this context, it is worth noting that the basic structure of the norm-conformative disposition provides precisely the "building blocks" needed for the development of what Robert Brandom refers to as "norms implicit in practice" (recalling the important role that *sanctions* played in this account of rule-following).[84] This in turn permits the creation of social practices such as the "game of giving and asking for reasons" described in chapter 4, section 6. Thus the development of a norm-conformative disposition can be seen as a crucial evolutionary step, allowing humans to pass from simple signaling systems to the emergence of fully compositional language. The emergence of language—and hence the intentional planning system—provides straightforward advantages to the individual (those associated with "the language upgrade"). This may help to explain the adaptive value of the particular combination of conformist social learning and moralistic punishment that we see among humans.

The emergence of language may also help to explain why altruistic behavior is more robust as a cultural pattern. Once compositional linguistic resources are in place, it then becomes possible for individuals to introduce elements of conscious guidance into the process of cultural evolution (for example, by allowing individuals to verbally contest norms that institutionalize a suboptimal behavior pattern, or by serving as a source of bias in the production of "mutations" in the cultural pattern). In other words, language makes possible rational deliberation about the desirability of potential norms. This may help to explain why even though in principle any behavior can be sustained as a cultural pattern, cooperative ones tend to occur with greater frequency than noncooperative ones (and why they continue to be favored in modern societies, in which group selection effects are highly attenuated, if not nonexistent).

6.6. Against Sociobiology

In retrospect, it should be easier to see why one need not endorse a sociobiological view in order to accept a naturalistic and evolutionary account of our
moral dispositions along the lines of the one presented here. The key to it lies in
the "dual inheritance" model of biological and cultural evolution that is being
posited, combined with the "dual process" theory of mind. However, in order to
see how this model allows one to escape the charge of sociobiologism, it is useful
to examine first some of the *invalid* arguments against sociobiology that philosophers have been known to make.

The most common error among philosophers is to assume that a biological
explanation for a particular trait must assume that anything genetic is "hardwired" (or canalized) and thus admits of no variation. As a result, they will often
point to simple behavioral differences from one human group to another as
evidence that a particular form of behavior is "cultural" and not "biological."[85]
(In other words, they claim that phenotypic variation in the absence of genetic
variation defeats the sociobiological hypothesis.) This ignores the fact that plasticity with respect to some characteristic is not only compatible with biological
explanation, but that such plasticity is itself a biological trait, one whose presence must be subject to evolutionary explanation. As E. O. Wilson puts it, the
sociobiological hypothesis in this case "is that genes promoting flexibility in
social behavior are strongly selected at the individual level."[86]

For example, the fact that desert locusts sometimes develop into brown grass-
hoppers and sometimes develop into yellow winged locusts does not pose any
obstacle to biological explanation. On the contrary, the developmental plasticity
required to become one or the other is itself the object of such an explanation. (As
it turns out, a very persuasive adaptive explanation is available. It is *crowding* that
triggers the development of the individual into a migratory locust rather than
a sedentary grasshopper. In effect, the species has a mechanism that tells individuals when it is a good idea to be moving on.) Similarly, an enormous amount
of variation can be explained by the simple fact that organisms are capable of
learning. There is nothing obscure about this, from a biological point of view,
since learning involves nothing more than a feedback relationship between the
organism and the environment during the course of development. All the sociobiologist needs to do is provide some explanation that shows how it is adaptive for
individuals to learn which behavior is best, rather than to have it be fixed.

That such explanations are available is already implicit in the universally
shared assumption that phenotype is a joint product of a complex developmental interaction between the organism's genotype and its environment (an environment that includes other cells within the organism, other members of the
same species, as well as the "parametric" physical environment). This makes it
easy for the sociobiologist to offer an explanation for differences among human
groups: it is simply a case of different environments (both social and nonsocial)
triggering different behaviors or characteristics, all of which are latent possibilities for all individuals. As Wilson puts it, "culture, including the more resplen-
dent manifestations of ritual and religion, can be interpreted as a hierarchical

system of environmental tracking devices."[87] Thus if we ask "why did so-and-so do such-and-such?" the proximate causes we appeal to by way of explanation need not refer to any adaptive features of the behavior. (In fact, the behavior can be quite maladaptive—so long as the acquisition of maladaptive phenotypes in the population overall does not reduce fitness to a level that would render plasticity in this domain maladaptive.) The sociobiologist is merely committed to the claim that if one were to pursue the chain of explanation back far enough, eventually one would hit on some factor that could only be explained through an adaptive genetic explanation.

The problem is that when formulated in this way, the sociobiological hypothesis risks becoming trivial. One can see this very clearly in Wilson's work. He argues:

> The channels of human mental development... are circuitous and variable. Rather than specify a single trait, human genes prescribe the capacity to develop a certain array of traits. In some categories of behavior, the array is limited and the outcome can be altered only by strenuous training—if ever. In others, the array is vast and the outcome easily influenced.[88]

The question then becomes: given the very high level of plasticity that humans exhibit, and granting that this plasticity, as a trait, is subject to evolutionary explanation, do evolutionary considerations place any *interesting* constraints on the "array" of traits that can develop within any a particular domain of human culture? Take, for example, the issue of food preference. We all come equipped with certain natural food aversions that are easy to explain in evolutionary terms. It is certainly not an accident that we are "instinctively" repulsed by the smell of rotten meat, or the taste of milk that has turned, or by the appearance of food that is moldy. Yet all of these reactions can be unlearned with sufficient effort (which is why we talk about some foods, like blue cheese, being "acquired tastes"). Thus it is not clear precisely what the evolutionary story contributes to our understanding of human diet. One can easily imagine that as our early ancestors migrated to different climates and regions, it became adaptive for them to become more flexible, so that they could acquire a taste for foods that had previously provoked highly aversive reactions (e.g., most preserved foods). Yet if this is the case, then we run the risk of saying that the only thing the evolutionary story really explains is the fact *that we eat*. In order to explain *why we eat what we eat*, one must turn to an entirely different set of factors. Furthermore, the idea that behavior must be adaptive imposes almost no constraints on this secondary explanation. It only requires that, on average and in general, the maladaptive consequences of all the bad dietary habits we acquire must not outweigh the overall advantages associated with our capacity to acquire tastes.

From this perspective, one can see the problems that positing a norm-conformative disposition creates for sociobiological forms of explanation. Because it is grounded in imitation, this disposition is essentially open to all forms of behavior (which is not to say that all forms of behavior are equally likely to be reproduced). Furthermore, it lays the groundwork for the cultural transmission of phenotype (and thus for "population-level effects"). A phenotype may prove to be culturally adaptive (i.e., successful at reproducing itself) even though it is not genetically adaptive. Thus when it comes to explaining a particular form of behavior, such as dietary taboos, the cultural explanation may wind up doing all the work. If we ask why Jews do not eat pork, Hindus do not eat beef, or Americans do not eat dogs, questions of genetic fitness simply need not enter into the story in any interesting way. The type of "just so" sociobiological explanations we are accustomed to hearing (such as speculation that taboos on pork may have "evolved" as a defense against trichinosis) are clearly invalid, since genetic evolution has clearly favored plasticity in the area of meat consumption. So while there are interesting questions to be asked about how these dietary taboos originated, and why they, rather than other cultural variants, succeeded in reproducing themselves, the evolutionary biological perspective places only trivial constraints on the range of possible explanations. Furthermore, there is no reason to expect that the cultural explanation will be a genetically adaptive one, simply because cultural evolution is governed by a different selection mechanism. In fact, many dietary restrictions are strikingly maladaptive at the genetic level (a large number of deaths from famine in India could have been averted if people had been willing to eat the cows). The problem, as Wilson acknowledges, is that "cultural behavior...seems to be a psychological whole invested in the brain or denied it in a single giant step."[89] This makes sense if one views cultural transmission as the product of a single social learning heuristic, namely, the disposition toward imitative conformity. Yet if this is the case, then human culture will be able to support an enormous amount of genetically maladaptive behavior, without making our capacity for culturally determined behavior itself fitness-reducing. As a result, there is simply no reason to favor "survival of the fittest" explanations when it comes to any form of behavior that falls within the "array" of human traits subject to cultural variation. As Kim Sterelny notes, sociobiologists have had a tendency to finesse the distinction between "selective explanations for behavior" and "selective explanations of capacities for behavior," in order to obscure the fact that, in most cases, they are only in a position to deliver the latter, not the former.[90]

Due to considerations of this type, combined with concessions in the direction of the dual-inheritance model, Wilson himself can no longer be classified as a sociobiologist. This emphasizes the point that, contrary to the assumptions of many sociobiologists, critics of that doctrine are not committed to the idea that the human mind is a "blank slate," or some type of domain-general learning mechanism for the acquisition of culture.[91] On the contrary, positing dual inheritance is perfectly consistent with the recognition that various features of human cognition are the product of evolutionarily adapted cognitive mechanisms, and that some of these mechanisms are even specialized for the acquisition of specific elements of the cultural system. The question is whether the "genes-environment" framework represents the most perspicuous one for explaining the types of behaviors that wind up getting propagated in these various domains. Although it is not false, strictly speaking, to describe culture as merely part of the environment, it is positively misleading to do so when that part of the environment constitutes a second inheritance system. Thus the only real sociobiologists remaining are those who deny that culture forms an inheritance system, or think that there is no codependence between the genetic and cultural evolutionary systems. These claims are, in my view, too weakly motivated to merit sustained discussion here (though others have dealt with them at great length).[92]

Given this situation, it is more useful to think of our biological heritage as an extremely rich source of *biases* in the domain of cultural reproduction. Even if we were to suppose that people can be socialized into any behavior pattern whatsoever, the fact remains that it is much *easier* to socialize people to do some things than it is others. In the same way, you can cut wood any way you like, but it is much easier to do so with the grain. Our biological heritage constitutes the grain here, asserting itself in the domain of culture by affecting the amount of effort (of various forms) that will be required in order to stabilize and reproduce a given pattern. For instance, there is no doubt an adaptive explanation for the fact that we have 10 fingers. And the fact that we have 10 fingers no doubt provides an explanation for the fact that we count in base 10. But this does not add up to a sociobiological explanation for the fact that we count in base 10. On the contrary, different cultures have used a variety of different bases. When Europeans arrived in Mesoamerica, they found both base 20 and base 8 systems in use. Each of these systems "competes" with the others in the cultural domain (the same way the metric system competes with the British imperial system). But the fact that we have 10 fingers biases the competition in favor of base 10. Thus the explanation for the success of base 10 is in terms of cultural evolution. Human biology provides part of the environment in which cultural evolution occurs, and thus affects the fitness of different cultural variants, but it does not act as a direct force of *selection*. It is not because people who count in base 8 had fewer children that the system passed out of use. It is because they were unable to attract as many imitators as did their base 10 rivals.

Thus the best way to think of the adaptive unconscious (and in particular, all the modular elements described by evolutionary psychologists) is as the environment in which cultural selection occurs. Some cultural patterns will do well precisely because they reinforce or amplify these evolved dispositions. Consider the case of sexuality, where one finds an enormous variety of practices at different times and in different cultures. Peter Berger and Thomas Luckmann observe:

> While man possesses sexual drives that are comparable to those of the other higher mammals, human sexuality is characterized by a very high degree of pliability. It is not only relatively independent of temporal rhythms, it is pliable both in the objects toward which it may be directed and in its modalities of expression. Ethnological evidence shows that, in sexual matters, man is capable of almost anything. One may stimulate one's sexual imagination to a pitch of feverish lust, but it is unlikely that one can conjure up any image that will not correspond to what in some other culture is an established norm, or at least an occurrence to be taken in stride.[93]

Recognizing the "immense variety and luxurious inventiveness" of human sexual practices, especially in similar environments, suggests that the more interesting explanations are going to be cultural, rather than biological. But this does not mean that biological factors should be ignored. What the argument from variety shows is that biology imposes no significant constraints on the "array of traits" that may be exhibited (i.e., the range of social practices that may be reproduced). At the same time, some sexual practices are much more *common* than others. Moderate polygyny, for instance, is exceedingly common; polyandry is not. Compulsory homosexuality is not unheard-of, but is far less common than compulsory heterosexuality. The best way to formulate a "biological" explanation for these phenomena is not in terms of the adaptiveness of the practices, but in terms of a set of unconscious cognitive structures or somatic responses that bias cultural reproduction in the direction of one or another practice (these underlying structures being, of course, subject to straightforward adaptive explanation).

Consider a related example involving mate preferences. There are obvious biological reasons, in species where males make some parental investment, that they might also be more likely to engage in "mate guarding" behavior than females. One can certainly find this sort of behavior in many mammalian species. It would also not be strange to think that this had something to do with various human traits that seem to be more pronounced among males, such as sexual jealously and possessiveness. Indeed, in an international study, with samples drawn from 37 different cultures, David Buss found that males were consistently more likely than females to regard "no previous sexual intercourse" as an important characteristic of a potential mate. In 23 of the 37 samples, males expressed a stronger preference in this regard than did females, while in the other 14 samples "no significant sex differences were found."[94] This is the sort of finding that is sometimes taken to be grist for the sociobiologists's mill, since it seems easy to produce an "evolutionary" explanation for this pattern. Yet the same study also found that the overall intensity of this preference varied even more dramatically—from China, where both men and women almost uniformly viewed a potential mate's chastity as "indispensable" (over 2.5 on a 3-point scale) to Sweden, where it was regarded by both sexes as practically "irrelevant" (around 0.25 on the same scale). Within both Chinese and Swedish cultures, however, men were more likely to identify this issue as a concern than women. Yet the difference was only about 0.1 in both cases. What this shows is that the cultural difference was two orders of magnitude greater than the gender difference. This proves that it is possible (perhaps even easy) to socialize men in such a way that they care far less about chastity than women—just raise the men in Sweden and the women in China (or even the United States). Thus culture provides, if not *the* explanation for the preference, certainly the most *interesting* explanation for the relative power of the chastity norm in each society. What the biological logic of parental investment explains is not the particular preference any one individual has, but rather the general bias that one can see, within the domain of cultural reproduction, toward a greater male preoccupation with sexual fidelity. (The norm has slightly greater "affective resonance" with men than with women.)[95]

The idea that biology should be understood as a source of bias in the cultural sphere in many ways undermines the polarization that has long characterized the culture/biology debate. In the same way that sociobiologists need not regard inherited traits as "hardwired," critics of sociobiology are in no way committed to viewing the mind as a "blank slate."[96] Much of the debate over the "innateness" of various characteristics is based on confusion in this regard. In general, human cognitive development is too complex for us to be able to tell what is innate and what is learned—or even to draw the distinction in any meaningful way. Furthermore, there is clear evidence of so-called Baldwinian evolution in the cognitive sphere.[97] Evidence suggests that the human brain has undergone biological evolution *since* the development of the cultural inheritance system. Thus a feedback relationship has developed between biological and cultural evolution. In particular, biological adaptations that accelerate cultural learning, or else bias the outcome in favor of dominant cultural traits, will tend to be genetically adaptive. (The canonical example is lactose tolerance—a biological adaptation that is generally thought to have been a reaction to the cultural practice of animal husbandry, along with migration into northern climes where sunlight no longer provides adequate vitamin D.)

Yet despite this, sociobiologists often use the speed or ease of acquisition of a particular competence as an indicator of its genetic basis. Thus they contrast, for example, the speed with which human infants acquire language (and the remarkable paucity of stimulus or instruction) with the difficulty that most of us have learning algebra or calculus.[98] Yet while this is no doubt an important phenomenon, it does not show that language itself, in the sense of semantic content or even just grammar, is innate.[99] It is important to remember that not only has public language served as part of the evolutionary environment of adaptation for humans—such that infants with innate heuristics allowing them to learn language more quickly would have been at an advantage—but languages themselves, as cultural artifacts, are also adapted to the cognitive machinery of human infants. In other words, languages that can get themselves learned more quickly—for example, by taking advantage of certain innate learning heuristics possessed by human infants—have a competitive advantage over ones that cannot. Thus, as Andy Clark argues, we need not postulate innate language modules, or any other "major and sweeping computational and neurological differences between us and other animals," in order to explain our facility at language learning:

> Instead, relatively minor neural changes may have made basic language learning possible for our ancestors, with the process of reverse adaptation thereafter leading to linguistic forms that more fully exploit pre-existing, language-independent cognitive biases (especially those of young humans). The human brain, on this model, need not differ profoundly from the brains of higher animals. Instead, normal humans benefit from some small neurological innovation that, paired with the fantastically empowering environment of increasingly reverse-adapted public language, led to the cognitive explosions of human science, culture, and learning.[100]

If this were the case, then "it would look for all the world as if our brains were especially adapted to acquire natural language, but in fact it would be natural language that was especially adapted so as to be acquired by us, cognitive warts and all."[101] It is worth keeping in mind, when considering the innateness hypothesis, that language has all the appearances of being a cultural artifact, not least because there are so many mutually unintelligible languages on the planet.[102] As Tomasello points out, "'language' has several thousand distinct variants in the human species that are fundamentally different from one another, including in the syntactic conventions, and an individual human being can acquire any one particular language only in the context of several years of particular types of linguistic experiences with other human beings."[103] The coadaptation story—we are adapted to learn language fast, languages are adapted to be learned by us fast—is able to explain why language is acquired so quickly and easily by human infants, but also why it varies so widely in both lexicon and ("surface") grammar from one human group to another.

6.7. Conclusion

It is important to keep in mind, when thinking about human sociality, that altruism is extremely uncommon in nature. In order to see how dramatic the contrast is, one need only compare the way cells cooperate with one another inside our own bodies—and the kind of complex internal division of labor that this level of cooperation is able to promote—with the very low levels of cooperation that one sees between, for example, domestic cats, along with the complete absence of social structure that this entails. The difference is that the cells in our body have a 100 percent coefficient of relatedness and so have nothing to gain from free riding. One can think of a multicellular organism as a society of clones who exhibit complete cooperation, and thus have a "social structure" that exhibits extraordinarily high levels of internal complexity and interdependence (such as differentiation into organs that cooperate with one another in order to sustain the life of the organism). Failures of cooperation in this context are so infrequent that we have a special word for them—cancer. At the other end would be a typical diploid species, where there is a very low level of relatedness even among kin, and so very little in the way of social structure and cooperation. Of course, we should not marvel at the fact that purely Darwinian natural selection is able to generate such practices as animal husbandry and farming among ants, since we already know that natural selection is able to produce even more fabulously complex things like livers and immune systems. What is unusual about ants is simply the fact that the complexity is social, rather than internal to the individual organism (where we usually take cooperation for granted). And this is simply a reflection of how difficult it is to achieve any sort of organization or interdependence among genetically unrelated individuals.

This is the background against which the problem of human ultrasociality should be addressed. Apart from the high levels of cooperation one finds among humans, there are three other features that set us apart as a species: superior intelligence, use of a propositionally differentiated language to communicate, and culture-dependence. Given the rather slight biological difference between us and our closest primate relatives, it is very unlikely that these *differentia* are unrelated. They are most likely to be part of a single complex, or at least all facilitated by a single adaptation. The dominant tendency in the literature has been to focus on superior intelligence as the driving force. The analysis presented here suggests that culture-dependence is the more fundamental. Once culture-dependence is established, in the form of a norm-conformative disposition (imitative conformity coupled with moralistic punishment), one can then explain the emergence of propositionally differentiated speech (as Brandom's pragmatic theory of meaning shows), which can in turn be used to explain the origins of mental content, intentional states, and finally the intentional planning system that is at the root of our superior practical intelligence. Finally, it is much easier to see how altruism (and ultimately, cooperation) could persist as a culturally transmitted pattern of behavior (although the details of this merit further analysis, and will be taken up in the final chapter). Thus norm-conformity appears to be the key that opens all the locks. We are not just intelligent creatures who happen to like following rules; rather, following rules is what makes us the intelligent creatures that we are.

7

Transcendental Necessity

The time has come for a brief digression into the realm of armchair micro-sociology. When I was young, supermarket parking lots used to be something of a mess. People would bring their groceries out to the car, put them in the trunk, then abandon their shopping cart right next to the car as they pulled out. Everyone used to do this, and no one thought twice about it. Stores used to hire local teenagers to roam the lots, picking up unused carts and stacking them in orderly rows by the front door. This was no doubt a nagging expense, as stores were constantly looking for ways to keep the carts under control. Some installed barriers to keep people from taking them into the parking lot, but that was grossly inconvenient for customers. Finally, someone came up with a devilishly clever (and now ubiquitous) invention. It is a simple clip and chain mechanism on the handle of the cart. You insert a quarter to release the chain, allowing you to roam about with the cart as you please. But to get your quarter back, you must insert the chain into the clip on another cart. Through this simple little invention, stores managed to get customers not only to return their carts to the front door, but to line them up nicely as well. All you need to do is put one clip at the front door, to get the sequence going. Once it starts, everyone must then bring their carts to that spot, and fold them together, in order to get their quarters back.

Thanks to this simple little invention, grocery store parking lots were transformed overnight from unruly obstacle courses of abandoned shopping carts into tiny miracles of coordination and efficiency. Furthermore, all of this was accomplished without any hectoring, threats, or moral suasion. At my local supermarket, there are no signs saying "Please return your cart"; the economic incentive appears to be sufficient. People want their quarters back, and are willing to push their shopping carts around for a bit longer in order to recover them. Or so it would seem. Yet one can also observe, on some days, a rather strange phenomenon. A homeless person will hang out in the parking lot, offering to take people's carts back for them, in return for being able to keep the quarter. Almost everyone accepts, many quite gratefully (many of whom would not give money to panhandlers). This suggests that many people are willing to pay a quarter to avoid taking their shopping cart back. So why don't they just abandon them? This got me thinking. The next time I was at the store, about to walk my cart back to the front door, I thought to myself "Is this really worth it?" I was far from the return depot, the lot was three inches deep in snow, so that the wheels on the cart barely turned. "Forget it," I thought. "I'll just leave it here, and forfeit the quarter."

In principle, there was nothing wrong with this decision. The cart return system is a purely economic transaction between the customer and the store: if you want your quarter back, you take your cart back, otherwise the store gets it. Yet I was surprised to find myself struck by a pang of guilt at the thought of abandoning my shopping cart in the middle of the parking lot. I pictured the other shoppers looking at me reproachfully as I slunk out of the parking lot. Abandoning the cart *felt* like an extremely antisocial thing to do. In the end, I pushed the cart back.

What happened to me? A mere *regularity* in the behavior of shoppers had triggered my normative control system. What made it noteworthy in this case was that there wasn't *technically* a social norm underlying this regularity, just a pattern of behavior brought about by incentives. Yet over time, imitative conformity had clearly transformed this mere regularity into a social norm. The cart-return system at my local supermarket achieves nearly 100 percent compliance. And yet obviously it works so well not because it provides everyone with a direct incentive to return their carts, but because it provides enough of an incentive to get enough people to return their carts that it displaces shoppers to the "normative expectations equilibrium" of universal cart return.

What does this have to do with moral philosophy? In a widely discussed article, Christine Korsgaard introduced a very useful distinction between two different forms of skepticism about practical reason.[1] The first is "content skepticism." This refers to skepticism about the possibility that the content of moral judgments could be well justified. The content skeptic is one who doubts that we are able to offer a compelling defense of our judgments, when we claim that a particular action is right or wrong, or that a state of affairs is good or bad. "Motivational skepticism" on the other hand adds a new layer of difficulty, by suggesting that even if it were possible to come up with justifiable moral judgments, it is still not clear why the agent should be moved to act on those judgments. Thus the motivational skeptic is one who regards it as perfectly coherent that someone could judge a particular action to be right, and yet have no motive to perform it (or that someone might judge a state of affairs to be good, yet have no motive to bring it about). Motivational skepticism is usually summed up with the question "why be moral?" (such that, even if we know what the moral course of action is, we can still ask the question "why pursue the moral course of action, and not some other?").

The discussion of contextualism in chapter 5 showed how one might begin to respond to the problem of content skepticism. A more complete discussion will be reserved for chapter 9. For now, my goal is to deal with the problem of motivational skepticism. It will be my contention that a careful analysis of the form of deontic constraint at work in the shopping cart return system—understood in the light of the theory of norm-conformity articulated in the previous chapter—can serve as the cornerstone of a philosophically compelling response to motivational skepticism about morality.

7.1. A Skeptical Solution

Hume famously declared " 'Tis not contrary to reason to prefer the destruction of the whole world to the scratching of my finger."[2] The challenge he poses to common-sense morality is immediate and compelling. There is, however, some ambiguity in the precise sense in which the challenge can be understood. Hume might have been saying "What argument is there to show that one is better than the other?" but he could also have been asking "How could you rouse me to care one way or the other, if I happen not to?" Of course, the Humean theory of practical rationality answers the second question by specifying that any convincing argument must take as premises something that the agent already cares about. This makes it easier to see why the agent might care about the conclusion, but it simply pushes the problem of motivational skepticism back one step. It suggests that if the agent does not already happen to care about any of the standard range of moral concerns, it will be impossible to persuade him to start doing so. There will simply be no way for moral arguments to get a toehold with someone who is not already concerned about morality.

It is, however, important to remember that in ethics, as in epistemology, Hume himself was not a skeptic. He advanced skeptical arguments as a way of clearing the ground for the introduction of his own positive views. He describes his overall strategy as one of providing a "skeptical solution" to the problems raised. The general idea was to show that with respect to some problematic class of judgment, even though we have no high-powered justification for doing things the way we do, this need not trouble us terribly. Most people do things in the way that we might hope they would. Furthermore, people are creatures of habit, with very firmly entrenched dispositions. Thus we do not have to worry about them reversing course anytime soon. Philosophical skepticism, for Hume, amounts to idle speculation. Once we leave the study and venture out into the company of men, all of these doubts fade away.

Hume calls this a "skeptical solution" because it takes as its point of departure an acceptance of the basic skeptical argument. Rather than denying the skeptic's claims, it seeks merely to show that accepting them is not as dire, in terms of its life consequences, as it might initially have seemed. In the case of morality, Hume tries to make this point by showing that as a matter of fact, virtuous dispositions are quite widely shared, and in cases where a person is not already disposed through "natural virtue" to act altruistically, natural sympathy has a tendency to generate approval of actions that promote the greatest happiness.

John Stuart Mill adopts a similar line of argument when considering the "ultimate sanction" of the principle of utility. In the abstract, we can imagine persons who are simply devoid of all moral sentiment ("on them morality of any kind has no hold but through the external sanctions"). But empirically, this is extremely uncommon. Furthermore, when it comes to concern for the welfare of others,

> Whatever amount of this feeling a person has, he is urged by the strongest motives both of interest and of sympathy to demonstrate it, and to the utmost of his power encourage it in others; and even if he has none of it himself, he is as greatly interested as any one else that others should have it. Consequently the smallest germs of the feeling are laid hold of and nourished by the contagion of sympathy and the influences of education; and a complete web of corroborative association is woven round it, by the powerful agency of the external sanctions.[3]

Thus people start out life with a certain level of natural altruistic feeling. These sentiments are cultivated and "enlarged" over the course of the child's development, so that a properly socialized adult winds up having considerable sensitivity to the welfare of others, along with a broader willingness to do his part in cooperative endeavors. The entire system is a stable equilibrium, as Mill implies, since even those who have very little natural sympathy still have an interest in seeing it encouraged in others.

It is worth stopping for a moment to consider such "skeptical solutions," and to ask precisely what is wrong with them. After all, it is possible to develop a much more sophisticated version using the evolutionary perspective developed in the previous chapter. Both Hume and Mill were inclined to treat morality as a unitary phenomenon, arising from a single primitive disposition. This not only introduced a powerful noncognitivist bias into their thinking about morality, it also led them to develop theories that failed to accommodate some of the most important structural features of our moral reasoning. In particular, neither of them was able to explain the deontological character of many of our moral intuitions. Contemporary developmental psychologists, however, are more inclined toward the view that "prosocial" behavior among humans has multiple roots.[4] Prelinguistic infants have spontaneous sympathetic reactions (e.g., they may become distressed on hearing someone else nearby in distress). Even the very young understand that a crying baby requires attention, and may try to attract the attention of an adult or to assist the baby themselves.[5] Yet there are other, more sophisticated forms of altruism that only begin to appear at much later stages of development. Many of them depend on role-taking abilities (the ability to see interactions from the perspective of others), along with the ability to understand that action occurs within a framework of generalized expectations.[6]

From an evolutionary perspective, it not surprising that what we call "morality" should have a complex internal structure. Indeed, we should expect that each of the three evolutionary mechanisms that can sustain altruism (kin selection, reciprocity, and norm-conformity) should be associated with a distinct set of dispositions, each of which is capable of disposing the agent toward "prosocial" behavior of a different form. It has often been noted, for example, that natural sympathy is extremely limited in scope, and tends to be easier to cultivate when the person who is suffering resembles us in some way, or exhibits neotenous characteristics. This would seem to be an obvious legacy of kin selection. Hume noted that "a man naturally loves his children better than his nephews, his nephews better than his cousins, his cousins better than strangers, where every thing else is equal."[7] This is, of course, almost a precise statement of the calculus of inclusive fitness. Yet both Hume and Mill assumed that human morality was constructed by building on and extending these sympathies—and thus that the task of socialization was to make people feel more sympathy for more people, more often. From an evolutionary perspective, this is implausible; it clearly takes a different sort of mechanism to sustain human ultrasociality.

Unlike kin selection, reciprocal altruism is a mechanism that requires a much higher level of cognitive sophistication to develop. In particular, it requires the capacity to distinguish those who have cooperated in the past from those who have not, along with the ability in many cases to keep a "running tab" on how balanced the cooperative exchange has been. Thus it would be no surprise to see this form of altruism emerge only later in the developmental process, after more sophisticated social reasoning skills emerge in the child. As I mentioned, it is plausible to suggest that the "friend/foe" orientation that people deploy in social interaction is one of the psychological dispositions associated with this form of altruism. Indeed, the basic concepts of virtue ethics can all find behavioral correlates in systems of social interaction structured by reciprocal altruism. At this level, prosocial behavior is essentially anchored in a disposition to cooperate with specific individuals, built up over time through repeated exchanges. One can imagine the concept of virtue and vice arising as essentially the "scorecard" used to keep track of these exchanges. Benefiting from an altruistic act performed by another generates a slight positive cathexis of that individual (one begins to like him, or to ascribe a "virtuous" character). Suffering from a selfish or aggressive act performed by another generates a negative cathexis (one begins to dislike him, or ascribe a "vicious" character). This is how we passively keep track of the benefits we are receiving. Liking someone, in turn, generates a highly generalized disposition to act altruistically toward him or her.

Finally, the disposition required for the cultural transmission of learned behavior explains the role that rules play in our moral reasoning. The two dispositions discussed above are both substantive, in the sense that they privilege particular types of moral obligations (e.g., to alleviate the suffering of those in distress, or to come to the assistance of a friend). Yet one of the features of morality that has dominated philosophical discussion since Kant is precisely the formal character of our moral obligations. Principles like the golden rule, which can be found in every major culture and religion, do not commit us to performing one particular type of action; they simply insist that each action be evaluated as a possible candidate for adoption as a general rule. This can be understood as a reflection of the fact that our normative control system is fundamentally a disposition toward conformist imitation, and is thus entirely vacuous with respect to content. Setting aside the question of how the content of our obligations is to be determined, we can see how, on the motivational front, the disposition to respect moral rules could be understood as an incentive to do one's duty for its own sake.

Of course, these hypotheses are intended only to be suggestive. It is worth observing, however, that the three concepts that have dominated moral psychology for centuries—sympathy, virtue, and duty—map quite nicely onto the three evolutionary mechanisms that have been posited to explain altruistic behavior. Thus if one wanted to provide a "skeptical solution" to the problem of motivational skepticism, there are a number of very powerful resources available, since nature provides much more than just "sympathy," when it comes to natural feelings that can be "laid hold of and nourished."

Furthermore, there would be no danger in committing the naturalistic fallacy in such an account. The goal of a skeptical solution is not to argue that one *ought* to care about morality, because of certain facts about human biology and evolution. The goal is simply to allay any anxiety produced through skeptical doubts, by showing that as a matter of fact, normally socialized adults *do* care about morality, and that because this constitutes a stable evolutionary equilibrium, it should not be expected to change anytime soon. The solution, in other words, does not give people a reason to care about morality; it just gives the philosopher a reason to stop worrying about the fact that people have no particular reason to care about morality.

Consider, for example, how a state-of-the-art "skeptical solution" along these lines could be developed using the "sentimental rules" framework elaborated by Shaun Nichols.[8] Nichols begins with the observation that moral action is in many cases overdetermined with respect to motive. People have a "normative theory": an internal representation of the dominant set of rules governing social interaction in the society (this is equivalent to what I have been calling the agent's set of "principles").[9] Yet in the case of actions prohibiting harm to others, these rules are paired with a strong affective response, which reinforces and strengthens the individual's adherence to the rule. In Nichols's view, the rules are a set of culturally transmitted social norms, more or less along the lines suggested by the "dual inheritance" model of gene-culture coevolution.[10] The affective response on the other hand is generated by a mechanism that is a direct product of natural selection (probably for reasons of inclusive fitness) at the level of the adaptive unconscious. (Nichols considers, for example, the hypothesis advanced by James Blair that people possess a "violence inhibition mechanism" that "turns off" the impulse toward aggressive behavior in response to certain "distress cues.")[11] In cases where the agent is acting intentionally (as opposed to spontaneously, or unreflectively) this module does not directly determine the individual's behavior. On the contrary, it is the explicitly represented "normative theory" at the level of the intentional planning system that motivates the action. The significance of the underlying affective structure is first, that it biases cultural evolution in such a way that norms prohibiting harm are more likely to be reproduced than norms encouraging violence, and second, that it makes deviation from the norm less attractive to the individual, and thus makes it more likely to be respected even when the individual suffers a failure of intentional control. Thus the biologically evolved structure at the level of the adaptive unconscious enhances the "fitness" of a particular norm with respect to the dynamics of *cultural* evolution, as well as making it easier to adhere to and enforce the norm at the level of everyday social practice. Altruistic dispositions cultivated at the level of the adaptive unconscious are thereby transformed, somewhat indirectly, into moral obligations, at the level of the intentional planning system.

This analysis has considerable merit. First, it does not try to provide an adaptive explanation, in terms of genetic fitness, for the possession of particular intentional states. It also explains the relationship between altruism and morality without any sort of reductionism. This makes Nichols's account preferable to that of David Sloan Wilson and Elliot Sober, for instance, who attempt to provide an evolutionary explanation for the fact that individual *x*, in situation *y*, has a desire to act cooperatively. This both assimilates morality to altruism and commits them to an implausible form of sociobiology with respect to intentional states. As we have seen, not only does biology favor plasticity in the domain of what people desire, but so does culture—there are all sorts of norms that enforce noncooperative behavior. Thus it is clearly preferable to frame the biological analysis in terms of biases in the sphere of cultural reproduction. Insofar as people have preferences that lead them to cooperate, it is because norms enforcing cooperation have enjoyed greater reproductive success in the *cultural* sphere than the other candidates.

The other central attraction of Nichols's account—one that ranks it above most other versions of evolutionary moral psychology—is that he is able to explain why we all exhibit substantially similar patterns of moral reasoning and judgment, despite the fact that our underlying "moral" dispositions are a grab bag of different structures, created for a variety of more or less unrelated evolutionary reasons. Psychologist Marc Hauser, by contrast, talks about individuals having a generative "moral organ" similar to the one he takes to be responsible for grammar.[12] Yet he includes in the list of moral rules generated by this "organ" all sorts of dispositions that could not plausibly be considered the result of a unified evolutionary process. For example, the incest taboo shows up on pretty much every list of moral rules that are thought to have an evolutionary foundation. Yet the incest taboo is related to a very distinct, domain-specific psychological phenomenon, namely, the Westermarck effect, through which children raised in close proximity to each other tend to be develop an aversive reaction to the thought of sexual relations with one another. (Thus biological siblings separated at birth often find one another attractive, whereas children raised together on a kibbutz find the idea of intracohort sexual relations repulsive.) There is an absolutely straightforward evolutionary explanation for this, but of course, it has nothing to do with reciprocal altruism, group selection, or any of the other special mechanisms posited in order to resolve "the mystery of altruism." So why would it be part of the "morality" module? Indeed, from an evolutionary psychology perspective, it is not clear why it should even be regarded as a moral norm. Yet it is universally regarded as such, even by those who adopt a very restrictive definition of the term moral.

Nichols's analysis provides a simple and elegant explanation. The unified framework of moral reasoning is a consequence of the fact that we are acting on the basis of a "normative theory" subscribed to at the level of the intentional planning system. The Westermarck effect functions at the level of the adaptive unconscious. It does not "strictly canalize" behavior, as witnessed by the various societies throughout history in which social norms permit or even encourage brother-sister marriage. Who you are allowed to have sex with and who you are allowed to marry is ultimately determined by social norms. Due to the Westermarck effect, however, norms that prohibit incestuous marriages have positive affective resonance. Norms that permit it, on the other hand, run "against the grain" (and are therefore at a competitive disadvantage in the domain of cultural reproduction). People regard the issue as a moral one, and apply the usual structural elements of moral reasoning (e.g., "Are they responsible? Did they know they were brother and sister?") because the incest prohibition is just one norm among many. It is merely an empirical consequence of the Westermarck effect, and the strength of the "yuck" response that it engenders, that the norm is practically universal in human societies.

The model can be applied in a similar way, in order to incorporate the three evolutionary precursors to morality outlined above. Like Robert Boyd and Peter Richerson, Nichols believes that, in principle, any sort of rule can be reproduced through a system of cultural inheritance. Thus "nasty" norms can be reproduced just as well as "nice" ones, as witnessed by the fact that most societies throughout human history, including our own, have at times considered it obligatory to impose what we now regard as absolutely gratuitous suffering on people. But don't worry, says the Humean, although "nasty" norms can do just as well as "nice" ones, as a matter of fact they tend not to. Thanks to inclusive fitness, we care about our families and those who are close to us. Thanks to reciprocal altruism, we believe in rewarding virtue and punishing vice. And thanks to imitative conformity, we believe that duty is its own reward, and that we should refrain from "making an exception of ourselves." More generally, cultural evolution exhibits directionality, toward a "softening of mores," as the cumulative effect of these biases acquires increased significance over time. There is, of course, no philosophical necessity about this; it is just a happy fact about the constitution of our nature. So while there is no response to the skeptical argument, this isn't such a problem, since the bias toward "nice" norms is not played out at the level of the intentional planning system anyhow, and so the failure to win this argument is unlikely to have any impact on the overall process of moral improvement in our society.

7.2. Problems with the Skeptical Solution

While recognizing that Nichols's theory does not claim to be more than it is, there are still some fairly pressing questions that a "skeptical solution" constructed along these lines fails to address.[13] First of all, it does not explain why we are content to have some of our affective responses reflected and amplified by our system of norms, but in other cases strive mightily to extinguish the natural affective reactions that we have. For example, the flip side of the "neoteny" response, which evokes a wide range of caring behavior in the presence of infants, is that the system in question seems also to be fairly finely attuned to detecting abnormalities in the child that might indicate low returns to parental investment. This is most obvious in the case of Down syndrome and craniofacial abnormalities, but people also make much more subtle (unconscious) discriminations. All of these deviations from "normal," neotenous appearance diminish the perceived attractiveness of the infant—both to parents and unrelated parties—which is associated in turn with lower levels of maternal attention, affection, responsiveness, and verbal interaction.[14] In other words, mothers have a tendency to automatically and unconsciously scale back their level of parental investment in a child that is perceived to be abnormal. It is not difficult to see how such an affective response could underlie certain practices of infanticide that have prevailed at various times in many cultures.[15]

It would be easy to multiply examples of "nasty" affective dispositions of this sort that we all share. For example, people have always enjoyed watching others being tortured, and "torture as entertainment" is as prevalent in our culture as it ever was; we simply substitute clever simulation for the real thing. Thus the mere fact that "nice" norms have affective resonance does not explain their reproductive success in the culture, since a lot of "nasty" norms have affective resonance as well. Nichols, however, treats the competition as though it involved only "nice" norms versus affectively neutral norms, and is thus unable to provide much reassurance when it comes to dealing with the problem of "nasty" ones. Thus his framework does not provide an adequate explanation for "the civilizing process," or the softening of mores.

There is also the fact that the dispositions we have often employ very crude heuristics, which are quite prone to misfire. Some of them are not very good at doing what they were supposed to do, in terms of enhancing genetic fitness, even in the environment of evolutionary adaptation. The neoteny response, for instance, is easily triggered by juveniles of other species. This has led to the emergence of several (arguably parasitical) species that take advantage of this human propensity. Dogs, for instance, are essentially wolves who have developed adaptations that freeze their development at a juvenile stage, thus preserving aspects of neoteny in their appearance and behavior (e.g., barking, playfulness, submissiveness). Regardless of what sort of use people might put dogs to, the fact remains that the development of a "care" orientation toward members of another species represents the misfire of an evolved disposition, from the standpoint of our selfish genes.

There is also the fact that we no longer live in the environment of evolutionary adaptation, and so all sorts of heuristics that might once have worked rather well can no longer be assumed to do so.[16] Bioethicists are constantly pressing people to look beyond the "yuck" factor, and to consider the reasons for and against particular practices. The reason is that the spontaneous affective responses we have are completely out of place in the context of a modern technological society. The invention of anesthetic, for instance, completely changed medical practice. Surgeons have to go through a long process of resocialization, so that they become able to make forceful and decisive interventions in cases where the ordinary person would hesitate (e.g., cutting someone's sternum open with a power saw, in order to do open-heart massage). This requires not only that the individual override her own spontaneous affective response, but that norms be changed as well, in reflection of the fact that our primitive affective responses are no longer appropriate.

Perhaps more important, there is simply no reason to think that these heuristics serve *our* interests, as opposed to the "interests" of our genes. As Keith Stanovich notes, "no human has optimizing genetic fitness as an explicit goal.... Thus, the revolt of the human survival machines—the robot's rebellion—consists of gene-built humans trying to maximize their own utility rather than the reproductive probability of their creators in situations where the two are in conflict."[17] Consider, for instance, the example of a mother who decides not to breast-feed for aesthetic or lifestyle reasons.[18] Having made this decision, any subsequent pangs of regret she may get when holding her baby can be thought of as her genes trying to assert their influence, at the expense of her own interests (as she defines them). Evolutionary psychologists, however, have often "tacitly colluded with the gene" by downplaying the potential divergence between instrumental rationality and evolutionary adaptation.[19]

Of course, if our altruistic dispositions were similar to our preference for green over blue food, then there would not be too much to worry about. In an age of food coloring, there is no particularly good argument for preserving an aversion to blue food, but there is no particularly good argument for changing it either. Unfortunately, with altruism, there is an obvious argument to be made for getting rid of whatever natural dispositions we may have. Like Jane Goodall's chimpanzee who woke up one day and realized that calling out to the others whenever he found food was not in his interest, we also are in a position to recognize that conflicts may arise between our altruistic dispositions and our self-interest. Do you really want kids messing up your beautiful condominium? Do you really want friends nagging you for favors all the time? Do you really want to let some promise that you made get in the way of advancing your career?

This is where doubts about the "skeptical solution" arise. The question is not exactly "why be moral?" but rather "why not become immoral?"[20] Why not unlearn or suppress whatever altruistic dispositions we have, and learn to ignore the "affective resonance" enjoyed by certain norms? Biology is not destiny, especially when it only serves as a source of biases in the cultural sphere. Ethical vegetarians and animal rights activists frequently publicize their cause using photographs of especially neotenous juveniles of other species (e.g., harp seals) in an attempt to expand our circle of moral concern. In the same way, antiabortion activists use photographs of late-term fetuses (e.g., sucking their thumbs) in an attempt to achieve the same effect. Since the intersection set of animal rights activists and antiabortionists is very close to empty, this means that almost everyone, in certain cases, is capable of disregarding the altruistic impulses that arise at the level of the adaptive unconscious. Why not go one step further, and get rid of (or ignore) these responses entirely? In particular, why not eliminate the open-ended cooperative disposition that most people seem to have (which leads them to cooperate in one-shot prisoner's dilemmas) and adopt a strictly instrumental orientation, cooperating only when external sanctions or potential reciprocation make it prudent to do so? There is an obvious argument from self-interest to be made in favor of doing so. Unless there is a compelling counterargument to be made in favor of altruism, then the broader disposition begins to appear as simply an artifact of our evolutionary history, a set of behavioral routines that served a useful function *prior* to our acquisition of the calculative and planning capacities needed to pursue our self-interest in a more differentiated fashion (in the same way, for example, that our seemingly natural tendency to discount future satisfaction may have served a useful purpose prior to our acquisition of the competences needed to calculate probabilities and weigh future risks, but now has become unhelpful).

My inclination is to grant that in the case of the dispositions linked to kin selection and reciprocal altruism, this argument from self-interest is difficult to counter, other than by reciting the usual platitudes about the good life, such as the satisfaction that comes from caring for others—arguments that have force only with people who already find such ethical concerns persuasive. A person who found preferences of this sort irksome could rationally choose to change them, using whatever psychological techniques were available. We may have good reason to discourage a person from doing so (along the lines suggested by Mill), but there is no guarantee that we can produce a knock-down argument. However, in the case of our normative control system, the situation is entirely different. Our norm-conformative disposition is not one that a rational agent could choose to eliminate. There is, as Kantians have long claimed, an internal connection between morality and rationality that the "skeptical solution" overlooks. In the remainder of this chapter, I will try to show how this conclusion can be established.

7.3. Transcendental Arguments

The Humean solution to the problem of motivational skepticism consists in granting that there is no knock-down argument to be made for having a motivational disposition to act morally, but that this is not something to worry about, because most people as a matter of fact do have the appropriate motivation most of the time. The problem with this response is that there is a powerful argument from self-interest to be made for losing any such disposition. So even if most people happen to have it, it is difficult to see why they should not also make efforts to eliminate it. If one identifies the agent's self-interest with his utility function, then a disposition to act morally shows up essentially as an expensive preference. It has a very high opportunity cost, in the sense that satisfying it requires a major sacrifice with respect to the agent's other preferences. Thus, like an addiction, it is a preference that one might find oneself motivated to eliminate.

In response to this difficulty, perhaps the most immediate temptation is to attempt a straightforward refutation, by challenging the argument from self-interest. If it could be shown that the preference in question is not in fact all that expensive, then it might be possible to give the agent a good reason for retaining it. This is obviously going to be difficult to do in the case of altruistic dispositions that involve sacrificing "the robot" in order to enhance the reproduction of the gene. However, in the case of altruistic dispositions that enable cooperation—defined in terms of the interests of the individual, not the gene—there would seem to be much greater chances of mounting a successful defense. Our norm-conformative disposition may have evolved for all sorts of reasons involving the genetic fitness of various social learning strategies, issues that are of no ongoing interest or concern to us as individuals. However, given that we have such a disposition, and given that it helps us to sustain wide-ranging systems of cooperation that generate significant collective benefits, is there not an argument from self-interest to be made for retaining it?

Unfortunately, the answer is no. In fact, posing the question in this way gets us right back to where we started at the beginning of chapter 2. If it were possible to produce a strictly instrumental argument for adopting (or keeping) a cooperative choice disposition, then some kind of rule-instrumentalism would prove to be correct. It would be possible to provide a strictly instrumental account of social order, and there would be no need to assign any sort of sui generis force to deontic constraints. The problem is that our self-interest encourages us to cooperate only when doing so is essential to securing reciprocity, and to defect when we are able to do so with impunity. Thus what instrumental rationality recommends to us is simply instrumental rationality, unfettered by any special choice dispositions or constraints.

Yet all is not lost. It may pay to reexamine the assumption that an argument in favor of our altruistic dispositions must appeal to the individual's self-interest, conceived of in instrumental terms, in order to be effective. As we have seen, the sort of rationality that individuals exhibit at the level of the intentional planning system is more complex than that. Furthermore, in the case of the normative control system, certain of the competencies that individuals rely on when engaged in the process of rational deliberation seem to presuppose the very motivational structures that are the object of deliberation. This suggests that a transcendental justification of the relevant disposition might be more successful than an appeal to self-interest. Yet this Kantian argument form, despite being widely used in attempts to defuse epistemological skepticism, has not received widespread attention in the debates over practical rationality.[21]

The basic transcendental strategy is not to refute the skeptic directly, but rather to neutralize skeptical doubts by showing that they are cognitively inaccessible. This can be achieved by showing that while these doubts appear plausible at first glance, on closer examination they turn out to violate certain conditions of possibility of thought. So while we have no *particular* reason for thinking the way we do, the alternatives are all demonstrably incoherent. The equivalent argument in the case of *motivational* skepticism would take a slightly different form. Since here the skeptic is making a pragmatic rather than a theoretical recommendation, a transcendental justification of norm-conformity would show that the skeptic's recommendations are pragmatically inaccessible to us. We have no *particular* reason, in the abstract, to follow the rules, but given that we are disposed to do so, we cannot coherently choose to abandon this disposition.

To see how a transcendental argument against motivational skepticism would go, it is helpful to recall the circumstances under which Kant pioneered this argumentation form. Kant's most significant argument of this type concerned our conception of the physical world as a causal nexus. In his epistemological work, Hume pointed out that observation alone is insufficient to give us a very rich conception of causality. All that we ever see, he argued, is a series of discrete events. The idea that there could be any underlying connection between them, much less one that would allow us to predict the outcome of future interactions, is not something that experience alone can furnish. He concluded, on these grounds, that our idea of a causal connection arises only from a certain habit of mind. Having seen events unfold in a certain sequence, he argued, we develop a tendency to expect the same sequence again under similar circumstances. This is the way we are inclined to think, and there is no reason that other people should not think differently. And if we encountered someone who didn't have this particular habit of mind, there isn't much we could do to recommend it to her. (Again, his "skeptical solution" is to say that since everyone we meet has this habit, there is not really anything to worry about.)

Kant responds to this argument by first granting the core of the "psychologistic" thesis. Causal relations are not something that, strictly speaking, we perceive; they are something that we "read into" experience. This does not entitle us, however, to regard them as arbitrary, or as merely a habit of mind. This is because, Kant claims, we would not be able to have a perceptual experience of an object if we did not also conceptualize it as something that fits into a causal nexus. So while we "happen" to treat objects as though they were causally connected, there is nothing arbitrary about this, since we would not be able to perceive them at all if we did not do so.

The argument that purports to establish this conclusion is the notoriously obscure transcendental deduction.[22] The details of this particular argument are not especially important here; it is the form that is of interest. The transcendental deduction does not attempt to justify directly our imputation of a causal ordering to events (i.e., it does not provide us with a reason why we should do so), and it is certainly not designed to convince someone who doesn't have this structure of mind that he should acquire it. In this respect, the transcendental deduction is not really a justification of our claims about causality.[23] The way Kant develops it, it is simply a way of disarming a certain sort of philosophical anxiety. He is claiming, in effect, that even if we can't justify the way things are, the alternative cannot be coherently conceptualized, and so we don't have to worry about it. Thus the task of philosophical justification is supplanted by the critique of metaphysics—"metaphysics" here denoting the temptation to speculate about what might happen under inconceivable circumstances.

The conclusion of Kant's argument can be clarified by reconstructing it within the framework of contemporary modal semantics. It is common these days to understand modal operators—necessity, possibility, impossibility—as a set of restricted quantifiers over possible worlds. They are restricted by an implicit accessibility relation.[24] Thus to say that *p* is necessary is to say that *p* is true at all possible worlds accessible to our own. Different accessibility relations then produce different concepts of necessity. If all worlds with the same laws of logic as our own are considered accessible, then this provides the notion of logical necessity. If all worlds with the same laws of physics as our own are considered accessible, then this provides the notion of physical necessity. Within this framework, transcendental necessity can be introduced simply by defining a new accessibility relation. According to this view, a proposition is transcendentally necessary if it is true at all possible worlds cognitively accessible to our own.

If we think that the limits of what can be coherently conceptualized are determined only by the laws of logic (i.e., anything noncontradictory can be conceived), then this transcendental accessibility relation will be redundant. But for Kant, this would be true only of a purely "discursive" intellect (i.e., God). As corporeal beings, we are restricted in what we can perceive. This imposes a broadly verificationist constraint on what we can conceive, which in turn makes the notion of cognitive accessibility much narrower than that of logical accessibility. Thus the set of cognitively accessible possible worlds are those containing states of affairs that could be objects of possible intuition (i.e., that could be perceived). The transcendental deduction attempts to show that a world in which there are no causal connections between events, while logically possible, is not transcendentally possible (because states of affairs in it could not be perceived, given the kind of mental equipment we have). Because our system of perception requires us to conceive of objects as causally linked, the existence of such connections is true at all possible worlds cognitively accessible to our own, and so it is transcendentally necessary.

While Kant was primarily interested in the constraints that the structure of perception imposes on conceptualization, the linguistic turn drew attention to the role that language plays in constraining the range of conceptualizable states of affairs. With Wittgenstein came the recognition that in order for a state of affairs to be cognitively accessible to us, it must be possible for us to *say* what that state of affairs consists in. This is the idea underlying his claim that "the limits of *language* are the limits of *my* world."[25] But not just anything can be said. Certain constraints must be satisfied in order to make an intelligible statement. As a result, many philosophers began to suspect that the question of which possible worlds are cognitively accessible to our own would be best answered by developing a theory of meaning.

One immediate consequence of this view is that any conditions that must be satisfied in order for language to function correctly will be transcendentally necessary. To take one example, Donald Davidson has argued that the interpretations we give to one another's linguistic behavior are severely underdetermined by the evidence available to us.[26] Any particular utterance can be interpreted in a variety of different ways, simply by varying the beliefs that we ascribe to the person who uttered it. And since these beliefs are propositional attitudes, the content of these beliefs can be varied by changing the interpretations that we give to these sentences. As a result, the only way we can possibly understand one another is if we privilege one of these interpretations. Davidson argued that we do so by selecting the ascription of meaning and belief that maximizes the number of true beliefs held by that individual—this is the famous "principle of charity."

It is a consequence of the principle of charity that belief is intrinsically veridical. In order to ascribe a set of predominantly false beliefs to an individual, one would have to interpret this person uncharitably (since it is always possible to make more of these beliefs come out true by changing one's assumptions about what the person means by what she says). But once the principle of charity is abrogated, there is no longer much left to go on in constructing an interpretation. People can be interpreted as saying or believing pretty much anything at all. This makes it impossible to figure out what the contents of these beliefs are, and as a result, gives us no reason to ascribe content to them in the first place. Thus a world in which people have predominantly false beliefs is not cognitively accessible to us.

This consequence is what underlies the Davidsonian response to Cartesian skepticism.[27] "Evil-demon" thought-experiments, in which one has been tricked into developing beliefs about the world that are systematically false, describe a state of affairs that is not logically contradictory, but is at the same time not conceivable. Under such circumstances, we would have to reinterpret these beliefs so that they come out predominantly true. As a result, such skeptical thought-experiments are metaphysical in the Kantian sense—they ask us to speculate about events that occur in possible worlds that are not cognitively accessible to our own.

Again, it is important to note that Davidson's transcendental argument in defense of the intrinsic veridicality of belief does not provide a positive justification for their having this status. What he says is something more like "well if they didn't, we wouldn't be having this conversation." It is a brute fact about us that we interpret one another charitably. But since we wouldn't be able to interpret one another at all without doing so, given that this principle provides the central criterion of the intelligibility of our utterances, any speculation about suspending it, or doing things some other way, is cognitively idle. And if we did happen to meet someone who didn't interpret utterances charitably, then we would not be able to persuade her that she should, simply because we would not be able to understand what she was doing at all.

7.4. The Argument

The question, then, is whether the motivational structures associated with norm-conformity are merely conventional, or whether they are transcendentally necessary. Because social norms prescribe particular actions, independent of their consequences in particular cases, the normative control system shows up as a form of deontic constraint on the agent's ability to pursue his or her objectives in an instrumental fashion. Thus it can also be conceived of as a disposition that results in our principles being assigned significant deliberative weight, relative to our desires. However, the analysis of the game of giving and asking for reasons, presented in chapter 5, section 4, suggests that this disposition to accord normative reasons for action deliberative priority is a precondition of all rational thought, and is therefore not something we can coherently opt to change.

The underlying picture of human rationality is as follows. Humans start out, much like other primates, relying on a massively parallel system of cognition, made up of a set of domain-specific heuristics that have evolved as a way of addressing particular problems that presented themselves with some frequency in the environment of evolutionary adaptation. All primates engage in social learning (whereby, instead of engaging in trial-and-error learning, they look to the behavior of conspecifics for clues as to the best strategy). Humans, however, hit on a particular heuristic—imitation with a conformist bias—that has significant adaptive value. In particular, the fidelity of the copying strategy is sufficiently great that it enables cumulative cultural change, and thus creates a cultural inheritance system.[28] It also creates the preconditions for genuine rule-following to emerge, and hence for the development of norms-implicit-in-practice. This creates the possibility of semantic intentionality, and propositionally differentiated language (whereby the meaning of propositions becomes independent of their immediate context of use). Thus language develops, initially, as an external social practice. However, the enhancement of our cognitive abilities associated with this "language upgrade" leads individuals to increased dependence on language as a tool for planning and controlling their own behavior. Thus the intentional planning system develops as the seat of conscious, rational action. Theories of rational action (such as decision theory) are not psychological theories that attempt to model underlying "springs of action." They are essentially expressive theories, which attempt to work out the normative commitments that are implicitly undertaken whenever we act on the basis of our beliefs and preferences. Thus they are part of the toolkit that is provided to us by the language upgrade.

The intentional planning system enjoys a certain measure of autonomy from other cognitive systems, in the sense that it has the capacity to override behavioral impulses arising from the adaptive unconscious. (The mechanism here is not fully understood, and is subject to considerable dispute.) We form linguistically explicit representations of our own bodily needs, affective responses, along with goals that we are disposed to seek. In so doing, we can choose to ignore, defer, sublimate, reschedule, and otherwise fiddle with our more primitive behavioral dispositions. Of course, one of these behavioral dispositions is our propensity to engage in imitative conformity. As we have seen, people rely on imitation in order to establish "default social behavior." As Ap Dijksterhuis puts it, "we are wired to imitate and we do it all the time, except when other psychological processes inhibit imitation."[29] The reason it is more noticeable in human infants is simply that they have not yet developed higher-order mental or cognitive processes able to override it. At the level of the intentional planning system, this imitative "reflex" receives explicit representation in the weight that we assign to social norms, relative to our concerns about the consequences of our actions. It becomes our "norm-conformative disposition," comparable to the discount rate we use to trade off present against future satisfaction.

The question then becomes: why do we not try to get rid of this imitative propensity, once we have developed the capacity for fully intentional, rational action? Why assign it any weight in our system of priorities, as opposed to trying to expunge or suppress it? Human infants may be "imitation machines," but once we've acquired the benefits of cultural inheritance, why not discontinue the learning mechanism? This is where the transcendental justification of our norm-conformative disposition comes in. One can imagine an argument having three steps, as follows.

1. *Language is a social practice.* It is a commonplace view among those impressed by the work of the later Wittgenstein that the meaning of linguistic expressions is determined by their use. The key point for the purposes at hand is that the use of such expressions is determined not just by conventions, but norms-implicit-in-practice. The most highly articulated version of this claim can be found in the work of Robert Brandom, who argues (as we have seen) that the meaning of linguistic expressions is determined by their inferential role. This role is to be understood as a kind of deontic status in the language game of assertion. Producing an utterance with assertoric force *commits* one to a series of further utterances. The utterance is permissible only if one has an *entitlement* to make it, on the basis of some other set of utterances. For Brandom, to understand the meaning of an expression is to grasp this set of commitments and entitlements.

It is a consequence of this view that the capacity to produce a meaningful utterance, that is, an utterance that will be understood by others, requires the capacity to take on and discharge such commitments. (Consider the case of a speaker who says "I'm going for a walk" but then does not acknowledge any of the inferential consequences of this utterance, or perform any of the actions that would be consistent with the kind of commitment undertaken. If one grants the speaker's sincerity, one has no choice but to suspect that he either meant something else by what he said, or else simply didn't understand what the words he used meant.) If language is grounded in a normatively regulated social practice, then it follows that only agents capable of making and respecting deontic constraints should be able to produce meaningful utterances. (Note the parallel to the Davidsonian position outlined above. Instrumentally rational agents could produce utterances that sound exactly like the utterances produced by agents exercising normative control. It is just that we would have no grounds for ascribing *content* to these utterances.)

2. *Intentional states are deontic statuses.* As we have seen, there is an internal connection between belief and assertion. A belief appears to achieve *in foro interno* what an assertion achieves *in foro externo*. While one tradition in philosophy of language seeks to explain assertion as the expression of a belief, the "social practice" perspective developed and defended here suggests that beliefs are best understood as a kind of deontic status. To say that someone believes that p is to say that this person is committed to the claim that p (and so could, for instance, be called on to display her entitlement to p, or acknowledge some of the further commitments that follow from p). In order to counteract the tendency to reify these sorts of intentional states (i.e., to think of them as something inside the agent's head), Brandom suggests that we use the term "doxastic commitment"

instead of belief.[30] From this, it follows that only an individual with a norm-conformative disposition can have contentful beliefs, because only such a person is able to respond to his deontic status (including his doxastic commitments). A person who doesn't follow rules provides others with no grounds for the ascription of contentful intentional states.

3. *To decide that one should reason purely instrumentally, and then do it, would be to respond to a deontic status, and so would be an exercise of normative control.* This puts things a little bit too neatly, but it conveys the general idea. In order to rationally reflect on one's norm-conformative disposition, one must acquire a series of doxastic commitments, and then track their consequences. This is what makes the process recognizable as *reasoning*, rather than just behavior. But as a result, our normative control system is not just a preference we happen to have; it is a capacity that we must *exercise* in order to carry out the process of rational reflection. Questioning our disposition to assign deliberative weight to normative reasons for action is therefore cognitively idle, because the very intelligibility of the question depends on a background exercise of precisely such a disposition. Similarly, the force of any conclusion that one might draw is cognitively idle, since it will only be implemented by an agent willing to follow through on commitments entailed by a given process of reasoning. Put otherwise, from the standpoint of rationality, normative control is transcendentally necessary. A rational agent could never choose to eliminate it, because normative control is a condition of possibility of thought.

It is always possible that we might opt to become a *homo economicus* through some kind of radical existential choice. The point is simply that this is not something that could rationally recommend itself to us. In the same way, we could cease to interpret people charitably. But in so doing, we would cease to interpret them at all, and so would be opting out of rational agency.

The key idea in this argument is that because rationality involves the use of language, and because learning language requires mastery of a normatively regulated social practice, normative control is a precondition of rational agency. This is not to deny that people can engage in acts of social deviance, or that they can rationally choose to do so. The claim is simply that because of the internal connection between normative constraint and rationality, it is impossible to argue oneself out of having a norm-conformative choice disposition. By the time one has the capacity to engage in this sort of deliberation, it's too late. (To use a computer metaphor, it's like trying to patch our own operating systems, when the files we are hoping to modify are in use, and we have no option to reboot. It is easy to look at such a system and wonder why it was put together the way it is, as opposed to some other way. But this is idle speculation, from a pragmatic perspective, once it is up and running.)

Immorality, in this context, is like false belief for Davidson. It is possible to persuade oneself that one has a few false beliefs. But one cannot persuade oneself that one's beliefs are systematically false, because this is inconsistent with the presuppositions of rational agency. Similarly, it is possible to persuade oneself to perform specific actions that are wrong, but it is impossible to argue oneself into a state where one no longer experiences the force of normative constraints.

Thus there is a significant asymmetry between the normative control system we acquire and any other disposition that is associated with altruistic conduct. We may be able to train ourselves to resist feelings of sympathy, or to unlearn many of the instincts that underlie virtue ethics, but we cannot choose to eliminate our normative control system in the same way. The difference is that the capacity for normative control functions as one of the building blocks that is *used* in the development of more sophisticated cognitive competences. This is why "inhibitory control" is regarded by psychologists as one of the most important characteristics of the intentional planning system as a whole, and not merely the normative control system.[31] Normative constraint and rationality are part of an evolutionary "package deal."

7.5. Objections

This argument gives rise to a number of fairly immediate objections. Three of them are worth discussing in detail:

1. *Even if all this is correct, couldn't we be disposed to respect only those deontic statuses that are needed to participate in the practices that constitute our linguistic abilities—and thus our capacity for rational deliberation?*

The assumption throughout this book has been that the agent's normative control system is perfectly general—that it constitutes a disposition to conform to norms in general, and not any one particular class of norms. There is, of course, a very plausible evolutionary story that can be told to explain the purely formal character of this disposition (drawing on its origins in imitative learning). Yet the skeptic might counter the transcendental argument by suggesting that the agent adopt a more flexible disposition, one that leads her to respect only "cognitive" norms, while systematically violating all other moral or social norms. Thus she might eliminate the disposition to act morally, while still preserving the disposition to respect those norms that are constitutive of the game of giving and asking for reasons, and thus the cognitive content of her intentional states.

When considering this possibility, it is important to keep in mind E. O. Wilson's observation that "cultural behavior . . . seems to be a psychological whole invested in the brain or denied it in a single giant step."[32] One simply does not find people who are socialized in such a way that they are disposed to conform to only one half of a culture, but not the other half. People may *dissent* from the culture, and may contest or reject specific norms, but they are still disposed to conform to norms generally. So while one can imagine evolution producing a creature that was motivated to respect cognitive norms only, or a race of intelligent machines designed in this way, neither would bear much resemblance to ourselves. There may be an element of evolutionary path-dependency in our own particular style of culture-dependence—so that once an open-ended imitative disposition is developed, it is very difficult to modify it in the direction of a more selective disposition (in the same way that once a compound eye has developed, it is difficult to move in the direction of a lensed eye, and vice versa). If so, then it is merely a happy accident of our nature that rational reflection does not undermine our motivation to act morally.

There are also philosophical reasons for thinking that there is a problem with the type of compartmentalization that would be required in order to obey only cognitive norms. One of the key features of the pragmatist order of explanation is the insistence that empirical content enters into the game of giving and asking for reasons through both language-entry *and* language-exit moves.[33] Language-entry moves typically consist of observations, and provide the representational dimension of linguistic meaning. Language-exit moves consist of actions, and provide the pragmatic content of meaning. Mastery of an expression involves familiarity with both the "upward" reasons that entitle one to it and the "downward" consequences of accepting it.[34] Producing intelligible utterances involves not only responding to one's environment in a certain way but also acting in a way that is consistent with these utterances (this is the point of the quotation from Sellars in chapter 5, section 7). Since these downstream consequences may involve any sort of action that falls under an intentional description, there is no discrete set of norms that constitutes "the" practice of assertion. Language is woven into the fabric of all social interaction, and so requires the capacity to respond to one's deontic status generally, not some specific set of such statuses. In the same way that there is no principled distinction between "knowledge of language" and "knowledge of the world" on the language-entry side, there is no principled distinction between "knowledge of language" and "knowledge of what to do" on the language-exit side.

This does not mean that a person must actually endorse the prevailing set of social norms in order to use language. It means only that a person must have a generalized disposition that results in her assigning normative reasons for action considerable deliberative weight. It is still possible for an agent who has such a disposition to reject some large set of the prevailing social norms, while accepting the more immediately "cognitive" ones (the same way a person might refuse to accept some significant segment of our everyday empirical beliefs). But such a person poses a different sort of problem from the one posed by the purely instrumental agent. The problem here is one of content skepticism, not motivational skepticism. The purely instrumental agent is someone who simply does not respond to his or her deontic status, and so will not feel the practical force of any moral argument. The deontically constrained maximizer who rejects some set of social norms feels the force of such arguments, but simply denies that they are sound. Thus he would be motivated to act in a norm-conformative fashion, if only he could be talked into accepting the relevant social norms. That the latter sort of people exist does not constitute an objection to the transcendental argument presented above, because this argument is intended only to preclude the former.

   2. *Does this argument not run the risk of proving too much? Is it not the case that we sometimes meet rational people who genuinely lack a norm-conformative choice disposition? After all, people often violate their duties.*

Far too many philosophers, including both Kant and David Gauthier, assume that moral agents must assign lexical priority to normative reasons for action, so that reasons that arise from the rules simply trump whatever concern one may have for the consequences. I am inclined rather to regard the normative control system as a disposition that assigns a certain weight to normative considerations. Principles are more or less important, just as desires can have greater or lesser priority. The choice disposition simply assigns a weight to these normative constraints relative to one's desires (in exactly the same way that one's prudential constraint, expressed in the form of a discount factor, assigns a weight to future preferences relative to present ones). As a result, it is possible to submit to temptation, without having this reflect any disturbance of the underlying choice disposition. In the same way that short-term satisfaction can simply overshadow the long-term consequences of an act, it can also overshadow concerns over its impropriety.

One no doubt encounters an enormous amount of variation in the strength of this normative control system from person to person, ranging from hyperconformism on one side to moral laxity on the other.[35] Most of the "everyday immorality" one encounters is, I would argue, the result of laxity, and not a fundamentally different choice disposition. It is also worth noting that most people do not respond to cases of serious moral laxity with argumentation alone. We generally respond to moral intransigence by *sanctioning* the offender. Although this sometimes takes the form of outright punishment, it is often more subtle. We cease to trust persons with poor moral character, we refuse to cooperate with them, we disassociate ourselves from them, and we symbolically censure their actions. This is just the mechanism of socialization at work. It is precisely through the internalization of these sanctions that the moral choice disposition is reinforced. Thus one does not always have to argue people into assigning moral considerations greater deliberative weight; one can also socialize them to do so.

An adult who genuinely assigns no weight to normative considerations is not someone who lacks a particular sort of sensitivity, but someone who has suffered a more general failure of socialization. Such persons no doubt exist, but the point to note is that this failure of socialization, which impairs their ability to feel the force of normative constraints, also impairs their ability to respond to rational argumentation. Argumentation is ultimately a form of moral suasion. A certain threshold level of normative constraint is needed in order to function as a fully rational agent. It is a mistake to assume that moral commitments, in order to be justified, need to be justifiable to those who fall below this threshold, since only those above the threshold are able to act as full participants in the game of giving and asking for reasons.

Finally, it should be noted that a lot of behavior that we are inclined to classify as evil is in fact rationalized. People who do bad things usually have some kind of story that purports to justify the conduct from the moral point of view. Rather than exhibiting straightforward deviance with respect to the prevailing set of social norms, what people more often do is make socially deviant use of what are, in principle, legitimate excuses.[36] For example, they will argue that they had "no choice" in the matter, or that they were merely punishing the victim, perhaps preemptively, for some other offense, or that they did it out of allegiance to some higher principle, and so on. These ex ante rationalizations neutralize the force of the agent's own normative judgments, and therefore allow the agent to "have his cake and eat it too," by retaining allegiance to the dominant system of norms and values, while at the same time exempting his own actions from its imperatives, thereby freeing him to pursue his self-interest in a relatively unconstrained fashion.[37] In many cases, a cognitive norm will be violated (e.g., "stealing" is described as "borrowing") in such a way as to allow the offender to claim that he was in compliance with a more heavily weighted moral or legal norm (e.g., "don't steal").The key point is that in such cases, agents are responding to accusations of impropriety, not by disavowing the norms, but by providing reasons for their actions that have force within the existing normative framework. The problem is that the reasons they provide are overly self-serving. Nevertheless, these people are not genuinely "opting out" of morality, in the way that the motivational skeptic imagines, they are merely behaving badly.

3. What about psychopaths?

The figure of the "psychopath" or "sociopath" sometimes shows up in philosophical discussions as a stand-in for the moral skeptic, proof that there are individuals who simply do not feel the force of moral constraints, even though they exhibit otherwise normal reasoning and social skills. They are completely amoral, and yet highly intelligent and manipulative. This in turn appears to suggest that "morality" is a relatively modular component of our neural architecture, one that can be removed without compromising cognition or intentional planning. This highly stylized characterization of psychopathy, however, is constructed largely for philosophical purposes. The clinical phenomenon is somewhat more complex.There are two threads that combine to produce the syndrome that is referred to as "primary psychopathy." The most important is the absence of certain social emotions, in particular, a lack of sympathy for others. In other words, what psychopaths appear to lack is not morality per se, but rather one of the more archaic roots of altruistic behavior among humans—the capacity for sympathetic identification (i.e., the altruistic disposition most likely to be the result of kin selection). It is not surprising that this capacity should be relatively "modular," that there should be variation with respect to it in the population, and that it could be removed without affecting general cognition. (And it is therefore unsurprising that, as Linda Mealey observes, psychopathology has an inheritable component, that the occurrence of primary psychopathy is relatively invariant across cultures, and that it occurs more frequently among men than women.)[38]

A person could have this sort of emotional deficit and yet still act perfectly "morally"—by virtue of respecting the prevailing set of social norms. The central characteristic of psychopaths in this regard, as Nichols observes, is that their incentives for respecting moral rules tend not to be overdetermined. Thus, insofar as they avoid harming others, it is not because they feel any sort of abhorrence at the prospect, but simply because they regard it as not the sort of thing that is done.[39] In a sense, their problem is that they have too much of a Kantian moral psychology. There is no fail-safe, in cases where their adherence to the rules fails. When they become disinhibited, for instance, they are capable of great violence, simply because they are unconstrained by any sort of fellow-feeling or sympathy.

The second aspect of psychopathy is a general weakness of normative control, manifested in the form of impulsivity, inability to respect commitments, "poor behavioral controls," and a "lack of realistic, long-term plans."[40] This is far more common in the population at large (where it is known as "subclinical antisocial personality" or "secondary sociopathy") and probably has no biological basis.[41] These people have weak normative control (or "moral laxity"), engage in antisocial behavior, but experience the normal range of social emotions. In this case, however, it is noteworthy that such individuals do suffer deficits in rationality, particularly when it comes to planning. They do not suffer simply from an absence of morality, but from very general weakness of their intentional planning system. This suggests that norm-conformity, unlike sympathy, is not simply a module that can be plucked out, leaving the rest of the individual's cognitive competences intact. Although there is a negative correlation between secondary sociopathy and general intelligence, what is more striking about these individuals is that they exhibit what Stanovich calls "dysrationalia."[42]

What links these two syndromes together in some individuals is the fact that children suffering the emotional deficit associated with primary sociopathy often develop a weak normative control system as a consequence, by virtue of the fact that the absence of social emotions makes them less responsive to certain types of rewards and punishments. Simply put, they are more difficult to socialize. It is the combination of the two that generates the more dangerous forms of psychopathy. Nevertheless, the two syndromes are distinct from one another, and many people suffer from one but not the other. The typical media image of the cool, calculating psychopath is that of an individual who lacks emotion, but suffers no deficits at the level of normative control. This is in fact not the typical profile of a psychopath. But either way, the existence of psychopathy as a syndrome poses no challenge to the empirical claims that serve as the basis for the transcendental argument advanced here. Psychopaths have important emotional deficiencies, which clearly prevent them from having a normal moral sensibility, but they are not rational amoralists—on the contrary, they are neither fully amoral nor fully rational.

7.6. Conclusion

The general point of the transcendental argument is to show that we need not worry about how to justify our norm-conformative choice disposition to individuals who do not feel the force of deontic constraints. As a result, the argument would not convince a Martian to become moral. The purpose of the transcendental argument is to show that we don't need to convince aliens in order to allay our doubts about the defensibility of our own moral commitments. Those who have attempted a direct refutation, therefore, take on an unnecessary burden of proof—and then find themselves unable to discharge it. The transcendental argument shows that the person who asks "What if you could take a pill that would make you a purely instrumental utility-maximizer?" is similar to the person who asks "How do you know that your beliefs aren't all false?" We do not require a step-by-step argument that excludes this claim. The question is intelligible only under assumptions that are metaphysical in the pejorative sense of the term. Our inclination to respect deontic constraints—to follow the rules—is therefore not given any sort of high-powered philosophical justification; it is simply shown to be inescapable for a rational agent.

In this respect, the norm-conformative choice disposition differs from the two other mechanisms that contribute to prosocial behavior among humans. There is nothing irrational about seeking to overcome one's natural feelings of sympathy, or one's inclination to reciprocate kindness that has been shown by others. It is vicious to do so, but it is not formally precluded by one's status as a rational agent. However, any attempt to overcome one's inclination to conform to social norms—to become a pure consequentialist—is formally precluded. Yet it is not irrational in the instrumentalist's sense of the term (i.e., contrary to one's self-interest, narrowly conceived). It is irrational because such a decision would constitute the rejection of rationality as well. The intentional planning system that we have is fundamentally dependent on the normative control system. As a result, we cannot escape the authority of norms without denying the authority of reason.

8

Weakness of Will

The purpose of demonstrating the transcendental necessity of a norm-conformative choice disposition is to show that the problem of motivating agents to act morally is not, strictly speaking, a *philosophical* problem. Insofar as they are rational, agents will be motivated to respect deontic constraints, by a disposition that broadly resembles what Kant called "Achtung fürs Gesetz." This disposition is completely neutral with respect to content. It enjoins us to do our duty, whatever that duty may be (or to act in accordance with our principles, whatever those principles may be).[1] The transcendental argument simply shows that this disposition is required in order to participate in the game of giving and asking for reasons, which is in turn the foundation of rational argumentation. Thus rational agency turns out to require a set of competencies that are a subset of those that are constitutive of moral agency. As a result, while one may need to argue with others in order to persuade them that some particular normative constraint is justified (such as the prohibition of adultery, theft, or lying), one need not argue with them about whether it is worthwhile being motivated to respect those norms that they do happen to recognize. A prior consensus on that point can safely be assumed, by virtue of the fact that one is arguing with them.

An enormous number of philosophers, however, have been persuaded that even after a decision has been made that one ought not, for example, commit adultery, it is still very much an open question whether or not one will act on this conviction. People seem to make resolutions and break them all the time, so obviously just deciding that one ought or ought not do something is not enough to settle the issue. The transcendental argument, therefore, appears to close up the gap between moral judgment and moral action in a way that is manifestly contrary to our everyday experience of temptation, not to mention self-consciously immoral conduct. Of course, the norm-conformative disposition assigns only a certain *weight* to particular social norms, and so can simply be outweighed by a sufficiently powerful desire. Agents are also capable of spinning very complex self-justificatory tales, in order to rationalize as a form of dissent what is ultimately just social deviance. Yet these explanations create the "space" for immoral action by essentially taking the original judgment to be only pro tanto, then introducing some other, stronger consideration that overwhelms it. Such explanations clearly do not handle the case of the individual who decides that, all things considered, he should do *x*, but then fails to do it. Does the moral philosopher not need something to say to this person?

In my view, the answer is no. This is a social control problem, not a philosophical problem. There is no question that people sometimes act contrary to their best judgments when they suffer a loss of intentional control, as when acting impulsively, in the heat of the moment, or in a disinhibited state. In such cases, we say that the person acted "without thinking," since it is his intentional planning system as a whole that has been preempted. (People also confabulate, and so provide intentional accounts of what was actually nonintentional action, without any awareness that they are doing so.[2] Thus the mere fact that they are able to supply an intentional explanation does not rule out the possibility that it was nonintentional behavior.) Obviously while they are out of control there is no point arguing with them. And when they have things back under control, it is pretty easy to make a case for "thinking before acting," since people who act contrary to their own intentionally formulated plans may ignore not only their moral obligations but also their self-interest (i.e., both their principles and their desires). Thus we engage in socializing practices aimed at ensuring that individuals, as much as possible, don't get into such states.

This answer seems unsatisfactory only because many philosophers have been inclined to think that people routinely act in ways that are *intentional*, and yet contrary to their own preferences. In other words, it is thought that people may choose not to maximize value with respect to their own beliefs, desires, and principles, by knowingly choosing to bring about a state of affairs that is ranked lower in their overall preference ordering than some other available alternative. The reason that such a tendency toward *intentional counterpreferential choice* has seemed plausible to many is that it is felt to be the only persuasive explanation for the phenomenon of *weakness of the will*. Many philosophers have accepted at face value the suggestion that the person who knows he shouldn't drink, but has another beer regardless, or who knows that she should go to bed early, but stays up late regardless, is intentionally choosing to act in a way that is contrary to his or her own all-things-considered judgment. According to this view, these agents have a preference, based on some prior exercise of practical reasoning, for either temperance or turning in early; they are simply not able to get themselves to act on the basis of this particular preference. In the terminology that has become increasingly standard in the philosophical discussion, it is said that they are unable to bring their *motivation* into proper alignment with their own (desiderative) *evaluation* of the situation.

It is easy to see how this analysis readmits noncognitivism into the theory of practical rationality through the back door. If a systematic misalignment of motivation and desiderative evaluation is possible, then establishing some sort of "cognitivist" thesis with respect to the content of desires achieves very little. The fact that one's desires are responsive to rational deliberation doesn't count for very much, if one's underlying motivations are completely unaffected. This whole picture, however, is based on a conceptual error, one that is aided and abetted by the tendency to overdiagnose weakness of the will. The thought that weakness of the will might be a common phenomenon is based, first, on a tendency to ascribe propositional content to states of the adaptive unconscious, and thus to describe any sort of teleological behavior as intentional action; and second, on a nearly complete neglect of the phenomenon of discounting, or time preference, which results in a failure to see why the agent's all-things-considered preferences at the point of decision might change from one moment to the next, even though her atemporal desires (e.g., those elicited through the usual hypothetical lottery procedure) remain constant.

8.1.   Akrasia

In a sense, skeptical arguments about moral temptation that take weakness of the will as their point of departure represent a radicalization of the preference noncognitivism discussed in chapter 5. In that chapter, the goal was simply to show that there is no reason to think that there is anything arbitrary, irrational, or irredeemably subjective about the process through which our preferences are generated. Our preferences are not necessarily more irrational than our beliefs, and there is no reason that people cannot have a perfectly cogent argument about the relative desirability of one outcome or another. From this perspective, Hume's claim that we cannot change our sentiments involves a conceptual confusion. If one identifies our "sentiments" with our desires, then there is no reason to think that they are any less changeable than our beliefs. On the other hand, if one identifies our "sentiments" with the somatic condition underlying certain desires (i.e., that serve as a basis of possible language-entry moves), then they do not serve as reasons for action, and so the fact (in cases where it is one) that they cannot be changed at will imposes no special constraints on our practical deliberations. Disambiguation of these two senses of the term "sentiment," combined with a rejection of the epistemic regress argument, is sufficient to undermine the standard forms of Humean skepticism about practical reason.

The more extreme skeptical position, however, does not claim that the *content* of our desires is somehow irrational, but rather that there is an irrational element in our motivational system, above and beyond what our desires may or may not contribute. This more subtle form of skepticism suggests that even if we can exercise some control over our desires, or rationally justify their content, desires alone are unable to motivate us to act.[3] In order to get something done, we must not only have the correct constellation of desires and beliefs in place, we must also be motivated to act on the basis of these particular desires (and not some other set). Alfred Mele, for example, has suggested that each of our desires has two priority levels: the first an evaluative one, which reflects our cognitive judgment concerning the relative urgency of that goal, and the second a motivational one, which reflects something like the level of libidinal cathexis associated with the goal.[4] The former determines what we say and think we should do, but the latter determines what we are actually able to summon up the energy to get done.

Of course, if these two scores always lined up, or more specifically, if either one were simply determined by the other, then there would be no point introducing this sort of *dédoublement* into our psychological theory. Mele's suggestion, however, is that the evaluative and the motivational systems often function quite independently of one another, and thus the two scores are often misaligned. In particular, the mere fact that we assign some goal a high evaluative score does not automatically translate into a high motivational score for that same goal. In fact, Mele thinks our motivational system functions in a quasi-noncognitive fashion (it represents something like our "animal spirits"). Because of this, we must employ all sorts of tricks and indirect strategies (such as "attention management") in order to get our motivational system into alignment with our evaluative one.

Taken to its logical extreme, what Mele's proposal implies is that there could be a truly systematic misalignment between what an agent *says* and what she *does*, such that she remains a helpless spectator in her own life, constantly observing herself doing all sorts of things that she claims not to want to do.[5] Naturally, this constitutes a prima facie violation of Sellars's dictum, mentioned already: "It is a necessary truth that people tend to do what they think they ought to do, for it is a necessary truth that people who occupy a linguistic position which means *I ought to do A now*, tend to do A. If they did not, the position they occupy could not mean *I ought to do A now*."[6] If someone never did what she said she wanted to do, what grounds would we have for ascribing to her a genuine desire to do it? Mele does not address this concern because he is a psychological realist about desires, and so takes their content as given. This is not an accident, since the sort of bifurcation between our cognitive and motivational systems that Mele posits is possible only if the content of our cognitive states is determined quite independently of our actions.

Given these theoretical difficulties, one might wonder what reason there could be to introduce this sort of partial redundancy into the psychological theory. If I decide that today I want to wear brown socks, then I usually just get up and put on a pair of brown socks. After I have made the decision, I do not need to engage in any sort of psychological manipulation to instill in myself the motivation to put on brown socks. The desire to do it just *is* the motive to do it. So why treat the two as though they were separate? The answer, of course, lies in weakness of the will. According to Mele, the fact that the evaluative and motivational systems are separate from one another is revealed in instances in which agents exhibit *akrasia*—where they make a decision, but then act contrary to their better judgment. Furthermore, the fact that "reason" finds itself neutralized in such instances demonstrates that the motivational system is noncognitive (or in Mele's more cautious formulation, that "the motivational force of wants typically is not under our control to the extent to which the evaluative ranking of wants is").[7] Thus Humean skepticism is given new lease on life.[8]

According to this analysis, a person who vows to go to bed early so that he will be well-rested in the morning, and yet finds himself staying up late, suffers from a misalignment of the evaluative score associated with "being well-rested in the morning" and the motivational score. Although he ranks being well-rested high in his overall list of priorities, this desire simply fails to *move* him to take the actions needed to achieve it. (This is perhaps compounded by the fact that "watching late-night television" has a motivational score that is much higher than its evaluative score.) Thus if one examines the individual's choice while tabulating only the evaluative score associated with his desires, the behavior seems mysterious. What one needs to do is ignore the evaluative score and focus on the motivational one, because that is what is called on to do the work of getting him off the couch and into bed.

This proposal does have certain elegant features. The most significant is that it allows Mele to define the concept of "self-control" very ingeniously, as the overall level of correlation between the evaluative and motivational scores associated with an agent's various desires (i.e., the degree of alignment between the two systems). A person who we would describe as being, by nature, very self-controlled, is one whose evaluations generate by default a reasonably high level of motivational cathexis. (Thus the fact that my desire to wear brown socks leads unproblematically to my putting on brown socks is a function of my level of self-control.) A person who is weak-willed, on the other hand, is someone who must engage in all sorts of indirect manipulation in order to bring about this alignment of the two systems (and often fails to do so). Thus Mele is able to affirm, in a very clear way, the everyday intuition that weakness of the will represents a failure of self-control.

The question is whether one is obliged to go so far—psychological bifurcation of the agent's intentional system—in order to explain these seemingly everyday occurrences of weakness of the will. I believe we should be more cautious. As Mele observes, the bifurcation strategy is only required to explain so-called strict akratic action, which he defines as action in which the agent *intentionally* acts contrary to her own all-things-considered judgment. There are many cases in which agents only *appear* to be doing so. They exhibit what we might loosely refer to as weakness of the will, but the actions do not exhibit strict akrasia, and so do not lend any support to the bifurcation strategy. These include:

1. *Nonintentional behavior.* Human behavior is governed by a number of different control systems, many of which are completely beyond our voluntary control. Others are under voluntary control, but are clearly not part of the intentional planning system. We have an enormous number of behavioral routines that function on "autopilot" with respect to our conscious mind (like catching a ball, putting on a turn signal while driving, etc.). This is the domain of the adaptive unconscious. Many of these routines can be stimulated directly by the environment before we've had a chance to think. Furthermore, under certain conditions, or in the presence of certain stimuli, one system may override

another. You can tell yourself not to flinch or close your eyes when someone throws a ball at you but then find yourself unable to control the impulse when the time comes. You can tell yourself not to cry during a sad movie (since after all, it's just a movie) but then find yourself doing so regardless (and so on). As I have argued already (chapter 4, section 2), it is a mistake to ascribe "full-blown" intentional states to the agent as a way of explaining such actions.

As a result, there is nothing mysterious about the fact that people sometimes do things that are contrary to their own desires, in cases where the behavior is not a product of their intentional planning system. Furthermore, the behavior in question need not be impulsive or simple. According to the standard dual-process view, the cognitive style of the adaptive unconscious is "automatic, heuristic-based, and relatively undemanding of computational capacity."[9] Among other things, this means that its operations can be carried out "while attention is directed elsewhere."[10] This is not true of intentional reasoning, which typically requires explicit awareness and concentration. Thus nonintentional behavior is often evoked when the agent is distracted, unable to concentrate, or simply doesn't have the time to think things through. For example, for a long time the first half of the route that I drove to work coincided with the route to the airport. Because of this, I often found myself driving to work when my plan was to go pick someone up at the airport, simply because I stopped paying attention to where I was going. This is a case of nonintentional counterpreferential behavior, involving a fairly complex sequence over an extended period of time. Of course, since I had no reason to go to work, the moment someone would ask me where I was going I would immediately reverse course and get back on the correct route. Thus there was no temptation to deploy a Mele-style explanation here, and suggest that even though my desire to go to the airport was high on my list of evaluative priorities, I simply lacked the associated motivation. (Although it is worth noting that there is absolutely nothing to *preclude* a Mele-style explanation here either—that I went to my office because I had a desire to do so, which despite having been given an evaluative score of zero, for some reason had a high motivational score. One could imagine treating Freudian explanations of action, which appeal to unconscious motives, as explanations having such a structure. The fact that such explanations are notoriously unfalsifiable could then serve as a cautionary note to anyone inclined to accept Mele's analysis.)

If, however, I was a workaholic, and so perhaps assigned going to work an evaluative score somewhat greater than zero, we might be inclined to regard my driving to work rather than to the airport as an instance of weakness of the will, which could then be explained as a consequence of an underlying misalignment of evaluations and motivations. Mele recognizes, however, that this sort of move would be theoretically otiose, given that far more plausible, theoretically conservative, explanations are available.

2. *Recalcitrant stimuli.* As we have seen, many desires are introduced into the intentional planning system through "language-entry moves" in response to some somatic stimulus, or else behavioral dispositions that arise at the level of the adaptive unconscious (such as sympathy). There is a certain amount of "free play" in how the individual responds to such stimuli within the scope of

the intentional planning system. For example, there will normally be multiple stimuli competing for attention, and so the individual will impose some type of scheduling on them (reflected in the relative priority level assigned to each desire). When I feel a hunger pang, I respond in the ordinary run of cases by acquiring a desire to eat something. If I am busy and do not have the time to stop and eat, then I may assign a relatively low priority to this desire. I may even decide to get rid of it entirely. Yet doing so does nothing to make the underlying stimulus go away—I still feel hungry. Thus despite having chosen not to eat, I may eventually reverse course, deciding to manage the stimulus by stopping to eat. Yet in so doing, I may still find myself thinking about how I really shouldn't be doing so. But this does not add up to a case of intentional counterpreferential choice, since my all-things-considered judgment at the point of decision is that I should stop and eat. The fact that I would rather not have to have the desire does not mean that acting on it involves choosing the "lesser good" under the circumstances.

Consider a similar case, in which I am trying to concentrate on a difficult task, which I am repeatedly failing to perform, and am feeling a sense of frustration mounting. (Of course, this somatic stimulus is merely one that I have learned over time to recognize as frustration. Thus I acquire an increasingly intense desire to stop doing what I'm doing, because the implicit model of my own somatic states that structures my desires leads to me infer that stopping the activity will lead to appeasement of that sensation.) When I first begin to feel this frustration, I may recognize that it is counterproductive, that I should be a more focused person, and so on. As a result, if and when I do succumb to my frustration and give up what I am doing, then I have in a sense exhibited weakness. But it is not a form of weakness that requires any special sort of explanation. I would prefer not to experience a certain somatic stimulus, but given that I do, it is best to deal with it in some way at the level of intentional planning. There is a loose way of talking, according to which my "better judgment" in this situation tells me that I should not give in to frustration. But my better judgment may also tell me that I should be immune to hunger or unafraid of heights.

Finally, there may be cases in which I have conflicting desires, but where I recognize that acting on one of them, rather than the other, is going to require greater effort (e.g., attention, concentration). This is often the case when one desire coincides with a behavioral disposition generated by the adaptive unconscious, whereas the other requires an exercise of inhibition over such dispositions. For example, I may have a desire to be a nice person, but also enjoy making fun of people. Acting on the former desire will initially require a greater exercise of attention, because I have to be constantly monitoring my own behavior in conversation (although I anticipate that over time niceness will become more of a habit). Thus I may decide to reschedule the first desire, to a time when conditions are more propitious. (For example, I may decide to work on it later, when my job is less stressful, or when I'm getting more sleep at nights, or when I've mellowed with age.) If one looks at things atemporally, my "best judgment" is that I should be nice (i.e., the desire to be nice is assigned the highest priority). But again, this does not mean that, at the time of decision, my all-things-considered preference is to be nice.

3. *Dynamic preference instability.* People often change their minds about what they want. I might decide in advance that I am not going to drink at the party, and then simply change my mind when I arrive. Or to use Mele's example: "A man who, after careful deliberation, forms the here-and-now intention to shoot his injured horse, may, while taking aim at its head, catch a glimpse of its doleful eyes and decide, due to weakness of the will, that it would be best after all to save it. His refraining from shooting the horse would, however, be a case of derivative akratic action, and, again, our concern is with strict akratic action."[11] The action is not strictly akratic, in Mele's view, because the man *changes his mind.* Of course, the change in preference may involve breaking a past resolution, because he may have vowed not to give in to feelings of sympathy for the horse. But it is not obvious that preference changes can be akratic in the same way that actions supposedly are. My beliefs and desires are structured by certain deontic scorekeeping practices, and are responsive to events outside the game of giving and asking for reasons. As a result, I cannot simply choose to adopt (or maintain) whatever beliefs and desires happen to suit my needs at a given moment. I may vow never to adopt superstitious beliefs, but then find that some mystical experience imposes them on me. Similarly, I may vow never to feel sympathy for an animal, but then find this commitment defeated under particular circumstances (e.g., due to a failure of affective forecasting). Of course, I may also find that this feeling disappears a while later, returning me to my previous preference ordering. But that does not make my action at the point of decision akratic. I did not intentionally choose the lesser good; I merely changed my mind about what constituted the greater good, under the pressure of circumstances.

This brief inventory suggests that for any putative instance of strict akratic action, there will always be alternative hypotheses. Furthermore, since these alternative hypotheses are theoretically more conservative, the question naturally arises as to whether *all* such putative instances could in fact be explained without positing strict akratic action. After all, it is enormously difficult to tell the difference between an intentional counterpreferential choice and a temporary preference reversal (i.e., where someone changes his mind, only to change it back again a moment later). If one looks at the typical behavior of, for example, smokers who are trying to quit, all the evidence suggests that what they are doing when they fall off the wagon is changing their minds, then returning to their previous preference ordering once the craving has subsided.[12]

Philosophers, however, have been loathe to draw this conclusion. The primary reason is that they have generally failed to see any good reason why an agent might undergo such a temporary preference inversion. In particular, if one regards the agent's preferences as a system of evaluations, there seems to be no reason that these evaluations should change from one moment to the next, when nothing in the world has changed. After all, if not-smoking is better than smoking overall, why should it not also be better from moment to moment? As a result, there has been a tendency to assume that peoples' desires are, by default, dynamically stable (such that any deviation from this pattern calls out for special explanation, like strict akrasia).

What has been missing from this discussion is an understanding of the phenomenon of *discounting*, along with the way that a time preference may interact with an agent's more mundane preferences in order to generate dynamic instability. As I will attempt to show, a more sophisticated understanding of discounting dramatically reduces the impulse to ascribe intentional counterpreferential choices to an agent. This in turns suggests that motivations cannot become detached from evaluation in the way that Mele supposes they can.

8.2. Discounting

It seems perfectly reasonable to suppose that, given a choice between receiving some particular quantum of satisfaction today and receiving it tomorrow, all things being equal, an agent might reasonably prefer to receive it today. More generally, agents might have a preference for satisfying their desires *sooner*, rather than *later*, independent of any concern over uncertainty. Yet despite the fact that these psychological propensities are so intuitively familiar to us all, philosophers have for a long time been suspicious of anything that might resemble a pure time preference.[13] If all things genuinely are equal, they have claimed, a genuinely rational agent should be indifferent as to when his preferences are satisfied. Agents, in other words, should not discount future satisfaction when they make decisions, unless this reflects some uncertainty about the future (in which case it should be factored into the agent's expected utility via her beliefs, and not imposed as a discount on the anticipated payoffs).

The strictest formulation of this claim is that of Henry Sidgwick, who claimed that rationality imposed a "principle of prudence":

> We might express it concisely by saying "that Hereafter *as such* is to be regarded neither less nor more than Now." It is not, of course, meant that the good of the present may not reasonably be preferred to that of the future on account of its greater certainty: or again, that a week ten years hence may not be more important to us than a week now, through an increase in our means or capacities of happiness. All that the principle affirms is that the mere difference of priority and posteriority in time is not a reasonable ground for having more regard to the consciousness of one moment than to that of another. The form in which it practically presents itself to most men is "that a smaller present good is not to be preferred to a greater future good" (allowing for difference of certainty): since Prudence is generally exercised in restraining a present desire (the object or satisfaction of which we commonly regard as *pro tanto* "a good"), on account of the remoter consequences of gratifying it.[14]

Of course, if one were an objectivist about value, it might be possible to build such a prohibition on discounting into the conception of rationality. But from any perspective that takes the agent's opinions about what is best for her seriously, it is difficult to see how a time preference could be precluded by the theory of practical rationality. Apart from the fact that time preference is a ubiquitous feature of human preferences (hence the obligation to pay back borrowed money with interest, even when the debt is secured by collateral), there is also the fact that it often arises in response to an underlying somatic state, for example, the feeling of impatience. Quite simply, we find *waiting* to be unpleasant.[15] Similarly, we often find that desires become more intense in the near term, when somatic states that are associated with them are triggered (e.g., hunger or sexual arousal), and so we assign greater priority to them. Although "time preference" is the term that is usually used to describe this, it might be more accurately be referred to as delay-aversion.

Regardless of the particular dynamics of our underlying somatic states, the question whether or not it is a good idea for us to have the underlying states that we have simply does not speak to the question of whether it is rational to act on them, given that we do. It is no doubt *unwise* for us to be too impatient, or to discount the future too sharply. There is actually good reason to think that delay-aversion is part of an evolutionary legacy that is maladaptive in our present cultural context. To see why, consider the analogy between impatience and a very closely related phenomenon, frustration. There is a very plausible biological explanation for the fact that we, and other higher mammals, experience frustration. Frustration serves the important function of preventing organisms from getting caught in infinite loops. The frequency with which computers get stuck in these loops (i.e., when they "crash") shows just how difficult it is to design a system that is immune to them. Less cognitively sophisticated organisms, such as ants, occasionally get caught in infinite loops (some of them fiendishly constructed by human experimenters) so that they repeat the same unsuccessful activity again and again until they die. Our brains, however, never "crash" in the way computers and ants do. This is because more sophisticated organisms track repeated failure, building resistance to an unsuccessful activity each time it is performed, leading them to eventually abandon it in cases where it is consistently unsuccessful. Thus the capacity to become frustrated has clear adaptive value, even though on occasion it may lead us to give up on certain efforts prematurely. (It may also have certain perverse side effects, such as making so-called occasional reinforcement activities, such as golf, oddly compelling.)[16]

Of course, from a certain point of view, there is no *reason* to feel frustrated while trying to get the baby to sleep, or thread a needle, or perfect one's backhand. In fact, we may have good reason to believe that eventually the baby will sleep, the thread will go through the eye of the needle, and the backhand will improve. In other words, we may know that we are not stuck in a loop, or performing an impossible task. And as a result, we may recognize that the feeling of mounting frustration is maladaptive, a cognitive "misfire." Yet simply knowing that doesn't make the underlying somatic stimulus go away. Thus there is nothing irrational about giving in to the frustration and deciding to give up on these activities or taking a break in order to return to them later with a fresh mind. We might also plan ahead, choosing to break up repetitive activities or to trade off tasks with other people, in order to avoid frustration. These are all just routine management techniques that we have learned, as part of our intentional planning system, for staving off mounting feelings of frustration (since we know that ignoring these feelings may eventually lead to a total loss of intentional control—hence the number of shaken babies and mangled tennis rackets). This sort of self-management is no different in principle from learning to take a nap when we start showing signs of fatigue, rather than soldiering on until we collapse from exhaustion.

Managing impatience through delay-aversion is no different. There are striking similarities between the way that humans and other animals discount satisfaction. When given a choice between a small amount of food after a short delay and a larger amount of food after a longer delay, animals will often choose the smaller-sooner option.[17] If one gradually increases the size of the larger amount, they will at some point switch to choosing the larger-later option. There are obvious evolutionary reasons for this. Given that these animals are incapable of calculating probabilities and factoring risk into their decisions, a feeling of impatience and a tendency to privilege the near-term is a good heuristic mechanism for coping with uncertainty. A bird in hand usually *is* better than two in the bush. Naturally, once humans come along and figure out how to do probability calculations, this underlying disposition may become maladaptive (hence the intuition, so appealing to philosophers like Sidgwick, that it is irrational to privilege the "Now" over the "Hereafter"). Yet while this may give us a reason to control the feeling, or to ignore it as much as possible, it does not make us irrational for responding to it or managing it, given that we have it.

There are interesting and important parallels between the phenomenon of delay-aversion and that of risk-aversion.[18] The latter is also a type of metapreference, through which all of an agent's other preferences are filtered, selectively reducing the priority of all desires associated with uncertain outcomes (above and beyond the "mathematical" reduction in value imposed by the probabilities). In fact, risk-aversion and delay-aversion are very closely related phenomena, since an individual facing an open-ended sequence of gambles is guaranteed by the law of large numbers to get a payoff close to the mathematical value of the lottery, so long as she is willing to wait long enough. Thus risk-aversion, which lowers the subjective utility associated with the gamble, winds up being equivalent to an unwillingness to wait for this convergence to occur. In the case of risk-aversion, the behavior can also be interpreted as a response to an underlying somatic stimulus, namely, the feeling of anxiety produced by the uncertainty of outcomes. One reason that people have a somewhat hypertrophied preference for the sure thing is that it allows them to stop worrying. They may regret their decision afterward, when having passed up on a good bet, they see the winners celebrating, or when having paid for insurance year after year, they wind up not having an accident. But that doesn't make the decision irrational, given their preferences at the time it was made.

The standard strategy for representing delay-aversion is formally quite similar to that of risk-aversion. We include within our set of preferences a metapreference, expressed in the form of a discount rate, sometimes implicit, at other times explicit, that reduces the present value of future satisfaction. Sometimes this takes the form of a vague downgrading of certain thoughts

("I'll worry about that when the time comes"); sometimes it is much more explicit (as when we decide what sort of savings rate to adopt). At other times, we simply impose a temporal "cutoff" on our planning, so that we ignore the consequences that our choices will have in the distant future. Either way, the rate that the agent employs represents a more or less extreme regimentation of our underlying dispositions, which tend to be inchoate. We use our capacity to formulate an explicit preference, using language, as a way of lending greater order to these underlying dispositions, and of producing more successful long-term plans.[19] In the same way that we try to avoid building up excess frustration, we also try to avoid the negative affect associated with excessively deferred gratification.

Because delay-aversion is such an important and ubiquitous phenomenon, economists and game theorists automatically include a discount rate in each agent's utility function whenever dealing with a temporally extended choice problem. Philosophers, however, perhaps because of the ambient disciplinary suspicion of discounting, have tended to ignore it. Thus there is a tendency, in the literature on practical rationality, to talk about "desires" as though they were timeless and eternal, and to assume that the agent's "better judgment" about what course of action should be taken will be largely invariant across time. There is a failure to recognize that each one of the agent's atemporal desires, such as a preference for chocolate over vanilla ice cream, must be "schematized" (to use the Kantian term) in order to be translated into a concrete preference ordering over some set of pragmatically accessible possible worlds. In other words, the desire must be inserted into the temporal sequence of daily events. In the process, it gets adjusted by the agent's aversion to delay, which in turn affects the priority level that will be assigned to that desire in the all-things-considered ranking. If the vanilla ice cream is ready to eat right now and the chocolate needs to thaw for half an hour, a rational agent may well choose the vanilla, even though she has an abstract preference for chocolate over vanilla. Half an hour later, when the chocolate is being served, she may even regret her decision, but that doesn't make it irrational for her to have made it.

As we have seen, the standard discount function used by economists is based on an analogy with interest rates, not any empirical observation of how individuals actually discount future satisfaction. With functions of this type, a discount factor (δ) is introduced that specifies the value in present payoffs of one unit of payoffs to be received one period in the future. If the present $t = 0$, the value of any payoff at time $t + x$ is then taken to be an exponential function of δ, namely, δ^{t+x}. This may seem obvious, but in fact it rests on several rather substantive psychological assumptions. In particular, it assumes that individuals have exactly the same attitude toward a delay of a given length, regardless of when the delay occurs (e.g., tomorrow, or in several years).

There is, however, a lot of empirical evidence to suggest that individuals do not actually treat all delays the same, and so do not discount the future in the way that standard economic models suggest. George Ainslie has illustrated this in a variety of very simple studies.[20] For example, given a choice between a check for $100 that can be cashed right away and a check for $200 that can be cashed in three years, many people will choose the former. But many of these same people, when given a choice between a $100 check that can be cashed in six years and a $200 check that can be cashed in nine years, will take the $200.[21] It's not difficult to imagine what they are thinking. In the first case, people think "three years is a long time, I might as well take the $100." In the second case, they think "since I'm already waiting six years, an extra three years is no big deal, I might as well go for the $200."

Thus there is what Ainslie calls a "warp" in the way we think about the future. We seem to become more averse to delay the closer we are to having to suffer that delay. Put otherwise, we are not merely impatient, but we suffer from *heightened impatience* in the near term. Thus a more empirically accurate representation of our discount rate would take the form of what Ainslie calls a "hyperbolic" discount function, one that discounts satisfaction much more sharply in the near term. A closer approximation of how people feel about money, for instance, can be achieved by taking the sum and dividing it by $t + 1$, where t is the number of years of delay. Thus the expected utility of $1,000 in one year is equal to the utility of $500 in the present (in two years, $333; in three years, $250; in four years, $200; etc.). More formally (where r reflects individual variation, a higher number indicating greater impatience):[22]

$$\sum_{t=0}^{n} \frac{u_t(a)}{1+r(t)} \tag{1}$$

The chief characteristic of this function is that it takes a huge "bite" out of anticipated satisfaction in the very near term, but that it flattens out considerably in the long term. Thus it is able to explain why a surprising number of people both run up credit card debt *and* save for their retirement. (If people discounted the future exponentially, any 40-year-old willing to borrow at an interest rate of 20 percent would not care at all what happens to him at age 75.)

If one looks at a hyperbolic discount function of this sort in the abstract, it is difficult to see anything inherently wrong with it. If one is willing to admit time preference into the model of practical rationality, on the grounds that reasonable persons can be averse to delay, then it is difficult to see why rationality should require them to feel the same way about all delays, regardless of how far off in the future they are. At very least, it would require a far more complete theory of preference-rationality than any that are currently available in the philosophical literature.

When we shift our attention away from the hyperbolic discount function itself, however, and look at some of the consequences of acting on the basis of such a discount function, the picture changes. As it turns out, one of the underappreciated features of exponential discount functions is that they guarantee dynamic stability of "schematized" preferences (by virtue of the *stationarity* property that they exhibit).[23] In other words, if option a is preferred to option b at time t, then it will be preferred at any other time as well. Even if individuals are extremely shortsighted, they will be consistently shortsighted. They will *always* favor the lesser, nearer good over the greater, further one.

Hyperbolic discounting, on the other hand, generates dynamic preference instability. The expected utility of a particular option will tend to "spike up" in the very near term (as the intervening delay becomes smaller and smaller), sometimes overtaking options that were previously taken to be superior. One can see this clearly with Ainslie's example of the $100 and $200 checks. With the people who opted for the $100 check right away but chose the $200 check cashable in nine years, one could presumably go back to them in six years and buy the $200 checks for $100 (ignoring potential endowment effects). Thus hyperbolic discounting is able to explain the phenomenon of precommitment and temptation. Hume described the phenomenology of this quite well when he wrote:

> In reflecting on any action, which I am to perform a twelve-month hence, I always resolve to prefer the greater good, whether at that time it will be more contiguous or remote; nor does any difference in that particular make a difference in my present intentions and resolutions. My distance from the final determination makes all those minute differences vanish.... But on my nearer approach, those circumstances, which I at first over-look'd, begin to appear, and have an influence on my conduct and affections. A new inclination to the present good springs up, and makes it difficult for me to adhere inflexibly to my first purpose and resolution.[24]

Hume, however, chooses to describe this not as a reversal of preference, but rather as an example of our judgment being overwhelmed by our passions. "Tho' we may be fully convinc'd, that the latter object excels the former, we are not able to regulate our actions by this judgment; but yield to the solicitations of our passions, which always plead in favour of whatever is near and contiguous."[25] Most philosophers have been inclined to follow him in this assessment, and to classify this sort of intemperance as strict akrasia. Ainslie's analysis on the other hand provides a *rationalizing explanation* (at least as far as the theory of *practical* rationality is concerned) of intemperance, as a consequence of preference reversal.[26] At the point of decision, the hyperbolic discounter who chooses the "lesser good" is acting in accordance with her own all-things-considered judgment.

Consider the following concrete example (figure 8.1), a situation in which a person of limited means has to choose between going to a movie on Saturday evening and having money for dinner on Sunday. The atemporal utility associated with eating dinner on Sunday (10) is greater than that of seeing the movie (7). The two graphs show the expected utility for these two outcomes on each day of the week preceding, starting on Monday. The left pane (a) shows an agent with an exponential discount function ($\delta = 0.8$ per day), while the right pane (b) shows an agent with a hyperbolic discount rate (utility divided by "number of days plus one" delay). Both individuals can see clearly that having money for dinner on Sunday represents the greater good. They also both start out, on Monday, with a preference for the greater good. The central difference is that for the hyperbolic discounter, that preference gets reversed on Friday, remains inverted throughout the day on Saturday, and then switches back again on

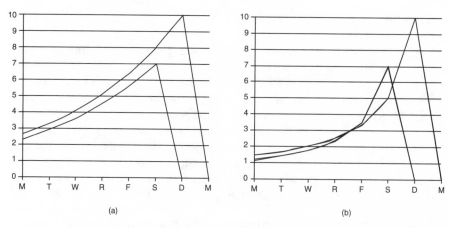

Figure 8.1 Exponential and hyperbolic discounting.

Sunday. So this person, left to his own devices, will resolve to save his money for dinner on Sunday, but then change his mind and go to the movie when the opportunity presents itself.

Obviously agents have all sorts of good reasons to want to avoid discounting future satisfaction hyperbolically. It may even be irrational, from the standpoint of preference-rationality, for individuals to exhibit the pattern of delay-aversion that generates a hyperbolic discount function. But regardless of all that, what Ainslie's model succeeds in showing is that the agent who "succumbs to temptation" in this way is not engaging in intentional counterpreferential choice at the point of decision. On the contrary, there is good reason to think that this person's all-things-considered preferences are dynamically unstable, because of the way that his aversion to delay interacts with his other preferences. Thus what appears to be strict akrasia is in fact temporary preference change.

For example, it could be that hyperbolic discounting involves a failure of affective forecasting (and that the preference reversal occurs when the individual corrects a past failure). People are, in general, not very good at anticipating the way that their own preferences will change with the passage of time. In one particularly elegant experiment, students were offered a choice of snacks during weekly classes, from a menu of six options over a period of three weeks.[27] Half were given the opportunity to decide at the beginning of each class what they wanted to have that day, the other half were offered a simultaneous choice of what they would have in each of the following three weeks (much like the "meal plan" choice in chapter 3, section 5). Almost two-thirds of those offered the simultaneous choice selected three different items for the three different weeks (and thus maximized variety in their consumption). However, of those who made the choices sequentially, fewer than 10 percent chose three different items on the three different weeks—they simply picked their favorite again (and again). A third control group, given a choice of three items for immediate consumption, almost all chose three different items. Thus the first "simultaneous choice" group exhibited a mistaken concern about satiation, ignoring the fact that over the course of the week their preferences would be "reset" to baseline.

Since most of the students offered the simultaneous choice made a mistake about their own future preferences, most of them would presumably have been willing to change their minds at a later date, if given the opportunity to do so. This would be perfectly rational, since all they would be doing is correcting their own past mistake. Yet one could easily tell the same story about the hyperbolic discounter. A person who takes the check for $200, cashable in nine years, on the grounds that, having waited for six years, three more years will be no big deal, is making a similar forecasting error. He is ignoring the fact that, in six years time, he will probably be just as averse to a three-year delay as he is currently to the prospect of an immediate three-year delay. Thus six years later, when he discovers that a three-year delay is in fact a big deal, he will want to change his decision. But in so doing, he is merely correcting an earlier forecasting error.

Of course, the explanation here depends on ascribing a cognitive bias to the agent, and so there is a *soupçon* of irrationality about the entire preference-reversal business. The important point is simply that when the agent makes the supposedly akratic decision she is not acting irrationally, or contrary to her own all-things-considered preferences. To take a more vivid example, one study of pregnant women who preferred not to use anesthetic during childbirth found that a majority reversed this decision once they went into active labor, but then drifted back toward their earlier preference one month postpartum.[28] I think anyone would hesitate to call this reversal "irrational" (or to authorize doctors to ignore requests for anesthetic made during labor). Yet unrealistic expectations about one's own tolerance for pain are no different in kind from unrealistic expectations about one's own ability to be patient. Thus the mere passage of time can serve as a source of rational preference change, simply because it "tests" one's patience.

There has been a curious tendency among philosophers to ignore this aspect of Ainslie's analysis. Mele, for example, recognizes that Ainslie's work provides a very plausible explanation for what agents are doing when they succumb to temptation. He therefore accepts Ainslie's basic analysis of discounting. But Mele incorporates it into his own theory by suggesting that hyperbolic discounting results in the "motivational" score associated with particular desires spiking up in the near term, leading us to act in ways that are contrary to our evaluations. He simply assumes that discounting is a noncognitive phenomenon, one that it leaves our evaluative judgments untouched. Yet the analysis presented above suggests that the preference inversions characteristic of hyperbolic discounting may be a consequence of agents engaging in rational reevaluation of their preferences. Among agents who exhibit delay-aversion, dynamic instability may be a natural feature of their system of preferences, even if their atemporal preferences remain unchanged. Thus Ainslie's analysis of discounting eliminates the need to associate separate "motivational" and "evaluative" scores with our desires, and raises serious doubts about whether strict akratic action ever really occurs.

8.3. Applications

One of the great attractions of Ainslie's analysis is that it provides a very compelling account of addiction. There is a popular tendency, widely shared among
philosophers, to confuse the phenomenon of addiction with the chemical dependency that the ingestion of certain substances creates. The assumption is that
certain substances, like nicotine, heroin, or alcohol, have chemical properties
that allow them to bypass the agent's rational faculties, forcing him to ingest
them even against his own will.[29] This is the so-called disease model of addiction, and it is no longer held in very high regard. Addiction is something quite
different from physical dependency. It takes only days to break the dependency
of the body on nicotine or heroin. Eliminating the addiction, on the other hand,
takes considerably longer. This is because the addiction arises from the pattern
of stimulation (i.e., pleasure) that the substance produces, and the power that
this exercises over the agent's own conscious decisions. What harmful addictive
substances have in common is that they offer a very quick burst of pleasure,
followed by significant negative aftereffects. If this pleasure is large enough and
comes fast enough, then an agent who sharply discounts the future will pay too
little attention to the aftereffects in her deliberations.

This is why smoking tobacco is so much more addictive than chewing it, and
why intravenous injection of heroin is so much more addictive than smoking
it. The body often receives the same dose of psychoactive substance in either
case; the question is simply how fast it gets into the bloodstream (and from
there, to the brain). Similarly, heroin and methadone are both opiates, and their
effects on the brain are essentially the same. The difference lies in the pattern of
stimulation that they provide. Methadone is ingested orally, rather than being
injected intravenously, and remains in the body longer. Thus it does not generate the euphoric sensation (the "hit") that heroin produces. Heroin addicts take
methadone in order to help themselves quit, because it allows them to work on
breaking their addiction without having to deal with the withdrawal symptoms
associated with eliminating their chemical dependency. On the other hand,
people who receive morphine for control of pain experience a very different
pattern of stimulation from the recreational user, and so often do not develop
an addiction. Even when they develop a physical dependence, and suffer acute
withdrawal symptoms when the morphine is discontinued, they generally do
not suffer from any cravings.[30]

Figure 8.2 shows the pattern of stimulation that characterizes an addictive substance.[31] The disutility generated at the tail end gets discounted, simply
because there is such a large spike of pleasure at the front end.

This analysis makes it clear that there are all sorts of things that can be addictive, and that they need not have any special chemical properties. Nicotine, alcohol, and heroin happen to be especially addictive, because of the increasingly
severe withdrawal symptoms, which amplify the individual's incentive to have
another "hit." But there is no difference in principle between these substances
and various forms of junk food, which are designed to generate precisely the
pattern of stimulation shown in figure 8.2. A variety of salty snack foods, for

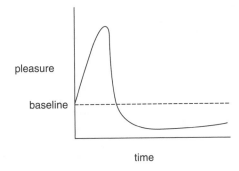

Figure 8.2 The pattern of addiction.

example, have been modified over time to maximize their surface area, so that there will be a greater burst of flavor at the very beginning (especially on the tongue, where the salt is tasted). A dull aftertaste then gives the individual an incentive to eat another one. This is the secret of everything from salted nuts to flavored tortilla chips.

One of the great virtues of Ainslie's analysis is that it shows just how pervasive the phenomenon of addiction is. The fact that we all, to a greater or lesser degree, discount the future hyperbolically means that we are all vulnerable to the lure of activities that, despite being ultimately unsatisfying, exhibit a particular pattern of reward that makes them difficult to resist. Any activity that is loaded up with satisfaction at the front end, followed by some protracted period of dissatisfaction, will tend to be chosen, even when, from an atemporal perspective, the latter is sufficient to outweigh the former. Similarly, any activity that has all the dissatisfaction at the front end, followed by some larger satisfaction, will tend to be passed over, even when, again from an atemporal perspective, the latter is sufficient to outweigh the former.

Of course even agents who discount the future exponentially can be lured into engaging in activities that generate a pattern of stimulation along the lines of figure 8.2. Thus one need not appeal to hyperbolic discounting to explain why agents engage in activities that are, broadly speaking, shortsighted or self-destructive. What hyperbolic discounting is needed to explain, however, is the pattern that addicts exhibit when, in a cool moment, they judge the activity to be self-destructive and resolve to quit, yet later change their minds and keep doing it. This sort of preference reversal cannot be explained as a consequence of mere discounting; it is a product of hypertrophied discounting in the short term.

The typical examples of weakness of the will that feature so prominently in the philosophical literature (smoking, having another beer at the party, staying up late, etc.) are all examples of activities that exhibit these patterns in the medium term. However, there are a variety of similar phenomena that occur in the short and long term. Adapting Ainslie's analysis somewhat, we might categorize these as shown in table 8.1.[32]

Table 8.1 Forms of Dysfunctional Behavior

Descriptor	Duration of cycle	Recognized as a problem	Examples
Compulsions	Months to years	Years to decades	Workaholism, constrictions of personality like miserliness, pedantry
Addictions	Hours to days	Days to years	Substance abuse, explosive emotional habits
Urges	Minutes to hours	Days	Bad habits such as "cable surfing," overeating, procrastination
Itches	Seconds	Minutes	Physical itches, obsessions, tics, mannerisms

Based on Ainslie, *Breakdown of Will*, p. 64.

The most important point is that Ainslie's discounting hypothesis provides an extraordinarily simple unifying explanation *for all of these phenomena*, without the need to posit strict akratic action on the part of agents. This is a good thing, since table 8.1 shows just how ubiquitous irrationality would be if Mele's analysis of weakness of the will were correct. Every time someone scratched a mosquito bite, ate a Dorito, or checked his email rather than working on his book, he would be behaving irrationally. If we want to avoid (for broadly Sellarsian reasons) positing pervasive misalignment of motivation and evaluation, then it makes more sense to explain these as preference reversals.

Ainslie's analysis can also be applied to explain various forms of immorality, which occur when agents succumb to temptation. The analogy between prudence and morality has been widely noted.[33] As the argument of chapters 6 and 7 has shown, properly socialized adults have a norm-conformative choice disposition, one that leads them to assign considerable deliberative weight to social norms in their conduct. This norm-conformative disposition can also be interpreted as a type of metapreference, which increases the priority level of the agent's preference over certain actions relative to outcomes (i.e., her principles relative to her desires). This means that an agent who accepts a particular norm as binding on her conduct will also be motivated to act in accordance with it; there is no need to go a step further to bring her animal spirits into alignment.

Many people will no doubt have had the experience of deciding, for example, that it is wrong to torment one's siblings, commit adultery, or evade taxes, and yet find that the urge to do so is irresistible when the opportunity presents itself. The "Humean externalist" would explain this by saying that one "knows" it is bad to do these things, but simply lacks the motivation to refrain—either because one lacks the preexisting motivations needed to transform the "external" reason licensed by the moral norm into a suitable "internal" reason, or because one has an appropriate "internal" reason, but somehow fails to secure a motivational score for that reason commensurate to its evaluative one. The explanation that I offered was more prosaic, namely, that the desire simply outweighed the principle, when it came time to determining a global preference ordering, either because one failed to take the principles as seriously as one might have, or because of moral laxity—a failure to assign principles in general adequate priority. There are very few people in this world who assign lexical priority to their principles over their desires, and so there usually exist incentives sufficient to induce immoral conduct in most people.

Ainslie's analysis provides additional support for the prosaic explanation, by offering an explanation for the fact that the "overwhelming" of one's principles by a desire often occurs in the heat of the moment, and thus generates the cycle of temptation, transgression, and regret that is familiar from the case of imprudence. After all, one is far more likely to be tempted by desires that exhibit the pattern of stimulation shown in figure 8.2 than by those that present merely a long-term gain in average satisfaction. Primarily, this is because the disposition to respect social norms generates a relatively "flat" pattern of satisfaction. Because norms are associated directly with actions, the valuation they confer tends to be invariant across time. Actions that are valued for the sake of outcomes on the other hand will tend to change in valuation as that outcome becomes either more proximate or more distant in time. Thus it is very easy to decide in advance that one will not, for example, tell a lie, and yet find that the temptation to do so increases dramatically at the time when the benefits of lying become most immediate. This is even more pronounced in the case of violence or sexual infidelity.

One exception to this claim about "flatness" involves the sudden flush of shame or discomfort associated with the violation of social norms. Breaking social rules is not as easy as one might think. Most people would be mortified by the thought of brazenly cutting into line at the movie theatre, tripping a complete stranger at the bus stop, or even just standing up and singing in a crowded restaurant.[34] One can easily imagine deciding to perform such actions (perhaps as a sociological experiment, in order to observe people's reactions) but then losing one's resolve when the time came.[35] The embarrassment associated with nonconformity is sometimes quite acute, enough to generate dynamic preference inconsistency. The positive gratification stemming from norm-conformity on the other hand appears to be far less unstable over time.

Of course, none of these examples are decisive, and people have wildly varying intuitions about what is going on in cases where we succumb to temptation. Ultimately, the question is simply how we want to describe the phenomenon of weakness of the will—as strict *akrasia* or as a temporary change of mind. It seems doubtful that introspection, linguistic intuition, or philosophical "analysis" will settle the question. There are, as I have suggested, powerful arguments stemming from the philosophy of language that speak in favor of the "temporary change of mind" hypothesis. Philosophers, however, have traditionally favored the strict akrasia explanation, simply because they have been unable to see what could possibly motivate apparently capricious changes of mind. If shooting the horse seemed like a good idea five minutes ago, then how could it not seem like a good idea now? Nothing in the world has changed, other than the fact that five minutes have elapsed. So why should preferences change?

This is why Ainslie's analysis, combined with a greater attention to the phenomenon of discounting, is so important. If the agent has a time preference, then it means that each of her preferences over states of the world must be time-indexed. This makes it easier to see how the fact that a week has elapsed could change the agent's evaluation of the situation. And if the agent's time preference has the hyperbolic structure that Ainslie has diagnosed, then it is easy to see how the agent's evaluations could exhibit the pattern of inconsistency over time that we have come to characterize as weakness of the will. This is, of course, not a decisive argument against the strict *akrasia* diagnosis. It does, however, eliminate the presumption in its favor that has, to date, heavily structured the philosophical discussion.

8.4. Self-Control

The argument so far has been based on my contention that discounting as such is not irrational, in the sense that it is not precluded by the theory of practical rationality. In this respect, it is like risk-aversion and norm-conformity. These are all metapreferences that may lead one, from the standpoint of one's atemporal preferences, to engage in what appear to be nonmaximizing courses of action. Thus an agent with such metapreferences may pass up some long-term gain in favor of short-term satisfaction, may prefer to take the "sure thing" instead of a mathematically superior gamble, and may choose to respect a norm, thereby passing up an opportunity to achieve some otherwise desirable outcome. If an agent has such preferences, there would appear to be no reason in principle that he or she should not act on them.

On the other hand, the fact that such metapreferences cannot be precluded in principle does not mean that agents cannot, and should not, reflect on and possibly change the particular preferences they have. In the case of the norm-conformative choice disposition, the transcendental argument of the previous chapter showed that such deliberation would be idle. Yet this is manifestly not so in the case of the agent's discount rate (and level of risk-aversion). In fact, there is good reason to believe that the discount rate that agents typically adopt creates all sorts of mischief in their lives, and that they may have good reason to try to change it. In particular, they may have good reason to adopt an exponential rather than a hyperbolic discount rate (or perhaps even a time preference of zero).

In this context, it is worth noting that a significant portion of the socialization process involves pressuring children to acquire the capacity to defer gratification (which is presumably part of the reason that impulsiveness declines steadily with age).[36] This reflects the widely held conviction among parents that their children's lives will go better if they discount the future less sharply. In particular, it will give them the ability to develop long-term plans and stick to them, or more generally, to live a life with fewer regrets. (Economists have spent considerable energy developing an analysis of education as a costly signaling system, allowing "high-ability" individuals to differentiate themselves from "low-ability" individuals in the job market. A more plausible analysis would be that the separating equilibrium distinguishes those with more capacity to defer gratification from those with less.)

In particular, the fact that a steep discount rate makes us more vulnerable to addictions and similar bad habits (such as staying up late, charging too much on your credit card, eating too much, procrastinating, overuse of pornography, excessive video game-playing, television watching, or net surfing) gives us all a reason to become more temperate individuals. Thus there will often be good arguments to be made against having the discount rate that implicitly structures many of our desires and preferences. And given that these desires are all open to modification through rational deliberation, the mere fact that primary socialization and habit provide us with a particular discount rate does not settle the question of what that rate should be. Of course, neither are we free simply to pick the rate that strikes us as ideal, because there is a somatic and libidinal system underlying our intentional planning system that must be tended to. Simply deciding one day not to discount future satisfaction is likely to be no more successful than simply deciding not to become frustrated. It takes a certain amount of self-control.

When thinking about self-control, it is perhaps useful to distinguish two senses of the term. Mele's definition of self-control (the level of default correlation between the agent's motivational and evaluative rankings of desires) is essentially passive. A person has a lot of self-control, on this view, if he tends always to do what he thinks it would be best to do. But there is also the question of how agents whose motivational and evaluative scores do not line up very well respond to that fact. Mele outlines a number of different strategies—attention management being the most important—that agents might adopt in response to such a situation.[37] This adverts to a more active notion of self-control, in which agents intervene, in some way, to ensure that their evaluative and motivational scores line up (or that their actions follow from their evaluations, and not necessarily their motivations). Nevertheless, there has always been something mysterious about the active form of self-control for partisans of strict akrasia. Aristotle perhaps put it best when he asked "if water chokes us, what must we drink to wash it down?"[38] Since weakness of the will is taken to represent the triumph of unreason over reason, it is not clear how more reasoning could be effective in counteracting it. There are good reasons not to act akratically, but if good reasons alone were decisive, then one wouldn't be acting akratically in the first place.

If, however, one regards weakness of the will as fundamentally a problem of temporary preference inversion, induced by hyperbolic discounting, then active self-control is much easier to understand. According to this view, a person who discounted the future exponentially (or in the limit case not at all), would be highly self-controlled in the passive sense of the term. He would always do what he thought it best to do. It is only hyperbolic discounters who want to do one thing but then change their minds later—and so have a present incentive to control what they do at a future date. Self-control in the active sense of the term, then, refers to the (rational) strategies that hyperbolic discounters adopt into order to control dynamic preference instability, or to control their own behavior in the face of dynamic preference instability. There is nothing mysterious or paradoxical about this.

Self-control in the active sense is essentially a type of precommitment strategy. Such attempts can be made either by ensuring that an anticipated preference inversion does not occur, that one's global preference ordering remains the same despite *local* preference inversions that may occur, or that one's actions conform to present preferences *despite* any preference inversions that may occur. What makes instances of the latter type examples of self-control, rather than simply the tyranny of a past self, is that the decision taken ex ante is also ratified ex post, once the temporary preference inversion has passed. (Of course, at the time the decision is taken, this anticipated ratification is purely speculative, and often mistaken. People often decide that a particular exercise of self-control was not worth the effort, once they have succumbed to temptation and failed to witness the anticipated ill effects. Thus one's planning can only be characterized reliably as an exercise in self-control when dealing with habits that have proven themselves to be consistently deleterious.)

It is important to recognize, in this context, that precommitment can be achieved through either internal or external mechanisms. It is helpful to distinguish, under the general rubric of self-control, strategies that involve an exercise of willpower from those that involve some sort of "work-around." Through an exercise of willpower, the agent may directly modify his (implicit or explicit) discount rate so that an anticipated preference inversion will not occur, or so that its effects will be attenuated. But rather than modifying his discount rate, the agent may also choose to avoid putting himself in the circumstances that he knows will generate a problematic preference inversion. Or if the circumstances are unavoidable, he may rearrange some other incentives, in such a way that they favor the action that is best, according to his *present* preferences. The latter are all *management* techniques. They do not correct the fundamental problem, which is the agent's tendency to discount the future hyperbolically. Instead, they work around it, and so despite leaving the fundamental problem in place, prevent it from generating manifestly dysfunctional behavior.

Self-control strategies can be analyzed under the following headings:

1. *Willpower.* While the agent's discount rate is responsive to underlying somatic conditions—such as a vague feeling of anxiety or impatience, or else the quickening of more particular somatic states like hunger or sexual arousal in the near term—it is not at all determined by these conditions. An agent who is experiencing hunger has considerable discretion in deciding how to respond. Normally, agents react to a feeling of hunger simply by modifying their intentional plans by adding a desire with the content "eat something" to their "to do" list. What they intend to eat and when they intend to eat will all be determined by the interaction of the desire to eat with other plans. Furthermore, agents retain the option of simply ignoring the somatic stimulus (especially if they have other, more pressing goals they must attend to). Later, if they find that the stimulus becomes more persistent and more distracting and begins to compromise their efficacy in achieving these other goals, they may "give in" to the desire and move "eat something" up in the list of priorities. On the other hand, they may continue to ignore it.

What exactly is going on here? Feeling hungry constitutes *pro tanto* grounds for adopting a desire to eat something. Usually this is a straightforward language-entry move—the agent responds to the somatic stimulus by adopting an intentional state, namely, a desire to eat, with a priority level that roughly reflects the perceived level of somatic arousal. However, the agent may also have *pro tanto* reasons for not eating, such as being on a diet, or wanting to get to work on time. She will then adjust downward the priority level associated with the desire to eat, in response to these reasons against. (Precisely how one wishes to characterize the dynamics of this mode of deliberation is not at issue here.) In so doing, she is choosing to "control" her need for food, by assigning that activity a lower priority in her plans than it would otherwise merit, were it to be based entirely on the somatic stimulus. This is what we normally think of when we talk about willpower.

This is why attention management is such an important component of effective self-control. The brain is normally inundated with stimuli, all of which must compete with one another for attention. The dynamic of this competition is largely outside of our control, although people are able to influence it to varying degrees. As we have seen, formulating explicit plans in the medium of language is an important device that we have at our disposal for doing so.[39] Thus as a particular somatic stimulus like hunger becomes stronger over time, it will begin to compete more effectively for attention. An agent who has other reasons for not eating, and therefore chooses to ignore her hunger pains, will therefore find this plan more and more difficult to carry out as time passes (and in the limit case, will suffer from a loss of intentional control). Thus one important technique for sticking to the plan is to prevent the hunger stimulus from securing attention, by becoming engrossed in some other activity or thought.

What does a *failure* of willpower look like in this view? Consider the case of someone who is working away on a report and begins to feel hungry. If she is engrossed in her work, she may not even notice this at first. When she does, she may then weigh the pros and cons of running across the street to buy a sandwich against continuing for a while longer with the work that she is doing. Suppose that she is feeling productive, and so decides not to take a break to eat for another two hours. She refocuses her mind on the report, and gets back to work. However, as time passes, she finds that she is becoming increasingly distracted by her hunger pains. She continues to refocus, but after an hour or so she relents and goes off to buy a sandwich. When she returns to work, her mind is no longer in it, and she regrets her decision.

The wrong way to characterize this would be as an instance of akrasia, or irrationality. It is not as though she has a nonintentional somatic state (hunger) and a desire (to work) and that when she goes off to buy the sandwich the former wins out over the latter, and so gets to determine her conduct. Nor is it the case that of her two desires (one to eat, the other to keep working) the former acquires greater motivational strength all on its own as the somatic stimulus increases. What we are dealing with is a rational change of mind, in response to a change in somatic stimulus. The agent has a *pro tanto* reason to eat, grounded in the somatic stimulus, and a *pro tanto* reason not to eat, derived from the importance of the report. The agent initially downgraded the priority of eating, in response to the latter, but miscalculated her ability to ignore the somatic stimulus over a two-hour period. When the agent "relents," it is because she changes her estimation of the priority that the somatic stimulus should confer on the desire to eat. There may or may not be irrationality involved in her changing the priority of a desire that she had initially vowed not to change, but there is certainly no irrationality in the action she takes, on the basis of the desire after it has been changed.

2. *Self-management.* Willpower, in its strictest form, involves simply deciding what one is going to do, according to the best reasons currently available, and then sticking to the plan, regardless of how one's somatic state (and perhaps even external circumstances) may change. At the limit, this can amount simply to imposing an exponential discount rate on one's deliberations, and ignoring whatever displeasure this may generate at the level of one's underlying somatic states. However, there is surely some truth in Hume's claim that "men are not able radically to cure, either in themselves or others, that narrowness of soul, which makes them prefer the present to the remote."[40] Most people, in other words, cannot simply impose a discount rate on themselves. Thus they have a range of indirect strategies and tricks that they employ in order to avoid the more problematic temporary preference inversions. Some of these, such as attention management, are so central to the exercise that they are best thought of as an element of willpower. Others, however, are more like work-arounds. Consider, for example, the use of substitute gratifications. Somatic stimuli tend to be extremely nonspecific, and we often rely on environmental cues in order to determine what they are, so that we may then go on to form desires with specific content. We have probably all had the experience of wandering around the kitchen, feeling the need to eat *something*, but not being sure what that something is. Even something as specific as a craving for a cigarette does not present itself as such, and can easily be misidentified as hunger. People who are trying to quit smoking can take advantage of this indeterminacy by eating snack food whenever they have a severe craving for a cigarette. (The reverse is true as well; people who are dieting often have a cigarette whenever they feel hungry.) It may not be as satisfying, but it does go some way toward keeping the somatic stimulus to a manageable level.

Similarly, people who are under considerable pressure to defer gratification in central areas of their life may choose to "go wild" in some more peripheral areas (by engaging in extreme sports, spending excessively in some consumption category, etc.). They may also choose to reward themselves for one exercise of discipline by relaxing discipline in some other area (e.g., treating themselves to a more expensive lunch, in return for finishing a report on time). In effect, they choose to manage their feelings of impatience and frustration by applying different implicit discount rates in different areas of their lives. The effectiveness of particular strategies may be specific to the individual in question, but there is no doubt that gratifications arising from one activity can have a spillover effect, reducing the level of stimulus associated with a related activity that the agent may be seeking to control. People may also simply choose not to attempt self-control in areas where they think the effort will create too much strain. Ainslie refers to this as a "lapse district," where past lapses have "foretold a broad loss of impulse control," and so the "person doesn't dare attempt efforts of will."[41] (He adds, helpfully, that when behavior in this lapse area becomes clinically noteworthy, it is referred to as a "symptom.")

The way people think about a particular decision can also have an important impact on the discount rate they apply. For example, it has been observed that individuals exhibit less dynamic instability in their preferences when dealing with questions in monetary terms. Ainslie has suggested one explanation for this, which is that money, because it is not consumed directly, but rather is transformed into consumption goods at the point of purchase, serves as a stand-in for a temporally extended sequence of satisfactions.[42] As a result, money effectively "bundles" together an entire set of preferences, some of which will be satisfied sooner, others later. Because of this, the temporary spike in desire for one good, caused by its temporal proximity, will tend to be smoothed out when combined with the desires for less proximate goods. Thus one of the best ways to exercise control over one's spending habits is to think of one's consumption in purely monetary terms: to think of each purchase in terms of its overall impact on the household budget, and so on.

3. *Environment management.* One of the most underappreciated aspects of self-control is the measures people take to avoid putting themselves in situations in which they will suffer from preference inversions. Mahatma Gandhi's approach to celibacy may have been to sleep between two naked young women (thereby making it an exercise in pure willpower), but most men who manage to refrain from adultery succeed because they never find themselves in such situations (and should such an unlikely situation arise, take evasive action). Indeed, there is something rather preening about Gandhi's "experiments in Brahmacharya," as though virtue were a demonstration sport, to be practiced competitively. For ordinary mortals, the standard way of avoiding succumbing to temptation is to avoid situations in which one will be tempted.

This sort of environmental management is so ubiquitous that much of it goes unnoticed. Sometimes there are explicit rules of thumb: Eat a full meal before you go grocery shopping. Flush your cigarettes down the toilet if you want to quit smoking. Get a new set of friends if you're trying to kick heroin. Unplug the internet if you want to get your thesis written. Don't carry cash if you don't want to spend it. More subtly, one can see in people's homes—environments they have created for themselves—many elements that serve as supports for habits and routines that the individual wants to cultivate or maintain. The type of food that is in the kitchen, the position of the television, the exercise equipment, the workspace are often "external scaffolding,"[43] designed to make certain activities easier, and others more difficult (or certain activities easier to combine with some than with others).

Of course, some people rely more heavily on their environments than others. Many people who have an enormous amount of self-control actually have very little willpower, but are able to control themselves through ingenious environmental management. One can see the importance of such external scaffolding by observing the extent to which their temperate habits are disrupted when they are placed in a different environment, such as a hotel (e.g., they might stay up too late watching television, simply because at home there is no TV in the bedroom).

4. *Cooperation.* One of the most underappreciated aspects of self-control is the way we recruit other people to assist us in abiding by our resolutions. Hume argued that our capacity to provide this sort of assistance to one another was in fact the foundation of "civil government and allegiance."[44] Once we have decided on the best plan, we can authorize others to punish us, constrain us, or even act on our behalf, in such a way as to guarantee that we stick to the plan. (Ulysses arranging for his sailors to tie him to the mast and then ignore all his subsequent orders is the classic example.)[45]

The extent to which we rely upon others to keep us on the straight and narrow is often overlooked. In the same way that our brains colonize elements of our physical environment (such as pencils, abacus beads, or linguistic symbols) in order to amplify our native cognitive abilities, we also use the cognitive abilities of other people for the same purposes, especially when there are complementarities available. Thus among spouses there is usually one person who keeps track of money, another who remembers birthdays, one person who acts as navigator in the car, and so on. Those who are able to divide up tasks effectively wind up being "smarter" when together than either is when alone. Less seldom noted is the way spouses divide up the burdens of exercising self-control by, either explicitly or implicitly, licensing one another to nag. One can also see it in the division of household labor—the person who is most likely to buy healthy food is the one most likely to be responsible for grocery shopping, the one most likely to save money and pay bills on time is the one most likely to be in charge of finances, and so on. There may be a number of different explanations for the fact that people who are married are, on average, happier than those who are single, separated, or divorced, but one factor must be the extent to which married couple are constantly working to correct each other's bad habits (a procedure that is, of course, painful in the short term but beneficial in the long term).

It is worth noting as well that many social institutions have traditionally been organized in such a way as to promote self-control, and to exercise it by proxy in cases where individuals fail. The best way to save, for example, is to authorize one's bank to make automatic withdrawals as soon as one's paycheck is deposited.[46] (This is also the best way to pay one's tax bill, which is presumably why the state imposes mandatory withholdings.) Employers usually pay out salaries in biweekly or monthly installments, rather than annual lump sums. They provide compensation to employees in the form of benefits, rather than simply cash. Bars in North America sell hard liquor by the shot, not by the bottle. The examples could be multiplied quite easily.

5. *Rule-making.* Finally, there is the well-known phenomenon of people making rules to constrain their own behavior. The best way to understand this sort of rule-making is to treat the individual as enlisting a principle as a *pro tanto* reason against performing a particular action, in order to bolster whatever desire-based reasons arise from the anticipated long-term consequences of that action.

Thus an agent who is tempted to eat a donut, and finds the mere contemplation of its long-term health consequences insufficient as a deterrent, might then scan about for some principles that such an action would violate. If this is successful, then he can take commitment to the principle and add it to the health consequences as reasons against eating it. Thus he brings his own normative control system into play on the side of temperate conduct.

Another simple strategy is to enlist others to help one develop good habits. Here one is not relying on the normative force that can be associated with certain actions, but with the positive cathexis that can be built up through repetition. Many people like to have routines—a set of actions that they perform each day—and deviation from them can be a source of displeasure, regardless of its consequences. Thus if one can get the right set of routines in place—healthy eating, regular exercise, a good night's sleep—then the gratification associated with adherence to the routine itself may be sufficient to outweigh any short-term temptations that may arise (especially given that the value of an action is normally undiscounted, simply because of its immediacy).

It is somewhat more difficult to understand the fact that agents often just invent rules for themselves, as a way of controlling their own behavior. There have been a large number of hypotheses advanced to explain this phenomenon.[47] One possible explanation, however, that has been widely ignored is that self-imposed rules represent internalized version of commitments initially adopted using the external scaffolding of interpersonal normative commitment. Part of the success of 12-step programs and support groups stems from the fact that individuals are able to commit themselves publicly before others to correcting dysfunctional behaviors. Having made a promise to the group, and having the sense that failure on one's part may let others down, provides additional normative grounds for compliance. More generally, simply being in a group of people all trying to correct the problem may trigger the agent's norm-conformative disposition.

I believe that the phenomenon of self-imposed rules essentially represents an internalization of this external mechanism of social control. Indeed, people will often describe these sorts of restrictions using the model of interpersonal interactions (e.g., in terms of "having made a promise to myself" or "having made a commitment to God.") There is also considerable reason to believe that the internalized version is not as effective as the interpersonal one. For example, there is a very strong negative correlation between social isolation and success in combating addiction.[48] This makes sense if rule-following is learned first in the form of compliance to external norms, after which normative self-control is acquired through internalization. This is further reason to believe that theorists who take the ability to plan, or to adopt intentional states, as primitives and then try to use these capacities to explain the emergence of rule-following and social norms get the explanatory order backward.

Because of this, there is often no sharp distinction between rule-making as an exercise of willpower and rule-making as a management technique. A marriage ceremony, for instance, combines elements of both in a seamless fashion. Making a promise in front of everyone in the world whose opinion you care about is simply not the same as making a promise in the privacy of one's own home. Both involve making a promise, and so imposing a rule on oneself. But the former also involves marshaling significant social and environmental resources to structure one's present and future incentives in such a way as to favor compliance with that rule.

8.5. Volitional Prosthetics

In chapter 4, I argued that there is no way to separate the "native" cognitive abilities of the human brain from the external mechanisms—the social, cultural, and physical resources—that we use to amplify them. Not only are the two not separable, but it is perverse to want to separate them, since to do so obscures the peculiar genius of the human mode of cognition. As Andy Clark writes:

> Advanced cognition depends crucially on our abilities to *dissipate* reasoning: to diffuse achieved knowledge and practical wisdom through complex social structures, and to reduce the loads on individual brains by locating those brains in complex webs of linguistic, social, political, and institutional constraints.... [Human brains] are not so different from the fragmented, special-purpose, action-oriented organs of other animals and autonomous robots. But we excel in one crucial respect: we are masters at structuring our physical and social worlds so as to press complex coherent behaviors from these unruly resources. We use intelligence to structure our environment so that we can succeed with *less* intelligence. Our brains make the world smart so that we can be dumb in peace! Or, to look at it in another way, it is the human brain plus these chunks of external scaffolding that finally constitutes the smart, rational inference engine that we call mind.[49]

These reflections on the nature of theoretical rationality have profound implications for our understanding of practical rationality as well. The most important piece of "external scaffolding" that goes into the construction of our intelligence is language, which we master first as a set of external symbols and social practices. It is mastery of language that gives us the capacity not only to count, to categorize, and to follow complex instructions but also to engage in intentional planning, and thus to impose a linear, coherent, rational order on our sometimes chaotic and conflicting behavioral dispositions. It is the internalization of these capacities that produces the rational, maximizing agent that decision theory seeks to model (and of course, as behavioral economists have shown, this internalization remains partial, and in some cases, fragmentary). This is why most of us, insofar as we do succeed in pursuing something like maximizing strategies in pursuit of our goals, manage to do so by "offloading" an enormous number of cognitive demands onto our physical environment (computers, stacks of paper, post-it notes, bank accounts, etc.) and onto other people (lawyers, stockbrokers, colleagues, spouses, etc.).[50]

Recognizing the importance of this external scaffolding must necessarily change the way we think about the "autonomous" individual. The philosophical (and Christian) tradition has tended to privilege the internal over the external, such that the only form of self-control that "counts" with respect to either prudential or moral temptation is willpower. Yet there is no clear distinction between the way we structure our environment to amplify our cognitive resources and the way we structure the environment to amplify our motivational ones. This sentence is being written on a laptop computer from which I have specifically uninstalled all the games, and which has been disconnected from the internet. It has been set up that way because I lack the willpower to refrain from gaming or surfing when I am supposed to be writing. Thus at many points, the *only* reason that I keep writing is that, in order to game or surf, I would have to get up, go downstairs, and boot up my desktop. In other words, I undergo a failure of "self-mastery" in the internal control sense, but I retain "self-mastery" through a prior organization of my external incentives in such a way as to favor actions that would be undertaken on the basis of the preference that I endorse on reflection (in a "cool moment"). To imagine that the internal strategy is somehow superior to the external one is simply to privilege arbitrarily one style of exercising self-control over another.

Many people treat their own willpower as something of a scarce resource, with only so much to go around.[51] Thus they make budgetary decisions, choosing which temptations to control directly and which ones to "offload" to the environment (in much the same way that we decide whether to commit something to memory or to write it down). Should I buy a case of beer, then ration my consumption? Or should I bring home only a six-pack? The fact that people buy beer by the six-pack, and pay more per bottle to do so, suggests that external control is an important feature of self-control. It means also that the all-night beer store is not an unmixed blessing. While providing increased convenience for some, it also pulls away a part of the external scaffold that many people use as part of their self-control system (namely, the unobtainability of more beer, after the six-pack is consumed). Thus late-night hours at the beer store should correctly be viewed as an innovation that *decreases* the autonomy of these people, by withdrawing a form of social cooperation that they at one time relied on to exercise self-control.

Joel Anderson has argued that these external scaffolds should be thought of as a type of *prosthetic*.[52] In this respect, we would have cognitive prosthetics, volitional prosthetics, moral prosthetics, and perhaps many others. There is a sense in which taking a false limb away from an amputee may constitute just as serious a threat to the integrity of that person as the initial loss of the limb. But what about taking away the eyeglasses of someone who is terribly shortsighted? Bullies do it all the time, and it is in most cases a far more damaging violation of the person than being punched or kicked. And what about taking away someone's clothing? The distinction between that which is "naturally" a part of the body and that which has been added to it is unhelpful when thinking about personal integrity. The situation is very much the same when thinking about autonomy and the will.

One further reason for not privileging internal control over external control strategies when thinking about the will is that different people make different choices about what tasks to offload onto the environment. Some people find it relatively easy to control food cravings, and so keep a house full of chocolates, candies, and snack food. Others find these cravings difficult to control, and so make sure that all of these items are banished from their house. They are, in effect, choosing to exercise control at the point of purchase, thereby creating a home environment that facilitates control at the point of consumption (or non-consumption, as the case may be). The fact that in the latter case, they are acting on the basis of external incentives, rather than internal control, is no reason to deprecate their motives. The important point is that they are acting on the basis of incentives that they have created for themselves.

Of course, the question of privileging the internal over the external is not terribly weighty in the case of prudential choice. It becomes more significant, however, in the case of resistance to moral temptation. Many philosophers have followed Kant in adopting an exceedingly strict definition of autonomy, according to which any influence of desire, rather than just principle, constitutes an affront to the autonomy of the agent. This of course maps onto his distinction between actions done *in accordance with duty*, and those done *from duty*. Such a distinction ignores the frequency with which agents, acting from duty, but knowing that they will later be subject to temptation that may defeat the motive of duty, arrange their incentives in such a way that it will later be in their interest to act in accordance with duty. In other words, they offload this particular exercise of willpower onto the environment. In Kant's view, this makes their later actions heteronomous, and deprives them of moral value. Thus the overwhelming majority of moral actions wind up being reclassified as amoral (Kant is surely right in saying that if his view is correct, there is no way of knowing whether any truly moral action has ever been performed).[53]

In the same way that the amount we can remember represents only a tiny fraction of the information we keep readily at our disposal in written form, the amount of moral fiber that most of us are able to summon up represents only a small percentage of what we have "offloaded" to the surrounding environment. This is why so many studies have shown that there are no stable personality traits associated with traditional "virtues" like honesty.[54] It also explains "the banality of evil" phenomenon—why people are willing to do abhorrent things when put in the right circumstances, and the right social environment. I have never met anyone who believes that he or she would have shocked a fellow human being to death, had she been one of the unfortunate participants in Stanley Milgram's famous experiments. Part of this is simply wishful thinking (the same way that 94 percent of college professors think their work is of above average quality, or that most people think they have above average driving skills).[55] But part of it also represents a genuine failure to perceive the extent to which we rely on our environment.[56] In the same way, most of us think we can do pretty complicated arithmetic, but if you take away all writing implements, calculators, and so on, it turns out that "we" can't do very much arithmetic at all. Similarly, we tend not to be very moral, when removed from the social context in which the preponderance of our moral actions occur. One way of responding to this is to assume that we are all bad people. The other possible response—the one I would recommend—is to rethink our traditional understanding of the moral will.

Of course, when doing arithmetic with a pen and paper, it is pretty easy to see where our operative short-term memory is being offloaded. Where does morality get offloaded? First and foremost, it is offloaded onto social institutions. The norms that govern our everyday practices, and that structure our expectations in routine social interactions, are the concrete embodiment of our moral life. Rather than think about the details of what we owe to one another, each and every minute of the day, most of us simply follow the rules. We conform to social norms. Not only does this lessen the cognitive load (because it frees us from the need to contemplate a broad swath of the consequences of our actions) but, because the norms are also socially sanctioned, it lessens the motivational load. It is both a cognitive and a volitional prosthetic. Assortative interaction is an important element of this. The best way to avoid committing a crime is to avoid socializing with criminals. More generally, the best way to prevent oneself from committing a certain type of action is to put oneself in a social context in which people regard that sort of action as particularly taboo. Not only does this bolster our impulse to conform, it also makes us apprehensive of the sanctions for failure to do so. The same way that most human knowledge is found in books, and only episodically in brains, most human morality is found in social institutions. Of course, the relationship between brains and norms is complex, and needs to be discussed in further detail. The point is simply that thinking of morality as some sort of abstract formula that we apply "on the fly," or in real time, to mediate social interactions, is to mistake, as Emile Durkheim put it, "the summit of morality for the base."[57]

9

Normative Ethics

In 1835, the crew of an Australian seal-hunting ship arriving in New Zealand made the mistake of mentioning that they had stopped over, en route, at a small group of islands where "there is an abundance of sea and shellfish" and where "the inhabitants are very numerous, but they do not understand how to fight, and they have no weapons."[1] In so doing, they alerted the Maori—the native population of New Zealand—to the existence of the Chatham Islands, along with some distant relatives, the Moriori. The two population groups, although descendants of the same Polynesian ancestors, had lost track of each other almost a thousand years earlier, and had since developed very different cultures. One of these differences was put on dramatic display when the Maori, on hearing of their new neighbors, responded by sending a war party of five hundred men to the Chathams. The Moriori, who had a tradition of peaceful dispute resolution, "decided in a council meeting not to fight back, but to offer peace, friendship, and a division of resources." The Maori on the other hand chose to attack. "Over the course of the next few days, they killed hundreds of Moriori, cooked and ate many of their bodies, and enslaved all the others, killing most of them too over the next few years." The Maori thought very little of this, since it was, as one conqueror explained, all done "in accordance with our custom."[2]

Here we have a typical example of an encounter between what one might call a "nice" culture and a "nasty" one. The presence of "nice" cultures on various Polynesian islands is well known. Reports from the earliest European voyages of exploration contained breathless accounts of societies in which the more unsightly features of European civilization were notably absent: no warfare, sexual repression, or aristocratic systems of rank. The existence of cultures in which such practices did not prevail was taken by many as evidence that these practices could be abolished at home as well. Yet few stopped to consider the possibility that it was not by accident that these "nice" cultures were to be found exclusively on remote Pacific islands. More specifically, they failed to consider the possibility that "nice" cultures could be found only on isolated islands for the same reason that flightless birds could only be found on such islands—the absence of natural predators. Of course, in the case of cultures, it was the "nasty" Maori that acted as the predators (much as Muslims did in North Africa, the Han Chinese did in Asia, the Aztec did throughout Mesoamerica, and Europeans did throughout most of the world.) Could it be an accident that every major human civilization has been, in essence, based on a "nasty" culture?

The moral of the story is this: evolutionary theorists are certainly not wrong to point out that some of the dynamics that limit the emergence and reproduction of altruistic behavior in the biological domain are also at work in the domain of culture. It is not clear how a system of social norms that prescribes an overly "nice" code of conduct can manage to avoid being supplanted by one that is much nastier. This is, in certain respects, counterintuitive. Because the "nice" system often generates Pareto-superior outcomes and the "nasty" one Pareto-inferior ones, there is an almost overwhelming tendency to think that reasonable people would automatically gravitate toward the former. History belies this assumption. Yet we are constantly at risk of committing, in the domain of culture, the same fallacy that leads us to think that patterns of altruistic conduct should emerge among animals in cases where it is "good for the species." The advantage of the evolutionary perspective is that it shows us that there is a *problem* explaining altruistic or cooperative conduct among humans, one which does not simply go away once we adopt a cultural rather than a sociobiological perspective. Most moral philosophers have not even seen the problem, and so have made little progress toward the development of a solution.

That said, many evolutionary theorists take things too far, assuming on these grounds that the same sort of games used to study the dynamics of biological systems can be unproblematically extended to handle cultural ones. I would like to begin by discussing the limitations of this strategy, before going on to elaborate a new one that adopts a less problematic attitude toward norm systems, and yet is still "realist" enough to accept the constraints that the need for replication imposes on the content of these systems.

9.1. Problems with Evolutionary Game Theory

Stories such as that of the Maori and Moriori lend credence to the view that the dynamics of cultural reproduction are subject to some of the same pressures that exist in the biological domain. In chapter 6, however, I took some trouble to show that evolutionary theories that attempt to explain particular social institutions in terms of their contribution to the genetic fitness of individuals are unhelpful. Evolutionary biology can play an important role in helping us to understand the emergence of culture-dependence in the human species. It can also help us to discern the structure of the biological "platform" that supports cultural transmission, namely, conformist imitation with moralistic punishment. The emergence of culture in turn permits the development of language, and of the intentional planning system. Yet once cultural transmission is in place, the forces of biological selection cannot "reach through" and determine the content of particular intentional states, simply because the *structure* of the cultural platform is so fitness enhancing that it permits the transmission of all sorts of *content* that is biologically maladaptive.[3] Biology may still serve as a source of powerful biases within the sphere of cultural reproduction, but it no longer serves a selective function. Otherwise put, biological factors may contribute to the *cultural* fitness of a behavior pattern, and thus exercise an influence on which patterns get selected, but they cannot act as a direct force of selection.

Thus it is inappropriate to treat "Cooperate in collective action problems" as a preference that could be directly cultivated by the forces of biological selection. To set up an evolutionary game with "Cooperate" and "Defect" as the strategies is therefore tacitly to commit oneself to a sociobiological framework that is empirically inappropriate for the analysis of human behavior. Of course, evolutionary game theorists have a response to this. It doesn't matter, they say, whether "Cooperate" and "Defect" are interpreted as genetically programed behavioral dispositions or as culturally transmitted memes, they are still subject to the same replicator dynamics.[4] And whether altruism is a gene or a meme, it will still face the same obstacles when it comes to propagating itself—since all the benefits go to others, it will have difficulty attracting imitators and discouraging free riders. Thus the same replicator dynamics can be applied in both cases, and the same game-theoretic models are valid, regardless of whether the "strategies" in question are biological or cultural.

This is almost true. The reason that the replicator dynamics can be used to model both biological and cultural systems is that these dynamics are extremely formal in nature. The standard equation simply states that the frequency of a particular variant i in the population p'_i at a given stage will be determined by the frequency at the previous stage, multiplied by the fitness of that variant f_i relative to that average in the population f:[5]

$$p'_i = p_i(f_i - f) \qquad (1)$$

There is nothing to take issue with here. This statement boils down to the claim that those things that are relatively good at reproducing themselves will tend to increase their share of a population over time, relative to those things that are bad at reproducing themselves. More important, it says nothing substantive about what "fitness" is, or how it is determined. Thus one can imagine all sorts of ways the replicator dynamics could be applied unproblematically to cultural phenomena. Consider, for example, an attempt to model the frequency of word use. One could record segments of a given length from the speech of a number of language users as they go about their daily business, and determine the frequency with which each word in their vocabulary occurs. One could then return to sample their speech after various intervals, in order to see how the vocabulary employed changes over time. One would no doubt encounter a certain drift, as some words pass out of use and others get introduced. One could then construct a model that assigned different "fitness" levels to different words, and then show how factors like their novelty, or topicality, lead to increased representation in the "population" of words produced by the speaker.

While I think that there would be nothing objectionable about such a model, one can see quite easily the problem it raises. What exactly determines the "fitness" of a word? Obviously certain expressions, like clichés, acquire their reproductive prowess in the same way that pop songs do—by sticking in one's mind. Trendy phrases move through the population like a virus, but then "burn out" once too many people begin to use them. Other expressions, like "dog" and "door," owe their fitness to the prevalence of dogs and doors in the environment, and to the pragmatic need to give directions that involve their manipulation or control. Other words, such as "the," acquire their fitness from grammatical conventions that are purely intralinguistic. Others, like "thanks" or "sorry," are determined by aspects of our social practices (e.g., Canadians say "sorry" on occasions where most English speakers say "excuse me").

Looking over these examples, it should be obvious that there is no simple property that constitutes the "fitness" of a word, other than its propensity to occur with a given frequency in speech. There is simply too much going on, in determining the speech pattern of a typical language user, to be able to pick out a simple set of factors that determines the frequency with which a given word will occur. As a result, the only way really to determine the "fitness" of a word is to see how well it is represented at time t_1 and at time t_2, then infer that the one with increased representation is more fit and the one with decreased representation is less so. At a strictly formal level, there is nothing to stop one from doing so. The only problem is that it turns the old "survival of the fittest" slogan into a tautology. The fit becomes nothing other than that which survives.

In biology, we have a relatively independent concept of fitness and reproductive success that allows us to make confident predictions about the effects that particular mutations will have on the representation of a particular allele in the population. When scientists "tweak" fruit flies so that they grow an extra pair of legs where their antennae should be, we can anticipate that this will reduce their fitness. We do not really need to mix them in with the general population, then check back in a few generations to see how many mutants are still in circulation. But with words, it is difficult to imagine making such predictions. For example, when the humorist Gelett Burgess began using the term "bromide" to refer to something boring or platitudinous, he also introduced the term "sulphite" to denote the contrary. While the former caught on, and has become a standard term, the latter did not. He also invented dozens of new words from scratch. The only one that entered general usage was "blurb." Who could have predicted any of this ex ante? And in what sense is it a characteristic of any one expression that it is more "fit" than the other? (What made "blurb" better than "igmoil" or "tashivate"?)

All of these puzzles arise with the comparatively simple case of word use. Now consider cultural reproduction. The discussion so far has been focused on imitation as the principal mechanism of cultural transmission. Nothing very specific has been said, however, about why individuals imitate certain forms of behavior and not others. Even during childhood—where there is very little cognitive evaluation of role models—the influences are extremely complex. An enormous amount of transmission occurs through primary socialization in the home, and therefore takes the form of straightforward vertical transmission. Yet once children begin venturing outside the home, the lines of transmission quickly become tangled. Not only peer groups but also high-status individuals and individuals in particular institutional roles (such as teachers) serve as major sources of influence. No one can say with any certainty what motivates the individual to associate with one group of peers rather than some other, to respond to one dimension of the status hierarchy over some other, or to respond positively or negatively to particular authority figures.

Once the child achieves something approaching an adult level of sophistication, cultural transmission is further complicated by the level of rational scrutiny the individual brings to bear on his own conduct. Instead of blindly imitating various cultural parents, he may begin to reflectively assess the merits of different behavior patterns. This may lead him to revise or reject cultural patterns that he has already adopted, to seek out behavioral patterns or belief systems that he has not been exposed to, or to engage in autonomous learning aimed at improving existing patterns. The memetics literature has tended to focus on noncognitive mechanisms of cultural transmissions (e.g., some forms of behavior attract imitators simply by drawing attention to themselves, others by promising social connections and recognition, others by offering more hedonic forms of gratification, others by exploiting cognitive biases, etc.).[6] Yet not only are all of these forms of behavior subject to rational evaluation but cognitive mechanisms also serve as an independent conduit for transmission. Individuals sometimes change their behavior when they become convinced, rationally, by others to do so.[7]

Thus what counts as "fitness" in models of cultural reproduction remains a black box, which contains dozens of different factors, all of them interacting in unknown and highly unpredictable ways. If we are interested in understanding morality, the primary question is whether what goes on "inside" that black box is more important than what goes on "outside" of it. Those who have tried to apply evolutionary models to the analysis of cooperation as a cultural pattern have assumed that cooperation will have low fitness in the cultural domain for roughly the same reason that altruism in other species has low fitness in the biological domain. This assumption is what justifies their use of the same replicator dynamics to analyze the conditions for the emergence and reproduction of cooperation among humans. They begin by assuming that the morality meme is unfit, because of the utility payoffs it generates for its host (usually glossing over the fact that utility for the host is not the same as "enhanced fitness" for the selfish meme).[8] They then go on to look for external structures—"outside" the black box of culture—that will sustain it (such as group selection). The unstated assumption is that we are able to make judgments, with some degree of confidence, about what will turn out to be fit and unfit in the cultural realm.

Yet how can we state with any confidence what is "fit" and "unfit" as a cultural replicator, when we have no general theory of cultural reproduction? It is helpful to keep in mind that suicide bombing is a very robust meme in some cultural contexts. Generations of ethnographers have documented the extraordinary diversity of social practices that have managed to establish and reproduce themselves in the cultural sphere. If headhunting, ancestor worship, human sacrifice, and vows of celibacy have, at times, been able to enjoy great success as memes, then why not peace, love, and mutual understanding?

In particular, we have very little scientific understanding of how status systems work. As participants, of course, we have an intuitive grasp of how the status system in our own society functions—and what it takes to move up or down. But no one is able to explain, much less anticipate, why some particular goods or symbols become markers of status and why others decline. Yet there is obviously an important connection between morality and status (since bad behavior on the part of high-status individuals often leads to a "fall from grace"). Status also serves as an important source of "biased" transmission in the cultural sphere, since people are more likely to imitate individuals with superior prestige.[9] So it is possible that morality is able to survive as a cultural pattern because it confers prestige, which in turn makes the cooperator more likely to become a cultural parent.

One might just as plausibly suppose that we are the victims of "magical thinking," a cognitive bias that leads us to believe that if we act cooperatively, it will cause others to do the same (or optimism bias, which could lead to the same conclusion).[10] Thus we might be more likely to act cooperatively because we chronically miscalculate the probability that our acts will be reciprocated. If this were the case, then the success of cooperation in the cultural sphere would be a consequence of certain intrinsic features of the meme, along with the "memespace" in which it operates. (It could even be a byproduct of a cognitive bias that is adaptive for some *other* function.) Thus cooperation would turn out to be highly "fit" as a cultural pattern, simply because the mechanism of cultural reproduction, along with the type of selective forces operative in that domain, are significantly different than those that prevail in the biological.

Shaun Nichols's version of "naturalized" moral sentiment theory works on a hypothesis of this sort. His claim is that the standard biological adaptations aimed at producing altruistic conduct, which determine our natural affective reactions, get amplified in the sphere of cultural reproduction.[11] While they are not especially robust in species that act only on the basis of an adapted psychology, they become more powerful in the cultural sphere by virtue of their ability to bias cultural reproduction. They produce what Richerson and Boyd refer to as a "content bias," which favors prosocial forms of behavior in the overall dynamics of cultural reproduction.[12] So even though our natural feelings of sympathy may not lead us to act all that sympathetically, they do make us far more likely to accept and reproduce rules that promote acting out of concern for the well-being of others. The motivating force of these rules may, in turn, lead to significantly higher levels of actual sympathetic behavior.

If a hypothesis such as this were correct, then it would turn out that, in the case of morality, everything interesting that is going on would be occurring *inside* the black box that evolutionary game theorists put over the determinants of "fitness." Thus replicator models would not provide any particular insight into the success of cooperation. They would help us to understand why altruistic behavior patterns among humans are *insulated* from the forces of biological selection that would otherwise press for their elimination, but beyond that they would tell us nothing about why these patterns succeed. In order to determine this, we would be better off adopting a participant perspective, and using our intuitive knowledge of the cultural sphere in order to isolate and analyze some of the factors that contribute to the success of cooperative social norms. The apparatus of evolutionary game theory would not provide any purchase on the question. (Indeed, one cannot help but suspect that the range of hypotheses entertained in the "evolution of cooperation" literature has been artificially constrained by the desire to develop a formal model of the mechanism that might sustain altruism as a cultural pattern.)

In any case, if these considerations were not sufficiently persuasive, then there is a final, decisive argument to be made against evolutionary game theory as an approach to the understanding of cultural patterns. These models start from the assumption that variation is effectively random.[13] In the case of culture, however, variation is often not random, especially when dealing with intelligent animals like humans. Even trial-and-error learning seldom involves random variation in behavior. Instead, it involves what Boyd and Richerson call "guided variation," in which the individual varies his behavior on the basis of intelligent hypotheses about what might work better. This significantly changes the dynamic of the evolutionary system. Natural selection functions as a "culling process" that eliminates unsuccessful variants.

> Guided variation works quite differently because it is *not* a culling process. Individuals modify their own behavior by some form of learning, and other people acquire their modified behavior by imitation. As a result, the strength of guided variation does not depend on the amount of variability in the population.... [Thus] while biased transmission has important analogies to natural selection, guided variation definitively does not. It is a source of cultural change that has no good analog in genetic evolution.[14]

This is clearly relevant to the status of morality. People can often see the advantages of cooperation quite clearly, even when they have difficulty achieving those advantages due to free-rider problems. Nevertheless, this means that cooperation will be a strong "attractor" for processes of guided variation, even though it might not be so for processes of random variation. People will often be looking to move in the direction of full cooperation (e.g., to end civil wars, to eliminate corruption, to secure law and order, etc.), and this may have a significant impact on the dynamics of cultural systems. Yet this factor is excluded by standard evolutionary game theory models.

9.2. Morality and Convention

If these observations are correct, then evolutionary game theorists have tended to overestimate the amount that can be learned about cooperation by adopting an objectivating perspective. The cultural inheritance system is not just a product of our capacity to conform to norms. Through the development of propositionally differentiated speech, it also confers on individuals the capacity to represent to themselves explicitly the content of these norms, and thus to develop "second-order" attitudes toward them. People reason about norms. Thus, part of the explanation for the fact that cooperative norms do better than noncooperative norms in cultural inheritance systems, as opposed to genetic ones, is that people have good reasons for adopting them. A theory of norm-rationality will therefore be more useful to use than a "memetic" model of cultural evolution—for the same reason that an epistemological account of belief-formation is more enlightening than an epidemiological one. (While it may contribute to the popularity of a scientific theory that it is "easy to remember" or has "affective resonance," one can only get so far explaining the history of science in such terms.) Furthermore, it does no good to recharacterize rationality as "just another set of memes," since rationality refers to the rules governing the game of giving and asking for reasons, and is therefore part of the structure underlying the reproduction of any linguistically formulated cultural contents.

Unfortunately, the type of foundationalism that has encouraged noncognitivist or subjectivist theories of preference has also tended to impede the development of a plausible account of norm-rationality. The problem here is twofold. First, the search for foundations (or *Letzbegrundung*) has generated a tendency to look for a simple formula that could be applied, in order to determine whether a particular course of action is moral or immoral (e.g., the categorical imperative, the greatest happiness principle, etc.). Second, foundationalist presuppositions have encouraged philosophers to downgrade the status of norms that don't seem as susceptible to foundational modes of justification (e.g., because they are culturally relative). Hence the introduction of a distinction between "morality" and other, merely "conventional," social norms, such as rules of etiquette. The end consequence is that moral philosophers wind up focusing their energies not on producing a general theory of norm-rationality, but rather on debating extremely abstract, heavily idealized principles or decision procedures that purport to specify, once and for all, how to tell right from wrong.

I think it is important that this tendency be rejected. As has been apparent throughout the preceding discussion, I do not believe that there is any hard-and-fast distinction between moral norms and social norms more generally. Those who believe the contrary tend to do so on the basis of an intuition that there is, as Philippa Foot puts it, a "special dignity and necessity" attached to moral rules that makes them different from other social norms, despite the fact that, on the surface, they appear quite similar.[15] Indeed Foot begins her discussion of the subject by noting that moral rules and rules of etiquette both take the form of "categorical imperatives." Thus imperatives grounded in rules of etiquette, even though "lacking a connexion with the agent's desires or interests," nevertheless do not stand "unsupported and in need of support"; they require "only the backing of the rule."[16] Yet she goes on to claim that "considerations of etiquette do not have any automatic reason-giving force," whereas "moral considerations necessarily give reasons for acting to any man."[17] This is based on the observation that in the case of etiquette, but not morality, "a man might be right if he denied that he had reason to do 'what's done.' "[18]

Yet this hardly constitutes a principled distinction. First of all, it is not at all clear that one is entitled simply to opt out of etiquette, without appeal to some overriding consideration. Furthermore, an appeal to self-interest doesn't seem appropriate. Saying "I was really hungry" does not *justify* one's having greedily started to eat before others were served. And it is unclear that professing disinterest in the rules of etiquette really helps to build one's case. Of course, one can have legitimate *moral* reasons for violating norms of etiquette, but one can also have legitimate moral reasons for violating rules of morality.[19] Many people think that any moral norm can be justifiably violated, given a sufficiently weighty set of rival moral considerations (or even sufficiently odious consequences). The fact that rules of etiquette are more *easily* trumped by moral concerns is nothing but a reflection of the fact that we use the term "morality" to refer to the set of norms that we regard as particularly important.

The idea that etiquette is optional, in a way that morality is not, has gone largely unquestioned in the philosophical literature, even though it is implausible on the face of it. Part of the unquestioned acceptance is no doubt due to *déformation professionnelle* among academic philosophers, who consider their own disregard for social convention as a symptom of intellectual profundity (a presumption that, strangely enough, they seldom extend to rude and disrespectful students). Part of it is also no doubt an effect of countercultural thinking, which encouraged people to regard these sorts of social conventions as stifling and repressive. Thus the philosophical literature is rife with denunciations of obsolete rules of etiquette (e.g., Foot ridicules a rule that probably most readers will never have heard of, namely, that "an invitation in the third person should be answered in the third person")[20], combined with a failure to mention any of the rules that play such an important role in structuring daily life (e.g., the rules that limit physical contact among strangers, or that govern behavior in queues, turn-taking in conversation, conduct during academic seminars, etc.). Philosophers also generally fail to notice that the highly ritualized disdain for etiquette in our society is itself normatively enforced (just as "casual" dress is often more strongly enforced by informal social sanctions than "formal" dress).

It takes only a moment's reflection to see how profound this misunderstanding of etiquette is. The rules of etiquette are organized around the twin notions of "being polite" and "being rude." Being rude, giving offense, or showing "bad form," is just another way of describing a failure to show respect for other persons.[21] Thus we quite naturally treat lapses of etiquette as moral faults. Of course, the precise *way* one shows respect for others contains conventional elements. But the same is true of morality. The way people respond to an ultimatum game in North America reflects an adherence to a principle of fairness; in New Guinea it reflects an adherence to the norms governing gift giving. The latter set of norms is classified as "etiquette" in our society, whereas the former is classified as "morality" or "justice." Yet obviously no one would want to say that people in New Guinea are immoral for allowing "mere" considerations of etiquette to override the demands of justice in the division of the money.

To take another example, most philosophers would not hesitate to classify sexual harassment as a moral issue. Yet sexual harassment is not the same thing as sexual assault. Harassment involves almost entirely the violation of rules of etiquette. These rules are not recent inventions; most have been around for centuries. As Judith Martin notes, "sexual harassment is the modern name for ungentlemanly behavior—two grievous violations of etiquette that everyone is trying to pretend are brand new."[22] What has happened, in the last few decades, is that these rules have been "promoted" from the status of etiquette to that of morality. (Similarly, a very large number of norms governing sexual behavior have been "demoted" from morality to etiquette.) The reason is simply that we now take sexual harassment more seriously, because of our commitment to gender equality in the public sphere. It is implausible to think that this has involved a change in the nature of the rules, just as it is implausible to think that everyone in our culture up until sometime in the late 1970s simply failed to "see" that sexual harassment is morally wrong.

The more fashionable reason for assigning special status to moral rules, in contemporary philosophical circles, is through appeal to the research tradition in moral psychology initiated by the work of Elliot Turiel, which purports to show that "even very young children" grasp the distinction between moral and conventional rules. In a large number of experiments, it has been shown that children treat moral norms, such as those that prohibit hitting others, as having greater authority than norms of etiquette, or rules that structure their daily routines. Obviously they regard violation of the conventional rules as less serious, but they also identify them as authority-dependent and culture-specific. Moral rules, by contrast, are regarded as "unconditionally obligatory, generalizable and impersonal."[23] So when asked whether it is okay to hit someone, if a teacher says you can, they will say no, but when asked whether it is okay to drink soup from the bowl, if the teacher says you can, they will tend to say yes. They are also inclined to ascribe universality to the moral rules (i.e., "they are the same in other countries") but not the conventional ones.

On the basis of such findings, several psychologists (including Turiel) have been drawn to the surprisingly strong conclusion that moral and conventional judgment are housed in completely separate cognitive modules, and that the two sets of rules constitute disjoint domains.[24] This seems highly improbable.[25] First of all, it should be noted that the set of moral norms that have been tested are quite narrow, involving relatively serious infractions with clearly identifiable harms to specific individuals.[26] Yet "morality" certainly extends far beyond this. Richard Joyce, for instance, after accepting the moral/conventional distinction on the authority of these experiments, goes on to use the following as examples of *moral* transgressions: "failing to return a borrowed book, being rude to an undeserving waitress, pinching a morning newspaper from a hotel corridor."[27] It strikes me as being far from obvious that a child would regard any of these norms as universal or authority-independent. (What if the librarian tells you it's okay not to bring the book back? What if the hotel manager tells you it is okay to grab a newspaper from the hall?)

It is also relevant to note that the examples of moral/immoral actions are all other-regarding, yet the permission comes from an uninvolved third party, not the person most directly affected. (It's the *teacher* who says it's okay to punch the other kid, not the kid being punched.) The conventional rules on the other hand typically involve self-regarding behavior.[28] It would be interesting to know how children feel about moral norms that prohibit consensual actions, or self-regarding behavior. A proper comparison would also have to look at other-regarding conventional norms, where the "harm" is not intrinsic, but rather defined by the convention. (Is it okay to spit on other kids? Urinate on them? Cut in line in front of them?)

As it turns out, it is relatively easy to find rules of etiquette that subjects treat as "unconditionally obligatory, generalizable and impersonal." Nichols has provided what amounts to a debunking of the moral/conventional distinction by showing that norms prohibiting disgusting actions tend to evoke exactly the same pattern of response as moral norms (i.e., people consider such violations to be "less permissible, more serious, and less authority contingent than the neutral violations").[29] Consider the case of someone who spits in his water glass at a dinner party, then drinks it. Although this is clearly a rule of etiquette, Nichols found that subjects were inclined to treat it differently from more neutral rules, such as those that prohibit drinking soup from the bowl. In particular, subjects judged that it was not acceptable to drink spit, even if your host told you that it was okay; that it would not be okay, even if there were no rule prohibiting it, and so on. In other words, they had the same sort of intuitions about this subset of etiquette rules that philosophers have had about morality.

Nichols's explanation is that the norms that prohibit disgusting acts, like the norms that prohibit harming others, have affective resonance. People not only judge the action to be unacceptable, they feel strongly about it as well. This leads them to treat the norm differently.[30] Thus according to Nichols, "the moral/conventional task really taps a distinction between a set of norms (harm norms) that are backed by an affective system and a set of norms (conventional norms) that are not backed by an affective system."[31] What Turiel and others have been investigating is not morality in general, but rather a very specific set of harm norms, which are backed by altruistic sentiment at the level of the adaptive unconscious. Yet there are many moral rules that are not backed by such sentiment, particularly those that involve significant diffusion of harm, or have anonymous victims. Even when the victim is identifiable, people exhibit far more permissive attitudes toward harms inflicted on "a stranger" than on "someone you know."[32] So even with harm norms, it is not a good idea to allow the morality of the norm to be too closely identified with the affective response that may or may not accompany its violation.

9.3. Postconventional Morality

The distinction between morality and convention, according to Turiel, involves a difference between two types of rules that people use to regulate their conduct. Philosophers on the other hand have been inclined to up the ante even further, by distinguishing morality not just from convention but also from what is sometimes described (confusingly) as "conventional morality."[33] This term refers to what people *take* to be morally right and morally wrong. The term "morality" (or perhaps "morality proper") is then reserved for what is *actually* right and wrong. For example, homosexuality has traditionally been regarded as "sinful," and is still viewed that way by a majority of Americans. But of course the question of whether is it actually immoral is not to be determined by public opinion poll. The conclusion that is usually drawn, on the basis of examples such as this, is that the norms that happen to prevail in our society are neither here nor there, from the standpoint of morality proper. Many societies, at many different times in history, have enforced immoral norms (or more precisely, *all* societies, throughout *all* of history, have enforced norms that secular enlightenment intellectuals currently regard as mistaken). To propose even a family resemblance between morality and existing social norms would be to risk "tainting" morality with empirical considerations, and thereby to undermine its normativity.

Yet there is a very closely related question concerning the status of conventional morality that typically elicits a less dismissive response. How seriously should we take conventional morality as a whole when developing a system of normative ethics? Should the fact that everyone thinks that some action is wrong *count for anything* when deciding whether or not it really is wrong, and thus, whether a system of normative ethics needs to account for the judgment? Some philosophers believe that if their account of morality conflicts with certain aspects of conventional morality, then that is simply too bad for conventional morality. This is consistent with the view that conventional morality is just glorified public opinion. Yet very few are willing to adhere consistently to this line. J. J. C. Smart, for instance, is famous for having "bit the bullet" with respect to the counterintuitive implications of utilitarianism.[34] Most other utilitarians have dedicated considerable energy to the task of showing that their doctrine really does not conflict with conventional moral constraints (or "moral intuitions"), such as the prohibition on cutting innocent people up for their organs.

Thus we wind up in an unusual situation. Most moral philosophers, while largely dismissive of conventional morality with respect to particular judgments, and while denying that it can serve as a source of genuine moral constraint, try to ensure that their own normative ethical systems generate judgments that coincide with the outcome of our conventional moral reasoning. But they do so, by and large, without specifying why they care so much about reconciling the two. What does it matter if utilitarianism recommends lynching the innocent, in cases where the victim's death is quick and painless, while the elation of the mob lasts for days? For that matter, what does it matter if Kant's categorical imperative can be taken to prove, as Hegel suggested, that helping the poor is morally impermissible ("if everyone did that, then there would be no poor"). What does it matter if David Gauthier's contractarianism implies that we have no obligations of justice toward children or the disabled?[35] If the philosophical arguments were really as good as their defenders claim, why should these conclusions not be heralded as discoveries? ("Look, it turns out we don't have to help those people after all.") In Gauthier's case, the conclusion simply echoes what many people have thought throughout human history. Thus the problem cannot be that it violates a timeless and eternal "moral intuition"—the problem is that it violates contemporary mores. So how can moral philosophers assign no normative status to conventional morality within the framework of their own theories, and yet turn around and use conventional moral intuitions to test the adequacy of the same theories?

The answer, I believe, lies in an improper understanding of the relationship between conventional morality and the more abstract theories that philosophers develop under the rubric of "normative ethics." One of the key characteristics of conventional moral reasoning is its rigidity (which is sometimes mistaken for a conservative bias). Conventional moral reasoners (which includes most people, most of the time) typically have no idea how to justify the rules they are adhering to. Often they are able to produce the first or second step of an argument, but become quickly "dumbfounded" when confronted by further requests for justification.[36] As a result, they are not very good at handling situations that generate a conflict among rules (stealing to help a friend, lying to save a family member, etc.).[37] Since they do not derive these rules from "first principles," they have little in the way of abstract resources to fall back on when it comes to resolving such conflicts. A small percentage of the population, however, when faced with such dilemmas, will engage in what Lawrence Kohlberg called "postconventional" moral reasoning. This group, rather than assigning ultimate authority to the prevailing set of social norms, will take these to be derived from more general principles. Thus when the norms conflict, they adopt a hypothetical attitude toward the set of conventional social obligations, analyze them all from the standpoint of these more general principles, and then decide which norms (if any) should prevail in the circumstance.

There is no hard-and-fast distinction between these two orientations. Conventional morality itself contains a number of very abstract principles, which can be applied in pretty much any circumstance (e.g., "love one another," "be honest," "be true to yourself," etc.) and can trump more specific norms. What determines the level of conventionality in an individual's moral thinking is the extent to which she is willing to adopt a hypothetical attitude toward certain concrete social norms, and to allow these obligations to be trumped by more abstract moral considerations. In this respect, moral philosophers have tended to locate "morality" somewhere out at the very far end of the conventional–postconventional spectrum, such that only the most postconventional forms of moral reasoning are taken to "count" as forms of moral reasoning at all. The standard view is that conventional morality exists only because of the "boundedness" of human rationality. There is an ideal process of reasoning that will lead to the morally correct answer to any given problem. Unfortunately, we do not have the time or the resources to calculate the correct answer in every circumstance, and so we adopt a set of rules, which over time have been shown to be adequate heuristics, helping us to wind up with approximately the right solution in the long run. (This structure is most apparent in the reasoning of contemporary consequentialists, most of whom believe that the morally correct solution is determined by calculating the outcome that maximizes the good, according to some conception, but which because of computational and epistemological limitations, we are often unable to do. Thus we adopt rules that have been proven, in general and over time, to maximize the good.)[38]

A number of different objections have been raised to these sorts of theories. However, the most fundamental assumption has gone largely uncontested, namely, the idea that conventional reasoning in some way depends on postconventional reasoning. Naturally, this dependence must be logical, not genetic. Developmentally, it is simply not the case that anyone ever acquires the ability to engage in postconventional reasoning without first mastering conventional morality, and going through a long stage of conventional moral reasoning.[39] So it is not the case that anyone actually derives conventional morality from postconventional resources. The view, rather, must be that conventional morality depends on postconventional morality for its validity, or for whatever normative authority it may enjoy. Even though we may learn conventional morality first, when we reach the age of reason and begin to question these dogmatically acquired convictions, we draw on postconventional resources in order to ratify or revise this moral code. Thus postconventional morality provides the justificatory foundation for conventional morality.

This view is, I believe, mistaken. Far from providing the foundations for conventional morality, postconventional morality in fact depends on conventional morality for its authority. Conventional morality is an extraordinarily complex cultural artifact, one that has been produced over the course of millennia, and incorporates a vast number of small or large changes that have been made, in order to adjust to the circumstances and challenges that people routinely encounter in social interactions. Influences include not only several major religious traditions and schools of philosophy but also works of literature (e.g., the novels of Jane Austen), social movements (e.g., feminism, or the 1960s counterculture), television shows and movies (e.g., police dramas, battles between good and evil), and historical events (e.g., the Holocaust, the civil rights movement). It may be helpful to think of conventional morality on analogy with the common law (although of course unwritten and less systematic). What conventional morality represents, ultimately, are the terms under which individuals are willing and able to interact with one another in daily life, while generating the minimum amount of misunderstanding and conflict. Most of the obligations are broken down and differentiated by social role: that of husband or wife, parent, sibling, friend, coworker, stranger, and so on, and most of the everyday questions that we may have about what we owe to one another are answered by reference to the obligations imposed by these roles. Being able to display adult competence in social interactions essentially involves mastery of the obligations specific to these roles (and, of course, having the underlying motivational structure needed to comply with them).

In the same way that etiquette develops and changes over time, so does conventional morality. Postconventional morality does not stand outside this process, rather it is a part of it. As Michele Moody-Adams writes, "much of the moral language that helps shape the economic, social, and political dimensions of the contemporary world is a product of distinctively philosophical efforts to articulate interpretations of the structure of moral experience."[40] According to this view, what we think of as postconventional morality is essentially an expressive vocabulary, designed to articulate the structure of obligations that are implicit in conventional morality. However, once we have the ability to articulate the structure of these obligations, it puts us in a position to criticize and possibly change the relevant norms. It is therefore an exercise in what Robert Brandom calls "expressive rationality," namely, "a way of bringing our practices under rational control, by expressing them explicitly in a form in which they can be confronted with objections and alternatives."[41] In this way, abstract concepts, which are initially introduced merely as a way of expressing the content of conventional morality, become tools for reform as well.

There is a significant analogy, in this case, between the role moral philosophy plays with respect to conventional morality and the role logic plays with respect to everyday patterns of inference. The game of giving and asking for reasons, as we have seen (chapter 5, section 4), is governed by a set of "material inference" rules. These are rules that specify, in very concrete terms, what sort of moves a person is entitled to make from a given position. For example, from the position "it's raining" one is entitled to assert "the sidewalks will be wet."[42] Initially, making an inference is something a person can *do*. The aim of introducing logical vocabulary, such as the conditional, into a language is that it "will let one say (explicitly) what otherwise one can only do (implicitly)."[43] For example, it permits us to represent the material inference above in the form of an explicit claim: "If it's raining, then the sidewalks will be wet." Yet in order to get vocabulary that allows us to talk about the inference, and not the rain or the sidewalk, it is important to introduce an argument schema that cannot be transformed from correct to incorrect through substitution of nonlogical for nonlogical vocabulary. "If x then y, x, therefore y" is a schema of this type. It allows us to talk about how one gets from the idea of rain to that of wet sidewalks, or how one gets from the idea of seeing lightning to that of hearing thunder, and so on. Yet there is a temptation to think, once this schema is introduced, that what was "really" going on, in each of the original material inferences, was an implicit application of this schema, and that the validity of those inferences was inherited from the validity of the inference rule. This gives rise to the widespread assumption that material inferences are enthymematic (with the conditional as a suppressed premise).

Brandom refers to this as "the formalist fallacy." The idea that everyday reasoning presupposes logic is exactly backward (which is why, from this perspective, it is entirely unsurprising that the "man on the street" employs "sparse (or absent) reasoning strategies" when confronted with problems that are formulated in terms of elementary propositional logic).[44] According to Brandom, "the formal goodness of inferences derives from and is explained in terms of the material goodness of inferences, and so ought not to be appealed to in explaining it."[45] Yet people consistently reverse the order of dependence, mistaking the process of constructing expressive vocabulary for that of discovering underlying cognitive machinery. The concept of "truth" provides a good example of this. Many philosophers regard "is true" as a piece of purely expressive vocabulary, introduced in order to permit the formation of "prosentences." The latter are required in order for us to be able to formulate natural-language sentences that contain propositional variables. These are, in turn, useful if one wants to quantify over assertions or intentional states. Yet this consistently generates the false impression that "truth" is an independent norm or ideal that we hold all our ordinary assertions and beliefs up to—complete with a yawning chasm between what is true and what we happen to believe is true—when in fact it is just a piece of expressive vocabulary that we use, in order to talk about the standards that we already implicitly hold those assertions and beliefs up to.[46]

The tendency to hypostatize "morality," and treat it as an independent ideal, divorced from conventional morality, arises from precisely the same "formalist fallacy." The only difference is that in the domain of morality, we have been less successful at crafting purely formal vocabulary (with the obvious exception of terms like "right" and "good," along with deontic modalities like "obligatory," "forbidden," etc.). Had any of Kant's formulations of the categorical imperative succeeded (so that one could not turn a materially good inference into a materially bad inference simply by substituting one type of action, e.g., "giving money to the poor," for another, "breaking a promise"), then there would have been no hesitation among Kantians to declare (mistakenly) that the categorical imperative is what *underlies* all of our ordinary moral judgments.

This process of crafting expressive vocabulary occurs at more intermediate levels of abstraction as well. For example, like every other society in the world, we have a large number of norms that are used to resolve distributional (or "who gets what") conflict. There are different rules, though, tailored to different circumstances, and people make very different judgments in cases that involve differential levels of individual status, contribution, need, desert, and so on.[47] There are "cutting the cake" problems, "joint production" and "team effort" problems, domestic division of labor problems, and so on. Yet philosophers, undaunted by all this variety, have attempted to develop a formulation of "the" principle of equality, by introducing concepts at a sufficient level of abstraction (e.g., "envy-freeness," "capability space," "choice/circumstance,") that a principle defined in such terms might subsume all the more particular norms. Thus the philosophical discussion has been almost entirely focused on developing an explicit formulation of the principle of equality that will not generate any problematic counterexamples.[48] Theorists will start out with certain familiar intuitions about how estates should be divided up, how investors should be rewarded, or how cakes should be cut. They will then attempt to formulate an explicit principle that generates the appropriate divisions in certain highly stylized cases. Critics respond by generating counterexamples, where the principle as formulated generates seemingly "unjust" divisions. These counterexamples often become sufficiently important that they acquire names in the literature: the "tamed housewife" problem, the "repugnant conclusion," the "expensive tastes" objection, and so on. The theorist then attempts to tweak the principle, in order to avoid arriving at these problematic conclusions. The same cycle then repeats itself, as critics develop counterexamples to the tweaked principle.

There is no guarantee that philosophers will succeed in this endeavor. This does not mean, however, that there is anything capricious about the judgments of equality that we make in everyday life. There is a lot of inferential vocabulary that logicians have never succeeded in systematizing either. For example, no one has ever succeeded in developing a formal semantics for "because," even though it is a hugely important inferential term. It is possible that no one will ever succeed, simply because the range of different inferences that the term figures in may not support that level of regimentation. But that does not mean we cannot keep making perfectly valid inferences, using this term.

There are several areas in normative ethics where systematization is also quite unlikely. For example, there are some domains in which we apply more "consequentialist" norms (e.g., redirecting trolleys) and others in which we are more "deontological" (e.g., pushing people). For over a century, philosophers of a Kantian or utilitarian persuasion have been trying to show that there are adequate expressive resources, within their own preferred framework, to articulate the logic of *all* these norms. None of these efforts has been particularly persuasive, and it is easy to show that the average person's moral reasoning contains both elements, and so can generate inconsistencies. But does the discovery of such "contradictions" undermine morality? Not at all—no more than the existence of irregular verbs undermines the integrity of French grammar. It merely shows that morality is a very complex cultural artifact, which cannot be summed up in a single rule of choice or justificatory schema.

Charles Taylor has argued that, thanks to this dynamic, most of the work being done in normative ethics winds up being little more than a sophisticated form of gerrymandering.[49] Proposed principles routinely get rejected on the grounds that they generate what are obviously the wrong answers to a variety of moral questions. So people fiddle with them some more, then go back out to solicit another round of counterexamples. This often results in principles like the following (from T. M. Scanlon):

> *Principle M*: In the absence of special justification, it is not permissible for one person, A, in order to get to another person, B, to do some act, X (which A wants B to do and which B is morally free to do or not do but would otherwise not do), to lead B to expect that if he or she does X then A will do Y (which B wants but believes that A will otherwise not do), when in fact A has no intention of doing Y if B does X, and A can reasonably foresee that B will suffer significant loss if he or she does X and A does not reciprocate by doing Y.[50]

The result reads like a parody of the "analytical" style of philosophy. But apart from the unintended humorousness of such proposals, what is even stranger is the thought that principles like this might be conceptually prior to, or more fundamental than, the social practice of promise keeping (since the principle has so obviously been gerrymandered, in an effort to accommodate all intuitions arising from that practice).

The question is, if we already know what the right and the wrong answers are to moral questions, prior to the formulation of an abstract principle, what is the point of formulating the principle? Why not simply try to articulate more clearly how we arrived at this judgment in the first place, rather than inventing fancy principles so that we can derive it from a nonmoral source, such as the structure of rationality, or the conditions of unanimous agreement? Taylor, however, goes on to misdiagnose the problem, when he claims that the gerrymandering arises out of an attempt to develop a purely formal or procedural conception of morality, rather than simply acknowledging the substantive moral commitments that underlie our moral intuitions. In fact, the substantive conception of morality Taylor goes on to develop, in particular his characterization of the "hypergoods" that animate modern societies, is just as open to the charge of gerrymandering as any formalist ethical system. It also suffers from the "formalist fallacy" of mistaking the expressive vocabulary he is inventing for the discovery of a deep structure underlying our social practices (albeit an axiological, rather than a deontological structure).

The real issue is not one of formal or procedural versus substantive approaches to morality, or of privileging the right over the good. It has to do simply with the levels of abstraction in moral vocabulary. What is important is that philosophers not lose sight of their task. The point of doing normative ethics is not to uncover the foundations of morality, but rather to develop expressive vocabulary that permits more robust thematization and critical reflection on our practices. Ultimately, it is our commitment to a shared conventional morality that makes it possible for us to develop such vocabulary. How else to explain the fact that there is such a high level of convergence when it comes to moral intuitions among moral philosophers, and yet absolutely nothing resembling unanimity on the higher-order principles from which these intuitions are supposedly derived? The fact that any particular social norm may, in the fullness of time, come to be rejected does not mean that we can suspend our commitment to the entire body of norms that structure our social life, and reconstruct them all in a non-question-begging way from first principles. Furthermore, if the only resources we had at our disposal in managing social interactions were the sort of abstract principles that are endorsed by the various schools of philosophy—if people really did reason using the various formulae that have been proposed over the years—then the social world would be a very chaotic place indeed.

9.4. The Moral Point of View

There are two primary objections to "institutional" theories that identify morality, first and foremost, with a set of social norms. The first is the problem of immoral institutions; the second is the problem of anomic interactions (or interactions that are institutionally unregulated). In the first case, the institutional theory makes it difficult to see how individuals can adopt a critical stance toward the society in which they live, in cases where there happens not to be any inconsistency between the problematic institutions and the rest of the system of social norms. In the second case, the institutional theory makes it seem as though individuals are free to do whatever they like, or to adopt a purely instrumental orientation, whenever they find themselves in unusual circumstances, or dealing with individuals who do not have any status within the normative system.[51] Both of these criticisms suggest that there must be some standards or criteria "outside" of conventional morality, from which all existing moral obligations can be evaluated, and from which new obligations can be derived when circumstances call for it. I have argued that there is no such Archimedean point. In this section, I would like to respond to the second objection, before going on to deal with the problem of "immoral" institutions.

The concern over normatively unregulated interactions refers to the fact that the system of norms governing social interactions in any given society has been developed only to handle situations that are relatively common for that group of people. Thus when we find ourselves in situations that are unprecedented, or at least highly unusual, the system of norms may give us no clear guidance on how to proceed. But that doesn't mean we are free to do whatever we like, or to act in a purely instrumental fashion. We may refer to this as the problem of "zebras."[52] For example, many of the most pressing issues in bioethics arise from technological developments that expand the range of possible action in ways that seem morally troublesome, but which are not clearly addressed by conventional morality. We know that we cannot kill people, but what about terminating fetuses? We know that we have a duty of rescue toward people in distress, but does this include heroic measures for terminally ill patients? A typical introductory "moral problems" textbook is usually little more than a compendium of such zebras. Yet if morality were actually derived from postconventional resources (or "first principles"), it is unclear why these cases should be so vexing. If, however, our moral convictions arise out of a culturally transmitted conventional morality, then it is much easier to see why these cases should be difficult. We don't have clear criteria to determine, for example, the boundaries of the concept of "personhood," because we haven't traditionally needed such criteria, and in the vast majority of cases we still don't (just as we don't need precise criteria to determine where red stops and orange starts).

In any case, it is not difficult to see how we deal with the appearance of such zebras within the framework of conventional morality. The primary strategy is to articulate at a higher level of abstraction certain ideas or principles that are implicit in our more entrenched normatively regulated practices (such as the idea of "respect" for persons, or of human "dignity") and then try to project them to the new cases. In many instances, it will be possible to formulate a principle sufficiently general that it can be extended to handle them. One can then explore systematically the consequences of subsuming these new cases under such a category, consider the pros and cons, and so on. (If one looks at the typical "moral problems" textbook, one can see that this is in fact what most philosophers approaching these questions are doing, even though this is often not their self-understanding.)

Thus the appearance of zebras does not present a serious problem for the institutional theory of morality. A more difficult question arises from the fact that many conventional moral codes have a strong in-group bias, and in some cases deny any moral standing to out-group members. Aristotle, most famously, drew a sharp distinction between Greeks and barbarians, and felt that the moral entitlements of the latter group ranged from weak to nonexistent. In this respect he was simply following the conventional morality of his day. This is also a fairly common feature of moral codes in tribal societies.[53] This gives rise to the following problem: if conventional morality stipulates that social interactions with certain classes of people are normatively unregulated, does this make it okay to treat them as abusively as one sees fit? Is it permissible to adopt an instrumental orientation toward a person, simply because the moral code of one's society denies that person moral standing?

The answer here is certainly no. The fact that one's system of norms does not prescribe specific obligations toward a person does not relieve one of all moral obligations toward him. The moral agent will continue to assign normative reasons for action deliberative priority over instrumental ones—it is just that the system of norms fails to supply any concrete reasons for action in this context. Yet the mere fact that there are no specific normative constraints does not make the normative control system entirely transparent. An agent who assigns normative reasons for action deliberative priority will remain concerned that the action he chooses remains at least a *candidate* for incorporation into a norm.

We think of the moral person as the one who typically assigns deliberative priority to his principles, relative to his desires. In the absence of culturally transmitted principles to govern an interaction, the moral person can therefore continue to exhibit this disposition by acting in a way that exhibits an openness to normative regulation—by refraining from acting in ways that the other person could not accept as a basis for a shared norm. Thus the normative control system imposes its own very weak form of constraint on conduct, even in the absence of norms. Hence the idea that there is a difference between "thinking morally" about an interaction and thinking instrumentally. It is this difference that philosophers have attempted to articulate when they talk about judgment from "the moral point of view." A person who lacks concrete normative guidance in a situation must put himself in the shoes of the other, consider how his actions look from that person's perspective, and decide whether or not they could be acceptable to the other. This does not mean that he cannot pursue his own interests; it simply means that he has to pursue them under the constraint of possible reciprocity.

Thus the existence of a "moral point of view" is a reflection of the fact that we are by fundamental disposition norm-following creatures, and so remain guided by a norm-conformative disposition even in the absence of settled norms. We do so by acting on the basis of a principle that could be a norm, and refraining from acting in ways that would obviously give rise to objections, and calls for normative constraint, from others. Kurt Baier articulates this conception of the moral point of view as follows: "being moral is following rules designed to overrule self-interest whenever it is in the interest of everyone alike that everyone should set aside his interest."[54] John Rawls articulates a "principle of reciprocity," which "requires of a practice that it satisfy those principles which the persons who participate in it could reasonably propose for mutual acceptance under the circumstances and conditions of the hypothetical account."[55] Perhaps the simplest expression of the idea can be found in Kant, where he glosses the categorical imperative as an injunction to avoid making an exception of oneself.[56] Scanlon appeals to a similar intuition with his injunction to act only in ways that others could not reasonably reject.[57] We often teach this structure of practical judgment to children as a complement to more specific forms of conventional moral reasoning. "How would you like it if someone did that to you?" we ask. Hence also the cultural universality of the golden rule in its various formulations.

What is attractive about the formulations that one finds in Kant and Scanlon is that they articulate the content of the moral point of view as a negative criterion: they do not say what you should do, they simply exclude certain possibilities (namely, the pursuit of self-interest where one would not be willing to countenance others doing the same). The problem with these formulations arises only from the fact that both philosophers go on to plead for the self-sufficiency of this perspective, as though once one had an appropriate articulation of the golden rule, one could then dispense with conventional morality (or that such a rule could provide the foundational principle from which all of conventional morality could be derived). Yet mechanical application of such a principle, no matter how carefully formulated, can easily lead to conclusions that are contrary to a number of deeply held moral convictions.

The problem is that the moral point of view is too weak to generate a moral code all on its own. Conventional morality is a complex cultural artifact, one that develops over the course of generations, and is guided by the specific circumstances of the world in which people find themselves: the type of cooperative enterprises they wish to embark on, the typical sources of conflict and competition, the characteristic forms of human vulnerability, and so on. Believing that all of this could be derived from a single principle is an instance of what Emile Durkheim called mistaking the "summit" of morality for the "base"—assuming that everyday morality *depends* on the sort of abstract principles philosophers develop:

> [Philosophers] are obliged to take as a point of departure for their speculations a recognized and uncontested ethic, which can only be the one generally followed during their time and in their environment. It is from a summary observation of this ethic that they extract the law which is supposed to explain it. It is this ethic that supplies the material for their inferences; it is also that which they recover at the end of their deductions. For it to be otherwise, it would be necessary for the moralist, in the silence of his study, to construct solely through the power of his thought the complete system of social relations, since the moral law penetrates all.[58]

The moral point of view, at best, partitions the space of possible principles of action, separating those that could be adopted as part of a shared moral code from those that would be unlikely to secure the consent of others. Thus reflection from the moral point of view can generate principles (in the sense of individual preferences over actions), but these are at best candidates for incorporation into social norms, and even then they are still defeasible. One should strive not to make an exception of oneself, yet at the same time, if it is possible to tell a good enough story about why an exception should be made in one's particular case, then there is no reason the relevant norm could not be accepted by others. Thus the moral point of view provides guidance in the case of normatively unregulated interactions, and it serves as a source of bias in cultural transmission (against, e.g., blatantly exploitative arrangements), but it cannot serve as the foundation of morality.

As an example of how weak the moral point of view is, consider the case of the Aztec and their neighbor, the Tlaxcalan, who—it has been claimed—maintained a ritual war throughout the sixteenth century so that both sides could secure a steady supply of sacrificial victims (since neither side regarded it as permissible to sacrifice members of their own group). In a sense, this semipermanent state of war was consensual and mutually beneficial. Both sides were doing unto others as they would have had done to themselves. Thus the arrangement was, as far as I am concerned, permissible from the moral point of view. There are, of course, *arguments* to be made against it. But these arguments must take a different form. There may be substantive moral principles internal to the conventional morality of either group that can be used to condemn warfare or human sacrifice. The arrangement is, of course, also suboptimal from the perspective of many typical systems of preference (although not all). The development of more complex forms of cooperation may eventually lead to the need for stronger cooperative norms (as the spirit of commerce replaces the spirit of war). Thus there are many things wrong with the arrangement under which two nations remain in a state of semiperpetual warfare, but violation of the golden rule need not be one of them.

9.5. Independent Moral Judgment

In 1951, psychologist Stanley Milgram began the series of experiments that would profoundly alter our understanding of immoral behavior.[59] His goal, in these experiments, was to test Hannah Arendt's thesis about the "banality of evil." While covering the trial of Adolf Eichmann in Jerusalem, Arendt became convinced that far from being the monster the prosecution had tried to portray him as, Eichmann was in fact just a bureaucrat, doing what he was told. Although he carried out his job with some zeal, he did it with no particular malice, nor any great ill will toward the victims of the Holocaust, whose deaths he was busy organizing. Although Milgram was initially skeptical about Arendt's analysis, the results of his experiments removed any doubts from his mind. The majority of individuals, he found, did not really possess what we would think of as independent moral judgment. To be sure, most of his experimental subjects did complain and voice doubts about what they were being asked to do—to which the experimenter overseeing the tests simply responded blankly, "The experiment requires that you proceed." On this basis, however, the majority went on to administer what they could only presume to be lethal doses of electricity to a person who, as far as they knew, was an experimental volunteer just like themselves. Yet the fact that they did so with evident discomfort shows that they were not evil in any strong sense of the term; they were merely conformists, going along with expectations in whatever social situation they found themselves in.

It would be difficult to understate the impact Milgram's findings had on Western culture and society. Thanks in large measure to Milgram, "conformity" came to be seen as a powerful vice (rather than simply a disposition that is neutral between virtue and vice—virtuous in the company of virtue, vicious in the presence of vice). Furthermore, the cultivation of independent moral judgment came to be seen as a matter of urgent concern—as the best way to avoid a repetition of moral catastrophes like the Holocaust. Independent moral judgment, in turn, came to be seen as the antithesis of conformity.

Against this background, any theory that attempts to *identify* morality with the disposition to engage in imitative conformity is likely to strike many people as implausible (if not preposterously wrongheaded). Yet the standard lesson that people have taken away from Milgram's experiments, which results in the condemnation of conformity, is not the only possible one. Milgram successfully demonstrated the important role that conformity plays in securing social order, and showed also that this conformist disposition is basically neutral between "good" and "evil," that is, it can be used to transmit any sort of behavior. The conclusion usually drawn is that in order to reduce the occurrence of evil, people should stop conforming, and begin to rely on their own judgment. What we might choose to infer, instead, is that when it comes to promoting "good" and discouraging "evil," *social context matters.*[60] In a sense, Milgram was the first to show how much human morality depends upon the scaffolding supplied by social institutions—take away the scaffolding that people are accustomed to, replace it with one that is perverse or evil, and you will find that people do not behave all that morally.

Thus the focus on nonconformity and independent judgment that is usually encouraged by the reading of Milgram's experimental findings privileges what goes on "in the head" of the agent over what occurs in her social milieu. This is what motivates the attempt to extirpate any and all conformist tendencies (a quest that has been and, as we have seen, must remain fruitless). If instead one maintains an institutional focus, and recognizes the extent to which the external environment provides the scaffolding for all of our moral conduct, then there is no reason to regard conformity as a vice. It is a disposition that is *as* likely (if not slightly *more* likely) to promote good as it is to propagate evil. It is important to recognize that Milgram's experimental setup was one in which people's own preferences—thanks to sympathetic identification with the victim—happened to be "good," while the pressure to conform was a source of "evil." In cases where experimenters have switched things around, so that individuals are tempted to behave in an antisocial manner (e.g., to free ride), yet pressured to conform to a more prosocial norm (e.g., to cooperate), conformity becomes an important source of "good" behavior.[61]

Thus it is unhelpful, when thinking about independent moral judgment, to start out by setting up a contrast with conformity. It can easily lead one to think that the individual must be free from the influence of her social environment, and of conventional morality, in order to be genuinely independent in her judgment. From this, it is but a short step to the idea that she must derive her judgment from foundational first principles. This is wrongheaded. What is really going on, when people take a stand against some aspect of conventional moral-ity, is that they appeal to some *other* feature of conventional morality (perhaps a more systemic one) in order to argue against it.

The question is, therefore, how we can acknowledge the inescapably contex-tual and "internal" character of moral deliberation, and yet still preserve our intuitive understanding of the difference between independent moral judgment and mere conformity to "real existing" morality (in the form of social institu-tions). The key to a solution lies in examining the way the specific dispositions acquired unreflectively through socialization are taken up into and deployed by the agent's intentional planning system. There are important parallels here between the way the agent's system of desires is formed and the way her system of principles develops. In early stages of development, the child's behavior is gov-erned almost entirely by the adaptive unconscious, each component of which is specialized at handling particular functions—eating, grasping and manipu-lating, avoiding physical damage, and so forth. These mechanisms are directly responsive to generalized somatic stimuli, such as states of hunger, frustration, pain, and so on. As the child develops linguistic competence, along with greater analytical abilities, she begins to integrate these behaviors into a more coherent system of planned actions. Symbolic representation of somatic states is a key element in this process, allowing her not only to respond to occurrent feelings of hunger, for example, but also act on the anticipation that she will be hungry in a couple of hours. It is with the development of these sorts of competencies that we begin to think of the agent as rational.

Thus the agent begins to acquire "desires"—in the strict sense of the term—when she linguistically represents the goal states of her behavior. However, the "input" into this process of linguistification, which results in the sort of compre-hensive and coherent preference ordering that decision theorists take as basic, is not only "bottom up," that is, coming from her somatic states, but also both "top down"—coming from her values, or conceptions of the good—and "lateral," coming from imitation of role models and other forms of cultural transmission. Not only is the "input" from below frequently indeterminate, it is often scram-bled and incoherent—precisely because the adaptive unconscious lacks a central integrative system. Intransitivities, for example, are common. Part of the process of developing a preference ordering therefore involves the active development of a logically consistent set of desires. But there is much more to it than that. If one looks at the development of an individual's sexuality, for example, one can see that it is not just occurrent states of arousal that determine the form of the individual's desires. The development of sexual desire is heavily structured by the values that the individual subscribes to, along with the norms determining appropriate and inappropriate conduct. Thus the way the individual conceives of human "dignity," for example, will play a large role in determining which urges he is willing to take up and incorporate into his planned activities, and which he chooses to suppress, ignore, or sublimate.

Through this process, the mature individual winds up with an "independent" system of desires. It is not simply a symbolic representation of a set of noncogni-tive somatic states, nor is it the imprint of some abstract conception of the good, nor is it adopted wholesale from a cultural parent or peer group. On the contrary, it is a hybrid of at least all three, a reconciliation that is more or less tailored to the individual's particular circumstances, developed through the exercise of her own judgment.

The way the individual develops a set of principles to govern her conduct is quite similar. We initially acquire a disposition to conform to a range of social practices in a completely unreflective manner. Some of the rules we learn are taught to us in symbolic form (as when we are told by our parents not to lie) while others are acquired through imitation of the example set by others (this is how we learn the proper speaking distance to maintain from a person in casual conversation, or what to look at in a crowded elevator). In any case, after 10 years of pretty much nonstop socialization, the typical child winds up with dispositions to respect a fairly extensive list of dos and don'ts (some learned at home, others at school, others from peers, etc.). The task of the intentional planning system is to integrate all of these prohibitions and permissions (rejecting some, taking up others), to develop a coherent set of principles that can govern everyday conduct, and yet still allow for reasonable satisfaction of the individual's desires.

Through the process of socialization, the individual acquires not only a propensity to respect particular behavioral patterns but also a set of more abstract ideas and principles (often communicated via religious doctrines and morality tales). Developing a coherent system of principles will therefore involve not only reconciling and prioritizing concrete behavioral norms but also structuring the overall system in accordance with these more abstract ideas. Thus, for example, the person who assigns great weight to the Christian injunction to "love one another" will develop a set of personal principles that may be different in both style and content from someone who thinks that the U.S. Constitution provides the template for thinking about all social relations. Such individuals can usually coexist quite happily within a framework of shared institutions, simply because these differences in personal principle are within each person's range of tolerance, and so are not likely to be misclassified as forms of social deviance.

Thus what begins as an unreflective disposition toward imitative conformity becomes, with the development of the intentional planning system, a reflexive and stable normative control system, as the agent begins to self-consciously apply explicitly formulated principles to constrain her choices. This coincides with the development of what we think of as the individual's "personal morality." Just as with our desires we regiment the incoherent bundle of natural urges and cultural influences that we have—imposing transitivity, scheduling satisfaction, imposing a "reality principle" in cases of conflict, and so on—so with norms, we distill out those we regard as most important, discard those that do not "fit" with the system, and strive to secure coherence among them all (not because we value coherence for its own sake, but because we want to engage in rational planning of action). We also engage in judgment from the moral point of view. Where we find large batches of norms problematic, we may imagine how they could be restructured, subject to the constraints of reciprocity imposed by the moral point of view, and informed by other principles that we regard as important. Through these processes, we develop a personal moral code, or set of principles, that is derived from, but possibly also at variance with, certain features of conventional morality.

This is what generates the possibility of dissent, as distinct from deviance. If one looks at the great movements of moral reform in history, such as the civil rights movement, dissent has always been formulated in the "thick" language of moral ideas that are already very widely shared in the culture. Effective dissidents do not engage in criticism of the prevailing social institutions from the "outside"; they attack them from within, using the language in which moral claims are already routinely articulated. It has often been observed that what characterizes the moral rigor of dissenters is not that they subscribe to principles that are different from those that are widely shared in the community. They usually subscribe to the same principles; they simply take them more seriously, and thus apply them in a more consistent and thoroughgoing manner, or else exhibit less tolerance for failure to respect them.

Thus an institutional theory of morality, combined with a contextualist theory of justification, does not commit one to quietism in the face of unjust norms. It constitutes nothing more than a recognition that there are no knock-down *philosophical* arguments against particular norms and practices. The absence of philosophical arguments, however, does not imply the absence of *moral* arguments. Content skepticism is defeated not by providing an ultimate foundation for some particular set of moral obligations, but merely by showing that there is no reason in principle to expect moral arguments to fail, given the rich background of resources that our social life provides. We cannot make up all of morality, on the spot, through the power of thought alone. We probably could not make up a system of communication that way either. Luckily we don't have to, because we have at our disposal a number of extraordinarily powerful and sophisticated cultural artifacts (conventional morality and natural language, respectively) that relieve us of the necessity. What we can hope to do is make a contribution to the development and refinement of these artifacts, so that posterity may benefit.

9.6. Conclusion

Moral philosophy in the modern period has been dominated by attempts to impose drastic axiomatizations on morality, to develop a maximally parsimonious set of principles from which all other more concrete obligations could be derived. Utilitarianism and Kantianism represent the extremes of this tendency, in that they both attempt to reduce all of morality to one single principle. The hope was that this very abstract principle could then be justified by something that stands "outside" of morality, such as the nature of human rationality, the structure of the social contract, the inherent telos of human action, or something of that nature. This would provide the basis for a non-question-begging response to the content skeptic.

Yet this sort of axiomatic treatment represents, as Durkheim correctly noted, a complete inversion of the relations of dependence that exist in our moral thinking. Thus theorists who have sought to analyze morality from an evolutionary perspective have been right about one thing. It makes more sense to treat morality as a cultural artifact, reproduced from generation to generation, than it does to analyze it as a set of deductive consequences of some abstract principle. Where evolutionary theorists have erred is in their decision to treat morality as a *simple* cultural pattern, such as a strategy that says "cooperate if others cooperate, defect if they defect." In fact, morality is an extraordinarily complex set of rules, one that we spend the better part of our childhood mastering. It is more like a language than a strategy. Because they misconstrue morality as a type of strategy, evolutionary theorists have erroneously assumed that it is possible to make simple generalizations about its "fitness" as a cultural pattern.

Indeed, it is the very vastness of morality as a cultural artifact that provides the basis for a compelling response to the content skeptic. Morality is such a ubiquitous feature of social life that we often see right through it, and so fail to perceive the extent to which all of our social interactions are structured by norms that have implicitly moral content. And thus we fail to see how much is taken for granted, not just in every interaction, but in every argument and debate over moral questions. It is precisely this background of shared norms—a necessary feature of any ordered social life—that provides the fund of "regress-stoppers" required for the justification of norms that have become contested or problematic. There is no need to introduce hypothetical imperatives, evaluative beliefs, or anything else into the justificatory chain. As far as our moral arguments are concerned, it is actually norms all the way down.

The most important feature of this institutional approach to understanding morality is that it serves to assuage an ontological anxiety that has, in effect, dominated moral philosophy in the modern period. What are our moral judgments *about?* What is their objective correlate? Medieval Christian philosophers had what was, for a long time, a compelling answer to this question. Moral judgments were about the good, and the good had its objective correlate in the *form* of any given object. It was this form that dictated the principles of movement of the object. Thus the form of a rock dictates that it should fall, and the good for a rock is therefore its being united with the earth. This makes morality an integral part of science, since the good would have to figure as part of any explanation of an event (in terms of final causation). What are we doing when we deliberate about the good? We are merely attempting to pursue self-consciously that which our own form dictates. And naturally, since God created the universe, along with all of the forms in it, these are merely the physical embodiment of divine intentions. Thus moral science and natural science are two different approaches to understanding a single ontologically unified phenomenon, namely, the providential order.

The particular details of this medieval synthesis are not important. What is important is that within this worldview, morality fits seamlessly into nature; there is no tension whatsoever between natural science, morality, and religion. Unfortunately, the place that morality occupies in this grand scheme is one of several that were obliterated by modern science. With the disappearance of the concepts of form and of final causation, there is no longer any obvious place to situate "the good" within the general ontology of nature. Thus many philosophers in the twentieth century simply assumed that an "error theory" of morality went hand in hand with an "error theory" of religion. When we begin to think of gravity as responsible for falling rocks, rather than the rocks themselves, then the good no longer has any role to play in our scientific explanations of the world. And if we were wrong to think that there is such as thing as "the good" for rocks, then we must have been wrong to think that there is such a thing as "the good" for humans as well.

As a result, the scientific revolution left philosophers (and society more generally) without a plausible moral ontology. While beliefs could be described as being "about" the physical world, in some sense, and desires could be "about" the passions, or some set of internal somatic states, it was no longer clear what moral judgments could be about. And no matter how much ingenuity has been deployed by moral realists, trying to show that evaluative judgments have some kind of empirical correlate, all of their labors seem only to reinforce the impression underlying John Mackie's judgment that values are "ontologically queer."[62] (The arguments of moral realists often bring to mind Wittgenstein's remark that on hearing G. E. Moore's proof of an external world, he began to understand why skepticism was such a problem.)

The institutional theory of morality eliminates the mystery. Social norms are the "ontological" correlate of moral judgments. Morality is "about" the rules that govern our interactions. It commands convergence in judgment—to the extent that it does—because we live under shared social institutions, all of which are shot through with both implicit and explicit moral content. Philosophers have largely overlooked this possibility, simply because of a tendency to think that conventional morality is not moral enough to count as morality. I have tried to show that this is a mistake. All of the resources that philosophers have traditionally drawn on, in order to articulate the shortcomings of conventional morality, are themselves a part of our conventional morality (or else expressive vocabulary, introduced in order to articulate implicit features of our conventional morality). We do not need to stand outside of this system of norms in order to criticize it, any more than we need to stand outside of our system of empirical beliefs in order to improve on them.

Conclusion

Human beings are the only species on the planet that exhibits large-scale cooperation among genetically unrelated individuals. We are also the only "moral animal." These are, as far as I am concerned, merely two different ways of describing the same phenomenon. More specifically, the latter is simply our way of describing, from a participant perspective, what it is like to *be* the former. The advantage of the ethological description is that it makes the central problems of moral philosophy seem tractable, in a way that centuries of hairsplitting over rights, duties, virtues, and values has not. The question "What makes us a moral animal?" is one that should have a relatively straightforward (although perhaps unobvious) answer. It is also a problem that social scientists have made definite progress in addressing over the past few decades. Unfortunately, evolutionary theorists have too often failed to understand that answering their empirical questions falls quite a way short of answering the questions that have traditionally bedeviled moral philosophers. Moral philosophers on the other hand have generally failed to see that the empirical work of evolutionary theorists *constrains* the range of plausible answers to their traditional questions.

For example, moral sentiment theory is often based on the claim that morality is grounded in a form of extended sympathy. But one can easily ask the question "Is large-scale cooperation in human societies based on extended sympathy?" The answer, we have seen, is a resounding no. Sympathy is simply not sufficiently robust as a mechanism to explain human sociability, nor is it easy to see how sympathy could be leveraged, through other devices, into a mechanism sufficiently robust to do the trick. So while sympathy is no doubt a *part* of our moral life, it cannot be the answer to the major question of how large-scale cooperation is achieved, and so does not explain what distinguishes us from other primates.

Philosophers have often been too quick to assume that because they are working in the realm of normative theory, empirical details are irrelevant to their concerns. Thus they take themselves to be free to engage in data-free speculation. Of course, they are right to decry the undergraduate error of deriving normative conclusions from factual premises. But the mere fact that normative conclusions cannot be derived from factual premises does not mean that a theoretical reconstruction of the normative structure of morality need not *cohere* with existing bodies of scientific knowledge, in fields ranging from evolutionary biology and cultural anthropology to developmental psychology and sociological theory. After all, doing normative theory is not the same as legislating the way things ought to be. The moral philosopher is offering a reconstructive articulation of the norms that are already implicit in everyday social interactions. Whether or not morality is a product of socialization, for instance, is an empirical question. If it is a product of socialization, then we need an empirical account of how it gets reproduced across successive generations, how it arose, and why it might change over time. These are all empirical questions, yet also questions whose answers impose constraints on the range of plausible metaethical and normative theories.

For example, if morality really were a system of virtues, then it should be possible to detect systematic differences in the behavior of individuals who do and do not satisfy the folk-psychological criteria for the ascription of such virtues. Furthermore, the presence or absence of these virtues should have predictive value when it comes to anticipating "moral" behavior. Yet empirical studies have shown, time and again, that there are, in general, no stable traits of character at the "medium" level of generality at which virtue theory operates (and that even if there were, they would easily be overwhelmed by situational factors).[1] Most psychologists who study the question can only agree on five personality traits that have any sort of useful predictive value. It is noteworthy that these traits (known as the "big five": neuroticism, extraversion, agreeableness, conscientiousness, and openness to experience) do *not* correspond to any of the traditional categories of virtue theory; they are at a far greater level of generality. There is also widespread agreement that people develop fairly stable "scripts" that they work from when dealing with very particular types of situations, but that these don't add up to anything like the sort of broad dispositions posited by virtue theory. (For example, I am scrupulously honest when it comes to filing my income taxes, but I evade consumption taxes whenever presented with the opportunity to do so. Thus I cannot usefully be described as either honest or dishonest, even when it comes to the narrow category of "paying taxes.") Finally, there is the fact that virtue theory accords no role to imitation or conformity, which is probably the most important psychological factor determining individual compliance with moral constraints. In other words, virtue theory simply does not fit with any of the major twentieth-century discoveries in the realm of human motivational psychology. Surely this must have consequences for moral philosophy, such that we cannot simply go on propounding theories using the language of Aristotle, long after the vocabulary of "virtue" and "vice" has been shown to be inherently misleading.

To take a more concrete example: why do people behave immorally when drunk? An impressive 40 percent of violent crimes in the United States are committed by individuals who are under the influence of alcohol.[2] So naturally, there is a considerable amount of research on the question of what effects alcohol has on the individual that increase the probability of such transgressions of the normative order. For instance, the hypothesis that alcohol might stimulate negative or violent emotions has been studied extensively and decisively refuted.[3] Most contemporary work is focused on variants of the "disinhibition" theory, which suggests that alcohol does not provoke any specific affect or behavior, it merely weakens normative control. To use an image that is common in the literature, it's not like stepping on the gas, but rather like taking one's foot off the brake. (It may be worth noting as well that alcohol diminishes normative control in general, making people more likely to behave impolitely, unconventionally, imprudently, *and* immorally.) This is a finding that, it seems to me, clearly counts against the Humean and in favor of a naturalistic Kantian theory of motivation. It suggests that morality is not about having the right sort of desires, but rather about vetoing the wrong sort of desires. Yet despite the obvious relevance of these sorts of empirical findings, philosophical debates on the subject have been played out entirely at the level of the synthetic a priori.[4]

Of course, it is not difficult to see why moral philosophers are inclined to disregard these sorts of scientific findings. While scientists may seek to understand morality, the typical philosopher also wants to *defend* it. In fact, this urge is often so strong that it overrides the quest for descriptive adequacy, leading philosophers to invent psychological or anthropological theories that they think will be most conducive to the goal of justifying moral obligations.[5] This inclination is aided and abetted by the fact that scientists often presuppose the correctness of some form of moral noncognitivism, and therefore operate within a theoretical framework that many philosophers feel comfortable dismissing ab initio. Philosophers therefore tend to regard the scientific study of morality as tangential to their concerns, in the same way that "prospect theory" is regarded as interesting but not particularly relevant to the work of mathematicians and logicians.

Evolutionary theorists have often made things worse by trying to "debunk" our common-sense understanding of morality (a tendency best expressed in Michael Ghiselin's slogan "Scratch an altruist, and watch a hypocrite bleed").[6] Even those who have a more charitable attitude toward our self-interpretations in this regard have often exhibited a surprising lack of concern over whether morality will survive the scrutiny they bring to bear on it. David Sloan Wilson and Elliot Sober, for instance, in *Unto Others*, present a sophisticated rearticulation of the doctrine of group selection, and try to show that such a mechanism may be responsible for the psychological system underlying human altruism. I have argued that their explanation is unpersuasive, but in any case, one might certainly hope that it is, because if their account is right, the only thing that sustains altruism among humans is the segmentation of the population into small endogamously reproducing groups, coupled with periodic recombination. This means that, in an era of global migration, social mobility, and racial integration, one can look forward to the ruthless eradication of any altruistic dispositions in the human population (and the collapse of all human civilization).[7]

Similarly, Keith Stanovich argues quite persuasively that culture-dependence creates all of the necessary preconditions for a "robot's rebellion" against the dictates of our selfish genes. We have a variety of biological impulses that it is no longer in our interest to submit to, and the development of an intentional planning system gives us the tools necessary to free ourselves from such imperatives. However, Stanovich goes on to say that we are not just the victims of selfish genes but also of selfish memes, which seek to reproduce themselves at our expense. In a bizarre Nietzschean twist, he argues that whenever these conflict with our self-interest, narrowly construed, we should stage a "robot's rebellion" against these culturally transmitted patterns of behavior.[8] He appears not to realize that he is implicitly recommending the abolition of morality (a move that would, inter alia, eliminate the basis of ultrasociality in our species, lead to the collapse of civilization, etc.). He is also assuming the existence of a standpoint outside of these memes, from which it is possible to separate "our" interests from those of the memes that we transmit.[9]

The tendency among evolutionary naturalists to think of morality as some sort of ruse perpetrated on us by Mother Nature is quite pervasive. Richard Joyce, for instance, argues that nature "has designed us to think of our relations with one another in moral terms." But he goes on to ask:

> Why has Mother Nature granted us this bounty? Not for any laudable purpose (so let's not sing her praises too loudly), but simply because being nice helped our ancestors make more babies. It is naïve to assume that these natural prosocial tendencies extend to non-cognitive feelings, behavioral dispositions, inclinations, aversions, and preferences, but not to *beliefs*. But acknowledging beliefs under the influence of natural selection raises epistemological concerns, for the faithful representation of reality is of only contingent instrumental value when reproductive success is the touchstone, forcing us to acknowledge that if in certain domains *false* beliefs will bring more offspring then that is the route natural selection will take every time. Moral thinking could well be such a domain.[10]

This is clearly another case of general skepticism ("you only believe that because your genes want you to") being deployed in opposition to a specific philosophical thesis, without regard for the more general epistemological problems it creates. Joyce doesn't seem inclined to think that our belief in an external world, or the existence of other minds, is merely another convenient fiction foisted on us by our genes. Why the difference? The problem is that morality is *normative*, and from a certain perspective, there is something about normative statuses that seems "unscientific," possibly even superstitious. (It doesn't help, of course, that the traditional explanation for the "oughtness" of these normative statuses involved tracing them back to divine commands. This lent considerable support to the presumption that the elimination of God from our ontology would result in the elimination of the entire domain of the normative as well.) Thus instead of trying to offer a naturalistic reconstruction of normativity, philosophers of a naturalistic temperament have typically tried to debunk, dismiss, or reduce it.

Yet it has turned out to be difficult to excise normativity from the field of scientific inquiry. Obviously, trying to get rid of normativity requires that our sense of moral obligation somehow be explained away.[11] But it also forces us to explain a variety of different phenomena, from the orderliness of social interaction to the contentfulness of intentional states, to the meaningfulness of linguistic expressions, without recourse to any irreducibly normative concepts. This is something that has not been achieved in any of these domains. Indeed, insofar as plausible-sounding "naturalistic" explanations have been produced, it is usually because some normative notion is being smuggled in through the back door.[12] "Representation," for instance, is an essentially normative notion, and yet it is often treated as though it were purely descriptive. "Causality" is also treated as though it were an explanatory primitive, something that requires no further explanation. Yet causality is a very complex, poorly understood relation, the ascription of which seems to depend essentially on a commitment to all sorts of counterfactuals. As Robert Brandom has observed, the modal relations underlying such counterfactuals are just as mysterious, if not more so, than the standard set of deontic modalities.[13]

It is because problems such as this have been cropping up in a variety of different fields that there has been a general move, over the past decade or two, away from the idea that normativity is something that needs to be eliminated from our worldview and toward the view that it needs to be better understood. Scientists and philosophers have been forced to get past their initial reaction to the "queerness" of normative claims. Of course, this does not mean that there isn't something genuinely odd about the normative, or about the way human sociality, language, rationality, and cognition depend on the normative. This is why the Kantian strategy of transcendental argumentation is so important. The Kantian is perfectly comfortable acknowledging that, from a certain perspective, there are arbitrary elements in the way that we experience the world, in the way that we reason, and in the way that we interact with one another. Given that our minds are the product of evolution, it would be very surprising if they didn't have somewhat quirky "design" features. Yet we only have genuine access to one perspective, namely, our own, and that is a perspective situated within the world that we experience, the forms of reasoning that we deploy, and the type of social interactions that structure our development. Thus many of the seemingly arbitrary elements are not actually arbitrary *for us*. It is too late to patch our own operating systems.

When deploying such an argumentation strategy in defense of morality, however, it is important to exercise restraint. A transcendental argument cannot be used to justify specific normative obligations, it can only be used to justify the phenomenon of deontic constraint in general—the fact that we have a normative control system, and hence a disposition to respect social norms. This is no small achievement, since the fact that morality takes the form of a system of duties—actions that must be performed for their own sake, and not for the sake of some anticipated reward—has often been regarded as one of its most puzzling features. I have also suggested that the normative control system imposes weak constraints on the content of possible norms, and thus that "the moral point of view" is also open to transcendental justification. But this does not provide us with the premises or procedures needed to derive the remainder of our moral obligations. It represents simply a specification of the psychological structures that must be in place in order for the individual to acquire and conform to conventional morality. The latter is an extremely complex cultural artifact, which has been produced and refined over the course of generations. Most of what we call moral argumentation draws on resources that are internal to this system of conventional morality.

Thus the transcendental argumentation strategy provides a response to motivational scepticism only. My response to content scepticism is perhaps less satisfying, since I do not think it is possible to provide a *philosophical* justification of any substantive moral principle. The only proper philosophical response is to show that all of the arguments in favor of content scepticism tacitly presuppose problematic epistemological theories—usually some form of foundationalism. Thus there is no particular reason to think that we should have difficulty providing a rational justification for some contested moral principle, given the depth of the resources provided by our shared conventional morality (and in intercultural contexts, given the pragmatic structure of interactions that call for normative regulation, along with the potential benefits of cooperation). There is no knock-down argument to show that some particular principle must emerge the victor from such deliberations, but neither is there any knock-down argument to show that *no* principle will emerge the victor.

The argument advanced here constitutes, as advertised, a defense of the phenomenon of deontic constraint, but not a complete theory of morality. This is why the discussion began with a critique of the instrumental conception of rationality, which claims that the rational agent values actions for their consequences only, and never for their own sake. My primary argumentation strategy was simply to show that consequentialists have failed to make their case. This was not so difficult, because the type of subjectivism about value that rational choice theorists have been inclined to adopt makes it very difficult for them to turn around and prohibit agents from caring about the intrinsic properties of their actions. Thus most of the work involved simply clearing up misunderstandings about technical aspects of the instrumental theory.

However, once one abandons the subjectivist pose, and begins to inquire into the origins of the content of the agent's intentional states, then the deeper problem with the instrumental theory starts to become apparent. The instrumental conception of rationality is, in many ways, merely an expression of the idea that we differ from our closest primate relatives only in that we are smarter, or have greater computational abilities, which in turn makes us better, as individual organisms, at calculating where our self-interest lies. According to this view, we have fundamentally the same mental equipment as other animals—the same sort of mental states, and the same sort of calculative abilities. The only difference is that we have bigger brains, and so we are able to make better use of these cognitive endowments.

The analysis developed here suggests that human intelligence—or more specifically, human rationality—is more of a "lateral" evolutionary development than a "vertical" move in the hierarchy of being. It is not produced through a quantitative augmentation of a set of systems shared by all higher mammals; rather, it is an indirect tweak that allows us to make somewhat unprecedented— and highly successful—use of cognitive machinery that was originally adapted for other uses. Fundamentally, it is the development of language as a tool of public communication that makes the "language upgrade" available to us, which is in turn the basis for the intentional planning system whose deployment theories of practical rationality seek to model. Thus our capacity for rational planning is somewhat different from many of our other psychological systems. Perhaps the most noteworthy difference is that it depends on certain kinds of social and cultural resources in a way that, for example, our perceptual system does not. This is why some of the constitutive features of our social environment—such as the norm-governed structure of social life—migrate inward, and become constitutive features of our psychological faculties. And this in turn explains why there is an indissoluble bond between rational practical deliberation and deontic constraint.

If human beings were nothing more than very smart chimpanzees, and human rationality was nothing more than an amplification of the cognitive abilities chimpanzees use when fishing termites out of a hole, then we probably would be instrumental reasoners. We would also be extremely uncooperative, have no culture or civilization to speak of, and live in primal hordes of no more than 150 individuals. But this image represents a misunderstanding of human intelligence. Our intelligence is not the pinnacle of evolutionary development, nor is there any obvious trend in that direction within the animal kingdom. We are more like a strange and somewhat improbable little offshoot.

In the same way that the search for extraterrestrial intelligence is motivated by a bad theory of terrestrial intelligence, a search for extraterrestrial morality would be equally ill conceived. Human morality is obviously a consequence of the specific type of sociality exhibited in our species, or more specifically, the way social integration is achieved in our species. A species that stood to benefit less from cooperation in large groups would have no need for it. A species with a higher average coefficient of relatedness would have no need for integration through shared culture, since biological mechanisms would suffice. Thus morality is a peculiarly human phenomenon. Yet it is, at the same time, *profoundly* human, such that we cannot imagine ourselves being human without it.

Notes

Introduction

1. Immanuel Kant, *Foundations of the Metaphysic of Morals*, trans. Lewis White Beck (Indianapolis: Bobbs-Merrill, 1959), p. 30 (Ak 414).

2. See David Sally, "Conversation and Cooperation in Social Dilemmas: A Meta-analysis of Experiments from 1958 to 1972," *Rationality and Society* 7 (1995): 58–92; also Richard H. Thaler, "Cooperation," in *The Winner's Curse* (Princeton: Princeton University Press, 1992).

3. See, for example, David McNaughton and Piers Rawling, "Agent-Relativity and the Doing-Happening Distinction," *Philosophical Studies* 63 (1991): 168–69.

4. For an example of this, see Jon Elster's highly influential *Nuts and Bolts for the Social Sciences* (Cambridge: Cambridge University Press, 1989), pp. 23–24.

5. Leonard J. Savage, *The Foundations of Statistics*, 2nd ed. (New York: Dover, 1972). The complete quotation in context is as follows: "If two different acts had the same consequences in every state of the world, there would from the present point of view be no point in considering them two different acts at all. An act may therefore be identified with its possible consequences. Or, more formally, an act is a function attaching a consequence to each state of the world," p. 14.

6. Naturally, it has not remained so. See, e.g., Peter Hammond, "Consequentialist Foundations for Expected Utility," *Theory and Decision* 25 (1988): 25–78. He observes that consequentialism in normal form games is relatively innocuous, but that in decision trees (i.e., temporally extended choice problems) it imposes implausible restrictions. He therefore recommends expanding the domain of "consequences" so that "consequentialism requires that everything which should be allowed to affect decisions to count as a relevant consequence," p. 26. I discuss this sort of expanded definition of consequences in chapter 3, section 2.

7. Robert Brandom, *Making It Explicit* (Cambridge, Mass.: Harvard University Press, 1994).

8. Derek Bickerton, "Resolving Discontinuity: A Minimalist Distinction between Human and Non-human Minds," *American Zoologist* 40 (2000): 864. As Peter J. Richerson and Robert Boyd write, "The macroevolutionary record is a stern test of explanatory hypotheses because the explanation has to get the timescale right.," *Not by Genes Alone* (Chicago: University of Chicago Press, 2004), p. 242.

9. For a helpful overview of this dispute, see Shelly Kagan, *Normative Ethics* (Boulder, Colo.: Westview Press, 1998).

10. Shaun Nichols, *Sentimental Rules* (New York: Oxford University Press, 2004), pp. 5–8.

11. Jurgen Habermas, *Moral Consciousness and Communicative Action*, trans. Shierry Weber-Nicholson (Cambridge, Mass.: MIT Press, 1990), p. 164.

Chapter 1

1. Thomas Hobbes, *Leviathan*, ed. Richard Tuck (Cambridge: Cambridge University Press, 1991), p. 13.

2. Hobbes, *Leviathan*, pp. 38–39.

3. Hobbes, *Leviathan*, pp. 38–46.

4. G. E. M. Anscombe, *Intention* (Oxford: Blackwell, 1959).

5. Hobbes, *Leviathan*, p. 39.

6. Hobbes, *Leviathan*, p. 39.

7. This usage is widespread in the rational choice literature, although not entirely standard among philosophers. Compare the following. Jon Elster, *Nuts and Bolts for the Social Sciences* (Cambridge: Cambridge University Press, 1989), writes: "Rational choice is instrumental: it is guided by the outcome of the action. Actions are valued and chosen not for themselves, but as more or less efficient means to a further end," p. 22. On the other hand, Jean Hampton, *The Authority of Reason* (Cambridge: Cambridge University Press, 1998), defines the instrumental conception of rationality as involving a commitment both to the claim that "a fundamental component of practical reasoning is reasoning that determines the best means to an end," and the claim that "practical reasoning plays no role in the setting of unmotivated ends of action," p. 169. The latter claim can, of course, be formulated in a way that makes it trivially true—simply by taking the content of intentional states to be outside the purview of practical rationality. But if it is intended substantively, as the claim that reason more generally plays no role in setting the ends of action, then it is the doctrine that I refer to as *preference noncognitivism*, not instrumental rationality.

8. See Leonard J. Savage, *The Foundations of Statistics*, 2nd ed. (New York: Dover, 1972), pp. 13–17. This partitioning, known as the "Savage trichotomy," will be discussed at greater length in chapter 3. Although it is not universally accepted among decision theorists, it is largely taken for granted by game theorists. See Roger Myerson, *Game Theory* (Cambridge, Mass.: Harvard University Press, 1991), pp. 5–12.

9. Georg Henrik von Wright, *An Essay on Deontic Logic and the General Theory of Action* (Amsterdam: North-Holland, 1968), pp. 58–68. "Impossible" is being used here in the sense of "false at all possible worlds physically accessible to our own, i.e., having the same laws of nature."

10. The fact that the agent does not know, at the time of decision, which node she is at is represented by the dashed line between the three nodes in figure 1.1, which shows that they belong to the same "information set."

11. Note that there are still only three outcomes, not nine. It is important that outcomes be specifiable independent of the actions that lead to them, for reasons that will become apparent in section 3 of chapter 3.

12. See Mark Kaplan, *Decision Theory as Philosophy* (Cambridge: Cambridge University Press, 1996), pp. 168–69.

13. Beliefs, on the other hand, can be fixed, by assuming that agents assign all tautologies a probability of 1, and all contradictions a probability of 0.

14. Erik Nord, *Cost-Value Analysis in Health Care* (Cambridge: Cambridge University Press, 1999).

15. John von Neumann and Oskar Morgenstern, *The Theory of Games and Economic Behavior*, 2nd ed. (Princeton: Princeton University Press, 1947).

16. My presentation of utility functions loosely follows R. Duncan Luce and Howard Raiffa, *Games and Decisions* (New York: Dover, 1957). Incidentally, this combination of ordinalism plus axiomatic constraints has generated a lot of needless confusion in the philosophical literature, by suggesting that decision theory involves a commitment both to a conception of practical rationality and a (thin) theory of preference-rationality. (See, for instance, J. David Velleman, "The Story of Rational Action," in Velleman, *The Possibility of Practical Reason* [Oxford: Clarendon, 2000]). Starting out with cardinally ranked preferences over outcomes eliminates the need for axiomatic constraints, and therefore makes it clear that decision theory is not in the business of deciding which beliefs and preferences are rational and which aren't.

17. Weak preference means that the agent either prefers one option to the other or is indifferent between the two.

18. Plato, *The Republic*, trans. Francis MacDonald Cornford (London: Oxford University Press, 1941), p. 25 (343b–344c).

19. Niccolo Machiavelli, *The Prince*, trans. Harvey C. Mansfield Jr. (Chicago: University of Chicago Press, 1985), p. 66.

20. Donald Davidson, "Mental Events," in Davidson, *Essays on Action and Events* (Oxford: Clarendon, 1980), p. 222.

21. Alisdair MacIntyre, *After Virtue*, 2nd ed. (Notre Dame, Ind.: University of Notre Dame Press, 1984), Charles Taylor, *Sources of the Self* (Cambridge, Mass.: Harvard University Press, 1989).

22. Von Neumann and Morgenstern, *Theory of Games and Economic Behavior*, pp. 11–12.

23. See Shaun Hargreaves Heap and Yanis Varoufakis, *Game Theory: A Critical Text*, 2nd ed. (London: Routledge, 2004), for a development of game theory that places particular emphasis on the "common knowledge of rationality" (CKR) constraint.

24. John Nash, "Non-cooperative Games," *Annals of Mathematics* 54 (1951): 289–95.

25. For overview, see Drew Fudenberg and Jean Tirole, *Game Theory* (Cambridge, Mass.: MIT Press), pp. 11–14.

26. For an accessible proof, see Fudenberg and Tirole, *Game Theory*, pp. 29–33.

27. Reinhard Selten, "Reexamination of the Perfectness Concept for Equilibrium Points in Extensive Games," *International Journal of Game Theory* 4 (1975): 25–55. It should be noted that even these basic refinements are problematic, because they all use conditionalization to assign probabilities to counterfactuals. Since conditional and counterfactual probabilities are in fact not equivalent, these refinement strategies have given rise to some predictable difficulties. For an overview, see Cristina Bicchieri, "Strategic Behavior and Counterfactuals," *Synthese* 76 (1988): 135–69.

28. John Harsanyi and Reinhard Selten, *A General Theory of Equilibrium Selection in Games* (Cambridge, Mass.: MIT Press, 1988).

29. Drew Fudenberg and Eric Maskin, "The Folk Theorem in Repeated Games with Discounting or with Incomplete Information," *Econometrica* 54 (1986): 533–54. See also Fudenberg and Tirole, *Game Theory*, pp. 150–60. Note that for such results to obtain players must not discount the future too heavily.

30. Joseph Farrell, "Meaning and Credibility in Cheap-Talk Games," *Games and Economic Behavior* 5 (1993): 514–31.

31. The term is due to Farrell, "Meaning and Credibility in Cheap-Talk Games." For summary and discussion, see Joseph Heath, "Is Language a Game?" *Canadian Journal of Philosophy* 25 (1995): 1–28.

32. Bicchieri, "Strategic Behavior and Counterfactuals," p. 138.

33. See Roger Myerson, *Game Theory* (Cambridge, Mass.: Harvard University Press, 1991), pp. 113–14.

34. Martin Hollis and Robert Sugden, "Rationality in Action," *Mind* 102 (1993): 1–35.

35. Garrett Hardin, "The Tragedy of the Commons," *Science* 162 (1968): 1243–48. See also Russell Hardin, *Collective Action* (Baltimore: Johns Hopkins University Press, 1981).

36. For example, see the articles collected in Richmond Campbell and Lanning Sowden, eds., *Paradoxes of Rationality and Cooperation* (Vancouver: University of British Columbia Press, 1985).

37. Thomas Schelling, *Micromotives and Macrobehavior* (New York: Norton, 1978), p. 32.

38. Hobbes, *Leviathan*, p. 89.

39. David Gauthier, *Morals by Agreement* (Oxford: Clarendon, 1986). Many philosophers have detected a hint of circularity in the thought that an individual might choose to adopt a set of principles to guide her choices (e.g., Velleman, *Possibility of Practical Reason*, p. 228.) On what basis could one make such a choice? Gauthier's early architectonic intuition was that since decision-theoretic reasoning always generates optimal results, instrumental reasoning could be regarded as unproblematic in this domain. The choice of principles to govern practical reasoning in social interactions could then be represented, and resolved (without circularity), as a decision-theoretic choice problem. The structure of this argument is most visible in David Gauthier, "Reason and Maximization," *Canadian Journal of Philosophy* 4 (1975): 411–33, reprinted in Gauthier, *Moral Dealing* (Ithaca: Cornell University Press, 1990), pp. 209–33.

40. For an overview, see Richard H. Thaler, *The Winner's Curse* (Princeton: Princeton University Press, 1992), pp. 6–20.

Chapter 2

1. Kant uses the phrase in "Idea for a Universal History with Cosmopolitan Purpose," in *Kant's Political Writings*, 2nd ed., ed. Hans Reiss (Cambridge: Cambridge University Press: 1991), p. 44.

2. The comparison between Bert Hölldobler and Edward O. Wilson's *The Ants* (Cambridge, Mass.: Harvard University Press, 1991) and any standard introductory textbook in social psychology will be highly unflattering to the latter.

3. Peter Berger and Thomas Luckmann, *The Social Construction of Reality* (New York: Doubleday, 1966), p. 51.

4. The persistence of the view that "shared values" are required for social integration is in fact a testimony to the frequently disavowed, but still lasting, influence of Talcott Parsons, not only in contemporary sociology, but in "folk sociology" more generally. See Talcott Parsons, *The Structure of Social Action*, 2 vols. (New York: McGraw Hill, 1937), and *The Social System* (New York: Free Press, 1951).

5. Thomas Hobbes, *Leviathan*, ed. Richard Tuck (Cambridge: Cambridge University Press, 1991), p. 117.

6. Thomas Schelling, *The Strategy of Conflict* (Cambridge, Mass.: Harvard University Press, 1960), "Threats," pp. 123–30, "Promises," pp. 131–37.

7. This is true in Canada at least. Elsewhere I am told people are more confrontational.

8. Pamela Oliver, "Rewards and Punishments as Selective Incentives for Collective Action: Theoretical Investigations," *American Journal of Sociology* 85 (1980): 1361. Thus Michael Taylor writes, in *The Possibility of Cooperation* (Cambridge: Cambridge University Press, 1987), that many proposed solutions to collective action problems are faulty, because they "involve the use of threats and offers of sanctions, and the creation and maintenance of the sanction system entails the prior or concurrent solution of collective action problems," p. 22.

9. Robert Boyd, Herbert Gintis, Samuel Bowles, and Peter J. Richerson, "The Evolution of Altruistic Punishment," in Herbert Gintis, Samuel Bowles, R. Boyd, and E. Fehr, eds., *Moral Sentiments and Material Interests: On the Foundations of Cooperation in Economic Life* (Cambridge, Mass.: MIT Press, 2003), pp. 215–28.

10. Robert Axelrod, *The Evolution of Cooperation* (New York: Basic Books, 1984). The strategy was actually submitted by Anatol Rappaport.

11. Tit-for-tat versus tit-for-tat is a Nash equilibrium, for the same reason (D, L) is a Nash equilibrium in figure 2.1. However, it is not a subgame-perfect equilibrium, because the course of action that it prescribes off the equilibrium path is not utility-maximizing (since the anticipated payoff associated with "punitive" defection is no different from the payoff associated with "parasitical" defection). For a more detailed discussion, see Eric Rasmusen, "Folk Theorems for the Observable Implications of Repeated Games," *Theory and Decision* 32 (1992): 161.

12. On the former, "Nash reversion strategy" (also known as the "trigger" or "grim" strategy), see James W. Friedman, "A Noncooperative Equilibrium for Supergames," *Review of Economic Studies* 38 (1971): 1–12. On the latter, see Drew Fudenberg and Eric Maskin, "The Folk Theorem in Repeated Games with Discounting or with Incomplete Information," *Econometrica* 54 (1986): 533–54.

13. Peter Richerson and Robert Boyd, "The Evolution of Human Ultra-Sociality," in Irenas Eibl-Eibesfeldt and Frank Salter, eds., *Ideology, Warfare, and Indoctrinability*, (New York: Berghan Books, 1998), pp. 71–95.

14. Jon Elster, *The Cement of Society* (Cambridge: Cambridge University Press, 1989), p. 131.

15. See Francis Fukuyama, *Trust* (London: Penguin, 1995), Robert Putnam, *Bowling Alone* (New York: Simon and Schuster, 2000).

16. Samuel Bowles and Herbert Gintis, "Origins of Human Cooperation," in Peter Hammerstein, ed., *Genetic and Cultural Evolution of Cooperation* (Cambridge, Mass.: MIT Press, 2003), p. 432.

17. Robert Boyd and Peter Richerson, "The Evolution of Reciprocity in Sizable Groups," *Journal of Theoretical Biology* 132 (1988): 337–56.

18. Rosaria Conte and Mario Paolucci, *Reputation in Artificial Societies* (Dordrecht: Kluwer, 2002), pp. 38–48.

19. See David Braybrooke, "The Insoluble Problem of the Social Contract," in Richmond Campbell and Lanning Sowden, eds., *Paradoxes of Rationality and Cooperation* (Vancouver: University of British Columbia Press, 1985), pp. 277–305.

20. The notion was popular for a while among political scientists that the collective action problem at the level of sanctions was less problematic than the one at the level of first-order cooperation, because imposing sanctions is less costly than cooperation.

But the issue, of course, is not whether things are more or less costly. As long as there is any net cost associated with imposing sanctions, then there is a collective action problem. The issue is only resolved if individuals have a positive preference for sanctioning others.

21. Bruno Verbeek, *Instrumental Rationality and Moral Philosophy* (Dordrecht: Kluwer, 2002) writes: "In normal circumstances, most people prefer more over less money, paying less taxes over paying more taxes, and so forth. Moreover, most people expect others to have these preferences in these circumstances. Contrary to the suggestion implicit in the objection, I do not believe we are so dead-wrong about these interests," p. 86.

22. See Ken Binmore, *Playing Fair: Game Theory and the Social Contract*, vol. 2 (Cambridge, Mass.: MIT Press, 1994), 1:104.

23. Binmore, *Playing Fair*, p. 95.

24. The primary significance of Gödel's incompleteness theorem is that it blocked Frege's logicist program, and therefore showed that arithmetic is not reducible to logic. For overview, see Stephen Kleene, "The Work of Kurt Gödel," in Stuart Shanker, ed. *Gödel's Theorem in Focus* (London: Routledge, 1988), pp. 48–73.

25. Donald Davidson, "The Structure and Content of Truth," *Journal of Philosophy* 87 (1990): 279–328. See also Daniel M. Hausman, "Revealed Preference, Belief, and Game Theory," *Economics and Philosophy* 16 (2000): 99–115.

26. There is also the fact that a large part of what makes the conception of preference that underlies the instrumental model plausible is that it corresponds roughly to the sort of desires that we have introspective access to, as witnessed by the fact that we grant agents a certain first-person authority in their reports. The doctrine of revealed preference suggests that agents are only able to ascertain their desires by observing their own behavior, then inferring post facto that they desired x or y. David Gauthier notes the absurdity of this suggestion, and proposes a framework in which revealed preferences would be weighted against "attitudinal preferences," those that are "expressed in speech." *Morals by Agreement* (Oxford: Clarendon, 1986), pp. 27–28.

27. Herbert Simon, *Models of Bounded Rationality*, 2 vols. (Cambridge, Mass.: MIT Press, 1982).

28. David Gauthier articulates this strategy most clearly in "Reason and Maximization," *Canadian Journal of Philosophy* 4 (1975): 411–33.

29. See David Gauthier's restatement of his views in "Assure and Threaten," *Ethics*, 104 (1994): 690–721; also Edward McClennen, *Rationaliy and Dynamic Choice* (Cambridge: Cambridge University Press, 1990). John Broome, "Are Intentions Reasons? And How Should We Cope with Incommensurable Values?" in Christopher Morris and Arthur Ripstein, eds., *Practical Rationality and Preference: Essays for David Gauthier* (Cambridge: Cambridge University Press, 2001), pp. 98–120.

30. Verbeek, *Instrumental Rationality and Moral Philosophy*, pp. 255–63.

31. This version drawn from Edward McClennen, "Rationalité et Règles," in Jean-Pierre Dupuy and Pierre Livet, eds., *Les Limites de la Rationalité* (Paris: La Découverte, 1997), p. 100.

32. Edward McClennen, "The Rationality of Being Guided by Rules," in Alfred R. Mele and Piers Rawling, *The Oxford Handbook of Rationality* (Oxford: Oxford University Press, 2004), pp. 234–35.

33. Gauthier, "Assure and Threaten," p. 716. See also Richard Holton, "Rational Resolve," *Philosophical Review* 113 (2004): 507–35.

34. For a more careful development of this argument, see Claire Finkelstein, "Rational Temptation," in Chrisopher W. Morris and Arthur Ripstein, eds., *Practical Rationality and Preference* (Cambridge: Cambridge University Press, 2001), p. 69.

35. Michael Bratman, *The Faces of Intention* (Cambridge: Cambridge University Press, 1999), p. 55n.

36. Gauthier, *Morals by Agreement*, p. 180.

37. Similarly, athletes wouldn't bother to train, knowing that the person with the most natural ability will win, regardless of whether *everyone* trains or *everyone* takes it easy. See Joseph Heath, *The Efficient Society* (Toronto: Penguin, 2001), pp. 95–97. On price competition, see p. 105.

38. Schelling, *Strategy of Conflict*, and David Lewis, *Convention* (Cambridge, Mass.: Harvard University Press, 1969).

39. Schelling, *Strategy of Conflict*, pp. 54–57.

40. Schelling, *Strategy of Conflict*, p. 55.

41. For the formal definition, see Lewis, *Convention*, p. 58.

42. For discussion, see Verbeek, *Instrumental Rationality and Moral Philosophy*, pp. 9–75.

43. Govert den Hartogh, *Mutual Expectations: A Conventionalist Theory of Law* (The Hague: Kluwer, 2002), is clear on this point, yet strives mightily to avoid the limitations that it imposes on "conventionalist" explanations of social order.

44. David Hume, *A Treatise of Human Nature*, 2nd ed., ed. L. A. Selby-Bigge (Oxford: Clarendon, 1978), p. 490.

45. Hume, *Treatise of Human Nature*, p. 521.

46. Hume, *Treatise of Human Nature*, p. 521.

47. See Robert Sugden, *The Economics of Rights, Co-operation and Welfare* (Oxford: Blackwell, 1986), pp. 172–73. Ken Binmore states the view with admirable clarity, when he writes: "the Game of Morals is nothing more than a coordination device for selecting one of the equilibria in the Game of Life," *Just Playing: Game Theory and the Social Contract*, vol. 1 (Cambridge, Mass.: MIT Press, 1998), 2:424.

48. For an overview, see Elinor Ostrom, "A Behavioral Approach to the Rational Choice Theory of Collective Action," *American Political Science Review* 92 (1998): 1–22.

49. Conte and Paolucci, *Reputation in Artificial Societies*, p. 63.

50. An incomplete sample: Friedrich Schneider and Werner W. Pommerehne, "Free Riding and Collective Action: An Experiment in Public Microeconomics," *Quarterly Journal of Economics* 96 (1981): 689–704; Oliver Kim and Mark Walker, "The Free Rider Problem: Experimental Evidence," *Public Choice* 43 (1984): 3–24; Mark Isaac, Kenneth F. McCue, and Charles R. Plott, "Public Goods Provision in an Experimental Environment," *Journal of Public Economics* 26 (1985): 51–74.

51. Herbert Gintis, "Strong Reciprocity and Human Sociality," *Journal of Theoretical Biology* 206 (2000): 169–79.

52. Robyn M. Dawes and Richard H. Thaler, "Anomalies: Cooperation," *Journal of Economic Perspectives* 2 (1988): 187–97.

53. Gerald Marwell and Ruth E. Ames, "Economists Free Ride, Does Anyone Else?" *Journal of Public Economics* 15 (1981): 295–310.

54. David Sally, "Conversation and Cooperation in Social Dilemmas: A Meta-analysis of Experiments from 1958 to 1972," *Rationality and Society* 7 (1995): 58–92.

55. Varda Liberman, Steven M. Samuels, and Lee Ross, "The Name of the Game: Predictive Power of Reputations versus Situational Labels in Determining Prisoner's Dilemma Game Moves," *Personality and Social Psychology Bulletin* 30 (2004):1175–85.

56. Joseph Henrich, Robert Boyd, Samuel Bowles, Colin Camerer, Ernst Fehr, Herbert Gintis, and Richard McElreath, "In Search of Homo Economicus: Behavioral Experiments in 15 Small-Scale Societies," *American Economic Review* 91 (2001): 76–77.

57. Alvin E. Roth, "Bargaining Experiments," in John H. Kagel and Alvin E. Roth, eds., *Handbook of Experimental Economics* (Princeton: Princeton University Press, 1995), pp. 253–348.

58. Henrich et al., "In Search of Homo Economicus," p. 76.

59. Henrich et al., "In Search of Homo Economicus," p. 76.

60. David A. Schroeder, Thomas D. Jensen, Andrew J. Reed, Debra K. Sullivan, and Michael Schwab, "The Actions of Others as Determinants of Behavior in Social Trap Situations," *Journal of Experimental Social Psychology* 19 (1983): 532.

61. On normative salience, see Cristina Bicchieri, *The Grammar of Society* (Cambridge: Cambridge University Press, 2005), pp. 70–76. On communication, see John M. Orbell, Alphons J. C. van de Kragt, and Robyn M. Dawes, "Explaining Discussion-Induced Cooperation," *Journal of Personality and Social Psychology* 54 (1988): 811–19; also Sally, "Conversation and Cooperation in Social Dilemmas," p. 69.

62. Jane Allyn Pilliavin and Hong-Wen Charng described, in 1990, "a 'paradigm shift' away from the earlier position that behavior that appears to be altruistic must, under closer scrutiny, be revealed as reflecting egoistic motives," "Altruism: A Review of Recent Theory and Research," *Annual Review of Sociology* 16 (1990): 27. This was probably premature, but the tendency they describe has since gathered considerable momentum.

63. Herbert Gintis, "A Framework for the Unification of the Behavioral Sciences," *Behavioral and Brain Sciences* 30 (2007): 2.

64. More formally, it arises out of the commitment to methodological individualism as Max Weber understood it. See Joseph Heath, "Methodological Individualism," in Edward N. Zalta, ed., *Stanford Encyclopedia of Philosophy* (2005), http://plato.stanford.edu/entries/methodological-individualism/.

65. Robert Brandom, *Articulating Reasons* (Cambridge, Mass.: Harvard University Press, 2000).

Chapter 3

1. Peter Hammond, "Consequentialist Foundations for Modern Utility," *Theory and Decision* 25 (1988): 25.

2. See Jon Elster, *The Cement of Society* (Cambridge: Cambridge University Press, 1989), p. 98. See also Jon Elster, "Rationality, Morality and Collective Action," *Ethics* 96 (1985): 136–55, where he distinguishes between "process-oriented" and "outcome-oriented" benefits, the former deriving from "participation in the action itself," p. 145.

3. Talcott Parsons, *The Structure of Social Action*, 2 vols. (New York: McGraw Hill, 1937), pp. 439–40.

4. Philip Pettit, "Institutional Design and Rational Choice," in Robert E. Goodin, ed., *The Theory of Institutional Design* (Cambridge: Cambridge University Press, 1996), pp. 54–89.

5. John Braithwaite sums up the consensus view, in *Crime, Shame and Reintegration* (New York: Cambridge University Press, 1989), when he writes, "you cannot take the moral content out of social control and expect social control to work. If there is no morality about the law, if it is just a game of rational economic trade-offs, cheating will be rife," p. 142. This is perhaps why those who declare themselves to be "rational choice" criminologists typically turn out not to be so, on closer inspection. Ronald L. Akers, for instance, "Rational Choice, Deterrence, and Social Learning Theory in Criminology: The Path Not Taken," *Journal of Criminal Law and Criminology* 81 (1990): 655, quickly reformulates the utility-maximization hypothesis as a special instance of a much broader "social learning theory," which "encompasses the full range of behavioral inhibitors and facilitators: rewards/costs; past, present and anticipated reinforcers and punishers; formal and informal sanctions; legal and extra-legal penalties; direct and indirect punishment; and positive and negative reinforcement, whether or not rationally calculated."

6. Justin Aronfreed, *Conduct and Conscience: The Socialization of Internalized Control over Behavior* (New York: Academic Press, 1968).

7. See Viktor Vanberg, *Rules and Choice in Economics* (London: Routledge, 1994), pp. 13–14. This is something of a misnomer, since the view in question was not held by either Emile Durkheim or Talcott Parsons (it is, however, quite similar to the view *ascribed* to Durkheim by Parsons). See Parsons, *Structure of Social Action*, pp. 380–88.

8. As Herbert Gintis writes, "culture therefore takes the form not only of new techniques for controlling nature, but also of *norms and values* that are incorporated into individual preference functions through the sociological mechanism known as *socialization* and the psychological mechanism known as *internalization of norms*." "A Framework for the Unification of the Behavioral Sciences," *Behavioral and Brain Sciences* 30 (2007): 2.

9. Vanberg, *Rules and Choice in Economics*, p. 15. He goes on to say that because the behavior is preprogrammed, "in some sense, the *very absence of choice* seems to be constitutive" of rule-following. This is a common inference, but an illegitimate one. I may have been preprogramed by my mother to eat healthy snacks instead of junk food, but that does not mean I lack choice when, feeling peckish, I walk to the health food store. The only difference between this case and the rule-following one is that in the latter, what has been inculcated through socialization is a direct preference for an action, rather than an outcome.

10. This usage is due to Durkheim. For a recent statement, see Chandra Sripada and Stephen Stich, "A Framework for the Psychology of Norms," in Peter Carruthers, Stephen Laurence, and Stephen Stich, eds., *The Innate Mind: Culture and Cognition* (Oxford: Oxford University Press, 2006), pp. 281–82.

11. See discussion in Parsons, *The Social System* (New York: Free Press, 1951), pp. 236–40.

12. Pace John Heritage, *Garfinkel and Ethnomethodology* (Cambridge: Polity Press, 1984), pp. 30–32.

13. Harold Garfinkel has put particular emphasis on this aspect of the social order. As he writes, in his inimitable style, "in exactly the way that a setting is organized, it *consists* of members' methods for making evident that settings' ways as clear, coherent, planful, consistent, chosen, knowable, uniform, reproducible connections—i.e., rational connections. In exactly the way that persons are members to organized affairs, they are engaged in serious and practical work of detecting, demonstrating, persuading through displays in the ordinary occasions of their interactions the appearances of consistent, coherent, clear, chosen, planful arrangements. In exactly the ways in which a setting is organized, it *consists* of methods whereby its members are provided with accounts of the setting as countable, storyable, proverbial, comparable, picturable, representable—i.e., accountable events," *Studies in Ethnomethodology* (Cambridge: Polity Press, 1984), p. 34.

14. Elster, *Cement of Society*, p. 100. The fact that Elster hedges this claim in the next sentence does little to dispel the sense that he fundamentally mischaracterizes the phenomenon of normative control. Cristina Bicchieri is similarly inclined to regard norms as unconscious scripts that "are activated in the right circumstances," *The Grammar of Society* (Cambridge: Cambridge University Press, 2005), p. 148.

15. Ernst Fehr and Joseph Henrich, "Is Strong Reciprocity a Maladaptation? On the Evolutionary Foundations of Human Altruism," in Peter Hammerstein, ed., *Genetic and Cultural Evolution of Cooperation* (Cambridge, Mass.: MIT Press, 2003), p. 68.

16. This discussion is drawn from the excellent analysis in Heritage, *Garfinkel and Ethnomethodology*, pp. 106–7.

17. One can see a theory of this type in Robert Nozick, *The Nature of Rationality* (Princeton: Princeton University Press, 1993).

18. The phrase comes from Allan Gibbard, *Wise Choices, Apt Feelings* (Cambridge, Mass.: Harvard University Press, 1990), p. 56, but there are few similarities between the way Gibbard conceives of the normative control system and the way that it is analyzed here.

19. Parsons, *Social System*, p. 206.

20. Bicchieri, *Grammar of Society*, p. 52.

21. Matthew Rabin, "Incorporating Fairness into Game Theory and Economics," *American Economic Review* 83 (2003): 1287. Rabin's model has an even more unusual feature, which is that he associates no positive value with mere compliance, but treats only supererogatory action and norm violation as payoff-relevant. Thus his model does not privilege symmetric cooperation over symmetric defection in a collective action problem (see p. 1288).

22. Ernst Fehr and Klaus M. Schmidt, "A Theory of Fairness, Competition and Cooperation," *The Quarterly Journal of Economics*, 114 (1999): 817–68.

23. Bruno Verbeek, *Instrumental Rationality and Moral Philosophy* (Dordrecht: Kluwer, 2002), pp. 102–3.

24. Verbeek, *Instrumental Rationality and Moral Philosophy*, p. 157.

25. Bicchieri, Rabin, and Verbeek further limit the generality of their models by building the conditionality of the agent's willingness to follow the norm (i.e., the fact that the willingness to comply is affected by the expectation that others will comply) directly into each agent's utility function, as opposed to treating it as a consequence of the strategic dimension of the interaction. This strikes me as being unmotivated. Why not retain a utility function that can be fully specified independent of any particular social interaction? As long as the agent retains some concern for payoffs (i.e., norm-conformity is not assigned lexical priority), an aversion to being "suckered" will emerge out of the interaction, as the agent contemplates the consequences of complying with the norm while others defect.

26. Gintis, "Framework for the Unification of the Behavioral Sciences," pp. 2–3.

27. For example, Robert Nozick used the term "side constraints" to describe the way rights function in deliberation. See Nozick, "Moral Constraints and Moral Goals," in Stephen Darwall, ed., *Deontology* (London: Blackwell, 2002), pp. 83–89.

28. Georg Henrik von Wright, *An Essay on Deontic Logic and the General Theory of Action* (Amsterdam: North Holland, 1968), p. 14.

29. Von Wright, *An Essay on Deontic Logic*, pp. 64–68.

30. The precise scale that is used makes no difference. One might be tempted to represent forbidden actions as having negative appropriateness. Similarly, one often represents outcomes as having negative utility. All of these functions remain unique through any positive linear transformation.

31. For concise exposition on lexicographic preferences, see Peter Ordeshook, *Game Theory and Political Theory* (Cambridge: Cambridge University Press, 1986), pp. 17–18.

32. Jean Hampton, *The Authority of Reason* (Cambridge: Cambridge University Press, 1998), p. 282.

33. This term is due to Isaac Levi, *Covenant of Reason* (Cambridge: Cambridge University Press, 1997), p. 74. See also Richard Jeffrey, *The Logic of Decision*, 2nd ed. (Chicago: University of Chicago Press, 1983), pp. 83–84.

34. Jordan Howard Sobel, *Taking Chances* (Cambridge: Cambridge University Press, 1994), p. 13.

35. Following Jeffrey's concept of desirability, *Logic of Decision*, p. 78.

36. Jordan Howard Sobel, "World Bayesianism: Comments on the Hammond/McLennan Debate," in Bertrand R. Munier, ed., *Risk, Decision and Rationality* (Dordrecht: Reidel, 1988), p. 539.

37. Levi, *Covenant of Reason*, p. 85.

38. Some confusion may arise from the fact that some "deontologists" in moral theory *do* argue that consequences are irrelevant to the moral evaluation of the rules we respect in everyday practice. Kant, for example, argued that consequences were irrelevant when it came to justifying particular duties derived from the categorical imperative. Yet he still thought that, at the action-theoretic level, rational agents would take consequences into account in their deliberations. Most obviously, if the categorical imperative licenses some set of actions as permissible, the agent is then free to choose the one that promotes his own happiness.

39. Levi, *Covenant of Reason*, pp. 76–77; also François Lepage, "Qu'est-ce qu'un acte jugé faisable?" *Philosophiques* 28 (2001): 369–80.

40. David McNaughton and Piers Rawling, "Agent-Relativity and the Doing-Happening Distinction," *Philosophical Studies* 63 (1991): 168.

41. For an example of this response, see Brian Skyrms, *Evolution and the Social Contract* (Cambridge: Cambridge University Press, 1996), p. 28.

42. Nonstrategic uncertainty is typically represented by adding "nature" to the game as "player 0," who moves with fixed probability.

43. One can find this recommendation made explicitly in Binmore, *Just Playing: Game Theory and the Social Contract*, vol. 1 (Cambridge, Mass.: MIT Press, 1998), p. 108.

44. Hampton, *Authority of Reason*, p. 264.

45. This "dropping out" of the consequential component of the agent's utility function may also help to explain the behavior that many agents exhibit when facing uncertain events. Experimental game theorists have observed that people are far more likely to cooperate in prisoner's dilemmas when they do not know what their opponent has chosen. Once they have been informed, rates of cooperation plummet, regardless of whether the opponent chose to cooperate or to defect. Eldar Shafir and Amos Tversky, "Penser dans l'incertain," in Jean Pierre Dupuy and Pierre Livet, eds., *Les Limites de la Rationalité* (Paris: La Découverte, 1997), 1:118–50, present the results of one study in which 37 percent of subjects cooperated when their opponent's choice was unknown. When informed of the other's choice, only 3 percent of the same subjects chose to cooperate when the other defected, but more surprisingly, only 16 percent chose to cooperate when the other cooperated (pp. 125–26). One possible explanation is that under conditions of uncertainty, agents are simply loathe to engage in the process of reasoning needed to determine the dominant instrumental strategy, and so simply "lop off" that whole segment of the choice problem. As a result, they are more likely simply to perform whatever action the relevant set of social norms prescribes, which is typically to cooperate.

46. In order to see why people might have "intrinsic" preferences for certain meeting-places over others, for instance, see Gordon H. Orians and Judith H. Heerwagen, "Evolved Responses to Landscapes," in Jerome Barkow, Leda Cosmides, and John Tooby, *The Adapted Mind* (New York: Oxford University Press, 1992).

47. Harry Frankfurt, "Freedom of the Will and the Concept of the Person," in Frankfurt, *The Importance of What We Care About* (Cambridge: Cambridge University Press, 1987).

48. Eugen von Böhm-Bawerk, *Capital and Interest*, trans. William A. Smart (London: Macmillan, 1890); also Irving Fisher, *The Theory of Interest* (New York: MacMillan, 1930).

49. See Eric Rasmusen, *Games and Information*, 2nd ed. (Oxford: Blackwell, 1989), p. 108.

50. This assumption is not as innocuous as it may sound, since it would be impossible to identify real-world violations of completeness or transitivity without it. See Paul Anand, "Are the Preference Axioms Really Rational?" *Theory and Decision* 23 (1987): 189–214.

51. Bicchieri adopts such a similar notational convention, *Grammar of Society*, p. 52.

52. This idea is inspired by the discussion in Henry Allison, *Kant's Theory of Freedom* (Cambridge: Cambridge University Press, 1990), pp. 126–27 (although Allison is presupposing a lexicographic ordering of types of reasons for action).

53. For an overview of different proposals, see Roger Myerson, *Game Theory* (Cambridge, Mass.: Harvard University Press, 1991), pp. 310–16.

54. See Matthew Rabin, "Incorporating Fairness into Game Theory and Economics," *American Economic Review* 83 (2003): 1281–1302; or Gary E. Bolton, "A Comparative Model of Bargaining: Theory and Evidence," *American Economic Review* 81 (1991): 1096–1136. Both of these models are too concrete, in that they build a concern for fairness directly into the agent's utility function.

55. Colin Camerer and Richard H. Thaler, "Ultimatums, Dictators and Manners," *Journal of Economic Perspectives*, 9 (1995): 209–19 at 212.

56. Some theorists, such as Verbeek and Bicchieri, consider it important that the model render the satisfaction that individuals receive from conforming to a norm conditional on the conformity of other players. This strikes me as being something that should remain an open question. For example, does the discovery that a competitor has cheated entirely vitiate the satisfaction that comes from having played fair? For example, do people not derive some satisfaction from voluntarily reducing their environmental footprint, even though they know that many others are not doing so?

57. Eric Rasmusen, *Games and Information*, 2nd ed. (Oxford: Blackwell, 1989), pp. 48–57. See also Bicchieri, *Grammar of Society*, p. 27.

58. Here I am using the term "trust" in the very general sense in which it is used in sociological theory (and especially the literature on social capital). Consider Francis Fukuyama: "Trust is the expectation that arises within a community of regular, honest, and cooperative behavior based on commonly shared norms, on the part of other members of the community," *Trust* (London: Penguin, 1995), p. 26. Naturally, more specific trust relationships can develop as agents acquire greater knowledge of the *particular* norms that individuals accept.

59. See the interesting experiment and discussion in Joyce Berg, John Dickhaut and Kevin McCabe, "Trust, Reciprocity, and Social History," *Games and Economic Behavior* 10 (1995): 122–42.

60. Peter J. Richerson, Robert T. Boyd, and Joseph Henrich, "Cultural Evolution of Human Cooperation," in Hammerstein, *Genetic and Cultural Evolution of Cooperation*, p. 379.

61. Harold Garfinkel, "A Conception of, and Experiments with, 'Trust' as a Condition of Stable, Concerted Actions," in O. J. Harvey, ed., *Motivation and Social Interaction* (New York: Ronald, 1963), pp. 187–238.

62. Compare David Gauthier, *Morals by Agreement* (Oxford: Clarendon Press, 1986), with David Gauthier, "Assure and Threaten," *Ethics* 104 (1994): 690–721.

Chapter 4

1. The former being the central innovation in Leonard J. Savage, *The Foundations of Statistics*, 2nd ed. (New York: Dover, 1972).

2. Michael Dummett, *Origins of Analytical Philosophy* (London: Duckworth, 1993).

3. Michael Dummett, "Language and Communication," in Dummett, *The Seas of Language* (Oxford: Clarendon, 1993), pp. 166–87.

4. Dummett, "Language and Communication," p. 166.

5. Edmund Husserl, *Cartesian Meditations*, trans. Dorion Cairns (The Hague: Martinus Nijhoff, 1977); Ludwig Wittgenstein, *Tractatus Logico-Philosophicus*, ed. D. F. Pears and B. F. McGuinness (London: Routledge, 1974).

6. Michael Dummett, "Frege's Distinction between Sense and Reference," *Truth and Other Enigmas* (Cambridge, Mass.: Harvard University Press, 1978), p. 117.

7. This is the celebrated hypothesis first advanced by Lev Vygotsky, *Mind in Society* (Cambridge, Mass.: Harvard University Press, 1978). See also Stephen Toulmin, "The Inwardness of Mental Life," *Critical Inquiry* 6 (1979): 1–16. For a careful formulation of the thesis, see Peter Carruthers, "Conscious Thinking: Language or Elimination?" *Mind and Language* 13 (1998): 323–42.

8. Andy Clark, *Being There* (Cambridge, Mass.: MIT Press, 1997), p. 195, discussing Laura Berk and Ruth Garvin, "Development and Private Speech among Low-Income Appalachian Children," *Developmental Psychology* 20 (1984): 271–86. See also Laura E. Berk, "Why Children Talk to Themselves," *Scientific American* (November 1994): 78–83.

9. The innateness issue needs to be separated from the externalism issue. The fact that humans pick up grammar so quickly does not mean that language is "built in." They may be adapted to learn from the environment more quickly. This will be discussed more extensively in chapter 6.

10. Michael Dummett, *Frege's Philosophy of Language*, 2nd ed. (Cambridge, Mass.: Harvard University Press, 1981), pp. 298–99.

11. Thomas Hobbes, *On the Citizen*, ed. Richard Tuck and Michael Silverthorne (Cambridge: Cambridge University Press, 1998), pp. 102–3 (sec. 8:1).

12. Dummett, *Origins of Analytical Philosophy*, p. 22.

13. Mark Richards, "Propositional Attitudes," in Bob Hale and Crispin Wright, eds., *Blackwell Companion to Philosophy of Language* (Oxford: Blackwell, 1997), p. 208.

14. A phrase coined by Jerry Fodor, *The Language of Thought* (New York: Crowell, 1975).

15. Roderick Chisholm, "The Problem of the Speckled Hen," *Mind* 51 (1942): 368–73. These problems are all descendants of Descartes's "chiliagon" argument in the sixth of his Meditations. See René Descartes, *Meditations on First Philosophy*, trans. John Cottingham (Cambridge: Cambridge University Press, 1986), pp. 50–51.

16. Saul Kripke, "A Puzzle about Belief," in Avishai Margalit, ed., *Meaning and Use* (Dordrecht: Reidel, 1979), pp. 239–83.

17. Richards, "Propositional Attitudes," pp. 213–16.

18. See Fred Dretske, *Explaining Behavior* (Cambridge, Mass.: MIT Press, 1988), pp. 120–21.

19. Crispin Wright, "How Can the Theory of Meaning Be a Philosophical Project?" *Mind and Language* 1 (1986): 33. Daniel Dennett has observed that we can explain the behavior of a wide range of different complex systems by adopting what he calls "the intentional stance" toward them, namely, explaining their behavior in terms of beliefs and desires. In many cases, we do so despite knowing that this language should not be taken literally. We can describe the decisions of a chess-playing computer in terms of a set of beliefs and desires. Similarly, we often describe the behavior of insects in intentional terms, even in cases where we know that there is no central neuronal processing involved. Thus we often talk about things having beliefs and desires in cases where we clearly do not "really" mean it.

20. Fodor, *Language of Thought*.

21. Keith Stanovich, *The Robot's Rebellion* (Chicago: University of Chicago Press, 2004).

22. Or "functionally specialized, content-dependent, content-sensitive, domain-specific, context-sensitive, special-purpose, adaptively specialized," John Tooby and Leda Cosmides,

"The Psychological Foundations of Culture," in Jerome Barkow, Leda Cosmides, and John Tooby, *The Adapted Mind* (New York: Oxford University Press, 1992), p. 93.

23. Timothy D. Wilson, *Strangers to Ourselves* (Cambridge, Mass.: Harvard University Press, 2002), pp. 17–41.

24. Stanovich, *Robot's Rebellion*, pp. 35–36. On the issue of conscious v. unconscious, see Peter Carruthers, *Language, Thought and Consciousness* (Cambridge: Cambridge University Press, 1996).

25. For an overview of the issues, see Peter Carruthers, "Modularity, Language, and the Flexibility of Thought," *Behavioral and Brain Sciences* 25 (2002): 657–719.

26. Jerry Fodor, *Psychosemantics* (Cambridge, Mass.: MIT Press, 1987), p. 99; also Jerry Fodor, *A Theory of Content and Other Essays* (Cambridge, Mass.: MIT Press, 1982), p. 55.

27. See, for example, Steven Pinker, *The Language Instinct* (New York: Morrow, 1994), pp. 18–21.

28. Pinker, *Language Instinct*, pp. 148–49. See also Michael Tomasello, "Language Is Not an Instinct," *Cognitive Development*, 10 (1995): 135–36.

29. This is generally taken to occur in sections 244–71 of his *Philosophical Investigations*, trans. G. E. M. Anscombe (Oxford: Blackwell, 1953), although even this is subject to dispute.

30. This way of structuring the analysis is due to Robert Brandom, *Making It Explicit* (Cambridge, Mass.: Harvard University Press, 1994).

31. Tim Thornton, *John McDowell* (Montreal: McGill-Queen's University Press, 2004), p. 60. Naturally, proponents of the "language of thought" hypothesis are aware of this. The primary attraction of that theory has always been the way that it can explain the semantic content of more complex symbols via their combinatorial syntax and the semantic value of some more primitive set of atomic symbols. The question of how atomic symbols get their meaning is usually relegated to the status of a promissory note, or an outstanding problem.

32. Crispin Wright, *Realism, Meaning and Truth*, 2nd ed. (Oxford: Blackwell, 1993), pp. 23–29.

33. Wittgenstein, *Philosophical Investigations* (Oxford: Blackwell, 1958), p. 92e (sec. 258). This point is emphasized by John McDowell, "Wittgenstein on Following a Rule," *Synthese* 58 (1984): 325–64.

34. "Stripping it down" is something of an understatement. The private language argument has generated a vast secondary literature, with serious controversy over the correct interpretation of Wittgenstein's claims. I am not hoping to defend one interpretation over others here; I am merely trying to pick out the strain of thinking in the argument that has led many philosophers to become disenchanted with the traditional "individualistic" order of explanation in the understanding of intentional states.

35. This is the point of Wittgenstein's *Philosophical Investigations*, p. 94e (sec. 265).

36. The possibility of such "deviant" interpretations of the rule is the focus of Saul Kripke's concern in *Wittgenstein on Rules and Private Language* (Cambridge, Mass.: Harvard University Press, 1982).

37. Jerry Fodor, *Psychosemantics*, p. 101.

38. The more difficult problem lies in distinguishing between terms that refer to disjunctive properties and those that refer only to one property, but can be mistakenly caused by another. See Fodor, *A Theory of Content*, pp. 59–60. There are a number of proposed solutions, but none have attracted much consensus.

39. Wittgenstein, *Philosophical Investigations*, p. 88e (sec. 241).

40. And thus, pace A. J. Ayer, "Can There Be a Private Language?" *Supplementary Proceedings of the Aristotelian Society* 28 (1954): 63–76, a "Robinson Crusoe child" could not invent a language.

41. It allows us to form what Robert Brandom calls "differential responsive dispositions," *Making It Explicit*, pp. 88–89. He distinguishes, following Wilfrid Sellars, between "responsive" classification and "conceptual" classification. This is analogous to the action-theoretic distinction between behavior and intentional action.

42. Brandom, *Making It Explicit*, p. 5.

43. See Thornton, *John McDowell*, p. 29.

44. Brandom, *Making It Explicit*, pp. 18–30.

45. Brandom, *Making It Explicit*, p. 20.

46. Brandom, *Making It Explicit*, p. 21.

47. Brandom, *Making It Explicit*, p. 28.

48. Brandom, *Making It Explicit*, p. 34. The text under discussion is John Haugeland, "Heidegger on Being a Person," *Nous* 16 (1982): 15–26.

49. Brandom, *Making It Explicit*, p. 36.

50. Brandom, *Making It Explicit*, p. 36.

51. Brandom, *Making It Explicit*, p. 36. Brandom uses a peculiarly noncommital phrase here: "might still be claimed." The significance of this is unclear.

52. This is the view advanced by Kripke, in *Wittgenstein on Rules and Private Language*.

53. Brandom, *Making It Explicit*, pp. 37–39.

54. Brandom, *Making It Explicit*, pp. 44.

55. Brandom, *Making It Explicit*, pp. 44. For a similar argument, see Mark Norris Lance and John O'Leary-Hawthorne, *The Grammar of Meaning* (Cambridge: Cambridge University Press, 1997), pp. 224–27.

56. These are explored further in Joseph Heath, "Brandom et les sources de la normativité," *Philosophiques* 28 (2001): 27–46.

57. This terminology, along with the general idea underlying the analysis, comes from Jürgen Habermas, *The Theory of Communicative Action* (Boston: Beacon Press, 1987), 2:19.

58. Dummett, *Frege's Philosophy of Language*, p. 6.

59. Donald Davidson, "Theories of Meaning and Learnable Languages," in Davidson, *Inquiries into Truth and Interpretation* (Oxford: Clarendon, 1984), pp. 3–16.

60. For discussion see Pascal Engel, *The Norm of Truth*, trans. Miriam Kochan and Pascal Engel (Toronto: University of Toronto Press, 1991).

61. This is one aspect of the "problem of universals." See Gyula Klima, "The Medieval Problem of Universals," in Edward N. Zalta, ed., *Stanford Encyclopedia of Philosophy* (2004), http://plato.stanford.edu/entries/universals-medieval/.

62. Immanuel Kant, *Critique of Pure Reason*, trans. Norman Kemp Smith (New York: St. Martin's Press, 1929), p. 105 (A68/B93).

63. Wittgenstein, *Tractatus Logico-Philosophicus*, p. 8 (sec. 2.0272).

64. Arthur Schopenhauer, *The World as Will and Representation*, 2 vols., trans. E. F. J. Payne (New York: Dover, 1969).

65. Davidson, "Radical Interpretation," in *Inquiries into Truth and Interpretation*, pp. 125–40.

66. "Intents and purposes" may well undergo the same process that turned "spit and image" into "spitting image" in the twentieth century. English contains a large number of these sorts of internally redundant expressions. Apparently the habit of speaking this way arose during the period in which speakers could not be counted on to understand Latin-root loanwords, and so speakers would use the Anglo-Saxon term as well in order to ensure comprehension (e.g., "ways and means," "various and sundry," "straight and narrow," "lo and behold"). Thus many of these expressions began their lives as phrases designed to be understood in terms of their literal meaning. When they became figures of speech, that meaning became "frozen." So while the word "sundry" has changed its

meaning, so that "sundry items" now refers to toiletries, it still means what it used to mean, centuries ago, when used in the phrase "items various and sundry."

67. As an example of this, I had a completely incorrect understanding of the word "nonplussed" for well over a decade—thinking that it meant "unimpressed" rather than "perplexed." The error was able to persist simply because it never led to a misunderstanding severe enough to warrant correction. I only found out the proper meaning one day when I looked the word up in a dictionary, to see whether it was spelled with one *s* or two.

68. See, e.g., Pinker, *Language Instinct*, pp. 57–58, 78–82.

69. Michael Dummett, "Can Analytical Philosophy Be Systematic, and Ought It to Be?" in *Truth and Other Enigmas*, pp. 437–58.

70. Dummett, *Frege's Philosophy of Language*, pp. 308–11.

71. Wilfrid Sellars, "Some Reflections on Language Games," in Sellars, *Science, Perception and Reality* (London: Routledge and Kegan Paul, 1963), p. 327. Sellars actually calls them "entry and departure transitions." The terminology has drifted somewhat since then among those influenced by Sellars's work.

72. Brandom, *Making It Explicit*, p. 168.

73. Brandom, *Making It Explicit*, pp. 378–81.

74. This emphasis on perception has had a number of curious side effects; one in particular is that it makes the concept of a desire, or preference, rather difficult to understand, precisely because intentional states of this type are not obviously representational, or at least not in the same sense in which beliefs are. Hence the inclination to think of them as a quite different sort of mental state, such as a "vital motion," or to identify them with the body more than with the mind.

75. David Lewis, *Convention* (Cambridge, Mass.: Harvard University Press, 1969), p. 144; also Joseph Heath, *Communicative Action and Rational Choice* (Cambridge, Mass.: MIT Press, 2001), p. 30.

76. Andy Clark, "Magic Words: How Language Augments Computation," in Peter Carruthers and Jill Boucher, eds., *Language and Thought* (Cambridge: Cambridge University Press, 1998), p. 162.

77. Clark, "Magic Words," pp. 169–73.

78. Clark, "Magic Words," p. 182.

79. Patricia W. Cheng and Keith J. Holyoak, "Pragmatic Reasoning Schemas," *Cognitive Psychology* 17 (1985): 391–416.

80. See Paul Harris and Maria Núñez, "Understanding of Permission Rules by Preschool Children," *Child Development* 67 (1996): 233–59; also Denise Dellarossa Cummins, "Evidence of Deontic Reasoning in 3- and 4-Year-Old Children," *Memory and Cognition* 24 (1996): 823–29. For discussion, see Shaun Nichols, *Sentimental Rules* (New York: Oxford University Press, 2004), pp. 101–3.

81. Cheng and Holyoak, "Pragmatic Reasoning Schemas," p. 396.

82. Denise Dellarossa Cummins, "Evidence for the Innateness of Deontic Reasoning," *Mind and Language* 11 (1996): 160–90; also Tooby and Cosmides, "Psychological Foundations of Culture," pp. 181–84.

83. Cummins, "Evidence for the Innateness of Deontic Reasoning," p. 174.

84. Daniel Dennett, *Consciousness Explained* (Boston: Little, Brown, 1991), p. 218. It is precisely the inefficiency with which this "serial machine" is implemented that accounts for the demanding requirements, in terms of attention and computational resources, associated with the operations of what Stanovich calls "the analytical system." Incidentally, I am setting aside here the controversial question of the relationship between this "serial virtual machine" and consciousness, since it is not important for the argument being developed here.

85. Stanovich, *Robot's Rebellion*, pp. 34–36.

86. Monica Bucciarelli, Sangeet Khemlani, and Philip N. Johnson-Laird, "The Psychology of Moral Reasoning," *Judgment and Decision Making* 3 (2008): 121–39, at 124.

87. Elizabeth S. Spelke and Sanna Tsivkin, "Language and Number: A Bilingual Training Study," *Cognition* 78 (2001): 81–82.

88. Peter Carruthers, "Practical Reasoning in a Modular Mind," *Mind and Language* 19 (2004): 29–278. Note that Carruthers differs from the view presented here, in that he finds it helpful to conceive of language as itself a module.

89. The suggestion is that this ability develops as an internalization of the practice of following instructions. Clark, "Magic Words," p. 168. Dennett is fond of the idea that language enhances self-control and planning through "autostimulation," essentially providing an external work-around to compensate for the absence of certain neural pathways, *Consciousness Explained*, p. 196. This idea has a long history, and was given its canonical formulation by George Herbert Mead, *Mind, Self and Society* (Chicago: University of Chicago Press, 1934), who argues that producing symbols gives the individual the power of "calling out the response he calls out in another," p. 108.

90. See Daniel Kahneman, Paul Slovic, and Amos Tversky, eds., *Judgment under Uncertainty* (Cambridge: Cambridge University Press, 1982).

91. For excellent discussion, see Stanovich, *Robot's Rebellion*, pp. 142–46.

92. Donald A. Norman and Tim Shallice, "Attention to Action: Willed and Automatic Control of Behaviour," in Richard J. Davidson, Gary Schwartz, and David Shapiro, eds., *Consciousness and Self-Regulation* (New York: Plenum, 1986), 4: 1–18.

93. See Dennett, *Consciousness Explained*, p. 215. This is because our own analytical system, to which we have introspective access, is what provided the inspiration for the von Neumann architecture of traditional computers. "This historical fact has left a particularly compelling fossil trace: computer programmers will tell you that it is fiendishly difficult to program the parallel computers currently being developed, and relatively easy to program a serial, von Neumann machine. When you program a conventional von Neumann machine, you have a handy crutch; when the going gets tough, you ask yourself, in effect, 'What would I do if I were the machine, trying to solve this problem?' and this leads you to an answer of the form, 'Well, first I'd do this, and then I'd have to do that, etc.' But if you ask yourself, 'What would I do in this situation if I were a thousand-channel-wide parallel processor?' you draw a blank; you don't have any personal familiarity with—and 'direct access to'—processes happening in a thousand channels at once, even though that is what is going on in your brain. Your only access to what is going on in your brain comes in a sequential 'format' that is strikingly reminiscent of the von Neumann architecture—although putting it that way is historically backwards," p. 215.

94. Dennett, *Consciousness Explained*, p. 190. On exaptation, see Stephen J. Gould and Elisabeth S. Vrba, "Exaptation—A Missing Term in the Science of Form," *Paleobiology* 8 (1982): 4–15. For a more detailed statement of the exaptation thesis, see Derek Bickerton, "How Protolanguage Became Language," in Chris Knight, Michael Studdert-Kennedy, and James R. Hurford, eds., *The Evolutionary Emergence of Language* (Cambridge: Cambridge Univeristy Press, 2000), pp. 266–70.

95. Tooby and Cosmides, "Psychological Foundations of Culture," p. 94.

96. Derek Bickerton, "Resolving Discontinuity: A Minimalist Distinction between Human and Non-human Minds," *American Zoologist* 40 (2000): 862–73.

97. Marc D. Hauser and Elizabeth Spelke, "Evolutionary and Developmental Foundations of Human Knowledge: A Case Study of Mathematics," in Michael Gazzaniga, *The Cognitive Neurosciences*, (Cambridge, Mass.: MIT Press, 2004), 3: 853–64.

98. Spelke and Tsivkin, "Language and Number," 81–82.

99. Roger Thompson and David Oden, "A Profound Disparity Re-visited: Perception and Judgment of Abstract Identity Relations by Chimpanzees, Human Infants and Monkeys," *Behavioural Processes* 35 (1995): 149–61; Clark, "Magic Words," p. 175.

100. This reification generates the position that Michael Williams refers to as "epistemological realism" (i.e. realism about the objects posited in epistemology). For a more comprehensive critique of this tendency, see his *Unnatural Doubts* (Oxford: Blackwell, 1992).

101. This argument has been advanced with considerable force by Robert Brandom, in "Modality, Normativity, and Intentionality," *Philosophy and Phenomenological Research* 63 (2001): 587–610. Brandom points out, in particular, that philosophers of a naturalistic temperament often help themselves to the notion of causality, without providing any sort of naturalistic account of the modal judgments (such as counterfactual claims) that all judgments of causality imply. They then use this concept of causality to explain normative ideas like representation. The pragmatist perspective, on the other hand, takes deontic modalities, explained in terms of social practices, to be primitive. The alethic (or doxastic) modalities are then derived from the deontic ones. (This explains the structural parallels noted in chapter 3, section 2.)

102. Clark, *Being There*, p. 191.

103. See Gilbert Harman, *Change of View* (Cambridge, Mass.: MIT Press, 1986).

Chapter 5

1. David Hume, *A Treatise of Human Nature*, 2nd ed., ed. L. A. Selby-Bigge (Oxford: Clarendon, 1978), p. 517.

2. St. Augustine, *The City of God against the Pagans*, ed. and trans. R. W. Dyson (Cambridge: Cambridge University Press, 1998), pp. 615–16 (bk. 14, chap. 17).

3. See Philip Pettit and Michael Smith, "Freedom in Belief and Desire," *Journal of Philosophy* 93 (1996): 429–49.

4. The term is used to describe moral discourse by Peter Railton, "Moral Realism: Prospects and Problems," in Walter Sinnott-Armstrong and Mark Timmins, eds., *Moral Knowledge?* (New York: Oxford University Press, 1996), pp. 59–60.

5. Amos Tversky, "Intransitivity of Preferences," *Psychological Review* 76 (1969): 31.

6. Leonard J. Savage, *The Foundations of Statistics*, 2nd ed. (New York: Dover, 1972), pp. 19–21.

7. See Stephen Toulmin, *The Place of Reason in Ethics* (Cambridge: Cambridge University Press, 1950), pp. 63–64.

8. Hume, *A Treatise of Human Nature*, p. 459.

9. Bernard Williams, "Internal and External Reasons," in *Moral Luck* (Cambridge: Cambridge University Press, 1981), pp. 101–13.

10. Thomas Nagel, *The Possibility of Altruism* (Princeton: Princeton University Press, 1970), p. 28.

11. Michael Smith, *The Moral Problem* (Oxford: Blackwell, 1994), p. 99.

12. Michael Smith, "The Humean Theory of Motivation," *Mind* 96 (1987): 54.

13. Nagel notices this: "Although it will no doubt be generally admitted that some desires are motivated, the issue is whether another desire always lies behind the motivated one, or whether sometimes the motivation of the initial desire involves no reference to another, unmotivated desire," *Possibility of Altruism*, p. 29.

14. Christine M. Korsgaard, "Skepticism about Practical Reason," in Korsgaard, *Creating the Kingdom of Ends* (Cambridge: Cambridge University Press, 1996), pp. 311–34.

15. R. Jay Wallace, "How to Argue about Practical Reason," *Mind* 99 (1990): 371.

16. Smith, "Humean Theory of Motivation," p. 59. Interestingly, Smith drops this iteration defense of the desire-in desire-out thesis in the rewrite of the article that appears in *The Moral Problem*. Unfortunately, he continues to refer to "underived" desires, even though he no longer presents an argument to show that such things exist.

17. For the former, see Wallace, "How to Argue about Practical Reason," the latter Korsgaard, "Skepticism about Practical Reason."

18. See Donald Davidson, "A Coherence Theory of Truth and Knowledge," in Ernest LePore, ed., *Truth and Interpretation: Perspectives on the Philosophy of Donald Davidson* (Blackwell: Oxford, 1986), pp. 307–19.

19. Aristotle, *Physics*, trans. Robin Waterfield (New York: Oxford University Press, 1996), pp. 207–11 (VIII 6: 258b10–259b20).

20. The distinction between "unmotivated" and "motivated" desires is due to Nagel, *Possibility of Altruism*, p. 29.

21. For an example of this view, based on a regress argument, see Paul Anand, "Are the Preference Axioms Really Rational?" *Theory and Decision* 23 (1987): 189–214.

22. David Hume, *Enquiries Concerning Human Understanding and Concerning the Principles of Morals*, 3rd ed., ed. L. A. Selby-Bigge (Oxford: Clarendon, 1975), p. 293.

23. William Alston, *Epistemic Justification* (Ithaca, N.Y.: Cornell University Press, 1989), p. 54.

24. For instance, Smith distances himself from what he calls "the phenomenological conception of desire," *Moral Problem*, pp. 104–11.

25. Thus, according to Bernard Williams, when arguing morality with an agent who does not already possess the right motives, the only "glue" that we have with which to stick the moral ought to the agent "is social and psychological," *Moral Luck*, p. 122.

26. St. Thomas Aquinas, *Summa Theologica*, trans. Fathers of the English Dominican Province (New York: Benzinger, 1947), p. 586 (Ia IIae, qu. 1, art. 4).

27. Christine Korsgaard, "Aristotle and Kant on the Source of Value," in *Creating the Kingdom of Ends*, 227. This regress argument also structures much of the discussion in Korsgaard, *The Sources of Normativity* (Cambridge: Cambridge University Press, 1996), where she posits the need for an "*intrinsically normative entity*...that brings a regress of justification to a satisfactory end," p. 111.

28. Nagel, *Possibility of Altruism*, p. 4.

29. See Warren Quinn, "Putting Rationality in Its Place," in Quinn, *Morality and Action* (Cambridge: Cambridge University Press, 1993), p. 244. Other theorists tempted by the idea that desires require supplementation by some higher-order principle or motive before they can provide reasons for action include Jean Hampton, *The Authority of Reason* (Cambridge: Cambridge University Press, 1998), pp. 127–28; Korsgaard, *Sources of Normativity*, p. 97; and Barbara Herman, *The Practice of Moral Judgment* (Cambridge, Mass.: Harvard University Press, 1993), pp. 194–95, 229. This argument is fine so long as one is thinking of desires as nonintentional somatic states. It is not an attractive strategy, I will argue, if one is using the term "desire" to refer to an intentional state, understood as a type of deontic status.

30. Wilfrid Sellars, *Empiricism and the Philosophy of Mind* (Cambridge, Mass.: Harvard University Press, 1997), p. 33.

31. This way of formulating the issue is due to Crispin Wright, *Truth and Objectivity* (Cambridge, Mass.: Harvard University Press, 1992).

32. W. V. O. Quine, *From a Logical Point of View*, 2nd ed. (Cambridge, Mass.: Harvard University Press, 1961).

33. Susan Haack, *Evidence and Inquiry* (Oxford: Blackwell, 1993).

34. Michael Williams, *Unnatural Doubts* (Oxford: Blackwell, 1992), pp. 117–18, Wittgenstein citation from *On Certainty* (Oxford: Blackwell, 1969), p. 33 (sec. 250).

35. Robert Brandom, *Making It Explicit* (Cambridge, Mass.: Harvard University Press, 1993), p. 222.

36. Brandom, *Making It Explicit*, pp. 218–20.

37. Ludwig Wittgenstein, *Philosophical Investigations* (Oxford: Blackwell, 1958), 117e (sec. 381).

38. Brandom, *Making It Explicit*, p. 223; W. V. O. Quine, "Epistemology Naturalized," in *Ontological Relativity and Other Essays* (New York: Columbia University Press, 1969).

39. Brandom, *Making It Explicit*, p. 223.

40. For the classic statement, see Alvin Goldman, *Epistemology and Cognition* (Cambridge, Mass.: Harvard University Press, 1986).

41. For the account of impressions, see Hume, *Treatise of Human Nature*, pp. 86–94.

42. Sellars, *Empiricism and the Philosophy of Mind*, p. 33.

43. See Timothy Wilson, *Strangers to Ourselves* (Cambridge, Mass.: Harvard University Press, 2002), pp. 97–98.

44. Wilson, *Strangers to Ourselves*, pp. 100–102.

45. Daniel T. Gilbert and Timothy D. Wilson, "Miswanting: Some Problems in the Forecasting of Future Affective States," in Sarah Lichtenstein and Paul Slovic, eds., *The Construction of Preference* (Cambridge: Cambridge University Press, 2006), p. 562.

46. Daniel Kahnemann, "New Challenges to the Rationality Assumption," in Lichtenstein and Slovic, *Construction of Preference*, 495.

47. Does it even make sense to treat desire as different from belief? Why not just say that desires are beliefs about what we want? The only problem is that this fails to capture the difference in "direction of fit" of the two intentional states. Thus it fails the test of expressive adequacy, by obscuring a distinction that plays an important part of our folk-psychological vocabulary (which is in turn introduced as a way of describing positions in the game of giving and asking for reasons).

48. Thus an objectivist like Quinn, who argues that one must bring in "an evaluation of the desired object as good" in order to get from the somatic state of thirst to a desire capable of "rationalizing" action, is just like the internalist in epistemology, who claims that one must execute a reliability inference regarding one's own perceptual capacities, in order to get from seeing a red ball to believing that there is a red ball (e.g. Lawrence Bonjour, *The Structure of Empirical Knowledge* [Cambridge, Mass.: Harvard University Press, 1985], pp. 118–19). Both of these moves arise in response to a solid philosophical intuition, namely, that there is a "gap" between the perceptual experience and the intentional state, since the latter is a normative status and the former is not. But to introduce a third principle, in order to baptize the perceptual experience and see it reborn with normative status, is simply to initiate a problematic regress. The notion of a "language-entry" move avoids this difficulty, by specifying that a move can be made directly from a position outside the game of giving and asking for reasons to a position inside. The normative status of the latter is due to the fact that the move is rule-governed, and hence defeasible. See Robert Brandom, "Non-inferential Knowledge, Perceptual Experience, and Secondary Qualities," in Nicholas H. Smith, ed., *Reading McDowell* (London: Routledge, 2002), pp. 95–97.

49. There is considerable merit in Herman's analysis of what she calls "the deliberative field," especially the suggestion "that we think of an agent's deliberative field as containing representations of her interests, projects and commitments that have been 'normalized' to varying degrees to the principles of practical agency, both moral and non-moral," *Practice of Moral Judgment*, p. 198. My inclination, however, would be to identify

the deliberative field with what I have been calling the intentional planning system, and thus to treat all preferences, including desires, as elements within this field.

50. For a very interesting survey of the psychological literature, see Michael Ross, "Relation of Implicit Theories to the Construction of Personal Histories," *Psychological Review* 96 (1989): 341–57. See also Timothy D. Wilson, *Strangers to Ourselves* (Cambridge, Mass.: Harvard University Press, 2002), pp. 86–91.

51. James R. Averill, "A Constructivist View of Emotion," in Robert Plutchik and Henry Kellerman, eds., *Emotion: Theory, Research, and Experience*, vol. 1 (New York: Academic, 1980), 305–39.

52. Wilson, *Strangers to Ourselves*, pp. 107–8.

53. See the articles in Rom Harré, ed., *The Social Construction of Emotion* (Oxford: Blackwell, 1986).

54. Wilson, *Strangers to Ourselves*, pp. 130–34.

55. See David C. McCLelland, Richard Koestner, and Joel Weinberger, "How Do Self-Attributed and Implicit Motives Differ?" *Psychological Review* 86 (1989): 690–702. They summarize the distinction nicely when saying that "implicit motives predict spontaneous behavioral trends over time, whereas self-attributed motives predict immediate specific responses to specific situations or choice behavior," p. 691.

56. For survey, see Timothy Wilson and Daniel Gilbert, "Affective Forecasting," in Mark P. Zanna, ed., *Advances in Experimental Social Psychology*, vol. 35 (San Diego: Academic Press, 2003), pp. 345–411. For a classic study on lottery winners, see Philip Brickman, Dan Coates, and Ronnie Janoff-Bulman, "Lottery Winners and Accident Victims: Is Happiness Relative?" *Journal of Personality and Social Psychology* 25 (1978): 917–27.

57. Wilson, *Strangers to Ourselves*, pp. 110–12. Also Kahnemann, "New Challenges to the Rationality Assumption," p. 495.

58. Peter R. Giancola, "Executive Functioning: A Conceptual Framework for Alcohol-Related Aggression," *Experimental and Clinical Psychopharmacology* 8 (2000): 576–97, at 582.

59. There is evidence that people with "low deliberative efficiency" use various affective heuristics when making complex decisions, but these are crowded out by rational deliberation; they do not underlie it. See Ellen Peters, "The Functions of Affect in the Construction of Preferences," in Lichtenstein and Slovic, *Construction of Preference*, p. 457.

60. See "Excuse Me. May I Have Your Seat," *New York Times* (Sept. 14, 2004), for interesting interviews with former students of Stanley Milgram, who participated in his experiment that involved asking strangers to give up their seats on the New York subway.

61. See, for example, Talcott Parsons, *The Structure of Social Action*, 2 vols. (New York: McGraw Hill, 1937), pp. 456–58. Recall also Jon Elster's claim, cited above, that "the operation of norms is to a large extent blind, compulsive, mechanical or even unconscious," *The Cement of Society* (Cambridge: Cambridge University Press, 1989), p. 100.

62. John Heritage, *Garfinkel and Ethnomethodology* (Cambridge: Polity Press, 1984), pp. 106–10.

63. J. L. Mackie, *Ethics: Inventing Right and Wrong* (London: Penguin, 1977), p. 79.

64. Mackie, *Ethics*, p. 44.

65. See Richard M. Hare, *The Language of Morals* (Oxford: Oxford University Press, 1963), pp. 28–30.

66. Ap Dijksterhuis and John A. Bargh, "The Perceptual-Behavior Expressway: Automatic Effects of Social Perception and Social Behavior," in M. Zanna, ed., *Advances in Experimental Social Psychology*, vol. 30 (New York: Academic Press, 2001), pp. 1–40. See also John A. Bargh and Tanya L. Chartrand, "The Unbearable Automaticity of Being," *American Psychologist* 54 (1999): 467–468.

67. Ap Djiksterhuis, "Why We Are Social Animals: The High Road to Imitation as Social Glue," in Susan Hurley and Nick Chater, eds., *Perspectives on Imitation: From Neuroscience to Social Science*, 2 vols. (Cambridge, Mass.: MIT Press, 2005), 2:217.

68. Shaun Nichols, *Sentimental Rules* (New York: Oxford University Press, 2004), pp. 20–21n9.

69. See Andy Clark, "Epilogue: A Brain Speaks," in Clark, *Being There* (Cambridge, Mass.: MIT Press, 1997).

70. Brandom, *Making It Explicit*, p. 245. Also Robert Brandom, *Articulating Reasons* (Cambridge, Mass.: Harvard University Press, 2000), p. 84.

71. This term is due to Donald Davidson, "Actions, Reasons and Causes," in Davidson, *Essays on Actions and Events* (Oxford: Oxford University Press, 1980).

72. Brandom, *Making it Explicit*, pp. 248–49.

73. Brandom, *Making it Explicit*, p. 249.

74. Brandom, *Making it Explicit*, pp. 97–102.

75. Allowing them to do so would create what Michael Bratman calls the "bootstrapping problem." Bratman, *Intentions, Plans and Practical Reason* (Cambridge, Mass.: Harvard University Press, 1987), pp. 24–27.

76. See Jonathan Dancy, "The Argument from Illusion," *Philosophical Quarterly* 45 (1995): 421–38.

77. Michael Bratman, "Robinson Crusoe," in *The Faces of Intention* (Cambridge: Cambridge University Press, 1999), p. 2.

78. Bratman, "Shared Intention," in *Faces of Intention*. See also David Gauthier, "Assure and Threaten," *Ethics* 104 (1994): 690–721.

79. Claire Finkelstein, "Rational Temptation," in Chrisopher W. Morris and Arthur Ripstein, eds., *Practical Rationality and Preference* (Cambridge: Cambridge University Press, 2001), p. 61.

80. Donald Davidson, "How Is Weakness of the Will Possible?" in *Essays on Actions and Events* (Oxford: Oxford University Press, 1980).

81. See Wilfrid Sellars, "Phenomenalism," in *Science, Perception and Reality* (London: Routledge and Kegan Paul, 1963), pp. 60–105.

82. Of course, many philosophers have argued that they simply fail to discharge this function. As Davidson writes, "introducing intermediate steps or entities into the causal chain, like sensations or observations, serves only to make the epistemological problem more obvious. For if the intermediaries are merely causes, they don't justify the beliefs they cause, while if they deliver information, they may be lying. The moral is obvious. Since we can't swear intermediaries to truthfulness, we should allow no intermediaries between our beliefs and their objects in the world. Of course there are causal intermediaries. What we must guard against are epistemic intermediaries," "Coherence Theory of Truth and Knowledge," p. 312.

83. Sellars, *Empiricism and the Philosophy of Mind*, p. 36.

84. Sellars, "Some Reflections on Language Games," in *Science, Perception and Reality*, p. 350.

85. Gregory Kavka, "The Toxin Puzzle," *Analysis* 43 (1983): 33–34.

Chapter 6

1. Unfortunately, this has been accompanied by a shift toward "behavioral economics," which drops the "rational actor" model entirely and seeks to predict behavior merely on the basis of observed regularities. This tacitly grants the traditional model of instru-

mental rationality a monopoly on the concept of "rationality." A more attractive strategy—the one pursued here—is to use these experimental results as a basis for revising the traditional *homo economicus* model of rationality.

2. E. O. Wilson, *The Insect Societies* (Cambridge, Mass.: Harvard University Press, 1974); also Donald.T. Campbell, "Conflicts between Biological and Social Evolution and between Psychology and Moral Tradition," *American Psychology* 30 (1975): 1103–26.

3. Peter Richerson and Robert Boyd, "The Evolution of Human Ultrasociality," in Irenaus Eibl-Eibesfeldt and Frank Kemp Salter, eds., *Indoctrinability, Ideology, and Warfare: Evolutionary Perspectives* (New York: Berghahn, 1998), pp. 71–95.

4. Robert Boyd and Peter Richerson, "Solving the Puzzle of Human Cooperation," in Stephen Levinson and Pierre Jaisson, eds., *Evolution and Culture* (Cambridge, Mass.: MIT Press, 2005).

5. In the spirit of W. D. Hamilton, "The Evolution of Altruistic Behavior," *American Naturalist* 97 (1963): 354–56; and Robert Trivers, "The Evolution of Reciprocal Altruism," *Quarterly Review of Biology* 46 (1971): 35–57.

6. E.g. see Vero Copner Wynne-Edwards, *Animal Dispersion in Relation to Social Behavior* (Edinburgh: Oliver and Boyd, 1962).

7. Lee Dugatkin, *Cheating Monkeys and Citizen Bees* (New York: Free Press, 1998), pp. 17–18.

8. George C. Williams, *Adaptation and Natural Selection: A Critique of Some Current Evolutionary Thought* (Princeton: Princeton University Press, 1966).

9. The observation is due to Ronald Fisher, *The Genetic Theory of Natural Selection* (Oxford: Clarendon Press, 1930), although he did not use these terms.

10. W. D. Hamilton, "The Evolution of Altruistic Behavior"; also J. Maynard Smith, "Group Selection and Kin Selection," *Nature* 201 (1964): 1145–47.

11. Richard Dawkins, *The Selfish Gene*, 2nd ed. (Oxford: Oxford University Press, 1989).

12. I remain agnostic, throughout this discussion, on the question of exactly what a "gene" is. See Lenny Moss, *What Genes Can't Do* (Cambridge, Mass.: MIT Press, 2003). Nothing important in my argument hinges on this question, so far as I am aware.

13. Dawkins, *The Selfish Gene*, p. 19.

14. Dawkins, *The Selfish Gene*, p. 2.

15. M. Soler, J. J. Soler, J. G. Martínez, T. Pérez-Contreras, and A. P. Møller, "Microevolutionary Change and Population Dynamics of a Brood Parasite and Its Primary Host: The Intermittent Arms Race Hypothesis," *Oecologia* 117 (1998): 381–90.

16. Joan B. Silk, Sarah F. Brosnan, Jennifer Vonk, Joseph Henrich, Daniel J. Povinelli, Amanda S. Richardson, Susan P. Lambeth, Jenny Mascaro, and Steven J. Schapiro, "Chimpanzees Are Indifferent to the Welfare of Unrelated Group Members," *Nature* 437 (2005): 1357–59.

17. Sarah Hall Sternglanz, James L. Gray, and Melvin Murakami, "Adult Preferences for Infantile Facial Features: An Ethological Approach," *Animal Behavior* 25 (1977): 108–15.

18. This hypothesis was first advanced by Konrad Lorenz. See C. F. Zachariah Boukydis, "Adult Perception of Infant Appearance: A Review," *Child Psychiatry and Human Development* 11 (1981): 245.

19. Anne Fernald, "Human Maternal Vocalizations to Infants as Biologically Relevant Signals: An Evolutionary Perspective," in Jerome Barkow, Leda Cosmides, and John Tooby, *The Adapted Mind* (New York: Oxford University Press, 1992), pp. 398–401.

20. Dugatkin, *Cheating Monkeys and Citizen Bees*, p. 18.

21. Boukydis, "Adult Perception of Infant Appearance: A Review," p. 242.

22. Lisa M. Debruine, "Facial Resemblance Enhances Trust," *Proceedings of the Royal Society: Biological Sciences*, 269 (2002): 1307–12.

23. Frans de Waal, *Primates and Philosophers* (Princeton: Princeton University Press, 2006), pp. 24–25.

24. Martin L. Hoffman, "Sex Differences in Empathy and Related Behaviors," *Psychological Bulletin* 84 (1977): 712–22; Mark H. Davis, *Empathy: A Social Psychological Approach* (Boulder, Colo.: Westview Press, 1994). There is also, unsurprisingly, evidence that women show a stronger response to babies and toddlers. See Katherine A. Hildebrandt and Hiram E. Fitzgerald, "Adults' Response to Infants Varying in Perceived Cuteness," *Behavioral Processes* 3 (1978): 169.

25. Terrence Deacon, *The Symbolic Species* (New York: Norton, 1998), p. 244.

26. Keith Stanovich, *The Robot's Rebellion* (Chicago: University of Chicago Press, 2004).

27. Trivers, "Evolution of Reciprocal Altruism." For a useful, recent survey, see Rajiv Sethi and E. Somanathan, "Understanding Reciprocity," *Journal of Economic Behavior and Organization* 50 (2003): 1–27.

28. Robert Axelrod, *The Evolution of Cooperation* (New York: Basic Books, 1984).

29. There has also been a recent surge of skepticism about the extent of reciprocity-based cooperation, based on more careful attention to the distinction between genuine reciprocity, pseudoreciprocity, and byproduct mutualism—the latter being cases in which traits arise that are individually advantageous yet also have spillover effects for some others, who in turn may develop traits that generate spillover benefits. An example would be butterfly larvae who "feed" ants, who in turn protect the larvae from predators. The behavior of the ants, however, is one that is exhibited with *any* food source. Thus there is no real reciprocity here, because the behavior of the ants has no evolutionary connection to what the larvae are doing, and the trait would not change even if the larvae were to disappear. See Olaf Leimar and Richard C. Connor, "By-product Benefits, Reciprocity, and Pseudoreciprocity in Mutualism," in Peter Hammerstein, ed., *Genetic and Cultural Evolution of Cooperation* (Cambridge, Mass.: MIT Press, 2003), pp. 203–22.

30. See Scott Woodcock and Joseph Heath, "The Robustness of Altruism as an Evolutionary Strategy," *Biology and Philosophy* 17 (2002): 567–90.

31. See Woodcock and Heath, "Robustness of Altruism as an Evolutionary Strategy"; also Robert Boyd and Peter Richerson, "The Evolution of Reciprocity in Sizable Groups," in Boyd and Richerson, *The Origin and Evolution of Cultures* (Oxford: Oxford University Press, 2005), pp. 152–58.

32. On the former see Drew Fudenberg and Jean Tirole, *Game Theory* (Cambridge, Mass.: MIT Press, 1991), pp. 172–74. For a concrete model of this type, see Joseph Heath, "A Multi-stage Game Model of Morals by Agreement," *Dialogue* 35 (1996): 529–52.

33. Richard Alexander, *Darwinism and Human Affairs* (Seattle: University of Washington Press, 1979); also Richard Alexander, *The Biology of Moral Systems* (New York: de Gruyter, 1987); Martin A. Nowak and Karl Sigmund, "The Dynamics of Indirect Reciprocity," *Journal of Theoretical Biology* 134 (1998): 561–74.

34. See, for instance, Brian Skyrms, *The Evolution of the Social Contract* (Cambridge: Cambridge University Press, 1996), pp. 102–3. He switches to an evolutionary framework in order to make the multiple-equilibrium problem in David Lewis–style signaling games go away (see chapter 1, section 3 here) and then suggests that this is a useful point of departure for thinking about human linguistic conventions.

35. Philip Kitcher, "The Evolution of Human Altruism," *Journal of Philosophy* 90 (1993): 497–516.

36. Philip Kitcher, "Games Social Animals Play: Commentary on Brian Skyrms's *Evolution of the Social Contract*," *Philosophy and Phenomenological Research* 59 (1999): 225.

37. Skyrms, *Evolution of the Social Contract*, p. 21. See Justin D'Arms, "Sex, Justice, and the Theory of Games," *Journal of Philosophy* 93 (1996): 623–24.

38. Kitcher, "Games Social Animals Play," p. 225.

39. Peter J. Richerson, Robert T. Boyd, and Joseph Henrich, "Cultural Evolution of Human Cooperation," in Hammerstein, *Genetic and Cultural Evolution of Cooperation*, p. 379.

40. Robert T. Boyd and Peter J. Richerson, "The Evolution of Reciprocity in Sizeable Groups," *Journal of Theoretical Biology* 132 (1988): 337–56; also Robert Boyd and Peter Richerson, "Punishment Allows the Evolution of Cooperation (or Anything Else) in Sizable Groups," *Ethology and Sociobiology* 13 (1992): 174.

41. Ernst Fehr and Joseph Henrich, "Is Strong Reciprocity a Maladaptation? On the Evolutionary Foundations of Human Altruism," in Hammerstein, *Genetic and Cultural Evolution of Cooperation*, pp. 55–82.

42. Franz de Waal, *Chimpanzee Politics*, rev. ed. (Baltimore: Johns Hopkins University Press, 1998).

43. Trivers moots this friendship hypothesis in "Evolution of Reciprocal Altruism," p. 48. See also Michael Argyle and Monika Henderson, "The Rules of Friendship," *Journal of Social and Personal Relationships* 1 (1984): 211–37. On group biases, see Henri Tajfel, *Differentiation among Social Groups* (London: Academic Press, 1978); also Henri Tajfel, *Human Groups and Social Categories* (Cambridge: Cambridge University Press, 1981).

44. Kitcher, "Games Social Animals Play," p. 225.

45. John C. Mitani, "Reciprocal Exchange in Chimpanzees and Other Primates," in Peter M. Kappeler and Carel P. van Schaik, eds., *Cooperation in Primates and Humans* (Berlin: Springer, 2005), pp. 113–14; De Waal, *Primates and Philosophers*, p. 43.

46. Joan Silk, "The Evolution of Cooperation in Primate Groups," in Herbert Gintis, Samuel Bowles, Robert Boyd, and Ernst Fehr, eds., *Moral Sentiments and Material Interests: On the Foundations of Cooperation in Economic Life* (Cambridge, Mass.: MIT Press, 2003), p. 17.

47. Joan Silk, "Cooperation without Counting: The Puzzle of Friendship," in Hammerstein, *Genetic and Cultural Evolution of Cooperation*, pp. 50–51.

48. De Waal, *Chimpanzee Politics*, p. 201.

49. See, e.g., Dugatkin, *Cheating Monkeys and Citizen Bees*. Philosophers have also been inclined to think that some extension of reciprocity must be at work. See Richard Joyce, *The Evolution of Morality* (Cambridge, Mass.: MIT Press, 2006), pp. 140–41.

50. This is the central problem with de Waal's argument, in his Tanner Lectures (*Primates and Philosophers*). He is at such pains to emphasize the continuities in social behavior between humans and other primates that he provides an account that is unable to explain the discontinuities—in particular, the fact that humans alone engage in large-scale cooperation among unrelated individuals.

51. Boyd and Richerson, "Evolution of Human Ultrasociality," p. 72.

52. Elliot Sober and David Wilson, *Unto Others* (Cambridge, Mass.: Harvard University Press, 1998).

53. Sober and Wilson, *Unto Others*, pp. 135–42.

54. Boyd and Richerson, "Evolution of Ultra-Sociality," p. 80.

55. Richard Bryne and Andrew Whitten, eds., *Machiavellian Intelligence* (Oxford: Oxford University Press, 1998).

56. A particularly striking instance of the failure to recognize this problem can be found in Peter Singer, *The Expanding Circle: Ethics and Sociobiology* (New York: Farrar, Straus and Giroux, 1981), pp. 100–101. How could "rationality" evolve, if one of its direct

consequences were to make individuals indifferent between their own welfare and that of some other unrelated person? As Kim Sterelny observes, "Machiavellian versions of the social intelligence hypothesis" are well-motivated. Since "increased cognitive sophistication brings improved strategies of deception, counter-deception and cabal formation," it provides obvious benefits to the individual. "Social Intelligence, Human Intelligence and Niche Construction," *Philosophical Transactions of the Royal Society: Biology*, 362 (2007): 719–30 at 721. The link between increased cognitive sophistication and increased cooperativeness, on the other hand, is far from clear.

57. Robin Dunbar, "Neocortical Size as a Constraint on Group Size in Primates," *Journal of Human Evolution* 22 (1992): 469–93.

58. Robert H. Frank, "If Homo-Economicus Could Choose His Own Utility Function, Would He Want One with a Conscience?" *American Economic Review* 77(1987): 593–604, Robert H. Frank, *Passions within Reason* (New York: Norton, 1988); and Richard Joyce, *The Evolution of Morality* (Cambridge, Mass.: MIT Press, 2006).

59. Silk, "The Evolution of Cooperation in Primate Groups.

60. Samuel Bowles and Herbert Gintis, "The Evolution of Strong Reciprocity," *Theoretical Population Biology* 65 (2004): 17–28.

61. Herbert Gintis, "Why Do We Cooperate?" *Boston Review*, February/March 1998, p. 38.

62. Fehr and Henrich, "Is Strong Reciprocity a Maladaptation?" pp. 61–62.

63. Herbert Gintis and Samuel Bowles, "Strong Reciprocity and Human Sociality," *Journal of Theoretical Biology* 206 (2000): 169–79.

64. Cristina Bicchieri, "Local Fairness," *Philosophy and Phenomenological Research* 59 (1999): 231.

65. In later work, Gintis subtly reclassifies the norms governing gift exchange as a type of "fairness" concern. Herbert Gintis, "Solving the Puzzle of Prosociality," *Rationality and Society* 15 (2003): 170. This makes the term "fairness" essentially vacuous, making it preferable to state simply that agents respect norms, rather than "norms of fairness," p. 170.

66. This discussion is drawn from Robert Frank and Philip J. Cook, *The Winner-Take-All Society* (New York: Penguin, 1995), p. 172.

67. For further discussion, see Joseph Heath, *The Efficient Society* (Toronto: Penguin, 2001), p. 96.

68. I use the term "maladaptive" here and throughout to mean genetically or biologically maladaptive. I do not use the term "maladaptive" in the context of cultural evolution, because of the prevailing ambiguity about what should count as reproductive success for a meme.

69. A celebrated example of the latter is the "blind spot" in the human eye. See Richard Dawkins, *The Blind Watchmaker* (London: Penguin, 1990), p. 93.

70. Robert Boyd and Peter J. Richerson, "Why Culture Is Common, but Cultural Evolution Is Rare," in Boyd and Richerson, *The Origin and Evolution of Cultures*, pp. 52–65.

71. Another well-documented example is mate guarding among male soapberry bugs, which is determined by the sex ratio of the population. See Robert Boyd and Joan B. Silk, *How Humans Evolved*, 3rd ed. (New York: Norton, 2002), p. 69.

72. Stephen Jay Gould, *Ontogeny and Phylogeny* (Cambridge, Mass.: Belknap Press, 1977), p. 400; quotation cited by Gould is from Morris Cohen, *The Meaning of Human History* (LaSalle, Ill.: Open Court, 1947), p. 174.

73. Robert Boyd and Peter J. Richerson, "Climate, Culture and the Evolution of Cognition," in Boyd and Richerson, *The Origin and Evolution of Cultures*, p. 77.

74. See Bennett G. Galef Jr., "Imitation in Animals: History, Definition and Interpretation of Data from the Psychological Laboratory," in Bennett G. Galef Jr. and Thomas R. Zentall, eds., *Social Learning* (Hillsdale, N.J.: Erlbaum, 1988), pp. 3–28.

75. Kathy Nagell, Kelly Olguin, and Michael Tomasello, "Processes of Social Learning in the Tool Use of Chimpanzees (*Pan troglodytes*) and Human Children (Homo Sapiens)," *Journal of Comparative Psychology* 107 (1993): 174–86. See also Michael Tomasello, *The Cultural Origins of Human Cognition* (Cambridge, Mass.: Harvard University Press, 1999), pp. 29–30.

76. Tomasello, *Cultural Origins of Human Cognition*, p. 159. In another important experiment, Andrew Meltzoff showed that human infants will imitate unusual and inefficient behavior. Experimenters showed one group of 14-month-old infants how to activate a button on a light panel by bending over and touching it with their foreheads. Two-thirds of the infants who had seen it done this way attempted to reproduce the behavior, versus none in the control groups. See "Infant Imitation after a 1-Week Delay: Long-Term Memory for Novel Acts and Multiple Stimuli," *Developmental Psychology* 24 (1988): 470–76. (The purpose of the one-week delay mentioned in the title of the paper was to show that imitation is an important learning strategy, not merely a passing reflex.)

77. Richard Dawkins, *The Extended Phenotype* (Oxford: Freeman, 1982), p. 111. See also Daniel Dennett, *Darwin's Dangerous Idea* (New York: Simon and Schuster, 1995), p. 363.

78. Peter J. Richerson and Robert Boyd, *Not by Genes Alone* (Chicago: University of Chicago Press, 2004), pp. 37–38.

79. Robert Boyd and Peter J. Richerson, "Social Learning as an Adaptation," in Boyd and Richerson, *The Origin and Evolution of Cultures*, pp. 19–34.

80. Robert Boyd, Herbert Gintis, Samuel Bowles, and Peter J. Richerson, "The Evolution of Altruistic Punishment," in Gintis et al., *Moral Sentiments and Material Interests*, pp. 215–27.

81. Richerson and Boyd, *Not by Genes Alone*, pp. 203–6.

82. This is, of course, a major explanatory advantage of their model, since every culture is ridden with norms of this type—it is hardly the case that all deviations from self-interested behavior involve attempts to achieve cooperative gains. Decades of criticism of functionalist anthropology (in the style of Bronislaw Malinowski) have established clearly that culture does not have an optimizing structure.

83. Richerson, Boyd, and Henrich, "Cultural Evolution of Human Cooperation," p. 378.

84. Robert Brandom, *Making It Explicit* (Cambridge, Mass.: Harvard University Press, 1994), pp. 18–30.

85. The most important source of this invalid argument is Marshall Sahlins, *The Use and Abuse of Biology* (Ann Arbor: University of Michigan Press, 1976).

86. E. O. Wilson, *Sociobiology* (Cambridge, Mass.: Belknap Press, 1975), p. 549.

87. Wilson, *Sociobiology*, p. 560.

88. E. O. Wilson, *On Human Nature* (Cambridge, Mass.: Harvard University Press, 1978), pp. 56–57.

89. Wilson, *On Human Nature*, p. 41.

90. Kim Sterelny, "Evolutionary Explanations of Human Behavior," *Australasian Journal of Philosophy* 70 (1992): 168.

91. For a variation on the "blank slate" accusation, see John Tooby and Leda Cosmides's characterization of the "standard social science model," in "The Psychological Foundations of Culture," in Jerome H. Barkow, Leda Cosmides, and John Tooby, eds., *The Adapted Mind* (New York: Oxford University Press, 1992), pp. 19–136.

92. For more complete discussion, see Boyd and Richerson, *Not by Genes Alone*, pp. 18–57.

93. Peter L. Berger and Thomas Luckmann, *The Social Construction of Reality* (New York: Anchor, 1966), p. 49.

94. David M. Buss, "Sex Differences in Human Mate Selection: Evolutionary Hypothesis Tested in 37 Cultures," *Behavioral and Brain Science* 12 (1989): 1–49; also David M. Buss, "Mate Preference Mechanisms: Consequences for Partner Choice and Intrasexual Competition," in Barkow et al., *Adapted Mind*, pp. 254–55.

95. Shaun Nichols, *Sentimental Rules* (New York: Oxford University Press, 2006), pp. 118–19.

96. Pace Tooby and Cosmides, "Psychological Foundations of Culture;" and Steven Pinker, *The Blank Slate* (New York: Penguin, 2002). See Boyd and Richerson, "Climate, Culture and the Evolution of Cognition," pp. 69–70.

97. Deacon, *The Symbolic Species*, p. 322.

98. Steven Pinker, *The Language Instinct* (New York: HarperPerennial, 1995). For an excellent critical discussion, see Michael Tomasello, "Language Is Not an Instinct," *Cognitive Development* 10 (1995): 131–56.

99. For a useful caution against both "naïve exaptationism" and "superficial adaptationism," see Anne Fernald, "Human Maternal Vocalizations to Infants as Biologically Relevant Signals: An Evolutionary Perspective," in Barkow et al., *The Adapted Mind*, pp. 394–95.

100. Andy Clark, *Being There* (Cambridge, Mass.: MIT Press, 1997), p. 212.

101. Clark, *Being There*, p. 212.

102. Richerson, Boyd, and Henrich, "Cultural Evolution of Human Cooperation," p. 380.

103. Tomasello, "Language Is Not an Instinct," p. 133. He goes on to point out, helpfully, that no nativist actually believes that "language" is innate. It is a theoretical posit, such as "universal grammar" or a "language of thought," that they take to be innate.

Chapter 7

1. Christine M. Korsgaard, "Skepticism about Practical Reason," in *Creating the Kingdom of Ends* (Cambridge: Cambridge University Press, 1996), pp. 311–34.

2. David Hume, *A Treatise of Human Nature*, 2nd ed., ed. L. A. Selby-Bigge (Oxford: Clarendon, 1978), p. 416.

3. John Stuart Mill, "Utilitarianism," in *Collected Works of John Stuart Mill*, vol. 10, ed. J. M. Robson (Toronto: University of Toronto Press, 1969), pp. 231–32.

4. Judith G. Smentan, Diane L. Bridgeman, and Elliot Turiel, "Differentiation of Domains and Prosocial Behavior," in Diane L. Bridgemen, ed., *The Nature of Prosocial Development* (New York: Academic Press, 1983), pp. 173–83.

5. Dale F. Hay and Harriet L. Rheingold, "The Early Appearance of Some Valued Social Behaviors," in Bridgeman, *The Nature of Prosocial Development*, pp. 81–82. See also Harriet L. Rheingold and Dale F. Hay, "Prosocial Behavior of the Very Young," in Gunther S. Stent, ed., *Morality as a Biological Phenomenon*, rev. ed. (Berkeley: University of California Press, 1980), pp. 93–123.

6. See Elliot Turiel, "The Development of Moral Concepts," in *Morality as a Biological Phenomenon*: 109–23.

7. Hume, *Treatise of Human Nature*, pp. 483–84.

8. Shaun Nichols, *Sentimental Rules* (New York: Oxford University Press, 2006).

9. Nichols, *Sentimental Rules*, pp. 16–18.

10. Nichols, *Sentimental Rules*, pp. 121–24.

11. Nichols, *Sentimental Rules*, pp. 11–16.

12. Marc D. Hauser, *Moral Minds* (New York: HarperCollins, 2006), p. xviii.

13. Nichols writes: "the Affective Resonance account is intended only as an explanation for why we have the harm norms we do. The account harbors no pretensions about providing a justification for our embracing the norms," *Sentimental Rules*, p. 165.

14. Judith H. Langlois, Jean M. Ritter, Rita J. Casey, and Douglas B. Sawin, "Infant Attractiveness Predicts Maternal Behaviors and Attitudes," *Developmental Psychology* 31 (1995): 464–72.

15. Katherine A. Hildebrandt and Hiram E. Fitzgerald, "The Infant's Physical Attractiveness: Its Effects on Attachment and Bonding," *Infant Mental Health Journal* 4 (1983): 10.

16. Keith Stanovich, *The Robot's Rebellion* (Chicago: University of Chicago Press, 2004), pp. 131–39.

17. Stanovich, *Robot's Rebellion*, p. 84.

18. Rebecca Eckler, *Knocked Up: Confessions of a Hip Mother-to-Be* (New York: Villard, 2005).

19. Stanovich, *Robot's Rebellion*, p. 131.

20. For a sharp formulation of this problem in these terms, see Geoffrey Sayre-McCord, "Deception and Reasons to Be Moral," *American Philosophical Quarterly* 26 (1989): 113–22.

21. The contemporary discussion in epistemology takes as its point of departure Barry Stroud, "Transcendental Arguments," *Journal of Philosophy* 65 (1968): 241–56. See also Peter Bieri and Rold P. Horstmann, eds., *Transcendental Arguments and Science* (Dordrecht: Reidel, 1979). On the use of transcendental arguments in moral philosophy, see A. J. Watt, "Transcendental Arguments and Moral Principles," *Philosophical Quarterly* 25 (1975): 40–57. Watt surveys a set of arguments all of which fail because they attempt to provide a transcendental justification of substantive moral principles. The argument to be presented here is different, in that it attempts to justify a purely formal choice disposition.

22. Immanuel Kant, *Critique of Pure Reason*, trans. Norman Kemp Smith (New York: St. Martin's Press, 1929), pp. 151–60 (B129–43).

23. Kant writes: "This peculiarity of our understanding, that it can produce *a priori* unity of apperception solely by means of the categories, and only by such and so many, is as little capable of further explanation as why we have just these and no other functions of judgment, or why space and time are the only forms of our possible intuition." *Critique of Pure Reason*, p. 161 (B146).

24. David Lewis, *Counterfactuals* (Oxford: Blackwell, 1973), p. 5.

25. Ludwig Wittgenstein, *Tractatus Logico-Philosophicus*, trans. D. F. Pears and B. F. McGuinness (London: Routledge, 1974), p. 57 (sec. 5.62). For both Kant and Wittgenstein, this distinction is the key to the critique of metaphysics. For both theorists, metaphysics starts when we attempt to make claims about what happens at possible worlds that are not cognitively accessible to our own. For Kant, this takes the form of treating noumena as phenomena. For Wittgenstein, it means trying to *say* something about that which can only *show* itself. In both cases, the key is to restrict one's speculations to the set of cognitively accessible possible worlds (for Kant, those that satisfy the conditions of possible experience, i.e. phenomena, and for Wittgenstein, those that can form the contents of propositions).

26. Donald Davidson, "Radical Interpretation," in his *Inquiries into Truth and Interpretation* (Oxford: Clarendon Press, 1984).

27. Donald Davidson, "A Coherence Theory of Truth and Knowledge," in Ernest LePore, ed., *Truth and Interpretation: Perspectives on the Philosophy of Donald Davidson* (Blackwell, Oxford, 1986), pp. 317–19.

28. Robert Boyd and Peter J. Richerson, "Why Culture Is Common, but Cultural Evolution Is Rare," in *The Origin and Evolution of Cultures* (Oxford: Oxford University Press, 2005), pp. 52–65.

29. Ap Djiksterhuis, "Why We Are Social Animals: The High Road to Imitation as Social Glue," in Susan Hurley and Nick Chater, eds., *Perspectives on Imitation: From Neuroscience to Social Science*, 2 vols. (Cambridge, Mass.: MIT Press, 2005), 2:207–20.

30. Robert Brandom, *Making It Explicit* (Cambridge, Mass.: Harvard University Press, 1994), pp. 157–59.

31. Stanovich, *Robot's Rebellion*, p. 36.

32. E. O. Wilson, *On Human Nature* (Cambridge, Mass.: Harvard University Press, 1978), p. 41.

33. Wilfrid Sellars, "Some Reflections on Language Games," in *Science, Perception and Reality* (London: Routledge and Kegan Paul, 1963), pp. 321–58.

34. Michael Dummett, *The Logical Basis of Metaphysics* (Cambridge, Mass.: Harvard University Press, 1991), pp. 282–83.

35. Talcott Parsons, *The Social System* (New York: Free Press, 1951), pp. 283–86.

36. See Gresham M. Sykes and David Matza, "Techniques of Neutralization: A Theory of Delinquency," *American Sociological Review* 22 (1957): 664–70. The authors argue that "much delinquency is based on what is essentially an unrecognized extension of defenses to crimes, in the form of justifications for deviance that are seen as valid by the delinquent but not by the legal system or society at large," p. 666.

37. Sykes and Matza, "Techniques of Neutralization," p. 667. For additional discussion, see Joseph Heath, "Business Ethics and Moral Motivation: A Criminological Perspective," *Journal of Business Ethics* (forthcoming).

38. Linda Mealey, "The Sociobiology of Sociopathy: An Integrated Evolutionary Model," *Behavioral and Brain Sciences* 18 (1995): 523.

39. Nichols, *Sentimental Rules*, p. 19.

40. Robert Hare, "A Research Scale for the Assessment of Psychopathology in Criminal Populations," *Personality and Individual Differences* 1 (1980): 115–16.

41. I've been told, on good authority, that some of the early research on sociopaths in prisons, in the 1970s, was done using guards as a comparison class. This practice was discontinued when it was discovered that, with the measurement instrument being tested, sociopathy turned out to be as common among the guards as among the prisoners. Fearing that publication of such research findings would result in denial of access to inmates, researchers switched to using control groups drawn from the general population.

42. On the relationship between antisocial behavior and intelligence, see James Blair, Derek Mitchell, and Karina Blair, *The Psychopath* (Oxford: Blackwell, 2005), p. 24. On "dysrationalia," see Stanovich, *Robot's Rebellion*, pp. 163–67.

Chapter 8

1. Naturally these are not exactly the same (more on this in chapter 9). The point merely has to do with the structure of the agent's motive.

2. Timothy Wilson, *Strangers to Ourselves* (Cambridge, Mass.: Harvard University Press, 2002), pp. 93–97.

3. Sarah Stroud refers to this view as "Humean externalism," in "Weakness of Will and Practical Judgment," in Sarah Stroud and Christine Tappolet, eds., *Weakness of Will and Practical Irrationality* (Oxford: Oxford University Press, 2003), pp. 126–31.

4. Alfred Mele, *Irrationality* (New York: Oxford University Press, 1987).

5. Stroud, "Weakness of Will and Practical Judgment," p. 143.

6. Wilfrid Sellars, "Some Reflections on Language Games," in *Science, Perception and Reality* (London: Routledge and Kegan Paul, 1963), p. 350.

7. Mele, *Irrationality*, pp. 38–39.

8. Donald Hubin argues, in "What's Special about Humeanism?" *Nous* 33 (1999): 30–45, that since evaluative judgments are useless if they are not accompanied by appropriate motivations, we might as well start with existing motivations when engaging in practical reasoning, rather than some abstract conception of the good that has no motivational force. Thus the Humean conception of practical reason is powerful, he argues, because it is the only deliberative procedure that will reliably produce desires that we are actually motivated to act on. Of course, this argument tacitly presupposes that the energy associated with motivation is communicated through practical reasoning in the same way that evaluative score is communicated—a textbook example of what Sellars called the confusion of the explanatory and justificatory (or causal and normative) orders.

9. Stanovich, *Robot's Rebellion*, p. 34.

10. Stanovich, *Robot's Rebellion*, p. 34.

11. Mele, *Irrationality*, p. 19.

12. Lennart Sjoberg and Tommy Johnson, "Trying to Give Up Smoking: A Study of Volitional Breakdowns," *Addictive Behaviors* 3 (1978): 149–64. The "reasons" given for smoking bear remarkable similarity to the "techniques of neutralization" used to excuse antisocial behavior (see chapter 7, section 5).

13. For philosophical discussion, see John Broome, "Discounting the Future," *Philosophy and Public Affairs* 23 (1994): 128–56. Some economists have also been suspicious of discounting; see Cecil Pigou, *The Economics of Welfare* (London: Macmillan, 1920), p. 25. For political scientists, see Jon Elster, *Nuts and Bolts for the Social Sciences* (Cambridge: Cambridge University Press, 1989), p. 44. The debate is sometimes tinged by an unhelpful confusion between an individual who discounts his or her own future satisfaction when calculating a utility-maximizing strategy and an individual who discounts the future satisfaction of *others* when doing a utilitarian calculation. The latter is problematic in several ways that the former is not.

14. Henry Sidgwick, *The Methods of Ethics*, 7th ed. (London: MacMillan, 1962), p. 381.

15. Usually, but not always. There is also the phenomenon of savoring and dreading, where the individual exhibits a negative discount rate.

16. See Howard Rachlin, *The Science of Self-Control* (Cambridge, Mass.: Harvard University Press, 2000), pp. 158–64.

17. Rachlin, *Science of Self-Control*, pp. 41–43; George Ainslie, "Impulse Control in Pigeons," *Journal of Experimental Analysis of Behavior* 21 (1974): 485–89. With these experiments, it is possible to calculate the implicit discount rate.

18. Rachlin, *Science of Self-Control*, pp. 150–55. In the case of an agent who faces an indefinite series of identical gambles, risk-aversion becomes equivalent to time preference, since the agent can be assured that if she is willing to wait long enough, her payoffs will converge with the mathematical value of the gamble. Thus Rachlin argues that the "paradoxes" of rationality created by discounting are no more paradoxical than the Allais paradox.

19. Even then, the imposition of a single discount rate across all domains of choice represents a fairly extreme stylization of our actual preferences. See Dilip Soman, George

Ainslie, Shane Frederick, Xiuping Li, John Lynch, Page Moreau, Andrew Mitchell, Daniel Read, Alan Sawyer, Yaacov Trope, Klaus Wertenbroch, and Gal Zauberman, "The Psychology of Intertemporal Discounting: Why Are Distant Events Valued Differently from Proximal Ones?" *Marketing Letters* 16 (2005): 354. A realistic model would allow greater context-specificity.

20. George Ainslie, *Picoeconomics* (Cambridge: Cambridge University Press, 1992).

21. George Ainslie, *Breakdown of Will* (Cambridge: Cambridge University Press, 2001), p. 33.

22. Rachlin, *Science of Self-Control*, p. 39. Ainslie, *Picoeconomics*.

23. George Lowenstein and Drazen Prelec, "Anomalies in Intertemporal Choice: Evidence and Interpretation," in George Lowenstein and Jon Elster, eds., *Choice over Time* (New York: Sage, 1992), p. 121.

24. Hume, *A Treatise of Human Nature*, 2nd ed., ed. L. A. Selby-Bigge (Oxford: Clarendon, 1978), p. 536.

25. Hume, *Treatise of Human Nature*, p. 535.

26. Ainslie, incidentally, does not accept this description. "Our relative overvaluation of nearer experiences does a lot more than make us prone to addictions," he writes; "in a culture where one of the basic properties of rationality is consistency, it makes us irrational from the outset." *Breakdown of Will* (Cambridge: Cambridge University Press, 2001), p. 161.

27. Itamar Simonson, "The Effect of Purchase Quantity and Timing on Variety-Seeking Behavior," *Journal of Marketing Research* 27 (1990): 150–62.

28. Jay J. J. Christensen-Szalanski, "Discount Functions and the Measurement of Patients' Values: Women's Decisions during Childbirth," *Medical Decision Making* 4 (1984): 47–58.

29. Watson, "Skepticism about Weakness of Will," *Philosophical Review* 86 (1977): 325.

30. Duncan Raistrick and Robin Davidson, *Alcoholism and Drug Addiction* (Edinburgh: Churchhill Livingston, 1985), p. 13.

31. Raistrick and Davidson, *Alcoholism and Drug Addiction*, p. 31.

32. Table 8.1 is based on Ainslie, *Breakdown of Will*, p. 64. The category of "urges" is one I have added. I have also eliminated the category of "pains," which Ainslie analyzes as a pattern of stimulation even more brief than itches. This is a fascinating theory, but one that seems to me rather speculative. Since nothing in my argument hinges on it, I have chosen to omit the analysis here.

33. Thomas Nagel, *The Possibility of Altruism* (Princeton: Princeton University Press, 1970), pp. 36–46.

34. This does suggest the interesting possibility that a lot of moral rectitude has the same structure as procrastination. People respect the rules because they "overvalue" the short-term discomfort of breaking them, relative to the long-term free-rider benefits. Many soldiers, for instance, report having experienced some distress at the discovery that it is quite "easy" to kill people, once the initial inhibition is overcome.

35. See Stanley Milgram, "On Maintaining Social Norms: A Field Experiment in the Subway," in *The Individual in a Social World* (New York: McGraw Hill, 1992). Harold Garfinkel also reported that many students instructed to perform far more minor "breaching experiments" at home could not bring themselves to carry out the assignment, on the grounds that they were "afraid to do it." *Studies in Ethnomethodology* (Cambridge: Polity, 1984), p. 47.

36. Rachlin, *Science of Self-Control*, p. 44.

37. Mele, *Irrationality*, pp. 51–52.

38. Aristotle, *Nichomachean Ethics*, trans. Christopher Rowe (Oxford: Oxford University Press, 2002), p. 191 (book VII.2 1146a).

39. Daniel Dennett, *Consciousness Explained* (Boston: Little, Brown, 1991), pp. 195–96.

40. Hume, *Treatise of Human Nature*, p. 537. This passage goes on to exaggerate the problem by saying "they cannot change their natures." The passage cited is correct only if one puts emphasis on the claim that men are not able *radically* to cure their tendency to prefer the present to the remote. This is not to say that they cannot influence it.

41. Ainslie, *Breakdown of Will*, p. 149.

42. Ainslie, *Breakdown of Will*, pp. 100–101.

43. This term is due to Andy Clark, *Being There* (Cambridge, Mass.: MIT Press, 1997). For further discussion, see the next section.

44. Hume, *Treatise of Human Nature*, p. 537.

45. See Jon Elster, *Ulysses and the Sirens* (Cambridge: Cambridge University Press, 1979).

46. More generally, see Cass R. Sunstein and Richard M. Thaler, "Libertarian Paternalism Is Not an Oxymoron," *University of Chicago Law Review* 70 (2003): 1159–1202.

47. For overview, see Ainslie, *Breakdown of Will*, pp. 78–85; Rachlin, *Science of Self-Control*, pp. 142–43.

48. Rachlin, *Science of Self-Control*, pp. 100–101.

49. Clark, *Being There*, p. 180.

50. Andy Clark, "Economic Reason: The Interplay of Individual Learning and External Structure," in John Drobak and John Nye, eds., *The Frontiers of the New Institutional Economics* (San Diego: Academic Press, 1996), p. 271.

51. They are probably right to do so. See Roy F. Baumeister, Ellen Bratslavsky, Mark Muraven, and Dianne M. Tice, "Ego Depletion: Is the Active Self a Limited Resource?" *Journal of Personality and Social Psychology*, 74 (1998): 1252–65.

52. Joel Anderson, "Neuro-Prosthetics," in Marcus Düwell, Christoph Rehmann-Sutter, and Dietmar Mieth, eds., *The Contingent Nature of Life* (Dordrecht: Springer, 2008).

53. Immanuel Kant, *Foundations of the Metaphysic of Morals*, trans. Lewis White Beck (Indianapolis: Bobbs-Merrill, 1959), p. 13 (Ak 397).

54. See Gilbert Harman, "Moral Philosophy Meets Social Psychology: Virtue Ethics and the Fundamental Attribution Error," *Proceedings of the Aristotelian Society* 99 (1999): 315–31; John Doris, *Lack of Character* (Cambridge: Cambridge University Press, 2002)); John Darley and C. Daniel Batson, "From Jerusalem to Jericho: A Study of Situational and Dispositional Variables in Helping Behavior," *Journal of Personality and Social Psychology* 27 (1973); Lee Ross and Robert Nisbett, *The Person and the Situation: Perspectives of Social Psychology* (New York: McGraw-Hill, 1991); Walter Mischel, *Personality and Assessment* (New York: Wiley, 1968).

55. Thomas Gilovich, *How We Know What Isn't So* (New York: Free Press, 1991).

56. Timothy D. Wilson, *Strangers to Ourselves* (Cambridge, Mass.: Harvard University Press, 2002), p. 98.

57. Emile Durkheim, *The Rules of the Sociological Method*, trans. W. D. Halls (New York: Free Press, 1982), p. 67.

Chapter 9

1. Jared Diamond, *Guns, Germs and Steel* (New York: Norton, 1999), p. 57.

2. Diamond, *Guns, Germs and Steel*, p. 54.

3. As Peter J. Richerson and Robert Boyd write, "cultural maladaptations arise from a design tradeoff. Culture allows rapid adaptation to a wide range of environments, but lead to systematic maladaptation as a result.... In creating a simulation of a Darwinian system using imitation instead of genes, natural selection created conditions that allow selfish cultural variants to spread." *Not By Genes Alone* (Chicago: Univerity of Chicago Press, 2005), p. 188.

4. For example, see Brian Skyrms, *The Evolution of the Social Contract* (Princeton: Princeton University Press, 1996), p. 11.

5. Herbert Gintis, *Game Theory Evolving* (Princeton: Princeton University Press, 2000), p. 195.

6. This is very much the tenor set by Richard Dawkins's initial discussion, in *The Selfish Gene*, 2nd ed. (Oxford: Oxford University Press, 1989), pp. 192–98.

7. See Maurice Bloch, "A Well-Disposed Social Anthropologist's Problems with Memetics," in Robert Aunger, ed., *Darwinizing Culture* (Oxford: Oxford University Press, 2000), pp. 189–203. There are a number of other useful essays in this volume.

8. Daniel Dennett, *Darwin's Dangerous Idea* (New York: Simon and Schuster, 1995), pp. 362–63.

9. Richerson and Boyd, *Not By Genes Alone*, pp. 163–64.

10. See Eldar Shafir and Amos Tversky, "Thinking through Uncertainty: Nonconsequential Reasoning and Choice," *Cognitive Psychology* 24 (1992): 449–74.

11. Shaun Nichols, *Sentimental Rules* (New York: Oxford University Press, 2006), pp. 155–57.

12. Richerson and Boyd, *Not By Genes Alone*, pp. 155–56.

13. Of course, even in biology it is not truly random, since the molecular structure of DNA makes certain changes more likely to occur than others. It is random only relative to the functional properties of the structures that are produced as the phenotypic expression of this DNA. Thus, for example, a mutation in a reptile with a three-chambered heart, although not purely random, is no more likely to move it toward a four-chambered heart than to make it "regress" to a two-chambered heart. Thus selection does all the work in determining the direction of evolutionary change.

14. Robert Boyd and Peter Richerson, *Not by Genes Alone* (Chicago: University of Chicago Press, 2005), p. 116.

15. Philippa Foot, "Morality as a System of Hypothetical Imperatives," in *Virtues and Vice* (Oxford: Oxford University Press, 1978), p. 160.

16. Foot, "Morality as a System of Hypothetical Imperatives," p. 160.

17. Foot, "Morality as a System of Hypothetical Imperatives," p. 161. She later takes it back even more, stating that considerations of etiquette "have no automatic reason-giving force independent of the agent's interests or desires," p. 176. David Brink echoes the idea, common among moral philosophers, that because the rules of etiquette are not imposed by the structure of rational agency, moral agents may not need to "live under the rules of etiquette at all." David O. Brink, "Kantian Rationalism: Inescapability, Authority, and Supremacy," in Farrett Cullity and Berys Gaut, eds., *Ethics and Practical Reason* (Oxford: Clarendon, 1997), p. 281.

18. Foot, "Morality as a System of Hypothetical Imperatives," p. 161.

19. Richard Joyce, *The Evolution of Morality* (Cambridge, Mass.: MIT Press, 2006), p. 193, suggests that "only people who have interests that will be served by following etiquette" have a reason to comply with the rules. But then the example he gives to show that the institution lacks "genuine binding force" is of a person speaking with his mouth full, in order to stop a friend from eating a wasp. This seems to me an obvious example of a moral rule trumping etiquette, not self-interest trumping etiquette. There are a fair

number of moral rules one could legitimately break as well, in order to prevent a friend from swallowing a wasp.

20. Foot, "Morality as a System of Hypothetical Imperatives," p. 160.

21. See Sarah Buss, "Appearing Respectful: The Moral Significance of Manners," *Ethics* 109 (1999): 795–826.

22. Judith Martin, *Miss Manners Rescues Civilization* (New York: Crown, 1996), p. 163.

23. Elliot Turiel, Melanie Killen, and Charles Helwig, "Morality: Its Structure, Functions and Vagaries," in Jerome Kagan and Sharon Lamb, eds., *The Emergence of Morality in Young Children* (Chicago: University of Chicago Press, 1987), p. 169.

24. Elliot Turiel, "Distinct Conceptual and Developmental Domains: Social Convention and Morality," in H. Howe and C. Keasey, *Nebraska Symposium on Motivation, 1977: Social Cognitive Development* (Lincoln: University of Nebraska Press, 1979), p. 77.

25. See Monica Bucciarelli, Sangeet Khemlani, and Philip N. Johnson-Laird, "The Psychology of Moral Reasoning," *Judgment and Decision Making*, 3 (2008): 121–39. They suggest, after a careful review of the evidence, that "moral reasoning is just normal reasoning about deontic proposititions that happen to concern morality" (p. 126).

26. For more detailed criticism along these lines, see Daniel Kelly and Stephen Stich, "Two Theories about the Cognitive Architecture Underlying Morality," in Peter Carruthers, Stephen Laurence, and Stephen Stich, eds., *The Innate Mind: Foundations and the Future* (Oxford: Oxford University Press, 2006),pp. 348–66.

27. Joyce, *Evolution of Morality*, p. 197.

28. J. G. Smentana and J. L. Braeges, "The Development of Toddlers' Moral and Conventional Judgments," *Merrill-Palmer Quarterly* 36 (1990): 329–46.

29. Nichols, *Sentimental Rules*, p. 22.

30. For more skeptical perspective on the role that emotional reactions play in moral judgment, see Joshua Greene, "The Secret Joke of Kant's Soul," in Walter Sinnott-Armstrong, ed. *Moral Psychology*, vol. 3: *The Neuroscience of Morality: Emotion, Disease, and Development* (Cambridge, Mass.: MIT Press, 2007), pp. 355–79.

31. Nichols, *Sentimental Rules*, p. 21.

32. Johannes A. Landsheer, Harm 't Hart, and Willem Kox, "Delinquent Values and Victim Damage: Exploring the Limits of Neutralization Theory," *British Journal of Criminology* 34 (1994): 52.

33. This concept has its origins in Jean Piaget, *The Moral Judgment of the Child*, trans. Marjorie Gabain (New York: Free Press, 1965). It was elaborated considerably by Lawrence Kohlberg, who used the term "conventional." See Kohlberg, *The Philosophy of Moral Development* (New York: Harper and Row, 1981), and *The Psychology of Moral Development* (San Francisco: Harper and Row, 1984). Note that Carol Gilligan's well-known critique of Kohlberg's model does not challenge the broad classification into pre-conventional, conventional, and postconventional levels; it only challenges the details of the "stages" within these levels.

34. Bernard Williams and J. J. C. Smart, *Utilitarianism: For and Against* (Cambridge: Cambridge University Press, 1973), pp. 69–72.

35. David Gauthier, *Morals by Agreement* (Oxford: Clarendon, 1986), p. 268.

36. This phrase was made popular by Jonathan Haidt, "The Emotional Dog and Its Rational Tail: A Social Intuitionist Approach to Moral Judgment," *Psychological Review* 108 (2001): 814–34.

37. Kohlberg, *Psychology of Moral Development*, pp. 171–205.

38. See Richard M. Hare, *Moral Thinking* (Oxford: Oxford University Press, 1981). See also the articles in Brad Hooker, Elinor Mason, and Dale Miller, eds., *Morality, Rules, and Consequences* (Edinburgh: Edinburgh University Press, 2000).

39. Kohlberg, *Psychology of Moral Development*, pp. 171–205.

40. Michele Moody-Adams, *Fieldwork in Familiar Places* (Cambridge, Mass.: Harvard University Press, 1997), p. 194.

41. Robert Brandom, *Making It Explicit* (Cambridge, Mass.: Harvard University Press, 1994), p. 106. Thus the "expressive rationality" perspective satisfies Moody-Adams's desideratum, that a philosophical contribution "steer a middle path between the anti-theorist's fetishism of 'everyday' moral thinking and argument and the systematic ethical theorist's fetishism of philosophical moral inquiry," *Fieldwork in Familiar Places*, p. 194.

42. Brandom, *Making It Explicit*, pp. 97–102.

43. Brandom, *Making It Explicit*, p. 108.

44. Denise Dellarossa Cummins, "Evidence for the Innateness of Deontic Reasoning," *Mind and Language* 11 (1996): 174.

45. Brandom, *Making It Explicit*, p. 105.

46. For a more developed example of this, involving what Richard Rorty called "the cautionary use" of the truth predicate, see Joseph Heath, *Communicative Action and Rational Choice* (Cambridge, Mass.: MIT Press, 2001), pp. 215–16.

47. See David Miller, "Distributive Justice: What the People Think," in *Principles of Social Justice* (Cambridge, Mass.: Harvard University Press, 1999), pp. 61–92.

48. See John Roemer, *Theories of Distributive Justice* (Cambridge, Mass.: Harvard University Press, 1996) pp. 183–93.

49. Charles Taylor, *Sources of the Self* (Cambridge, Mass.: Harvard University Press, 1989).

50. T. M. Scanlon, *The Importance of What We Care About* (Cambridge: Cambridge University Press, 1998), p. 298.

51. Scanlon, *Importance of What We Care About*, p. 297.

52. A "zebra" is a term used by doctors to refer to an unusual medical condition, almost never seen outside of textbooks. The term is derived from an old saying, "When you hear hoofbeats, think of horses, not zebras"—the thought being that the patient's symptoms are more likely to be caused by a common condition, rather than an exotic one. Another useful saying in the medical profession, normally used to curtail the excesses of enthusiastic medical students, is "common things are common." Moral philosophers could learn something from this. Typical "moral problems" textbooks often inadvertently promote moral skepticism (or at least subjectivism) among students, simply because they focus entirely on hard cases—abortion, euthanasia, cloning, etc.—while ignoring the vast number of completely unproblematic moral judgments that we make every day.

53. Richerson and Boyd, *Not By Genes Alone*, pp. 221–24.

54. Kurt Baier, *The Moral Point of View* (Ithaca, N.Y.: Cornell University Press, 1959), p. 314.

55. John Rawls, *Collected Papers* (Cambridge, Mass.: Harvard University Press, 1999), p. 208.

56. Immanuel Kant, *Foundations of the Metaphysic of Morals*, trans. Lewis White Beck (Indianapolis: Bobbs-Merrill, 1959), p. 42 (Ak 425).

57. T. M. Scanlon, "Contractualism and Utilitarianism," in Amartya Sen and Bernard Williams, eds., *Utilitarianism and Beyond* (Cambridge: Cambridge University Press, 1982), pp. 103–28.

58. Emile Durkheim, *The Division of Labour in Society*, trans. George Simpson (New York: Free Press, 1933), p. 435 (translation altered).

59. Stanley Milgram, *Obedience to Authority* (New York: Harper and Row, 1974).

60. This is the central lesson of John Doris's *Lack of Character* (Cambridge: Cambridge University Press, 2002) as well.

61. One can find some evidence for this hypothesis in Jeffrey M. Smith and Paul A. Bell, "Conformity as a Determinant of Behavior in a Resource Dilemma," *Journal of Social Psychology* 134 (1994): 191–200.

62. J. L. Mackie, *Ethics: Inventing Right and Wrong* (London: Penguin, 1977).

Conclusion

1. For example, see Bibb Latané and John M. Darley, *The Unresponsive Bystander* (New York: Appleton-Century Crofts, 1970). Doris, *Lack of Character*, provides a useful summary of the relevant literature.

2. Lawrence A. Greenfeld, *Alcohol and Crime* (Washington, D.C.: U.S. Department of Justice, Bureau of Justice Statistics, 1998).

3. Robert Nash Parker and Linda-Anne Rebhun, *Alcohol and Homicide* (Albany: State University of New York Press, 1995), pp. 34–36.

4. There are some signs that this is changing, e.g., see John Doris and Stephen Stich, "As a Matter of Fact: Empirical Perspectives on Ethics," in Frank Jackson and Michael Smith, eds., *The Oxford Handbook of Contemporary Philosophy* (Oxford: Oxford University Press, 2005), 114–52.

5. See Stephen Darwall, Allan Gibbard, and Peter Railton, "*Fin-de-siècle* Ethics: Some Trends," *Philosophical Review* 101 (92): 188–89.

6. Michael Ghiselin, *The Economy of Nature and the Evolution of Sex* (Berkeley: University of California Press, 1974), p. 247. See also Michael Ruse and Edward O. Wilson, "The Evolution of Ethics," in Michael Ruse, ed., *Philosophy of Biology* (London: Macmillan, 1989), pp. 313–19. Incidentally, the problems with these arguments stem from bad biology, not necessarily bad philosophy. See also Michael Ruse, "The New Evolutionary Ethics," in Matthew H. Nitecki and Doris V. Nitecki, eds., *Evolutionary Ethics* (Albany: State University of New York Press, 1993), pp. 133–62.

7. Eliot Sober and David Wilson, *Unto Others* (Cambridge, Mass.: Harvard University Press, 1998).

8. Keith Stanovich, *The Robot's Rebellion* (Chicago: University of Chicago Press, 2004), pp. 192–94.

9. Daniel Dennett, *Darwin's Dangerous Idea* (New York: Simon and Schuster, 1995), writes: "But if it is true that human minds are themselves to a very great degree the creation of memes, then we cannot sustain the polarity of vision we considered earlier; it cannot be 'memes versus us,' because earlier infestations of memes have already played a major role in determining who or what we are. The 'independent' mind struggling to protect itself from alien and dangerous memes is a myth," p. 365.

10. Richard Joyce, *The Evolution of Morality* (Cambridge, Mass.: MIT Press, 2006).

11. Modern Darwinians, in their eternal battle with the defenders of religion, almost uniformly presuppose that the question is to be settled through reference to the explanatory adequacy of evolutionary theory. Yet they systematically fail to apprehend that the failure of the modern scientific worldview to explain normatively phenomena—in particular, to offer a reconstructive explanation, rather than a debunking, of the binding force of moral obligations—constitutes the primary reason for the persistence of religious worldviews among educated persons.

12. Mark Norris Lance and John O'Leary-Hawthorne, *The Grammar of Meaning* (Cambridge: Cambridge University Press, 1997), pp. 344–47.

13. Robert Brandom, in "Modality, Normativity, and Intentionality," *Philosophy and Phenomenological Research* 63 (2001): 587–610.

Index